Studies in Outdoor Recreation
Search and Research for Satisfaction

SECOND EDITION

Studies in Outdoor Recreation
Search and Research for Satisfaction

SECOND EDITION

by Robert E. Manning

 Oregon State University Press
Corvallis

Partial support for publication of this book was provided by the
National Park Service Social Science Program.
The Oregon State University Press is grateful for this support.

The paper in this book meets the guidelines for permanence and durability of the Committee on Production Guidelines for Book Longevity of the Council on Library Resources and the minimum requirements of the American National Standard for Permanence of Paper for Printed Library Materials Z39.48-1984.

Library of Congress Cataloging-in-Publication Data
Manning, Robert E., 1946
Studies in outdoor recreation.
Bibliography: p
Includes index
1. Outdoor recreation—Research—Evaluation.
I. Title.
GV191.6.M314 1985   306′.483   85-15447
ISBN 0-87071-463-5

Oregon State University Press
101 Waldo Hall
Corvallis OR 97331-6407
541-737-3166 •fax 541-737-3170
http://.osu.orst.edu/dept/press

To my colleagues,
past and present,
whose research and writing make this book possible.

Preface

This book is a study of the social science research in outdoor recreation — the characteristics, attitudes, and behavior of people who visit parks and related areas. A large number of theoretical and empirical studies in outdoor recreation have been conducted over the past several decades, but these studies have been highly diverse in disciplinary approach and methods, and widely dispersed over space and time. With the exception of normally cursory reviews at the beginning of most published papers, little effort has been devoted to integrating this expanding scientific literature. This study attempts to synthesize this literature, and develop and present a body of knowledge on major outdoor recreation management and research issues.

The book is designed for students, scholars, and managers of parks and related outdoor recreation areas. For students, the book provides an historical perspective on outdoor recreation research, introduces a number of important issues and concepts in outdoor recreation, and provides entree into the scientific literature. For scholars and researchers, the book integrates and synthesizes the literature on a number of important topics in outdoor recreation, with special attention to theoretical and methodological issues. For managers, the book develops the practical implications of outdoor recreation research, and concludes with a chapter on principles and practices of outdoor recreation management.

The first edition of this book was written while I was on sabbatical leave at Grand Canyon National Park, and was published in 1986. Although sabbatical leaves present unusual opportunities to read, think, and write, I had no intention of writing a book. The manuscript that was published as the first edition of this book was more like a long letter to myself, attempting to organize and understand a diverse academic literature. This second edition has given me an opportunity to more purposeful in preparing this book. I have revised and updated the original nine chapters, and added four new chapters. This edition is illustrated more fully with tables and figures. I have added important new material on issues of race/ethnicity and gender, and their relationships to outdoor recreation. The book concludes with a new section, "Notes on Sources: A Guide to the Social Science Literature in Outdoor Recreation," an outline of how the scientific literature in outdoor recreation is organized, and where this material can be found. I hope this new edition is more useful and more readable.

I am grateful to a number of people and institutions for helping make this study possible. First and foremost, this study would not have been possible without the strong program of research and writing conducted by my colleagues, past and present, known and unknown. Once again, the generous sabbatical program of the University of Vermont provided me the time needed to conduct the study. I am grateful to Lawrence Forcier, former Dean of the School of Natural Resources, and Donald DeHayes, current Dean, for their encouragement and support. The National Park Service again provided me an opportunity to spend my sabbatical in a suitably inspirational setting to conduct my study. Special appreciation is expressed to B. J. Griffin and Stanley Albright, former and current Superintendents, respectively, Yosemite National Park. Park staff, including Chip Jenkins, Russell Galipeau, and Laurel Boyers, generously extended me many professional courtesies, as did Jan Van Wagtendonk of the Yosemite Science Center. Gary Machlis, Chief Social Scientist of the National Park Service, kindly arranged for distribution of the book throughout the national park system.

The study required locating and gathering many publications not in my possession. This was greatly facilitated by the staff of the Bailey/ Howe Library at the University of Vermont. Special thanks are expressed to Laurie Kutner, Reference Librarian. Jennifer Treadwell, Graduate Research Assistant, also helped locate a number of references. Several people were particularly helpful with technical aspects of preparing the book. Robyn Rooney and Claudette LaPlume patiently typed the manuscript, and William Valliere, Research Assistant, prepared several figures. Jo Alexander, Managing Editor of the Oregon State University Press, skillfully guided the manuscript into print.

Robert Manning

Table of Contents

1

Search for Satisfaction
An Introduction to Outdoor Recreation Research

Objectives of the Book

An early paper in the outdoor recreation literature challenged researchers to demonstrate and strengthen the scholarly significance and practical implications of their studies. Pointedly titled "Recreation Research—So What?," this paper called upon the research community to build a body of knowledge that would enhance our understanding of outdoor recreation and contribute to solving a variety of management problems (P. Brown et al. 1973). This book examines the outdoor recreation literature in an effort to meet that challenge.

The primary purpose of this book is to review, synthesize, and integrate the literature on social science aspects of outdoor recreation. While social science research in outdoor recreation does not have a long history, a relatively large number of studies have been conducted and published over the past several decades. However, with the exception of normally cursory literature review sections at the beginning of most published papers, little effort has been aimed at integrating this literature into an emerging body of knowledge.

The integrative study underlying this book is warranted for several reasons, all stemming from the inherent diversity of the field of outdoor recreation. First and foremost is the multidisciplinary nature of the subject itself. Issues in outdoor recreation are conventionally dichotomized into environmental science concerns (e.g., ecological impacts) and social science concerns (e.g., crowding and conflicting uses). But even within the social science domain, issues may be approached from a variety of disciplinary perspectives, including sociology, psychology, geography, political science, and economics. Integration of these discipline-based studies can be complex. Indeed, simply locating the research in the variety of journals and other publication sources in which it is reported can be difficult. Outdoor recreation research also tends to be isolated in space and time; studies are widely scattered geographically and are conducted over varying time periods. At least on the surface, an early study of developed campgrounds in an Eastern park can be difficult to integrate with a more recent study of wilderness use in the West. Yet they are both studies in outdoor recreation and will contribute more to a body of knowledge when integrated and synthesized than in isolation. Finally, outdoor recreation has been subject to wide methodological diversity. Even though the dominant research approach has been to survey on-site visitors, there has been substantial variation in sampling techniques, the scope of such studies, and the way in which important variables have been conceptualized and measured. Attempts to integrate studies are often frustrated by these inconsistencies. Still, the basic thrust of such studies can often be brought together to build evidence for or against a relationship, hypothesis, or theory. Moreover, a large-scale synthesis is likely to highlight methodological inconsistencies and, ideally, enhance the comparability of future research.

One result of this book, it is hoped, is a response to criticism that studies of outdoor recreation have few broad implications (e.g., P. Brown et al. 1973). Applied to individual studies, this observation may be largely true. But in a broad and interdisciplinary field such as outdoor recreation, this is probably how it should and must be. The essence of the scientific method is to divide issues into small and manageable components for study. Only after a critical mass of information has been created in this manner can the synergistic effects of the research process begin to emerge. The resulting body of knowledge then becomes more than the sum of its parts. In this book, the findings from a large number of studies are synthesized and integrated into knowledge and understanding. In this manner, management implications begin to be apparent.

The book is organized in thirteen chapters, most of which focus on a major theme in the literature. Though the book is divided primarily by subject matter, it also has a historical bent. Emphasis on one theme often evolves from development of another. The research on crowding (Chapter 5) which emerged in the late 1970s, for example, has its roots in the concept of carrying capacity (Chapter 4), which was applied to outdoor recreation beginning in the previous decade. Moreover, recent research on indicators and standards of quality employing normative theory and methods (Chapter 6) can be linked to concern with crowding. In addition, the development of most new fields of study follows a similar pattern as they evolve from basic descriptive approaches to more theoretical and analytical efforts. This pattern is reflected throughout the course of the book.

The first chapter briefly reviews the history of social science research in outdoor recreation and notes the emphasis on establishing and maintaining satisfaction among visitors, although definitions of satisfaction have changed over time. Research on the broad issue of visitor satisfaction has identified many closely related concepts and issues, and these make up many of the themes of subsequent chapters. Chapters 2 and 3 focus on social and descriptive studies. Topics included are some of the most basic issues in outdoor recreation: recreation activity patterns; social and cultural influences on recreation participation; and visitor attitudes, preferences, and perceptions regarding outdoor recreation areas. Chapter 4 examines the adoption of carrying capacity as an organizing framework in outdoor recreation. Borrowed from the biological sciences of wildlife and range management, the concept of carrying capacity has been found useful in the field of outdoor recreation, but only after extensive modification. An underlying concern of recreation carrying capacity suggests that satisfaction of visitors may decline with increasing use levels. The large group of studies exploring crowding in outdoor recreation is the focus of Chapter 5. Chapter 6 addresses indicators and standards of quality for outdoor recreation. Indicators and standards of quality are central to contemporary outdoor recreation management frameworks and have been explored through applications of normative theory and techniques. The seventh chapter examines motivations for outdoor recreation. Understanding of outdoor recreation is deepened when it is viewed from a "behavioral approach," emphasizing why people participate in recreation activities and the experiences and benefits attained. A recurring conclusion in the literature is that public tastes in outdoor recreation are diverse. Chapter 8 reviews several conceptual systems designed to ensure diversity in outdoor recreation, including the Recreation Opportunity Spectrum. Chapter 9 focuses on conflict in outdoor recreation. There are many examples of such conflict—hikers and stock users, cross-country skiers and snowmobilers, canoeists and fishers—and these can be understood more fully and managed more effectively in light of the conceptual and empirical research directed at this issue. Chapters 10 and 11 address two very specific issues in outdoor recreation—substitutability and specialization. As the name suggests, substitutability refers to the extent to which one recreation activity might be substitutable for another with regard to the experiences and/or benefits attained. Specialization refers to the evolution in some recreation activities as manifested in experience and commitment levels of participants. Chapter 12 explores management practices in outdoor recreation. The outdoor recreation literature suggests that a variety of management strategies and tactics can be used to manage outdoor recreation, and provides some indication of their relative effectiveness. The final chapter focuses on developing management implications from the outdoor recreation literature. Based on the studies reviewed and synthesized, a series of principles and practices for outdoor recreation management are developed and presented.

Like all studies, the review and synthesis reported in this book has limits. Though the study is multidisciplinary within the social sciences, perspectives are drawn primarily from sociology, psychology, geography, and to a limited extent, economics. Similarly, the study covers the time period from the early 1960s through the present; this is primarily a function of when outdoor recreation research has been conducted. The emphasis of the study is on published research. Confidence in research findings is enhanced when they have seen the light of critical review. Moreover, these materials are more generally available to readers who may wish to consult primary sources. Finally, the study is oriented to research that addresses use and management of public parks and related outdoor recreation areas.

Research in Outdoor Recreation

Outdoor recreation is not a discipline in the conventional academic sense. That is, it is not a basic branch of knowledge like biology, mathematics, or sociology. It is an applied field of study focused on an issue or problem that has attracted the attention of a broad segment of society. Though research in outdoor recreation can be traced back fifty years or more (e.g., Meinecke 1928, Bates 1935), sufficient attention was not focused on outdoor recreation for it to emerge as a field of study until after World War II. During the 1950s, rapid gains in economic prosperity, ease of transportation, increasing leisure time, and other social forces conspired to produce dramatic and sustained increases in the use of outdoor recreation areas. Problems in the form of environmental impacts and crowding began to attract the attention of both professionals and the public as manifested in articles in national magazines and professional journals (e.g., DeVoto 1953, Clawson 1959). Outdoor recreation as a field of study had its genesis in this period.

The beginning of serious social scientific study of this field began with the Outdoor Recreation Resources Review Commission (ORRRC) reports. ORRRC was a presidential commission established in 1958 to assess the status of outdoor recreation in America. It published its summary report, *Outdoor Recreation for America*, in 1962 along with twenty-nine special studies. The paucity of outdoor recreation research prior to that time is evident in one of the special studies which surveyed the outdoor recreation literature. The introduction of the report stated:

> The outline prepared as a guide for the bibliographic search assumed the existence of a substantial body of material relating rather directly to outdoor recreation. As the actual hunt progressed, the true situation—that the field (if it is yet that) of outdoor recreation has been but sketchily treated—became more and more evident (Librarian of Congress 1962:2).

The bibliographic catalog of the Library of Congress had no subject heading, "outdoor recreation." Fewer than ten entries were found in this study that referred to outdoor recreation in their titles.

Most of the early research in outdoor recreation was ecologically oriented. This was due, at least in part, to the fact that most outdoor recreation managers were professionally trained in the traditional biological disciplines or fields of study, including forestry and wildlife biology (Lime 1972a, Hendee and Stankey 1973). Moreover, most early social scientists traditionally paid little attention to the broad issue of leisure and recreation (Lundberg et al. 1934). The multidisciplinary nature of outdoor recreation, however, gained recognition in the post-World War II period. Social problems such as crowding began to supplement traditional concerns for environmental impacts, and participants in outdoor recreation activities were recognized as having socioeconomic characteristics, attitudes, and preferences that might be of interest to park and outdoor recreation managers. Emphasis on the social aspects of outdoor recreation was furthered in the 1960s and early 1970s by a series of calls for research on outdoor recreation in several major social science disciplines, including sociology (Catton 1971, Hendee 1971), economics (Clawson and Knetsch 1963), psychology (Driver 1972), geography (L. Mitchell 1969), and a general multidisciplinary approach (Lucas 1966).

Early social science research in outdoor recreation and leisure in general was primarily descriptive, focusing on the activities and social characteristics of participants. The ORRRC studies noted earlier are examples of this type of research. Early observers criticized this work as "little else than a reporting of survey data" (Berger 1962) and "sheer empiricism" (Meyersohn 1969). Absence of a strong theoretical foundation, along with an overemphasis on applied problem-solving, has been a continuing criticism of outdoor recreation research (Moncrief 1970, J. Hendricks and Burdge 1972, P. Brown et al. 1973, S. Smith 1975, Crandall and Lewko 1976, Burdge et al. 1981, Driver and Knopf 1981, Knopf 1983, Riddick et al. 1984, Witt 1984, Heywood 1986, Iso-Ahola 1986a, Reid 1987). For example, an analysis of papers published in the *Journal of Leisure Research* from 1978 through 1982 concluded that two-thirds "lacked an explicit statement about the theoretical basis of the study" (Riddick et al. 1984).

However, evidence suggests that this has changed over time as outdoor recreation research has developed and matured. As early as 1970, it was noted that the field of outdoor recreation was beginning to move beyond the descriptive phase and into more sophisticated explanatory studies (Moncrief 1970). Moreover, synergistic effects of outdoor recreation and leisure research were beginning to materialize. A study of participation in water-based recreation published in 1974 noted that "in the investigation of any problem area there must be a systematic and rigorous effort by many so that studies are progressive and research findings are accumulative, if a critical mass of theoretical and substantive knowledge is to emerge" (Field and Cheek 1974). The authors concluded that "In the study of leisure, we are coming of age." The same year, an assessment of research published in the *Journal of Leisure Research* reached a similar conclusion: "The study of leisure is approaching the threshold of real accomplishment" (Burdge 1974).

Progress in recreation research is evident in more recent analyses. An examination of papers published in four recreation-related journals from 1981 through 1990 found that most included a theoretical or conceptual framework (Henderson 1994a). Moreover, there is evidence that recreation research has proven effective and efficient. A study of the U.S. Forest Service found that the most important innovations in outdoor recreation management were derived from research (D. Anderson and Schneider 1993, Schneider et al. 1993). The study concluded that "recreation resource management research. . . is considered important and successful by managers and researchers." A second U.S. Forest Service study assessed the value of social science more broadly and concluded that "social science research can help managers work more effectively with their clients and partners to increase 'customer satisfaction,' increase support for resource management programs and policies, reduce controversy and conflict, reduce the need for restrictive rules, laws, and regulations relating to resource management and use, and reduce management costs" (Jakes et al. 1998). The effectiveness of recreation research in the U.S. National Park Service has also been documented (Machlis and Harvey 1993). Finally, an economic study suggests that, on the basis of efficiency, society may be underinvesting in outdoor recreation-related research (Bengston and Xu 1993).

Evidence suggests that recreation research has also become multidisciplinary, even interdisciplinary. Early analyses of outdoor recreation noted its inherent multidisciplinary nature, and that research should span the traditional social science disciplines (National Academy of Sciences 1969, Van Doren and Heit 1973, Crandall and Lewko 1976). A study of scholarly journals in recreation suggests that research has moved in this direction (Burdge 1983). Authors and editors of these journals reveal a trend away from a disciplinary approach to outdoor recreation to a more multidisciplinary treatment. Contributions from the traditional social science disciplines of sociology, psychology, and economics have declined relative to contributions from researchers in the broader park, recreation, and related departments, whose studies are broader in nature and more appropriate to problem solving in an inherently interdisciplinary field.

If the quality of outdoor recreation research is debatable, the quantity is not. Just eleven years after the scant literature base uncovered by the ORRRC studies, a bibliography on outdoor recreation carrying capacity was developed, containing 208 citations (Stankey and Lime 1973). A 1978 bibliography on the subject of river recreation contained 335 citations (D. Anderson et al. 1978). More recent bibliographies include nearly a thousand or more citations (Echelberger et al. 1983a, Kuss et al. 1990, Daigle 1993). Despite this apparent increase in outdoor recreation research, basic information on use and users of parks and related areas remains spotty at best. A recent survey of areas managed by the U.S. National Park Service found that most parks lacked basic visitor-related information, including socioeconomic characteristics, residence, and satisfaction (Manning and Wang 1998).

Research in outdoor recreation has, then, evolved in the classic manner of most emerging fields of study. Most early studies were descriptive and exploratory, substituting data for theory, and were disciplinary-based. An expanding database allowed more conceptual and analytical development, and ultimately a more multidisciplinary and interdisciplinary approach. These trends are evident in the scholarly journals in which recreation research is reported. The early studies of the 1950s and 1960s are found in journals of sociology, psychology, economics, and forestry. As research activity expanded, the developing field of outdoor recreation created its own multidisciplinary scholarly publication outlets, including the *Journal of Leisure Research* in 1969, *Leisure Sciences* in 1977, and the *Journal of Park and Recreation Administration* in 1983.

As the quantity of research has grown, so has its application. Research has led to greater understanding and appreciation of outdoor recreation as social behavior, and has created the foundation for a number of conceptual and organizing frameworks that underlie much of contemporary outdoor recreation management. However, many theoretical and methodological issues need further exploration, and findings from these studies need wider application across the broad spectrum of parks and outdoor recreation areas.

Search and Research for Satisfaction

As in most other areas of life, "quality" has been the underlying goal of those involved in outdoor recreation. Managers want to provide high-quality outdoor recreation opportunities, and visitors want to have high-quality outdoor recreation experiences. Researchers want to understand what contributes to and detracts from high-quality outdoor recreation experiences. As a consequence, the concept of quality is contained, explicitly or implicitly, in the goals and policies governing most outdoor recreation areas and is an underlying objective of most outdoor recreation research. But how is quality defined and measured?

The principal measure of quality in outdoor recreation has traditionally been visitor satisfaction. Beginning with the ORRRC studies, quality in outdoor recreation has often been measured in terms of user satisfaction (ORRRC 1962). Satisfaction as a measure of quality in outdoor recreation has been confirmed and reconfirmed throughout the literature:

> Providing recreation opportunities . . . for the constructive
> and satisfying use of leisure by all the nation's people is a

primary public purpose (National Academy of Sciences 1969:1).

. . . human satisfaction stands as the ultimate goal of resource programs directed toward providing camping opportunities (Bultena and Klessig 1969:348).

. . . the principal goal of recreation management is to maximize user satisfaction consistent with certain administrative, budgetary, and resource constraints (Lime and Stankey 1971:175).

. . . we assume the goal of recreation management is to maximize user satisfaction (Lucas and Stankey 1974:14).

The objective of recreation management . . . is to maximize user satisfaction within specified constraints of budget or physical resource or agency policy (Bury 1976:3).

In recent years . . . the most widely used conception of recreation quality has been that of satisfaction (More and Buyhoff 1979:1).

. . . a major goal of recreation . . . is to contribute to individuals' satisfaction (Beard and Ragheb 1980:21).

Satisfaction has often been identified as the principal product of the recreation experience and the major goal of recreation resource management (Drogin et al. 1990:167).

Satisfaction is one of the most central concepts in the study of recreation behavior (Floyd 1997:83).

The focus on satisfaction arises out of the need for some evaluative communication between visitors and managers. Because outdoor recreation in the public sector is traditionally free or priced at a nominal level, managers generally lack the clear feedback mechanism available in the private sector in the form of "price signals." Most managers recognize the potential usefulness of visitor opinions and evaluations, within the constraints of resource and management factors, in meeting the quality objectives of outdoor recreation areas.

The dominant conceptual basis for defining and measuring satisfaction in outdoor recreation has been rooted in expectancy theory (Vroom 1964, Lawler 1973, Fishbein and Ajzen 1975). Expectancy theory suggests that participants engage in recreation activities with the expectation that this will fulfill selected needs, motivations, or other desired states. The congruence between expectations and outcomes is seen to ultimately define satisfaction. This conceptual base is clearly reflected in an early and often cited definition of satisfaction as "a function of the degree of congruence between aspirations and the perceived reality of experiences" (Bultena and Klessig 1969:349).

Measurement of satisfaction, however, has proven to be more complex than anticipated (LaPage 1963, 1968, Propst and Lime 1982, LaPage 1983a, b, Noe 1987, Williams 1989). Several conceptual and methodological issues contribute to this complexity. First, general or overall measures of satisfaction may be too broad to be useful to either managers or researchers.[1] Satisfaction is a multidimensional concept, affected by a number of potential variables, some under the control of managers and many not. Measures of overall satisfaction may not be sensitive enough to detect changes in the variables of interest to managers and researchers. This issue has been illustrated in a number of wide-ranging studies that have found overall satisfaction to be influenced by elements of the biophysical, social, and managerial environments (Dorfman 1979, Foster and Jackson 1979, Beard and Ragheb 1980, Connelly 1987, Rollins and Chambers 1990, Williams et al. 1991, Floyd 1997, Burns et al. 1998). Multiple-item scales have been developed to measure alternative dimensions of satisfaction, and these have proved more useful than global, single-item measures (Ditton et al. 1981, Ditton et al. 1982, Graefe and Fedler 1986, Rollins and Chambers 1990, Vaske et al. 1991).

Second, satisfaction is a relative concept that is subject to substantial interpretation. One of the most commonly occurring themes in the outdoor recreation literature is that visitors to outdoor recreation areas often differ in ways that fundamentally affect the perceived quality of recreation opportunities, and alternately, satisfaction.[2] Visitors have varying socioeconomic characteristics, are exposed to different cultural preferences, and have varying levels of experience, and may have widely ranging attitudes, motivations, and norms. While objective elements of recreation opportunities (e.g., type of facilities provided, use level) can be important in influencing satisfaction, they are often filtered by subjective interpretations of individual visitors (Graefe and Fedler 1986).

This issue can be illustrated graphically as shown in Figure 1-1. Situational variables—resource, social, and managerial settings—can influence overall satisfaction, but these influences are mediated by the subjective evaluations of individual visitors. Empirical data tend to support this conceptual model. For example, whitewater boaters on the Cheat River, WV, reported their overall satisfaction by means of a

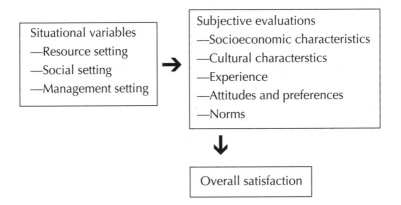

Figure 1-1. A conceptual model of recreation satisfaction. (Adapted from Whisman and Hollenhorst 1998.)

composite six-item satisfaction scale (Whisman and Hollenhorst 1998). Respondents also reported their subjective evaluations of several elements of the whitewater boating experience. Finally, several measures of objective situational variables were included in the analysis, such as use level of the river and water flow level. Regression analysis was used to determine the extent to which situational variables and subjective evaluations influenced overall satisfaction. Analysis yielded a path model of overall satisfaction for private (noncommercial) boaters, as shown in Figure 1-2. This model indicates that the combination of situational variables and subjective evaluations explains most (54%) of the variance in overall satisfaction. Moreover, these independent variables are statistically linked. For example, use of the river (a situational variable) is positively correlated (B = 0.47) with perceived crowding (a subjective evaluation), and perceived crowding is negatively correlated (B = -0.16) with overall satisfaction.

This issue may suggest reinterpretation of outdoor recreation from a "commodity metaphor" to a more "transactional" perspective (Williams 1989). Traditionally, recreation has been conceptualized as a production process: park and recreation agencies provide selected resource, social, and managerial settings, and these settings "produce" related types of recreation experiences and, ultimately, satisfied recreationists. A more transactional interpretation of recreation suggests that settings provided by park and outdoor recreation managers are important in influencing visitor satisfaction, but the ways in which these settings are perceived and evaluated by visitors may be equally important. Thus, satisfaction is a function of both recreation settings and participants.

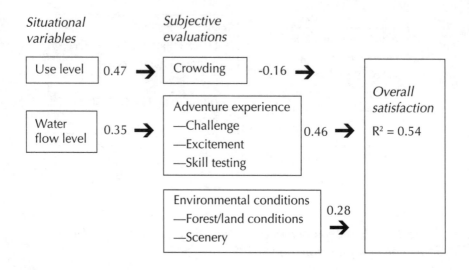

Figure 1-2. Path model of the influence of situational variables and subjective evaluations on the overall satisfaction of private whitewater boaters on the Cheat River, WV. (From Whisman and Hollenhorst 1998.)

A third, but closely related issue suggests that reliance on visitor satisfaction as a primary measure of quality may ultimately lead to diminished quality, or at least a level of quality as defined by a low common denominator. The relative nature of satisfaction as described above suggests that some visitors may be more sensitive to environmental or social impacts of increasing use levels. If such visitors are "displaced" by those who are less sensitive to recreation-related impacts, then satisfaction may remain high despite a substantive change in the type or quality of recreation opportunities (Dustin and McAvoy 1982).[3]

Fourth, most studies have found very high levels of satisfaction among visitors to a variety of recreation areas (ORRRC 1962, Brewer and Gillespie 1967, LaPage and Bevins 1981, Vaske et al. 1982a, Greenleaf et al. 1984, Applegate and Clark 1987, Drogin et al. 1990, Rollins and Chambers 1990, Vaske et al. 1991, Bevins 1992, J. Dwyer 1993a). This may be related to the broad and relative nature of satisfaction as described above. However, it should not be surprising as recreation experiences, by definition, are self-selected by visitors. This suggests that most visitors would choose recreation opportunities that are in keeping with their tastes and preferences. Despite the underlying reasons, uniformly high levels of overall satisfaction are of only limited usefulness to recreation managers and researchers interested in understanding relationships between outdoor recreation opportunities and experiences.

A final issue concerns methodological aspects of measuring satisfaction. It was noted above that multiple-item measures of satisfaction have proven more useful than general, single-item measures. However, no standardized measures have been developed and advanced. Concern has also been raised about when such measures should be administered. In the broadest sense, recreation experiences are dynamic and evolve over time. Research suggests that satisfaction and other evaluative measures also change and evolve over the duration of the experience (Hull et al. 1992, Stewart et al. 1992). However, it is unclear as to what is the most appropriate time to administer measures of satisfaction—during the experience, immediately after, or at some later period.

Research has led to new approaches to studying and defining quality and satisfaction in outdoor recreation. From the standpoint of an individual, quality and satisfaction involve the conditions of recreation settings and the characteristics of participants. Research and management attention must be applied to both of these factors. From the standpoint of a broader society, satisfaction might be equated with a diversity of recreation opportunities and experiences. Outdoor recreation might best be viewed as a system of opportunities providing a variety of visitor experiences. Each opportunity within the system should be managed explicitly for the experiences most appropriate for that area. Management of each recreation area would be changed only by conscious decision, not by a process of "creeping incrementalism" possible under general satisfaction monitoring. Under this interpretation, quality in outdoor recreation is defined as the degree to which each opportunity satisfies the experiences for which it is managed. In this way, total satisfaction of all outdoor recreationists might be truly optimized.

Interest in visitor satisfaction has helped stimulate a wide-ranging body of literature on outdoor recreation. The multifaceted nature of satisfaction has suggested a spectrum of variables and issues, ranging from the characteristics of visitors to the conditions of recreation settings, that advance understanding of outdoor recreation and influence the quality of outdoor recreation. The remaining chapters of this book explore these variables and issues.

Summary and Conclusions

1. The purpose of this book is to review and synthesize the literature on social science aspects of outdoor recreation into an integrated body of knowledge.

2. The need for this study stems from the multidisciplinary nature of outdoor recreation and the spatial, temporal, and methodological diversity of outdoor recreation research.

3. Management implications of outdoor recreation research become more evident when studies are integrated into a body of knowledge.

4. The first twelve chapters of this book focus on major themes in the outdoor recreation literature and include state-of-the-art knowledge of basic outdoor recreation concepts. The final chapter applies this body of knowledge by developing a series of principles and practices for planning and managing outdoor recreation.

5. Outdoor recreation is not an academic discipline but an interdisciplinary, applied field of study.

6. Research in outdoor recreation, particularly empirically based social science, began in earnest in the early 1960s when outdoor recreation was recognized as important and potentially problematic by a broad segment of society. Research has expanded greatly in recent years.

7. Outdoor recreation research has evolved in the traditional pattern of developing fields of study. Early studies tended to be descriptive, exploratory, and disciplinary-based, while more recent studies have tended to be more conceptually based, explanatory, and multidisciplinary.

8. Recent evidence suggests that outdoor recreation research is generally efficient and effective.

9. High quality is the underlying goal of outdoor recreation managers, visitors, and researchers. Visitor satisfaction, defined as the congruence between expectations and outcomes, has been the traditional measure of quality. However, measures of overall visitor satisfaction may be inadequate for several reasons, including:

   A. Overall satisfaction is a broad, multidimensional concept and may not be sensitive enough to detect changes in variables of interest to managers and researchers.

B. Overall satisfaction is a relative concept that is subject to interpretation. This suggests that satisfaction is a function of both objective characteristics of recreation settings—resource, social, and managerial conditions—and subjective evaluations of visitors as illustrated in Figure 1-1.

C. The relative nature of overall satisfaction suggests that it may remain high even when the type or quality of recreation opportunities change.

D. Overall satisfaction levels of visitors are often uniformly high, limiting their usefulness for understanding relationships between recreation opportunities and experiences.

10. Conceptual and methodological issues suggest that multiple-item measures of satisfaction may be more useful than general, single-item measures.

11. It is unclear when satisfaction measures should be administered—during the experience, immediately after, or some time later.

12. Quality in outdoor recreation has evolved from overall measures of satisfaction to the degree to which outdoor recreation opportunities satisfy the experiences for which they are planned and managed.

13. Research on satisfaction in outdoor recreation has helped reveal a variety of variables and issues that advance understanding of outdoor recreation. These variables and issues range from objective characteristics of recreation settings to subjective evaluations of recreation visitors and are described in subsequent chapters of this book.

Notes

1. This issue is discussed more fully in Chapter 5.
2. The issue of diversity in outdoor recreation is discussed more fully in Chapter 8.
3. The issue of displacement is discussed more fully in Chapter 5.

2

Social Aspects of Outdoor Recreation
Use and Users

Recreation Use and Users

Information on recreation use and users was recognized early as potentially important for a number of reasons (e.g., Bury 1964). For example, even relatively simple data from campground registration forms might be useful in the planning and design of recreation facilities. Information on size of camping groups, for instance, can be important to campground planners and designers. Several studies have developed illustrations and guidelines supporting the way in which information on recreation use and the characteristics of users can and should be integrated into recreation management (Lime and Buchman 1974, Plumley et al. 1978, Knopf and Lime 1984). Applications range from monitoring the popularity of recreation activities so as to more efficiently plan budgetary, personnel, and other resource needs to determining the residence and education of users in order to more effectively conduct public information and education programs.

A related issue concerns the desirability of collecting this type of information on a regular basis in order to determine trends in outdoor recreation. Outdoor recreation research has been conducted for a long enough period to begin to document such trends. A number of important trend-related studies can be found in the literature. For example, a comparison of five recreation use studies conducted over a twenty-five-year period at Yosemite National Park, CA, found a substantial shift in use toward single-day hikers (Van Wagtendonk 1980). Day users and other short-term visitors have distinct facility and service needs, and these should be reflected in management programs. Trend-related research on wilderness use in general suggests that, while there is considerable variation among individual areas, use tended to increase rapidly in the 1960s and 1970s, level off or even decline in the 1980s, and began to climb again in the 1990s (Lucas 1985, Roggenbuck and

Lucas 1987, Cole 1996). A series of national conferences on trends in outdoor recreation was begun in 1980 and has continued to meet every five years. Proceedings of these conferences represent a valuable source of information on trends in a variety of specific outdoor recreation activities and in outdoor recreation in general (LaPage 1980, Wood 1985, Thompson et al. 1995).[1] In addition, several papers on outdoor recreation trends have been prepared by senior researchers and provide valuable perspectives on outdoor recreation (Clawson 1985, Lucas 1985, Merriam 1986, Beaman 1997).

This and the following chapter examine social and descriptive aspects of outdoor recreation. This chapter focuses on measures of recreation activity and characteristics of recreationists, including their social characteristics and cultural influences on their recreation activity and behavior. Chapter 3 addresses attitudes, preferences, and perceptions of visitors to outdoor recreation areas.

Outdoor Recreation Activity

The first and most straightforward form of research into social aspects of outdoor recreation was measurement of recreation activity. Initial efforts, going back for some areas and agencies well before World War II, were primarily simple head counts of visitors to recreation areas. Larger efforts became more sophisticated, including length-of-stay measures and categorization of visits by specific activities such as camping and hiking.

Use measurement is often difficult due to the dispersed nature of outdoor recreation activity. A number of studies beginning in the 1960s have developed and evaluated various use sampling procedures.[2] Many recreation areas, particularly backcountry and wilderness areas, rely on use permits and self-registration as a primary source of information. However, a variety of relatively sophisticated use sampling and measurement techniques have also been developed, including mechanical and electronic counting devices, optical scanners and cameras, direct and indirect observation, and self-administered, personal interview, telephone, and mail surveys. The literature on alternative methods for monitoring recreation use, particularly in backcountry and wilderness, has been compiled into a manual that outlines advantages and disadvantages of alternative measurement approaches (Hollenhorst et al. 1992). For example, use permits allow collection of extensive and accurate use data, but can be costly to administer and may be burdensome to visitors. Self-registration can also provide extensive data, but noncompliance must be monitored to assess its accuracy. Indirect counts using electronic or mechanical devices along with self-registration can meet most research and management needs by providing data on both amount and type of use.

Many outdoor recreation areas and agencies have developed relatively standard use measurement procedures based on these techniques. But there are often substantive differences among areas and agencies. Figure 2-1, for example, shows annual use of areas administered by two major federal outdoor recreation agencies—the National Park Service and the U.S. Forest Service. But these data include

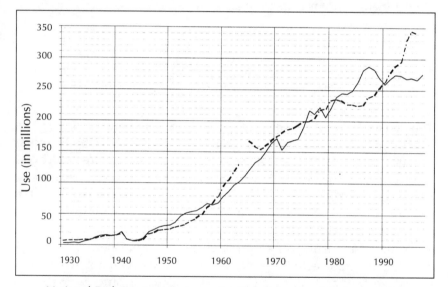

——— National Park Service. Data are "visits," defined as " the entry of any person into an area."

– – – U.S. Forest Service. Data from 1930 to 1964 are "recreation visits," defined as "the entry of any person into an area for recreation." Data from 1965 to 1996 are "recreation visitor-days," defined as "the recreation use of national forest land or water that aggregates 12 visitor hours. This may entail one person for 12 hours, 12 persons for one hour, or any equivalent combination of individual or group use, either continuous or intermittent."

Figure 2-1. Annual use of areas administered by the National Park Service and U.S. Forest Service.

two basic measurement units—"visits," and "visitor-days." A "visit" is generally defined as the entry of a person into a recreation area, and can include all visitors or just those who are participating in recreation activities. A "visitor-day" is generally defined as the presence of a person in a recreation area for twelve hours or any combination of visitors and hours that equals twelve. Each of these measurement units has advantages and disadvantages (Beaman and Stanley 1992). However, they also confound efforts to compare use among areas and agencies and sometimes even over time as agencies change use-measurement procedures.

Household surveys represent another basic approach to measuring outdoor recreation activity. They are more likely to be representative of recreation participation patterns of the general population than are on-site studies. The first large-scale national household survey of outdoor recreation was conducted in 1960 as part of the ORRRC studies, and was a nationwide survey of persons eighteen years and older (Ferriss 1962). The purpose of this survey was to determine the relative popularity of outdoor recreation activities as a guide to establishing priorities for further development of recreation facilities and services. The federal government has conducted or sponsored similar nationwide surveys on a periodic basis as part of its outdoor recreation planning responsibilities. Summary results for each of the six major nationwide surveys are shown in Table 2-1. In addition, the Land and Water Conservation Fund Act of 1964 has required states to conduct comprehensive recreation planning to qualify for matching federal grants. Many states conduct household surveys patterned after the federal studies as a part of their planning process.

While the surveys reported in Table 2-1 provide a measure of the outdoor recreation activities in which participation is most widely distributed, their usefulness in recreation planning and management has been limited by a number of conceptual and methodological problems. The first of these stems from consideration of these surveys, either explicitly or implicitly, as studies of demand for recreation activities (Knetsch 1969, Burdge and Hendee 1972). Data from these surveys are measures of participation in recreation activities, not necessarily demand. They do not take into account existing recreation opportunities and their effect on participation rates. It is likely that high participation rates will correlate with abundant opportunities, especially when these opportunities are priced at nominal levels, as is traditional in the public sector. Treatment of participation surveys as measures of demand may lead to a feedback model whereby supply or opportunity

Table 2-1. Nationwide participation rates in selected outdoor recreation activities, 1960–1994.

	1960[a]	1965[b]	1972[c]	1977[d]	1982-3[e]	1994[f]
	Percent participating					
Picnicking	53	57	47	72	48	49
Driving for pleasure	52	55	34	69	48	—
Sightseeing	42	49	37	68	46	57
Swimming	45	48	—	—	53	—
Pool	—	—	18	63	43	44
Other	—	—	34	46	32	39
Walking and jogging	33	48	34	68	53	67
Playing outdoor games	30	38	22	56	—	—
Golf	—	9	5	16	13	15
Tennis	—	16	5	33	17	11
Fishing	29	30	24	53	34	29
Attending outdoor sports events	24	30	12	61	40	47
Other boating	22	24	15	34	6	—
Bicycling	9	16	10	47	32	29
Nature walks	14	14	17	50	—	—
Bird watching	—	5	4	—	12	27
Wildlife photography	—	2	2	—	—	—
Attending outdoor concerts, plays	9	11	7	41	25	21
Camping	8	10	—	—	24	—
Developed	—	—	11	30	17	21
Backcountry	—	—	5	21	5	14
Horseback riding	6	8	5	15	9	7
Hiking or backpacking	6	7	5	28	—	24
Waterskiing	6	6	5	16	9	—
Canoeing	2	3	3	16	8	—
Sailing	2	3	3	11	6	—
Mountain climbing	1	1	—	—	—	4
Visiting zoos, amusement parks	—	—	24	73	50	—
Off-road driving	—	—	7	26	11	14
Other activities	5	—	24	—	4	—

a Ferriss (1962); b Bureau of Outdoor Recreation (1972); c Bureau of Outdoor Recreation (1973); d Heritage Conservation and Recreation Service (1979); e Van Horne et al. (1985); f Cordell et al. (1996, 1997); — Data not available creates high participation rates, which in turn encourage more supply, and so on (Chappelle 1973). Indeed, the supply of recreation opportunities has been found to have statistically significant effects on participation rates in at least two empirically based studies (Cicchetti et al. 1969, Beaman et al. 1979).

Another conceptual problem with participation surveys is their exclusive focus on activities rather than the underlying meanings these activities have for participants. Recent theoretical and empirical work has shown that people participate in outdoor recreation activities to satisfy certain motivations; that is, recreation activities are more a means to an end than an end in themselves. Overemphasis on activities ignores the potential for one activity to substitute for another in fulfilling the same motivations. The issues of motivations for recreation and substitutability of recreation activities are discussed more fully in Chapters 7 and 10, respectively.

Finally, participation surveys have been plagued by a host of methodological problems. The empty cells in Table 2-1 illustrate one such problem: the same activities are not always included in participation surveys. This lack of consistency limits comparisons over time and, therefore, the identification of trends. Not apparent from Table 2-1, however, are other methodological inconsistencies. The way in which activities are defined can substantially affect the participation rates reported. The distinction between walking and hiking, for example, is often unclear, sometimes being left to the discretion of the respondent. The time period covered by the survey can also be a source of bias in participation surveys. Some surveys cover an entire calendar year, while others focus on a single season. Other methodological issues include varying data collection techniques (e.g., personal interview, telephone, or mail surveys), sample size and response rate, age of respondents, recall period, and question wording and sequence.

Two studies in particular illustrate these methodological problems. The first study examined twenty-two national outdoor recreation participation studies conducted between 1959 and 1978, including those in Table 2-1, along with several U.S. Forest Service camping market surveys, U.S. Fish and Wildlife Service surveys of hunting and fishing, and a number of market surveys conducted by private organizations (Bevins and Wilcox 1979). Data on twenty-eight activities were explored, revealing some apparent trends, but a number of methodological issues as well. For example, participation in bicycling was included in thirteen surveys, but the range in nationwide participation varied from a low of 9% to a high of 47%, and no clear trend was apparent from the data.

Results for camping and hunting were somewhat more consistent, but there was still considerable variation among studies. It is often impossible to distinguish which differences are caused by varying survey methods and which reflect real trends. A second comparative study of recreation surveys concluded that examination of nationwide outdoor recreation participation surveys "may tell us more about the effects of alternative survey designs than about trends in participation" (Stynes et al. 1980).

Use Distribution and Dynamics

Research on recreation use has also addressed the distribution and dynamics of outdoor recreation activity over both space and time. An early study of the Boundary Waters Canoe Area, MN, mapped the spatial distribution of use and noted its uneven pattern (Lucas 1964a). Over half of all visitors were found to use only one-tenth of the access points to the study area. Uneven spatial distribution of recreation use has been a nearly universal finding of subsequent studies. Most such studies have focused on wilderness or related areas (Stankey et al. 1976, Lime 1977b, Leonard et al. 1978, Plumley et al. 1978, Lucas 1980, Manning and Powers 1984, Roggenbuck and Lucas 1987, Cole 1996, 1997a).

To quantify spatial distribution patterns more closely, a concentration index can be developed which relates amount of use to available area. The concentration index for the trail system of the Spanish Peaks Primitive Area, MT, for example, is shown in Figure 2-2. To compute the concentration index, trail segments are ranked by amount of use, and use is summed and graphed, starting with the trail segments most used. The 45-degree diagonal represents perfectly evenly distributed use (i.e., 50% of all trail miles account for 50% of use), while the curved line plots the actual distribution of use. In Figure 2-2, 50% of all trail miles account for approximately 80% of all use. The concentration index is calculated on the basis of area A as a proportion of area A + B. Index values range from 0 (perfectly even distribution) to 100 (perfectly uneven distribution). The concentration index for the Spanish Peaks Primitive Area is fifty-three, indicating relatively uneven distribution of use. Concentration indexes for the trail systems of seven wilderness areas ranged from fifty-three to seventy-eight (Lucas 1980).

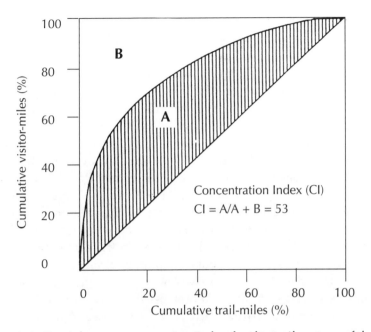

Figure 2-2. Spatial use concentration index for the trail system of the Spanish Peaks Primitive Area, MT. (From Lucas 1980.)

Spatial distribution of use of developed recreation areas also tends to be highly uneven. Occupancy rates for campsites within Vermont State Park campgrounds were found to vary dramatically, ranging from less than 10% to greater than 80% (Manning et al. 1984).

Recreation use has also been found to vary sharply among recreation areas (Stankey et al. 1976, M. Peterson 1981, Roggenbuck and Lucas 1987). Comparison of use among ten wilderness areas within the national forests, for example, found that visitor-days of use varied dramatically. Even when use was related to acreage, some areas received nearly 500 times as much use as others (Stankey et al. 1976, Roggenbuck and Lucas 1987).

Several studies have examined the distribution of recreation use over time. As with the spatial distribution of use described above, these studies have usually found highly uneven patterns of recreation use (Lucas 1980, Roggenbuck and Lucas 1987, Glass et al. 1991, Glass and Walton 1995). Most recreation areas, of course, are used most heavily in the summer, though areas that are heavily used for hunting, skiing, or other highly seasonal activities may be an exception. Even within the summer period, however, use can be highly skewed toward weekends and holidays. For example, weekends and holidays accounted for the majority of all summer use in nearly all roaded recreation areas studied within the national forests of Oregon and Washington (Hendee et al. 1976). Moreover, temporal use concentration indexes (using the same measurement approach as spatial use concentration indexes described above) for state park campgrounds in Vermont and New Hampshire ranged from twelve to forty-five, indicating relatively uneven distribution of use over time (Manning and Cormier 1980).

Research suggests that both spatial and temporal use of outdoor recreation areas tend to be distributed in a highly uneven fashion. This phenomenon creates several potential problems. Recreation facilities and services developed to meet peak loads may be largely unused at other times, resulting in inefficient resource use. In addition, the potential for crowding and conflicting uses is enhanced when a relatively large percentage of all visitors are concentrated in the same areas and/or time periods. And it may be that environmental impacts of recreation use are exacerbated by excessively concentrated patterns of use.

A final issue related to the temporal distribution of outdoor recreation concerns its dynamic nature. Early conceptual research suggested that outdoor recreation can be interpreted as an experience as much as a discrete activity such as hiking or camping (Clawson and Knetsch 1963, 1966).[3] Outdoor recreation was theorized as being comprised of five basic phases—anticipation, travel to a park or site, on-site experience, return travel, and recollection. Empirical research has tended to support the multiphase nature of outdoor recreation (More and Payne 1978, Hammitt 1980, Hull et al. 1992, Stewart 1992, Stewart and Hull 1992, Hull et al. 1996). For example, students on a college field trip tended to register distinct mood changes associated with each of the five phases of outdoor recreation noted above (Hammitt 1980). In a more directly recreation-related study, hikers were asked to record measures of mood, satisfaction, and aesthetic beauty at multiple points during their recreation experience (Hull et al. 1992). These measures were found to vary over time in meaningful ways. Moreover, study findings suggest that temporally based elements or phases of the recreation experience can be influenced by management actions. The dynamic nature of outdoor recreation suggests that both researchers and managers should address the multiple phases of the recreation experience.

Social Correlates of Outdoor Recreation

Along with the amount and distribution of recreation activity, social scientists have also examined the social characteristics of outdoor recreation participants. Special emphasis has been placed on basic demographic and socioeconomic characteristics such as age, education, income, and occupation. This information is fundamental to an eventual understanding of more sophisticated issues such as why people participate in outdoor recreation, and is also important in predicting future recreation patterns and evaluating issues of social equity.

Research into the social characteristics of participants in general leisure activities began as early as the 1930s. These studies multiplied in the 1950s and the 1960s when increased leisure became more generally available. Total participation in leisure activities, as well as in selected types of leisure activities, was generally found to be related to a variety of socioeconomic factors, particularly social class differences and occupational prestige (e.g., MacDonald et al. 1949, Reissman 1954, White 1955, Clarke 1956, Thomas 1956, Havighurst and Feigenbaum 1959, Gerstl 1961, DeGrazia 1962, Dowell 1967, Bishop and Ikeda 1970).

Publication of the ORRRC reports in 1962 extended this work more directly to outdoor recreation. Two ORRRC studies in particular focused on social correlates of outdoor recreation participation. One of these reviewed 48 studies relating to this issue conducted between 1950 and 1962. Five socioeconomic variables were found to be related to outdoor recreation patterns: age, income, occupation, residence, and stage of family life cycle (Sessoms 1961, 1963).

This study was supplemented by a nationwide household survey of outdoor recreation participation (Mueller and Gurin 1962, Hendee 1969). Participation in outdoor recreation activity was found to be "remarkably widespread," with about 90% of adults engaging in one or more activities in the course of a year. General participation was found to be statistically related to several demographic and socioeconomic variables: age, race, region of residence, place of residence, education, income, and stage of family life cycle. However, with the exception of age, relationships were only of weak to moderate strength. All demographic and socioeconomic variables combined explained about 30% of the variance in overall participation in outdoor recreation activities. Similar findings by Ferriss (1970) led to the conclusion that socioeconomic characteristics "provide only a moderately satisfactory basis for predicting outdoor recreation participation."

Research conducted since the ORRRC studies has generally tended to corroborate and extend these findings. Three types of studies comprise this literature. First, many on-site surveys at a variety of outdoor recreation areas have measured selected demographic and socioeconomic characteristics of visitors. To the degree they are comparable, a number of these studies are summarized in Table 2-2.[4] While all of these studies found a diversity of visitors, they also found that certain demographic and socioeconomic categories were commonly over-represented compared to their distribution throughout the general population. Visitors to outdoor recreation areas, especially more resource oriented areas such as national forests, national parks and wilderness, tend to be young to middle age and to be of relatively high socioeconomic status as defined by income, occupation, and especially education (Roggenbuck and Lucas 1987, Stankey 1971).

A second type of study has used general population surveys to examine selected demographic and socioeconomic characteristics of participants in a variety of recreation activities (Burdge 1969, Lindsay and Ogle 1972, T. White 1975, Bultena and Field 1978, Jackson 1980, Kelly 1980, R. Young 1983, More et al. 1990, Walker and Kiecolt 1995). Many of these studies have found statistically significant relationships between recreation participation and selected demographic and socioeconomic characteristics. For example, an early study surveyed residents of Allegheny County, PA, concerning their participation in selected leisure and outdoor recreation activities and their occupations (Burdge 1969). Occupational prestige was classified into four levels. Persons in the highest two occupational levels were found to have significantly higher participation rates in thirteen of the sixteen outdoor recreation activities studied. In addition, study findings suggest that different types of outdoor recreation activities appeal to different occupational classes. Six recreation activities described as potentially more expensive and less generally available were statistically related to the highest occupational prestige level, while four activities deemed more generally available were statistically related to the second highest occupational level. Moreover, two of the three recreation activities that were unrelated to any occupational prestige level were likely the most generally available of all.

A general population survey of visits to national parks in the Pacific Northwest offers further insight into the relationship between outdoor recreation and socioeconomic variables (Bultena and Field 1978). The percentage of respondents who had visited one or more national parks rose progressively with increased socioeconomic status. Socioeconomic status was then broken into its three component variables (income, education, and occupation), and each was tested for its relationship to national park visits. To isolate each of these three variables, statistical controls were applied to the other two. While education and occupation retained their statistically significant relationship with national park visits, income did not.

A large-scale analysis of a nationwide survey of recreation participation has generally corroborated the findings described above and placed them in a more comprehensive perspective (Kelly 1980). Thirty outdoor recreation activities were studied and divided into three types: forest-based activities, water-based activities, and outdoor sports activities. Seven socioeconomic characteristics of respondents (stage of family life cycle, income, sex, race, age, occupation, and education) were related to a statistically significant degree to outdoor recreation participation. However, these relationships were generally weak; these seven variables in aggregate explained less than 10% of the variance in overall participation in any of the three types of activities. However, a second phase of this study examined relationships between demographic and socioeconomic variables and participation in specific recreation activities. A number of stronger relationships were found, including:

1. Age is strongly and inversely related to recreation activities requiring physical strength and endurance.

2. Income affects only a few recreation activities that have relatively high cost thresholds.

3. Sex is related to recreation activities that have historically been associated with masculinity, such as hunting.

4. Education is moderately related to only a few recreation activities, such as sailing, golf, and cross-country skiing.

5. Occupation is strongly related to only one recreation activity, cross-country skiing.

6. Race is strongly related to a number of resource-oriented recreation activities, including camping, waterskiing, downhill skiing, and snowmobiling.

7. Stage of family life cycle is highly inter-correlated with age so that its effects on recreation activities are similar to those of age.

A final type of study is literature reviews that attempt to integrate and synthesize findings from other studies (Zuzanek 1978, Kelly 1980, O'Leary et al. 1982, Roggenbuck and Lucas 1987). Once again, these studies have generally corroborated the above findings. Selected demographic and socioeconomic characteristics are often related to

Table 2-2. Selected socioeconomic characteristics of outdoor recreationists.

Study	Area	*Predominant characteristic of the sample population[a]*			
		Income	*Education*	*Occupation*	*Age*
J. A. Wagar 1963b	2 national forest recreation areas	Middle	Middle to high	—	Young to middle-aged adults
Etzkorn 1964	1 California campground	—	High	Professional/ technical	—
Love 1964	12 national forest campgrounds	—	—	—	Children to young adults
E. Shafer 1965	4 state park campgrounds	Middle to high	—	—	—
King 1965, 1968	National forest campgrounds	Middle	High	Middle to high prestige levels	—
Burch and Wenger 1967	A variety of camping areas	High	High	White collar/ skilled	—
Hendee et al. 1968	3 wilderness areas	—	High	—	Young to middle-aged adults
Boster et al. 1973	Colorado River, Grand Canyon National Park, AZ	High	—	—	—
Murray 1974	Southern Appalachian Trail	High	High	Professional/ technical and students	Teenage to young adults
R. Lee 1975	Yosemite National Park, CA	—	High	Professional/ technical	—
Vaux 1975	4 wilderness areas	High, except students	—	—	—
Echelberger and Moeller 1977	National forest backcountry	Middle to high	Middle to high	—	Young adults
Towler 1977	Grand Canyon National Park, AZ, backcountry	High	High	Professionals/ students	Young adults

Predominant characteristic of the sample population[a]

Study	Area	Income	Education	Occupation	Age
Manning 1979a	4 Vermont rivers	—	—	—	Young to middle-aged adults
Stankey 1980a	2 wilderness areas	—	High	—	Young to middle-aged adults
Lucas 1980	9 wilderness areas	Middle to high	High	Professional/ technical and students	Young to middle-aged adults
Furuseth and Altman 1991	Greenway users, Raleigh, NC	Middle to high	High	—	Young to middle-aged adults
Watson et al. 1992	Cohutta Wilderness, GA	High	High	—	Young to middle-aged adults
	Caney Creek Wilderness, AR	High	High	—	Young to middle-aged adults
	Upland Island Wilderness, TX	High	High	—	Young to middle-aged adults
Cole et al. 1995	Boundary Waters Canoe Area Wilderness, MN	High	High	—	Young to middle-aged adults
	Shining Rock Wilderness, NC	—	High	—	Young to middle-aged adults
	Desolation Wilderness, CA	High	High	—	Young to middle-aged adults
Watson et al. 1996a	Eagle Cap Wilderness, OR	—	High	—	Middle age

a. The socioeconomic categories reported in this table are highly generalized to enable reasonable comparison among studies and over time.
— Data not available.

outdoor recreation participation, but these relationships tend to be only of weak to moderate strength. Demographic and socioeconomic variables generally explain only a small portion of the variance in overall participation in outdoor recreation, but may be related more strongly to participation in specific recreation activities.

Two methodological issues have been raised with regard to a number of the studies discussed in this section. First, on-site studies often focus exclusively on the "leader" of a recreation group, and this may constitute a source of bias (Lucas and Oltman 1971). A test of this hypothesis was conducted on the Anaconda-Pintlar Wilderness Area, MT, by interviewing both party leaders and all party members over age fourteen (Jubenville 1971). Statistically significant differences were found between the two samples with regard to five socioeconomic variables. Party leaders were more likely to be males, to have higher income and educational levels, to be in professional and technical occupations, and to have more years of recreation experience.

Another issue of concern focuses on differences between on-site studies and more broadly based surveys of the general population. It was noted earlier in this section that a nationwide household survey found that 30% of the variance in outdoor recreation activity could be explained by seven demographic and socioeconomic variables (Mueller and Gurin 1962). This study, by definition, included both participants and non-participants in outdoor recreation. Another household survey examined participation in water-based recreation activities in the Pacific Northwest (Field and O'Leary 1973). When non-participants were excluded from the analysis, a group of seven of the most important demographic and socioeconomic variables explained less than 12% of the variance in participation among the four water-based activities studied. The implication of this finding seems to be that much of the variation in socioeconomic characteristics found in household surveys is a function of distinctions between outdoor recreation participants and non-participants. When non-participants are eliminated (as they are by definition in on-site studies), the resulting populations are more homogeneous, at least with respect to traditional demographic and socioeconomic measures. Two other household surveys have generally corroborated these findings (O'Leary and Pate 1979, O'Leary and Weeks 1979).

The broad implication of these findings is that on-site studies of recreation visitors may sample a relatively limited diversity of the general population, at least as defined by demographic and socioeconomic characteristics. More broadly based studies of the general population may also be needed to assess satisfaction and other aspects of outdoor recreation opportunities on a more comprehensive basis.

Cultural Influences on Outdoor Recreation

The studies described in the preceding section have examined a number of social correlates of outdoor recreation. However, the relationships are generally of moderate strength at best and fail to explain a large percentage of the variation in outdoor recreation participation. Early observers described the results of this research as "both productive and disappointing" and went on to suggest an alternative perspective for outdoor recreation research (Burdge and Field 1972). It was noted that a basic tenet of the social sciences is that human behavior is culturally influenced, and this suggests that studies of outdoor recreation behavior include a component that focuses on the cultural context of recreation participation (Burch 1970).

Social Groups. Perhaps the earliest work in this area theorized that outdoor recreation, like most other behavior, is largely a function of the groups in which one operates:

> The same individual who goes hunting with an all-male group will behave differently than when he is taking his family fishing. Furthermore, these two groups will have different auxiliary activities and make different demands on the resource and recreation facilities. In other words, there is something in the nature of a recreation group that structures the group member's behavior (Burch 1964a:708).

Using primarily observational techniques, Burch (1964a) found preliminary empirical support for the notion that recreation activities are often characterized by the group structure of their participants, with different groups having different objectives and needs. Further theoretical development led to a "personal community hypothesis" of recreation: that participation in recreation is influenced by one's "social circles of workmates, family, and friends" (Burch 1969).

Consideration of the cultural influences on recreation has expanded considerably since the early 1970s, concentrating largely on social groups. An early review of the sociology of leisure, for example, noted that most social research in recreation has been based on random samples of individuals whereby the "connectedness of humans is carefully sampled out" (Meyersohn 1969). The potential shortcoming of this traditional approach was demonstrated by noting the prevalence of social groups in outdoor recreation. A study of visits to local parks by adult males, for example, found the vast majority (81%) came in social groups rather than alone (Cheek 1971). This finding has been consistently corroborated for most outdoor recreation areas and activities. The dominance of social groups in outdoor recreation environments is suggestive of the influence of group context on recreation behavior (Cheek and Burch 1976, Cheek et al. 1976). Empirical tests have consistently borne out this influence.

For example, a study of participation in four water-based recreation activities compared the influence of conventional demographic and socioeconomic variables and a measure of social groups (classified as family, friends, or family and friends) (Field and O'Leary 1973, Field and Creek 1974). Examined independently, none of the nine demographic and socioeconomic variables studied accounted for significant differences in participation rates in two of the four activities studied; for the third activity, only one variable was related to participation rates. Examined in a multivariate context, the nine demographic and socioeconomic variables explained less than 5% of the variance in the three activities and 26% in the fourth. When type of social group was analyzed, however, significant differences were found in participation rates. Moreover, when the measure of social group was added to the nine demographic and socioeconomic variables in a multivariate analysis, the amount of variance explained in participation rose to between 12% and 39% for the four types of activities.

A later general population study also compared the relative influence of demographic/socioeconomic variables and social groups on recreation behavior (Dottavio et al. 1980). Using a state-wide sample of Indiana residents, participation rates in twelve outdoor recreation activities were related to two independent variable sets: seven conventional demographic/socioeconomic variables, and social group (measured as alone, family, friends, family/friends) combined with age and sex of respondent. The second set of variables explained substantially more variance in absolute frequency of participation than the first. It should be noted, however, that when the dependent variable of participation rate was dichotomized into high/low participation, the difference between the two independent variable sets was reduced.

While the above studies indicate that social groups influence recreation participation, there is less evidence as to why such influences exist. However, two studies are suggestive. One study has attempted to illuminate this issue by examining both social group influences on and motivations for recreation participation (Buchanan et al. 1981).[5] Using a sample of visitors to a multiple-use reservoir, social group (defined as family, friendship, and family/friendship) was related to participation in three water-based activities and nineteen potential recreation motivations were rated by respondents. Results indicated that social groups varied in the frequency with which they participated in the three activities studied. Moreover, this variability appeared to be related to the different motivations associated with these activities. The activity most heavily predominated by one social group also had the least variability in motivations assigned to it, and the activity with the greatest mix of social groups participating had the greatest variability in motivations. These findings may indicate that social groups are attracted to recreation activities based on motivations inherent within the group.

A second study of kayakers obtained similar but expanded findings (Schuett 1995). Type of social group (e.g., by oneself or with family, friends, or organized groups) was found to be related to trip motivations as well as other personal characteristics, such as experience level and importance or centrality of kayaking.

Recent research has explored expansion of social groups to locate such "personal communities" within the larger framework of society (Stokowski 1990, Stokowski and Lee 1991). This theoretical approach suggests that individuals are socialized into recreation styles not only by means of the social groups within which they participate, but by their broader social contacts and relationships as well. Using social network analysis, an initial exploratory study suggests that broad social relationships can both facilitate and constrain recreation and leisure behavior. For example, individuals with social ties to multiple types of groups, such as immediate family, extended family, and friends, were involved in a broader range of recreation activities than individuals with social ties to only one group type.

Socialization, Community, and Status Group Dynamics. While a predominant focus of research into cultural influences on outdoor recreation has been social groups, several other variables have also received attention. Three of these variables include childhood experiences as part of the socialization process, effects of community type, and status group dynamics.

Several studies have examined childhood influences on outdoor recreation behavior in later life, all finding significant effects. For example, an early study examined childhood experience with nature and its relationship to the style of camping selected as an adult: easy access camping, remote camping, or a combination of the two (Burch and Wenger 1967). Both those who had childhood hiking experience and—perhaps more surprisingly—those who had participated in auto camping as children were more likely to practice remote or combination camping than easy-access camping. Easy-access campers were more likely to be people without either hiking or auto camping experience as children. The study concludes that:

> . . . activities pleasantly familiar to a person in his childhood tend to attract his leisure-time interest as an adult. Furthermore, an adult with previous familiarity with the out-of-doors apparently prefers more challenging camping experiences, at least part of the time, than does the person new to the out-of-doors (Burch and Wenger 1967:18).

The importance of childhood experiences was corroborated by a later household study of recreation participation (J. Christensen and Yoesting 1973). The total number of recreation activities participated in as a child was combined with seven other independent variables (mostly conventional demographic and socioeconomic measures) to explain 46% of the variance in adult recreation participation. Moreover, total childhood recreation activities were more important in explaining this variance than all the demographic and socioeconomic variables combined. This study was later replicated, and very similar results were obtained: 36% of the variance in adult recreation activities was explained by the number of recreation activities participated in as a child (Yoesting and Christensen 1978). The authors of this study point out, however, that participation in specific activities does not carry over from childhood as well as the general level of activity, and that socialization in recreation is apparently a lifelong process, influenced by a number of variables including social group.

A more recent study used in-depth interviews with participants and nonparticipants in canoeing and kayaking to determine the effects of socialization (Bixler and Morris 1998). Several types of socialization, including family experiences, summer camps, and scouting, were found to influence participation in these outdoor recreation activities. The authors conclude that "While there was tremendous variation in socialization experiences, canoeists and kayakers had 'accumulated' large numbers of outdoor experiences by the time they had reached their teens," and that "this 'outdoor capital' provides a solid experiential foundation for adopting water-based wildland recreation activities." A number of other studies have also found a relationship between childhood recreation activities and adult recreation participation (Sofranko and Nolan 1972, Yoesting and Burkhead 1973, Kelly 1974, McClaskie et al. 1986, McGuire et al. 1987, O'Leary et al. 1987).

Type of community has also been found to exert an influence on recreation behavior. The studies described in the preceding section of this chapter demonstrated relationships between selected demographic and socioeconomic characteristics of the individual and recreation participation. However, these relationships have been found to be mitigated by the social class structure of the community in which the individual resides (Bultena and Field 1980). Household samples were drawn from two communities varying distinctly in social class structure—one a predominantly middle-class community, the other a predominantly working-class community. Visitation rates to national parks were studied in both communities. Working-class people in the predominantly middle-class community were found to visit the parks significantly more frequently than their class counterparts in the predominantly working-class community. Conversely, park visitation rates of middle-class people in the working-class community were lower than their class counterparts in the middle-class community.

The theory of status group dynamics has also received attention as a cultural influence on recreation. This theory suggests that participation in recreation, particularly in "faddish" activities, is diffused through the population on a social class basis. The theory is based on the classic work of Veblen (1912), who observed that upper-class styles of leisure, as well as more general taste and consumption behavior, are often emulated and adopted by those of the lower classes as a means of status mobility. Several studies have tested this theory, finding it useful in predicting and explaining outdoor recreation participation patterns (West 1977, 1982a, 1983, 1984, 1985). These studies have found a number of outdoor recreation activities, such as bicycling, canoeing, and cross-country skiing, to be diffused over time from higher to lower social groups.

Race and Ethnicity. Interest in effects of race and ethnicity on recreation have been evident since the very early stages of outdoor recreation research. Two of the ORRRC studies in the early 1960s, for example, reported significant differences in outdoor recreation participation between blacks and whites (Hauser 1962, Mueller and Gurin 1962). Interest in this issue expanded in the 1960s and early 1970s as a function of the civil rights movement (Floyd 1998). Racial unrest in this period was attributed, at least in part, to poor quality and inequitable distribution of recreation opportunities (National Advisory Commission on Civil Disorders 1970, Washburne 1978, Kraus and Lewis 1986). Concern over issues of equity and social and environmental justice have continued to focus research attention on this matter. Interest in this subject area is likely to continue to grow in intensity and importance as minority populations of several types continue to expand relative to the traditional white, European-American majority (Floyd 1998). Research tends to fall into one of two basic categories: (1) studies that explore differences in recreation patterns between or among racial and ethnic groups, and (2) studies that attempt to explain such differences.

However, before these two basic categories of research are described, attention should be focused on the meaning of several key words or concepts, including race, ethnicity, and nationality. Though these words are sometimes used interchangeably, they have distinctly different meanings (Hutchison 1988, West 1989, Pfister 1993, Johnson et al. 1997a). Race refers to a set of genetic and biological characteristics that tend to characterize groups of people. Therefore, differences in recreation participation between blacks and whites would address a racial issue, at least in theory. However, it should also be noted that the existence of different races of humans is uncertain and controversial. While race has long-standing usage, some scientists argue that there is insufficient genetic variation within humans to support the notion of different races. Ethnicity is a more cultural concept and refers to groups of people who share distinguishing characteristics such as religion, language, customs, and ancestry. Nationality is also a cultural concept, though it is more narrowly defined than ethnicity, and refers to citizenship in a particular country on the basis of birth and/or naturalization. All of the above terms are used in the literature described in this section, and this can be confusing. However, the concept of ethnicity seems to be the most broadly applicable to the question under study: do groups in society share cultural characteristics that influence their recreation-related behavior? Some studies have adopted the more generic word "subcultural" to describe this broad concept and to avoid the confusion and ambiguity that may be associated with the terms race, ethnicity, and nationality.

Research on recreation patterns associated with subcultural groups has been conducted in a variety of contexts and has employed varying research methods. However, study findings have been nearly universal in their conclusion that whites participate more often than minority populations (particularly blacks and Hispanics) in traditional outdoor recreation activities (Hauser 1962, Mueller and Gurin 1962, Cheek et al. 1976, Washburne 1978, Kelly 1980, Washburne and Wall 1980, Klobus-Edwards 1981, McMillen 1983, Stamps and Stamps 1985, Van Horn et al. 1986, West 1989, Hartman and Overdevest 1990, J. Dwyer 1992, 1993b, Gobster and Delgado 1993, Scott 1993, M. Brown 1994, J. Christensen and Dwyer 1995, Cordell et al. 1996, J. Dwyer and Gobster 1997, C. Johnson et al. 1997b, Finn and Loomis 1998). The ORRRC studies noted above were the first to document this pattern, and it has been found to persist over time. A national survey conducted in 1977, for example, found that blacks participated less than whites to a statistically significant degree in several outdoor recreation activities, including camping, boating, hiking/backpacking, hunting, skiing, and sightseeing at historical sites or natural wonders (Washburne and Wall 1980). Similarly, a more recent on-site survey conducted at a nationwide sample of federal and state parks and outdoor recreation areas found that blacks comprised only 2% of all visitors while representing 11.7% of the U.S. population (Hartman and Overdevest 1990).

In addition to participation rates, studies have also found a variety of differences in recreation patterns and preferences among subcultural groups (Kelly 1980, Washburne 1980, Hutchison and Fidel 1984, Hutchison 1987, J. Dwyer and Hutchison 1990, Irwin et al. 1990, Baas 1992, Blahna 1992, J. Dwyer and Gobster 1992, Baas et al. 1993, Gobster and Delgado 1993, Gramann et al. 1993, Scott 1993, Taylor 1993, Chavez et al. 1995, Hospodarsky and Lee 1995, J. Dwyer and Gobster 1997, Pawelko et al. 1997, Wallace and Smith 1997). Most of these studies have addressed differences between whites and minority subcultural groups, particularly blacks and Hispanics. Findings suggest that, compared to whites, minority subcultural groups tend to:

1. Use and prefer "urban-oriented" recreation facilities and services.

2. Participate in larger groups that often include extended family and friends and comprise more diverse age groups.

3. Use and prefer more highly developed facilities.

4. Participate in activities that are more fitness- and sports-oriented.

5. Have a longer length of stay.

6. Use areas that are closer to home.

7. Use land-based rather than water-based areas.

8. Make more intensive use of facilities and services.

A second basic area of research has focused on why there are differences in recreation behavior among subcultural groups. Research in this area has been both theoretical and empirical. Three basic theories have been advanced to explain differences in recreation behavior among subcultural groups. The first two theories were developed in a seminal study by Washburne (1978). This study suggested what were perceived to be the competing theories of marginality and ethnicity. The theory of marginality suggests that minority subcultural groups, particularly blacks, suffer from economic and related disadvantages as a result of historic discrimination. These disadvantages act to inhibit participation in outdoor recreation by means of cost, transportation, information, location, and other barriers. The theory of ethnicity, on the other hand, suggests that differences in recreation behavior are a function of subcultural values; subcultural groups such as blacks and ethnic minorities reflect cultural values that are different than the dominant white, European-American culture, and these values manifest themselves in recreation behavior.

A third basic theory has been developed more recently and focuses on racism or interracial relations (West 1989, 1993). This theory suggests that minority subcultural groups may experience personal or institutional forms of discrimination that inhibit their participation in selected recreation activities.

A number of studies that have addressed and tested these three basic theories are compiled in Table 2-3. Tests of the marginality and ethnicity theories are often addressed in the same studies. The most common research approach is to measure recreation behavior across two or more subcultural groups while statistically controlling for a variety of socioeconomic variables such as income and education. This allows direct comparison of individuals of similar socioeconomic status. The theory of marginality is supported if differences in recreation behavior are reduced or eliminated in such tests, while the theory of ethnicity is supported if differences in recreation behavior persist. Several studies have also asked respondents more directly about barriers to participation in outdoor recreation as a means of testing the marginality and ethnicity theories. Tests of the interracial relations theory generally rely on surveys to determine the extent to which minority subcultural groups report having been subject to personal or institutional discrimination, and the degree to which this is a barrier to participation in outdoor recreation.

The studies outlined in Table 2-3 indicate some support for all of the three basic theories described above. This has led to a more contemporary view that the relationship between recreation behavior and subcultural factors is complex and can be understood only through consideration of multiple and possibly interrelated influences (J. McDonald and Hutchison 1986, West 1989, C. Johnson et al. 1997a, 1998). For example, it is clear that there are strong interrelationships between subcultural groups and socioeconomic status: historic patterns of segregation and discrimination are reflected in lower socioeconomic status of blacks and other minority subcultural groups. It is reasonable to suggest, therefore, that subcultural values may be influenced by socioeconomic status and that both the marginality and ethnicity theories may influence recreation behavior.

Research in this area has raised several other theoretical and methodological issues. One cluster of issues concerns the extent to which race, ethnicity, and nationality are adequate measures of subcultural groups (Allison 1988, 1992, 1993, Pfister 1993, Floyd and Gramann 1995). More specifically, such measures may be too simplistic to isolate groups that share a distinctive set of social values. More recent studies have begun to adopt more sophisticated measures of ethnicity which include ancestral origins, generational status, acculturation (the degree to which a minority group has acquired the cultural characteristics— language, religion, diet—of the dominant group), and assimilation (the degree to which a minority group has been incorporated into the social institutions—economy, education, government—of the dominant group) (Woodard 1988, Carr and Williams 1992, 1993a, b, Floyd and Gramann 1993, Tierney 1995, Shaull and Gramann 1998). Findings from these studies have contributed to the literature by suggesting that minority subcultural groups are not homogeneous populations; rather, they may exhibit distinctive recreation behaviors based upon the kinds of variables noted above.

A related issue concerns the potential differences among minority subcultural groups. Most research has focused on the potential differences between blacks and whites. However, there may also be important differences in recreation behavior among minority subcultural groups. Recent studies have begun to examine the recreation-related behavior of Hispanic and other subcultural groups (Hutchison 1988, J. Dwyer 1992, Floyd et al. 1994, Floyd and Gramann 1995, Heywood and Engelke 1995, Shinew et al. 1995, Yu 1996, Wallace and Smith 1997, Shaull and Gramann 1998, Stodolska and Jackson 1998).

A third issue concerns choice of appropriate "dependent variables" (Floyd 1998). Most recreation research on race and ethnicity has focused on participation rates in selected recreation activities. However, other related variables may be equally important, such as the underlying meanings of recreation activities, and how such meanings might be influenced by cultural factors such as race and ethnicity.[6] Several studies,

text continues on page 42

Table 2-3. Support for alternative theories of subcultural differences in recreation behavior. (Adapted from C. Johnson et al. 1997b.)

Study	Population/Area	Theory supported
Craig 1972	Black and white rural residents in Florida	Ethnicity/subcultural values
Jaakson 1973	Mexican American and Anglo employees	Ethnicity/subcultural values
Cheek et al. 1976		Marginality
Wagner and Donahue 1976	Black and white Chicago households	Marginality; Ethnicity/ subcultural values
G. Peterson 1977		Ethnicity/subcultural values
Washburne 1978	Black and white residents of California urban areas	Marginality; Ethnicity/ subcultural values
Washburne and Wall 1980	Black and white US households	Marginality; Ethnicity/ subcultural values
Klobus-Edwards 1981	Black and white households in Lynchburg, VA	Ethnicity/subcultural values
Hutchison and Fidel 1984	Mexican American and Anglo visitors to 13 Chicago parks	Ethnicity/subcultural values
Stamps and Stamps 1985	Black and white US households in a northern community	Ethnicity/subcultural values
Hutchison 1987	Black, Hispanic, and white visitors to 13 Chicago parks	Ethnicity/subcultural values
Woodard 1988	Black households in Chicago	Marginality
West 1989	Black and white Detroit households	Racism/interracial relations
J. Dwyer and Hutchison 1990	Black and white Chicago households	Marginality; Ethnicity/ subcultural values
Irwin et al. 1990	Mexican American and Anglo campers at one national forest	Ethnicity/subcultural values
J. Dwyer 1992	Ethnically diverse households in Illinois	Marginality; Ethnicity/ subcultural values
Blahna and Black 1993	Ethnically diverse students	Racism/interracial relations

Study	Population/Area	Theory supported
Carr and Williams 1993a, 1993b	Hispanic visitors to two national forests	Ethnicity/subcultural values
Chavez 1993	Ethnically diverse visitors to two national forests	Racism/interracial relations
J. Dwyer 1993b	Ethnically diverse households in Illinois	Marginality; Ethnicity/ subcultural values
Floyd et al. 1993	Mexican Americans in Arizona	Racism/interracial relations; Marginality
Gobster and Delgado 1993	Ethnically diverse visitors to a Chicago park	Ethnicity/subcultural values
Hutchison 1993	Hmong households in Wisconsin	Ethnicity/subcultural values
Scott 1993	Black and white visitors to Cleveland parks and surrounding residents	Marginality; Ethnicity/ subcultural values
Floyd et al. 1994	Black and white US households	Marginality; Ethnicity/ subcultural values
Hospodarksky and Lee 1995	Hispanic and Anglo visitors to one national forest	Marginality
Shinew et al. 1995	Black and white US households	Marginality
Shinew et al. 1996	Black US households	Marginality
C. Johnson et al. 1997b	Black and white rural residents in Florida	Ethnicity/subcultural values
Stodolska and Jackson 1998	Polish residents of Edmonton, Alberta	Racism/interracial relations
C. Johnson et al. 1998	Black and white residents of 6 rural counties in northwest Florida	Combination of marginality and ethnicity/subcultural values

for example, have found differences among racial and ethnic groups with regard to reasons for participating in fishing (M. Miller and Van Maanen 1982, M. Campbell 1989, Blahna 1992, West et al. 1992, Toth and Brown 1997). Blacks and Hispanics have reported emphasizing fishing for consumption and socializing more than do whites, while whites have emphasized fishing more for sport and diversion than do minority groups.

A final issue concerns the lack of consistency in research methods, including the way that study variables are defined and measured. A recent comparative analysis of studies concluded that:

> Differences in sampling, research focus, and analyses have produced a body of ethnic recreation literature that is somewhat difficult to compare. Because approaches vary, attributing recreation differences to a single dominant perspective is nearly impossible (C. Johnson et al. 1997b:13).

As research in this area matures, more consistent study designs will enable more direct comparisons across areas, populations, and time.

Research on race and ethnicity suggests several potential management implications. To the extent to which the marginality theory is valid, special efforts should be made to ensure equal access to outdoor recreation. Potential actions within the scope of individual managers include provision of public transportation, location of parks and outdoor recreation areas closer to minority populations, and development and marketing of recreation programs more directly to minority subcultural groups. Management implications of the ethnicity theory are quite different. To the extent that this theory is valid, recreation facilities and services should be designed to meet the recreation-related values of minority subcultural groups. Such adaptations might include an emphasis on more developed facilities closer to home and facilities that are designed for larger groups and more active uses. Finally, the racism or interracial relations theory suggests that managers should re-examine their agencies and programs for evidence of institutional discrimination (e.g., discriminatory pricing policies) and should be proactive in furthering programs to promote racial harmony.

Sex and Gender. There are strong parallels in social science research between sex and gender issues and race and ethnicity as described in the preceding section. These parallels are probably linked to traditional under-representation on the part of minority groups and women, along with the relatively recent emergence of the contemporary civil rights and women's movements. As with race and ethnicity, differences in recreation participation between males and females was observed in the early ORRRC studies on nationwide participation in a variety of recreation activities (Hauser 1962, Mueller and Gurin 1962). Initial research was primarily descriptive, documenting similarities and differences in recreation behavior between males and females. Only recently has this research expanded into an explanatory phase that attempts to understand and develop the implications of such recreation patterns.

Like race and ethnicity, attention should be focused on the meaning of key words or concepts in this body of literature. Though sex and gender are often used interchangeably, they have distinctly different meanings (Henderson 1994b). Sex refers to the genetic and biological differences that distinguish males and females. Gender refers to social and cultural distinctions between males and females that are learned in society. Differences in recreation behavior between males and females may be influenced by both sex and gender, though recent research suggests that cultural distinctions associated with gender may be especially useful in studying and understanding such differences.

As noted above, a number of studies of recreation participation and behavior have examined similarities and differences between males and females. Several review studies have attempted to integrate and synthesize a large number of these studies (Zuzanek 1978, Kelly 1980, O'Leary et al. 1982, Roggenbuck and Lucas 1987, Hartmann and Cordell 1989). Two general conclusions can be drawn from this body of descriptive literature. First, as applied to participation in broad leisure activities, the similarities between males and females are more striking than the differences (e.g., H. Christensen et al. 1986). Primary differences suggest that women may participate in fewer leisure and recreation activities than men and may be more oriented to culturally based and family-centered activities. Second, differences between males and females are more pronounced for some outdoor recreation activities, particularly those that may be considered more strenuous or traditionally masculine, such as hunting, fishing, and backcountry or wilderness-related activities. For example, a nationwide study of visitors to a variety of state and federal outdoor recreation areas found that males comprised over 90% of all hunters and nearly 60% of all backpackers (Hartmann and Cordell 1989). However, participation in other outdoor recreation activities such as developed camping and day hiking was nearly equally divided between men and women. Similarly, most studies of wilderness use report that males comprise between 70% and 85% of all visitors (Roggenbuck and Lucas 1987).

More recent research has begun to explore the reasons for such differences and their implications. Again, several review studies have attempted to integrate and synthesize this body of literature (Henderson et al. 1989, Henderson 1990, 1994b, Shaw 1994a, Henderson 1996). Several themes have emerged from this research.

First, traditional definitions and conceptualizations of leisure and recreation may be less appropriate for women than for men (Wearing and Wearing 1988, Henderson 1990). This issue might be manifested in several ways. Traditionally, leisure and recreation connote time free from employment or other obligations. However, for women, many of whom historically have not been employed outside the home and who have continuing obligations to family, leisure and recreation may simply not resonate as powerfully. Research on leisure and recreation patterns may misrepresent participation by females through use of standardized checklists of activities that are oriented primarily to male conceptions of leisure and recreation (Henderson et al. 1989, Henderson 1990). Even when such research identifies similar or dissimilar patterns of participation in recreation activities, the experiences of males and females may not be comparable. For example, participation in an activity such as swimming may represent a freely chosen recreation activity, but may also reflect an obligation to participate and/or supervise a children's activity (Henderson et al. 1989).

Second, leisure may be more constrained for females than males. Due largely to family and household obligations, women may have less leisure time than men, and available leisure time may be more highly fragmented (Witt and Goodale 1981, Gilligan 1982, Searle and Jackson 1985, Shaw 1985, Deem 1986, Henderson and Rannells 1988, Horna 1987, Henderson 1990, Henderson and Allen 1991, Harrington et al. 1992, Shaw 1992, E. Jackson and Henderson 1995, Culp 1998). Due to traditional lack of opportunities for employment outside the home, as well as differential earnings, women may also face more significant economic barriers than men to participation in selected leisure and recreation activities (Searle and Jackson 1985, E. Jackson 1988). For these and other reasons, fewer recreation facilities and services may be developed and offered expressly for females (Deem 1982, Searle and Jackson 1985, E. Jackson 1988). Some studies have also suggested that women's leisure may be constrained by fear of violence in parks and related areas (Westover 1986, Green et al. 1987, Hutchinson 1994, Scott 1995), insecurity over physical appearance (Wolf 1991), and by traditional gender stereotypes that are perpetuated in the mass media (Shaw 1994b).

Third, alternative feminist perspectives on leisure and recreation have evolved in response to the issues described above. The dominant perspective might be described as liberal and argues that women deserve and should be granted equal access and opportunities for leisure and recreation (Glyptis 1985, Chambers 1986, Westover 1986, Allison and Duncan 1987, Henderson et al. 1989, Henderson 1997). A second perspective can be labeled socialist in that it advocates changes in the larger society that will lead to enhanced social standing for women and, therefore, a stronger leisure environment. A third perspective is defined as radical because it rejects the traditional concept of leisure as androcentric (Deem 1986, Lenskyj 1988, Bella 1990, Henderson 1997). The traditional dichotomy between work and leisure/recreation may be viewed as less applicable for women than men because many women have historically not worked outside the home and have enduring responsibilities to home and family.

Fourth, as suggested in the previous section on subcultural groups, there may be important differences in leisure and recreation within cultural groups, including those based on gender. In fact, differences in leisure and recreation among women may be more significant than those between men and women (Henderson 1996). Such differences may be magnified for women who are in nondominant groups (based on age, income, disability, race, or other characteristics) or who exist at the margins of society.

The studies examined in this section demonstrate that recreation behavior, particularly participation in recreation activities, can be more fully understood through consideration of the cultural context in which individuals operate. This is in keeping with the views developed in the broader social science disciplines that human behavior is, in large part, culturally determined.

Summary and Conclusions

1. Information on recreation use and users has many potential applications in recreation management, including monitoring the popularity of recreation activities; designing recreation facilities and services; planning budgetary, personnel, and other resource needs; conducting public information and education programs, and evaluating the efficiency and equity of public outdoor recreation.

2. Information on recreation use and users should be collected on a regular basis to monitor trends in recreation use patterns.

3. The first and simplest form of research on social aspects of outdoor recreation was on-site use measurement. Relatively long historical records of use are available for some areas and agencies. These data suggest that use of federal parks and outdoor recreation areas tended to increase rapidly in the 1960s and 1970s, level off or even decline in the 1980s and begin to climb again in the 1990s. However, interpretation and comparison of these data are limited by lack of standardization in measurement units and methods.

4. Use measurement in outdoor recreation is often difficult due to the dispersed nature of outdoor recreation activity. However, a variety of use measurement techniques have been developed, including observation, self-registration, surveys, electronic and mechanical counters, optical scanners, and cameras.

5. Recreation use can also be measured by means of general population or household surveys. Periodic national surveys provide estimates of the relative popularity of a variety of recreation activities. However, interpretation and application of these survey findings are limited by the confounding effects of supply on participation, emphasis on activities rather than experiences or underlying meanings of recreation, and a number of methodological inconsistencies.

6. Use of outdoor recreation areas tends to be distributed in a highly uneven fashion over both space and time. This pattern of use has resulted in inefficiencies of resource use and has exacerbated problems of crowding and environmental impacts.

7. Outdoor recreation is a dynamic activity comprised of multiple phases, including anticipation, travel to a site, on-site experience, return travel, and recollection. Recreation management can influence all of these phases of recreation activity.

8. Demographic and socioeconomic variables—for example, income, education, and occupation—are generally not powerful predictors of overall participation in outdoor recreation. However, such variables are often more strongly related to specific outdoor recreation activities. For example, age tends to be inversely related to recreation activities requiring physical strength and endurance, while use of backcountry and wilderness areas is directly related with socioeconomic status, especially education.

9. Cultural context also influences outdoor recreation participation and behavior. Potentially important cultural influences include one's social group and other social relationships, childhood experiences and other elements of socialization, the type of community in which one lives, a general social class tendency toward status emulation, race and ethnicity, and sex and gender.

10. Whites tend to participate more often than blacks and other racial and ethnic minorities in traditional outdoor recreation activities. Blacks, Hispanics, and other subcultural groups have also been found to exhibit distinctive recreation behaviors and preferences, including preference for more developed and urban-oriented recreation facilities and participation in large groups that may include extended family and friends.

11. Three basic theories have been advanced to explain differences in recreation participation and patterns between whites and blacks and other subcultural groups. The theory of marginality suggests that blacks and other subcultural minorities suffer from economic and related disadvantages as a result of historic discrimination, and that this inhibits participation in certain outdoor recreation activities. The theory of ethnicity suggests that differences in recreation behavior are a function of subcultural values; blacks and other racial and ethnic minority groups reflect cultural values that are different from the traditional white, European-American culture. The theory of racism or interracial relations suggests that minority subcultural groups may experience personal or institutional forms of discrimination that inhibit their participation in outdoor recreation activities. Empirical research suggests that all three theories may be operative to some degree and may be interrelated.

12. Research on the role of gender in recreation suggests that there are more similarities than differences between males and females with regard to recreation participation and behavior. However, evidence suggests that females may tend to participate in fewer recreation activities than males, may favor more cultural and family-centered activities, and participate less often in outdoor recreation activities that may be considered strenuous or traditionally masculine, such as hunting, fishing, and backcountry or wilderness-related activities.

13. Reasons for gender-based differences in recreation may include constraints on leisure time for women due to continuing family and household obligations, and barriers to leisure and recreation for

women, including economic impediments, fear of violence, and gender-based stereotypes. Alternative feminist perspectives have evolved based on these and related issues. These perspectives include a liberal philosophy that suggests that women deserve and should be granted equal access and opportunities to leisure and recreation; a socialist philosophy that advocates changes in the larger society which will lead to enhanced social standing for women and, therefore, a stronger leisure and recreation environment; and a radical philosophy that rejects the traditional dichotomy between work and leisure/recreation because women have traditionally not worked outside the home and have enduring responsibilities to home and family.

Notes

1. Proceedings of the 1990 trends symposium were recorded and distributed on computer diskettes only.
2. These studies include Bury and Hall 1963, James and Ripley 1963, Lucas 1963, Bury and Margolis 1964, Tombaugh and Love 1964, J. A. Wagar 1964, Wenger 1964, Wenger and Gregerson 1964, James and Rich 1966, James and Tyre 1967, James 1968, James and Henley 1968, J. A. Wagar 1969, J. A. Wagar and Thalheimer 1969, Cordell et al. 1970, Elsner 1970, James 1971, James and Schreuder 1971, James et al. 1971a, b, Lucas et al. 1971, Lucas and Oltman 1971, James and Quinkert 1972, James and Schreuder 1972, Rugg 1973, Lime and Lorence 1974, Lucas 1975, Schreuder et al. 1975, Marnell 1977, Hogans 1978, Aldrich 1979, Tyre and Siderlis 1979, R. Becker et al. 1980, Leonard et al. 1980, More 1980, Echelberger et al. 1981, Leatherberry and Lime 1981, Lucas and Kovalicky 1981, Saunders 1982, Lucas 1983, M. Petersen 1985, Rawhauser et al. 1989, Chilman et al. 1990, Glass et al. 1991, Mengak and Perales 1991, Glass and Walton 1995, Marnell 1977.
3. The experiential nature of outdoor recreation is discussed more fully in Chapter 7.
4. Comparisons across studies have been hampered by lack of consistent or uniform categories of income and other socioeconomic and demographic variables (Stankey 1970).
5. The subject of motivations for recreation is examined more fully in Chapter 7.
6. The underlying meanings of outdoor recreation are addressed more fully in Chapter 7.

3

Descriptive Aspects of
Outdoor Recreation
Attitudes, Preferences, Perceptions

Visitor Attitudes and Preferences

Along with outdoor recreation activity patterns and their relationship to social and cultural influences, the attitudes and preferences of visitors were an early focus of research. Recognition of recreation as social behavior led naturally to the notion that information on visitor attitudes and preferences for facilities and services would be desirable in guiding recreation management. Research in this area was further stimulated by the suggestion that the attitudes and preferences of visitors may differ in substantive ways from how they are perceived by managers.

As might be expected, a relatively large number of studies on visitor attitudes and preferences have addressed a wide variety of recreation activities and areas and have incorporated varying research approaches. Review and synthesis of these studies is challenging. However, two relatively large and traditional areas of study have emerged. One area addresses developed recreation areas, especially campgrounds. The other area addresses backcountry or wilderness recreation and also incorporates information on camping. A special issue within this body of research concerns visitor perceptions of environmental impacts, especially those impacts caused by recreation use. And finally, as noted above, a number of studies have explored the relationship between visitor attitudes and preferences and those of managers. These four subjects comprise this chapter.

Developed Areas

Studies of attitudes and preferences of visitors to developed recreation areas have used two basic research approaches: 1) surveys in which visitors are asked to report their attitudes and preferences, usually in a close-ended format, and 2) observation of visitor behavior. In several cases, both approaches have been used simultaneously, providing insights into the validity of study findings.

Results of several studies that can be compared reasonably directly are summarized in Tables 3-1 and 3-2. Table 3-1 presents data on desirable characteristics of campsites. Most campers find partial-to-full shade to be desirable, strongly prefer flush toilets, prefer spacing between campsites in the 50- to 100-foot range, prefer to be located between 100 and 200 feet from both comfort station and drinking water supply, strongly prefer vegetative screening between campsites, and favor fireplaces constructed of metal. Table 3-2 presents data on the characteristics of campgrounds that have been found to contribute to or detract from their popularity. Nearness to water or other major tourist attraction was an important factor common to all the studies. The size of the campground (number of campsites) was found to be related to campground use in two studies, but in opposite directions.

It should be noted, however, that while these studies generally report majority opinions, there is often considerable diversity within the data. Authors of these studies have been careful to point this out. The study by Cordell and Sykes (1969), for example, states that study findings "represent majority opinion, but there are many campers who would prefer something quite different." And Lucas' 1970 study of twenty-two national forest campgrounds concludes that because of diversity in preferences, "A standard pattern of development does not seem appropriate." Perhaps no study has emphasized and illustrated this issue as well as E. Shafer (1969), whose study was titled "The Average Camper Who Doesn't Exist." The study points out that statistical averages sometimes obscure real diversity and create a model of reality that no visitors actually fit.

Another issue concerns correspondence of findings from studies using survey and observational techniques.[1] Studies using both techniques simultaneously have met with mixed results. An early study of camping, for example, surveyed visitors to a campground asking

Table 3-1. Visitor preferences for developed area campsite conditions

Study	Area	Research approach	Campsite condition						
			Shade[1]	Flush toilets[2]	Campsite spacing[1]	Distance to comfort station[1]	Distance to drinking water[1]	Screening between sites[2]	Type of fireplace[1]
Love 1964	12 national forest campgrounds	Observation	—	—	>100 ft	—	< 200 ft	84%	—
E.Shafer and Burke 1965	4 Pennsylvania state parks	Survey	Partial	85%	50-100 ft	—	—	—	—
Cordell and Sykes 1969	1 national forest campground	Survey	—	93%	Approx. 80 ft	100-200 ft	<100 ft	90%	Metal
James and Cordell 1970	1 national forest campground	Survey & Observation	Partial	—	—	—	—	—	—
Cordell and James 1972	1 national forest campground	Survey & Observation	Partial	—	Approx. 80 ft	100–200 ft	100-200 ft	—	Metal
Knudson and Curry 1981	3 Indiana state parks	Survey	—	—	40-65 ft	—	—	—	—
McEwen 1986	17 Tennessee Valley Authority campgrounds	Survey	Full	Majority	—	—	—	Majority	—
Bumgardner et al. 1988	29 Army Corps of Engineers campgrounds	Survey	Heavy	—	—	—	—	—	—

1. Condition preferred by majority of respondents; 2. Percent of respondents preferring this condition; — Data not available

about preferred campsite characteristics, while at the same time observing actual campsite selection patterns (Cordell and James 1970, James and Cordell 1970). The study reported "a comforting amount of parallelism" in the findings from both research approaches; campers tended to select campsites with the characteristics they said they preferred. Other studies have reported similar findings (Klukas and Duncan 1967, E. Shafer 1969).

However, other studies have obtained more varied findings. A study of thirty-one national forest campgrounds found that, while both survey and observational techniques revealed a strong influence of water-orientation in campground selection, there was less agreement about the influence of other variables (Lime 1971). And an experimental study also found differences between stated preference and observed behavior of recreation visitors in relation to vegetative screening and groundcover at campsites (Hancock 1973). When surveyed, campers stated a nearly unanimous preference for existing conditions, but observation showed that occupancy rates of the study campsites increased after screening had been thinned. The survey technique seems most appropriate for study variables of which respondents are consciously aware, such as water-orientation, and for questions that are not hypothetical, as well as those where there is little reason to expect bias. The most valid approach is to rely on a balance between research techniques, each acting as a check on validity for the other.

Finally, it should be noted that all of the studies reported are highly site-specific, and the degree to which their findings can be generalized to other areas and facilities may be limited. There is considerable evidence in these studies that visitors tend to respond favorably to the facilities they find. As described in Chapter 1, this is reflected in the generally high levels of satisfaction reported by visitors to a variety of recreation areas. The reason for this is not clear. However, it is likely that, to a large extent, visitors may sort themselves among areas and facilities according to their preferences. Preferences might also be based largely on the type of areas and facilities previously encountered. A study of river recreationists, for example, found that preferences for management actions were diverse, but that they seemed to be associated with management systems under which respondents had previously operated (McCool and Utter 1981). Unless attitudes and preferences are found to be relatively consistent over a variety of areas and facilities, it may be unwise to generalize findings from this type of research.

Table 3-2. Characteristics related to developed campground use.[1]

Study	Area	Campground characteristics	Relationship to campground use
Beardsley 1967	21 national forest campgrounds	Presence of a recreationally useable body of water within 1/4 mile	Positive
E. Shafer and Thompson 1968	24 New York state parks	Number of sites	Positive
		Location proximate to a major tourist attraction	Positive
Lucas 1970	22 national forest campgrounds	Number of sites	Negative
		Yards of beach	Positive
		Type of water located close by	In decreasing order of preference: canoeable rivers, lakes, large rivers, creeks
		Distance from Great Lakes	Negative
Lime 1971	34 national forest campgrounds	Percent of waterfront campsites	Positive
		Reputation for good fishing	Positive
		Length of time open	Positive
Bumgardner et al. 1988	29 Army Corps of Engineers campgrounds	Presence of utilities	Positive
		View of lake	Positive
		Access to lake	Positive
		Presence of covered picnic table	Positive

1. All studies listed used the research approach of observation.

Backcountry and Wilderness Areas

Results of several studies of backcountry visitor attitudes and preferences that are relatively comparable are summarized in Tables 3-3, 3-4, and 3-5. Studies of backcountry visitor attitudes toward management policies (Tables 3-3 and 3-4) suggest that:

1. Most visitors favor use limitations. It should be noted, however, that the general form of this question is posed in terms of whether use limits would be favored or opposed if the study area were "overused."

2. There is no consensus on the method by which use limits should be administered. A lottery appears to be the least-favored alternative.

3. Attitudes are mixed on fixed travel routes or itineraries.

4. A majority of visitors support self-registration.

5. Reaction is mixed on zoning by method of travel, lowering trail standards, and restricting or downgrading access routes.

6. Most visitors favor limits on party size.

7. Most visitors do not favor prohibition of campfires.

8. Most visitors do not favor a policy requiring use of designated campsites.

Studies of backcountry visitor preferences for facilities and services (Table 3-5) suggest that:

1. Relatively low-standard trails are preferred to high-standard trails.

2. Most visitors prefer to find bridges at large streams that might be difficult or dangerous to ford.

3. Information signs (e.g., trail names, directions, and distances) are favored along trail systems, while campsite and interpretive signs are less favored.

4. Fireplaces and picnic tables are generally not preferred at campsites, while fire rings are.

5. Opinion is mixed on pit toilets and other types of sanitary facilities at campsites.

6. Opinion is mixed on trail shelters.

7. Special facilities for horse use such as corrals and hitching racks are generally not favored.

8. Emergency telephones are generally not favored.

9. The majority of visitors prefer to have maps and informational pamphlets available.

10. The majority of visitors favor the presence of wilderness rangers.

All of the above studies have relied on survey techniques as the basic research approach since observational techniques are difficult in

Table 3-3. Percentage of visitors favoring selected rationing systems.

Study/Area	Use limits	First-come, first-served	Reservation	Lottery	Merit
Hendee et al. 1968 3 wilderness areas	50	—	—	—	—
Stankey 1973 4 wilderness areas	—	28	18	48	—
Echelberger et al. 1974, Tuckerman Ravine, NH	—	—	—	—	m
Towler 1977 Grand Canyon National Park, AZ	M	—	—	—	—
Stankey 1980a Spanish Peaks Primitive Area, MT	76	41	29	18	—
Stankey 1980a Desolation Wilderness Area, CA	92	57	59	11	57
Bultena et al. 1981a Mt McKinley National Park, AK	85	82	37	6	26
Utter et al. 1981 Salmon River, ID	—	—	M	M	M
Shelby et al. 1982 Snake River, ID	—	25	95	50	37
Shelby et al. 1982 Eagle Cap Wilderness Area, OR	—	50	73	28	42
Shelby et al. 1982 Mt. Jefferson Wilderness, OR	—	51	74	30	49
D. Anderson and Manfredo 1986 3 wilderness areas	54	—	—	—	—
D. Anderson and Manfredo 1986 3 rivers	49	—	—	—	—
Cole et al. 1995 Desolation Wilderness, CA	M	—	—	—	—
Cole et al. 1997a 3 high use wilderness areas	m/mx	—	—	—	—

M = majority; m = minority; mx = mixed; — Data not available.

Table 3-4. Percentage of visitors favoring selected backcountry management policies.

Study /Area	A	B	C	D	E	F	G	H	I
Hendee et al. 1968 3 wilderness areas	40	—	—	—	—	—	—	—	—
Stankey 1973 4 wilderness areas	23	8	—	47	41	—	mx	—	—
Echelberger and Moeller 1977 Cranberry Back-country, WV	15	—	54	—	—	—	—	—	—
Towler 1977 Grand Canyon National Park, AZ	M	—	—	—	—	—	M	—	—
Lucas 1980 9 wilderness areas	—	—	M	—	—	—	—	m	—
Stankey 1980a Spanish Peaks Primitive Area, MT	—	25	23	—	50	45	51	—	—
Desolation Wilderness Area, CA	30	17	—	—	43	53	81	—	—
Bultena et al. 1981a Mt McKinley National Park, AK	11	—	—	—	—	—	—	75	—
Shelby et al. 1982 Snake River, ID	66	—	—	—	—	—	—	—	—
Eagle Cap Wilderness Area, OR	66	—	—	—	—	—	—	—	—
Mt. Jefferson Wilderness, OR	55	—	—	—	—	—	—	—	—
D. Anderson and Manfredo 1986 3 wilderness areas	—	—	—	—	—	—	80	28	—
3 rivers	—	—	—	—	—	—	46	8	27
Martin 1986 White Mountain National Forest, NH	11	—	—	—	—	—	—	—	—

A = Entrance fee; B = Fixed itinerary; C = Registration; D = Zoning by method of travel;
E = Lower trail standards; F = Restrict access; G = Limit party size; H = Prohibit camp fires;
I = Designated campsites
M = majority; m = minority; mx = mixed; — Data not available.

Study /Area	A	B	C	D	E	F	G	H	I
Stewart 1989									
Grand Canyon National Park, AZ	—	82	—	—	—	—	—	—	—
Saguaro National Monument, AZ	—	77	—	—	—	—	—	—	—
Cole et al. 1995									
Shining Rock Wilderness, NC	—	—	—	—	—	—	—	M	m
Desolation Wilderness, CA	—	—	—	—	—	—	—	—	M
Cole et al. 1997a 3 high use wilderness areas	—	—	—	—	—	—	—	—	M

A = Entrance fee; B = Fixed itinerary; C = Registration; D = Zoning by method of travel;
E = Lower trail standards; F = Restrict access; G = Limit party size; H = Prohibit camp fires;
I = Designated campsites
M = majority; m = minority; mx = mixed; — Data not available.

backcountry environments where use is generally light and widely dispersed. A few studies of backcountry visitor preferences, however, have used observational techniques (Pfister 1977, Canon et al. 1979, Heberlein and Dunwiddie 1979, Cole 1982). An important finding from several of these studies is that visitors tend to camp at previously used sites rather than seeking out and establishing new sites.

Unfortunately, no studies of backcountry visitor attitudes and preferences have employed both survey and observational methods, nor are the few observational studies directly comparable to any of the survey-based studies. Thus, little is known about the validity of either type of study.

As with developed recreation areas, caution should be used in interpreting the findings of the above studies and incorporating them into management policy. The data reported are often averages, which tend to obscure the underlying diversity. Moreover, a number of studies have shown substantive differences of opinion among visitors depending upon visitor characteristics such as mode of travel (Stankey 1973, Lucas 1980), whether they are participating in a commercial trip (Utter et al. 1981, Shelby et al. 1982), the extent to which visitor attitudes conform to institutional definitions of wilderness (Hendee et al. 1968, Stankey 1972, Tarbet et al. 1977, Schreyer and Roggenbuck 1981), and

Table 3-5. Percentage of visitors favoring selected backcountry facilities and services.

Wildland Research Center 1962

Mt. Marcy. NY	Pit toilets, sanitary facilities	70
	Emergency telephones	50
Boundary Waters Canoe Area, MN	Pit toilets, sanitary facilities	50
	Emergency telephones	26
High Sierras, CA	Pit toilets, sanitary facilities	36
	Emergency telephones	45
Hendee et al. 1968, 3 wilderness areas	High standard trails	m
	Information signs	M
	Interpretive signs	m
	Fireplaces	25
	Picnic tables	40
	Trail shelters	60
	Corrals	20
	Maps/pamphlets	M

Merriam and Ammons 1968

Bob Marshall Wilderness, MT	High standard trails	25
	Information signs	90
	Fireplaces	34
	Picnic tables	34
	Trail shelters	15
	Emergency telephones	62
Mission Mountains Primitive Area, MT	High standard trails	32
	Information signs	62
	Fireplaces	24
	Picnic tables	24
	Trail shelters	34
	Emergency telephones	32
Glacier National Park, MT	High standard trails	10
	Information signs	67
	Fireplaces	52
	Picnic tables	52
	Trail shelters	76
	Emergency telephones	12

Stankey 1973

Boundary Waters Canoe Area, MN	High standard trails	37
	Pit toilets, sanitary facilities	63
	Maps/pamphlets	60
	Wilderness rangers	70
Bob Marshall Wilderness, MT	High standard trails	35
	Bridges across large rivers	67
	Campsite signs	52
	Pit toilets, sanitary facilities	43
	Corrals	25
	Hitching racks	26

	Maps/pamphlets	52
	Wilderness rangers	58
Bridger Wilderness, WY	High standard trails	31
	Bridges across large rivers	65
	Campsite signs	30
	Pit toilets, sanitary facilities	22
	Corrals	4
	Hitching racks	4
	Maps/pamphlets	60
	Wilderness rangers	68
High Uintas Primitive Area, UT	High standard trails	35
	Bridges across large rivers	62
	Campsite signs	26
	Pit toilets, sanitary facilities	25
	Corrals	11
	Hitching racks	16
	Maps/pamphlets	55
	Wilderness rangers	67
Murray 1975, Appalachian Trail	Low standard trails	M
Echelberger and Moeller 1977	Interpretive signs	50
Cranberry Backcountry, WV	Trail shelters	35
	Wilderness rangers	63
Plumley et al. 1978, Appalachian Trail	Trail shelters	49
Lucas 1980, 9 wilderness areas	High standard trails	m
	Low standard trails	M
	Bridges across large rivers	M
	Information signs	M
	Fireplaces	mx
	Fire rings	M
	Picnic tables	m
	Pit toilets, sanitary facilities	m
	Corrals	mx
	Maps/pamphlets	M
	Wilderness rangers	M
D. Anderson and Manfredo 1986 3 wilderness areas	Information signs	68
	Picnic tables	41
	Maps/pamphlets	74/90
	Wilderness rangers	62
3 rivers	Wilderness rangers	16
Cole et al. 1995, Desolation Wilderness, CA	Low standard trails	M
	Bridges across large rivers	M
	Interpretive signs	M
	Fireplaces	mx
	Fire rings	M
	Pit toilets, sanitary facilities	mx

M = majority; m = minority; mx = mixed; — Data not available backcountry experience (Towler 1977, Vaske et al. 1980, Hammitt and McDonald 1983).

Furthermore, findings of studies on backcountry areas, like the studies of developed areas, are site-specific. There is often diversity of opinion among visitors to different backcountry areas, which tends to limit the degree to which such data are generalizable to other areas. In addition, findings from the above studies are subject to widely varying methods of investigation (e.g., question wording and sampling procedures) and therefore may not be directly comparable. Thus, they may have little application beyond the study area.

Given these important limitations, elements of commonality can nevertheless be found from some groupings of studies. The conclusions outlined above based on studies of developed campgrounds and backcountry areas are examples. Two other studies based on selected components of the outdoor recreation literature are also suggestive. One of these examined studies that address attitudes and preferences of visitors to legally designated wilderness areas (Stankey and Schreyer 1987). This study reported several areas of commonality across a number of studies:

1. Wilderness visitors may be evolving toward a more "purist" orientation, emphasizing more appreciative and less consumptive uses, and expressing more support for use restrictions when and where conditions warrant.

2. Visitors tend to support the status quo, and this will require managers to educate visitors about needed changes in management policy.

3. Many visitors do not have well-developed attitudes and preferences regarding management issues, and this represents an opportunity for managers to educate visitors about needed changes in management policy.

4. Visitor attitudes and preferences are often related to visitor characteristics such as recreation activity, mode of travel, and level of experience. Recognition of such relationships can be useful in defining relatively similar types of visitors and tailoring management to meet their attitudes and preferences.

A second study focused on backcountry campsites using a combination of literature review and empirical study (Brunson and Shelby 1990). Campsite attributes preferred by visitors were identified by examining the findings of several studies of camping. These attributes were then included in a study of campers along the Deschutes River, OR, by asking respondents to rate their importance. A general hierarchy of importance was revealed, suggesting that campsite attributes fall into three categories. These attributes include (1) "necessary" attributes that are considered vital (e.g., flat ground, shade), (2) "experience" attributes that are considered important in determining the quality of the experience (e.g., good fishing, adequate screening), and (3) "amenity" attributes, which are less important, but which may help campers choose among otherwise acceptable campsites (e.g., amount of bare ground).

Perceptions of Environmental Impacts

A small group of studies has focused on visitor perceptions of environmental impacts, particularly those caused by recreation use. A review of this literature has suggested that visitors' perceptions of recreational impacts tend to be limited (Lucas 1979). With the exception of litter, visitors rarely complain about site conditions and usually rate the environmental conditions of recreation sites as "good" or better. This appears true for impacts on campsites and trails, as well as other resource impacts such as water pollution and wildlife disturbance. A study in the Boundary Waters Canoe Area, MN, for example, found that campers seldom commented on campsite impacts other than litter, and that there was no correlation between visitor ratings of campsite physical conditions and expert ratings of the severity of environmental impacts (Merriam and Smith 1974). Hikers in the Selway-Bitterroot Wilderness Area, ID/MT, reported that they were well satisfied with trail conditions, despite the fact that some trails were severely eroded (Helgath 1975). Only 1% of floaters on the Pine River in the Manistee National Forest, MI, were concerned with streambank erosion (which was very prominent), while 4% listed viewing and enjoying eroded banks as the high point of their trip; litter was far and away the most objectionable environmental condition reported by users (Solomon and Hansen 1972). The only impact reported by more than 50% of visitors to roaded forest lands in the Pacific Northwest was litter (Downing and Clark 1979). Finally, only one in four campers viewed vegetation impacts as a problem at four heavily used developed campgrounds in Pennsylvania (Moeller et al. 1974).

Two other studies generally corroborate these findings. One study reviewed visitor perceptions of environmental impacts at three Indiana state park campgrounds that were subject to varying levels of impact

(Knudson and Curry 1981). The majority of campers rated ground cover conditions as "satisfactory" to "excellent," even in areas where over three-fourths of the campsites were 100% bare or disturbed. Even the minority of respondents who rated ground cover "poor" or below reported that these conditions did not affect their enjoyment of the area. Moreover, two-thirds of respondents did not notice damage to trees or shrubs even though such damage was actually extensive in several areas. Finally, a study of river recreation surveyed floaters on several Southeastern rivers regarding their perceptions of five environmental impacts (Hammitt and McDonald 1983). Experience level of respondents was positively related to perceptions of impacts, but a large majority of floaters, even those classified as having high experience, failed to notice or report any of the five impacts studied.

Visitor Versus Manager Perceptions

At the beginning of this chapter, it was suggested that objective information on visitor attitudes, preferences, and perceptions is needed because this may differ from perceptions of recreation managers. Studies of this issue have addressed three broad aspects of recreation: the meanings or motivations associated with recreation areas or activities, perceptions of recreation impacts and problems, and attitudes toward recreation area management.

Several studies have found rather consistent differences between visitors and managers with regard to the meanings of outdoor recreation.[2] Two of the earliest studies illustrate these findings. One of these studies surveyed visitors and managers of selected developed campgrounds in Washington State (Clark et al. 1971a). Visitors reported generally high ratings on a number of traditional camping values such as experiencing "solitude and tranquility" and appreciating "unspoiled beauty." However, managers substantially underestimated the importance of such values to campers, apparently unable to rationalize these values with the use of developed campgrounds. The apparent incongruity of visitor values is evident in response patterns to two motivation items in particular. Nearly two-thirds of visitors rated "solitude and tranquility" as very important, while only about one-quarter rated "getting away from people other than my camping party" as very important. Apparently, solitude and tranquility are relative values and are defined by visitors to developed campgrounds somewhat differently than their traditional interpretation in outdoor recreation.[3] These changing values are apparently not well understood by managers. In a similar study of Minnesota state parks, visitors were found to define these areas primarily in terms of recreation, while managers defined them in terms of natural areas designed for preservation (Merriam et al. 1972). A third study of this issue focused on an urban landscape resource, the University of Washington Arboretum (Twight and Catton 1975). Visitors were found to be more oriented to preservation and naturalness of the area than managers and less oriented to scientific, educational, and horticultural aspects. In all three studies, visitors define the study areas primarily in terms of what they use them for rather than the purposes for which the areas may have originally been designed.

Two other studies have added additional insight to this issue. The first of these studies explored how well managers were able to predict the motivations of visitors to two national park areas: Cape Hatteras National Seashore, NC, (a recreation area with substantial off-road vehicle use), and Shenandoah National Park, VA, backcountry (a natural area) (Wellman et al. 1982b). Statistically significant differences were found between visitor and manager ratings on sixteen of twenty-two motivation items at Cape Hatteras and eight of twenty-five motivation items at Shenandoah. The authors suggest that the greater convergence of visitor and manager perceptions at Shenandoah might be explained by the fact that this area is more traditional in environment and use within the national park system than Cape Hatteras. Tentative support for this hypothesis is offered by a similar study of ski touring on national forest lands in Colorado (Rosenthal and Driver 1983). Very close agreement was found in this study between visitor motivations and manager predictions. This study area was primarily undeveloped backcountry more conventionally associated with outdoor recreation.

Several studies have included components that examine and compare visitor and manager perceptions of recreation impacts and related problems. Study findings have been generally consistent: managers tend to be more perceptive of such issues than visitors in all areas studied, including developed campgrounds (Clark et al. 1971a), backcountry campsites (Martin et al. 1989), wilderness (G. Peterson 1974, Shin and Jaakson 1997), roaded forest lands (Downing and Clark 1979), non-motorized recreation areas (Lucas 1979), and state parks and related areas (Manning and Fraysier 1989). Impacts and problems studied included litter, vandalism, theft, human waste, environmental impacts at campsites and along trails, water pollution, wildlife disturbance, excessive noise, rule violations, and conflicts among recreationists. Managers also tend to rate such issues as greater problems than do visitors.

The third broad aspect of recreation investigated by this group of studies is attitudes and preferences for area management. The first of these studies focused on visitors and managers of three western wilderness areas (Hendee and Harris 1970). Visitors were asked to rate the extent to which they agreed with an extensive list of wilderness attitude statements, policy and management alternatives, and a list of appropriate behaviors. Wilderness managers were asked to predict visitor responses. Broad agreement was found on two-thirds of the items, but disagreement on the remaining items illustrated several important misconceptions of managers. Managers overestimated visitor support for facility development and the prevalence of "purist" attitudes (e.g., many visitors did not object to the use of helicopters for management purposes, although managers thought they would). Managers also anticipated strong opinions from visitors who were actually neutral or had no opinion on management issues. Lastly, managers underestimated the responsiveness of visitors to measures of behavioral control (e.g., camp clean-up requirements and restrictions on trail shortcutting). Differences in area management preferences between visitors and managers were also found by Clark et al. (1971a), though they are not consistent with the results of the last study since they report that managers overestimated visitor opposition to increased area development. However, the differences in study areas may explain the apparent inconsistency of these two studies: the former was conducted in wilderness areas, while the latter focused on developed campgrounds. Finally, significant differences were found between visitors and managers regarding attitudes toward several use rationing practices (Wikle 1991). River users rated advance reservations and merit (demonstrated competence) more favorably than did managers, while managers rated zoning more favorably than did river users.

Nearly all of the above studies have speculated on why differences in perceptions exist between managers and visitors. A popular theory suggests that managers are more oriented to the natural environment and traditional conceptions of outdoor recreation by virtue of their professional training in the natural sciences (biology, forestry, wildlife biology), their rural residence, the professional missions under which they operate, and their experience with the natural environment, both generally and specifically on study sites. Another theory suggests a process of selective perception reinforcing managers' attitudinal and perceptual predispositions; managers may tend to notice and remember elements of visitor behavior that reinforce preconceived notions. Inaccurate assessments of visitors may also result from the fact that managers most often come into contact with vocal and opinionated visitors who may not be representative of most visitors with more moderate or less-developed views. And, finally, managers' own attitudes may affect their perceptions of recreation visitors: a manager's own opinion of what visitors *should* prefer may well influence his or her view of what visitors *do* prefer (Heberlein 1973, Absher et al. 1988). But regardless of the reason why, it is evident that managers and visitors to outdoor recreation areas can have different perceptions. Neither can be considered "correct." However, objective information on visitor attitudes, preferences, and perceptions appears to be an important prerequisite to informed outdoor recreation management.

Summary and Conclusions

1. Information on visitor attitudes and preferences can be useful in guiding recreation management.

2. Studies on visitor attitudes and preferences have been conducted in a variety of developed and backcountry recreation areas. These studies have led to some common findings concerning visitor attitudes toward alternative recreation management policies and preferences for selected facilities and services. However, caution should be used in generalizing such findings. Substantial diversity of opinion is often found within studies and across study areas.

3. More observational studies are needed, especially in backcountry areas, as a check on the validity of survey-based techniques.

4. Visitors to outdoor recreation areas tend not to be highly perceptive of environmental impacts caused by recreation. Visitors are most perceptive of litter.

5. Managers' perceptions of visitors have been found to be inaccurate in several ways, including the meanings or motivations associated with outdoor recreation, attitudes, and preferences for management, and perceptions of recreation impacts and problems. These findings reinforce the need for objective information from and about visitors.

Notes

1. This issue is discussed in additional detail in Chapter 5.
2. This issue is discussed more fully in Chapter 7.
3. This issue is discussed more fully in Chapter 5.

4

Carrying Capacity
An Organizational Framework

Origins of Carrying Capacity

Rapidly expanding recreation in the 1950s and 1960s gave rise to concerns over appropriate use levels of outdoor recreation areas. While interest in the impacts of recreation on the natural resource base predominated, there was also emerging attention on the effects of increased use on the quality of the recreation experience. The early studies described in the preceding chapters prompted theorists to search for a way such issues might be fit into an organizational framework to help formulate outdoor recreation policy. A resulting paradigm was the concept of carrying capacity.

Carrying capacity has a rich history in the natural resource professions, substantially predating its serious adoption in the field of outdoor recreation. In particular, the term has received wide use in wildlife and range management, where it refers to the number of animals of any one species that can be maintained in a given habitat (Dasmann 1964). But, in its most generic form, carrying capacity is a fundamental concept in natural resources and environmental management referring to the ultimate limits to growth as constrained by environmental factors (Odum 1959). In this generic form, carrying capacity has been applied to broad-ranging issues, including the ultimate population level of humans (e.g., Borgstrom 1965, Meadows et al. 1972) and general environmental planning (e.g., Godschalk and Parker 1975).

Perhaps the first suggestion for applying the concept of carrying capacity to outdoor recreation was recorded in the mid-1930s. A National Park Service report on policy recommendations for parks in the California Sierras posed the question, "How large a crowd can be turned loose in a wilderness without destroying its essential qualities?" (Sumner 1936). Later in the report, it was suggested that recreation use of wilderness be kept "within the carrying capacity." A decade later, a paper on forest recreation suggested that, "In all forest recreation, but particularly in zones of concentrated use, carrying capacity is important (J. V. Wagar 1946)." A follow-up article listed carrying capacity as one of eight major principles in recreation land use:

> Forestry, range management, and wildlife management are all based upon techniques for determining optimum use and limiting harvest beyond this point. Forest recreation belongs in the same category and will be more esteemed when so treated (J. V. Wagar 1951: 433).

The concept of carrying capacity became a more formal part of the outdoor recreation field when it was listed as a major issue by Dana (1957) in his widely read problem analysis of outdoor recreation, and as a result of its prominence in the deliberations and writings of the Outdoor Recreation Resources Review Commission (ORRRC 1962).

Carrying Capacity and Recreation

The first rigorous application of carrying capacity to outdoor recreation came in the early 1960s with a conceptual monograph (J. A. Wagar 1964) and a preliminary empirical treatment (Lucas 1964). Perhaps the major contribution of Wagar's conceptual analysis was the expansion of carrying capacity from its dominant emphasis on environmental effects to a dual focus including social or experiential considerations:

> The study reported here was initiated with the view that the carrying capacity of recreation lands could be determined primarily in terms of ecology and the deterioration of areas. However, it soon became obvious that the resource-oriented point of view must be augmented by consideration of human values (J. A. Wagar 1964: preface).

Wagar's point was that as more people visit an outdoor recreation area, not only the environmental resources of the area are affected, but also the quality of the recreation experience. Thus, carrying capacity was expanded to include consideration of the social environment as well as the biophysical environment. The effects of increasing use on recreation quality were illustrated by Wagar by means of hypothetical relationships between increasing use level and visitor satisfaction. This analysis suggested that the effects of crowding on satisfaction would vary, depending upon visitor needs or motivations.[1]

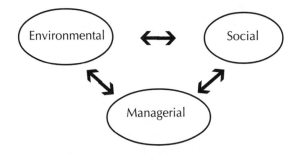

Figure 4-1. Three dimensions of recreation carrying capacity. (From Manning and Lime 1996.)

A preliminary attempt to estimate the recreation carrying capacity of the Boundary Waters Canoe Area, MN, followed shortly, and found that perceptions of crowding varied by different user groups (Lucas 1964b). Paddling canoeists were found to be more sensitive to crowding than motor canoeists, who were in turn more sensitive to crowding than other motorboaters. A range of carrying capacities was estimated depending upon these different relationships.

Wagar's original conceptual analysis hinted at a third element of carrying capacity, and this was described more explicitly in a subsequent paper (J. A. Wagar 1968). Noting a number of misconceptions about carrying capacity, it was suggested that carrying capacity might vary according to the amount and type of management activity. For example, the durability of biophysical resources might be increased through practices such as fertilizing and irrigating vegetation, and periodic rest and rotation of impact sites. Similarly, the quality of the recreation experience might be maintained or even enhanced in the face of increasing use by means of more even distribution of visitors, appropriate rules and regulations, provision of additional visitor facilities, and educational programs designed to encourage desirable user behavior. Thus, carrying capacity, as applied to outdoor recreation, was expanded to a three-dimensional concept by the addition of management considerations (Figure 4-1).

This three-dimensional view has been retained in contemporary analyses of carrying capacity, though it is sometimes described in terms of three types of carrying capacity. One writer, for example, offers definitions for three kinds of recreation carrying capacity; resource-bearing, visitor, and facilities (Alldredge 1973). Another study discusses three types of capacity, labeled ecological, social, and facilities (Heberlein 1977). A fourth type of capacity termed "physical" is also suggested, referring to the constraint imposed by sheer limits of physical space. This concept, however, is less often of concern in management of outdoor recreation.

Limits of Acceptable Change

Carrying capacity has attracted intensive focus as a research and management concept in outdoor recreation. Several bibliographies, books, and review papers have been published on carrying capacity and related issues, and these publications contain hundreds of citations (Stankey and Lime 1973, Graefe et al. 1984, Shelby and Heberlein 1986, Stankey and Manning 1986, Kuss et al. 1990). Yet despite this impressive literature base, efforts to apply carrying capacity to recreation areas has often resulted in frustration. The principal difficulty lies in determining how much impact or change should be allowed within each of the three components that make up the carrying capacity concept: environmental resources, the quality of the recreation experience, and the extent and direction of management actions.

The growing research base on outdoor recreation indicates that increasing recreation use often causes impact or change. This is especially clear with regard to environmental, natural, or biophysical resources. An early study in the Boundary Waters Canoe Area, MN, for example, found that an average of 80% of ground cover vegetation was destroyed at campsites in a single season, even under relatively light levels of use (Frissell and Duncan 1965). The biophysical and ecological impacts of outdoor recreation have been summarized and synthesized in a number of studies (e.g., Cole 1987, Kuss et al. 1990, Hammitt and Cole 1998). The remaining chapters in this book review and synthesize the ways in which increasing use levels can impact or change the quality of the recreation experience. Research suggests that increasing recreation use can also change the management environment through development and implementation of more intensive management practices (Manning et al. 1996a). Despite increasing knowledge about recreation use and resulting impacts, the critical question remains: how much impact or change should be allowed?

This issue is often referred to as the "limits of acceptable change" (Frissell and Stankey 1972). Some change in the recreation environment is inevitable, but sooner or later the amount, nature, or type of change may become unacceptable. But what determines the limits of acceptable change?

This issue is illustrated graphically in Figure 4-2. In this figure, a hypothetical relationship between visitor use and impacts to the biophysical, social, and management environments is shown. This

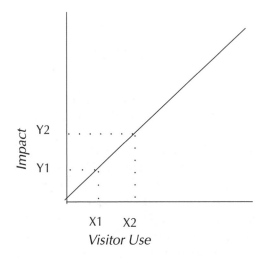

Figure 4-2. Hypothetical relationship between visitor use and impact to the recreation environment. (From Manning and Lime 1996.)

relationship suggests that increasing recreation use can and often does cause increasing impacts in the form of damage to fragile soils and vegetation, crowding and conflicting uses, and more direct and intensive recreation management actions. However, it is not clear from this relationship at what point carrying capacity has been reached. For this relationship, X1 and X2 represent alternative levels of visitor use that result in corresponding levels of impact as defined by points Y1 and Y2, respectively. But which of these points—Y1 or Y2, or some other point along the vertical axis—represent the maximum amount of impact that is acceptable?

To emphasize and further clarify this issue, some studies have suggested distinguishing between descriptive and prescriptive components of carrying capacity (Shelby and Heberlein 1984, 1986). The descriptive component of carrying capacity focuses on factual, objective data such as the relationship in Figure 4-2. For example, what is the relationship between the amount of visitor use and perceived crowding? The prescriptive component of carrying capacity determination concerns the seemingly more subjective issue of how much impact or change in the recreation environment is acceptable. For example, what level of perceived crowding should be allowed?

Management Objectives and Indicators and Standards of Quality

Recent experience with carrying capacity suggests that answers to the above question can be found through formulation of management objectives and associated indicators and standards of quality (Lime and Stankey 1971, Frissell and Stankey 1972, Lucas and Stankey 1974, Bury 1976, P. Brown 1977, Hendee et al. 1977b, Lime 1977a, 1979, Stankey 1980b, Boteler 1984, Stankey et al. 1985, Stankey and Manning 1986, Graefe et al. 1990, Shelby et al. 1992b, Shindler 1992, Lime 1995, Manning et al. 1995a, c, Manning and Lime 1996, Manning et al. 1996b, Manning 1997, National Park Service 1997). This approach to carrying capacity focuses on defining the type of visitor experience to be provided. Management objectives are broad, narrative statements defining the type of visitor experience to be provided. Indicators of quality are more specific, measurable variables reflecting the essence or meaning of management objectives. They are quantifiable proxies or measures of management objectives. Indicators of quality may include elements of the biophysical, social, and management environments that are important in determining the quality of the visitor experience. Standards of quality define the minimum acceptable condition of each indicator variable.

An example may help illuminate these ideas and terms. Review of the Wilderness Act of 1964 suggests that areas contained in the National Wilderness Preservation System are to be managed to provide opportunities for visitor solitude. Thus, providing opportunities for solitude is an appropriate management objective for most wilderness areas. Moreover, research on wilderness use suggests that the number of other visitors encountered along trails and at campsites is important in defining solitude for wilderness visitors. Thus, trail and camp encounters are potentially good indicators of quality. Research also suggests that wilderness visitors may have normative standards about how many trail and camp encounters can be experienced before opportunities for solitude decline to an unacceptable degree.[2] For example, a number of studies suggest that wilderness visitors prefer to see no more than five other groups per day along trails. Thus, a maximum of five encounters per day with other groups along trails may be a good standard of quality.

Management objectives and indicators and standards of quality should be formulated on the basis of several considerations. In keeping with the three-dimensional model of carrying capacity illustrated in Figure 4-1, these considerations can be organized into three broad categories.

1. Natural Resource Considerations. The biophysical characteristics of the natural resource base help determine the degree of change in the environment that results from recreation use. While even light levels of use may cause change in the environment, some resource bases are inherently more fragile than others. These biophysical resource characteristics should be studied and may become important guides in formulating management objectives and indicators and standards of quality.

2. Social Considerations. The needs and wants of visitors are important in determining appropriate outdoor recreation opportunities. Studies of visitors to outdoor recreation areas may suggest appropriate types and levels of outdoor recreation use. Such studies should be incorporated in carrying capacity analysis.

3. Management Considerations. Legal directives, agency mission statements, and other policy-related guidelines may suggest appropriate management objectives and related indicators and standards of quality. Moreover, financial, personnel, and other management resources may also suggest the types and levels of recreation use that are possible or feasible.

The types of information described above can be important in formulating informed and thoughtful management objectives and associated indicators and standards of quality. However, there is ultimately a value-based element of recreation carrying capacity that must also be addressed. While research can help illuminate the relationships between increasing use levels and change in the recreation environment as illustrated in Figure 4-2, determining the point at which change becomes unacceptable will usually require some element of management judgement. The natural resource, social, and managerial considerations described above can help shape such management judgments.

Carrying Capacity Frameworks

The literature described above has given rise to several frameworks for determining and applying carrying capacity to outdoor recreation. These frameworks include Limits of Acceptable Change (Stankey et al. 1985, McCool and Cole 1997a), Visitor Impact Management (Graefe et al. 1990), Visitor Experience and Resource Protection (Manning et al. 1996b, Hof and Lime 1997, National Park Service 1997), Carrying Capacity Assessment Process (Shelby and Heberlein 1986), Quality Upgrading and Learning (Chilman et al. 1989, 1990), and Visitor Activity Management Process (Environment Canada and Park Service 1991). All of these frameworks incorporate the ideas about carrying capacity described above and provide a rational, structured process for making carrying capacity decisions.

The basic steps or elements of the three most widely applied carrying capacity frameworks are shown in Table 4-1. While terminology, sequencing, and other aspects may vary among these frameworks, all share a common underlying logic. Core elements of these frameworks include:

1. Definition of the types of recreation opportunities to be provided. Recreation opportunities should be defined as specifically and quantitatively as possible through indicators and standards of quality.

2. Monitoring of indicator variables to determine whether existing conditions meet standards of quality.

3. Management action when and where monitoring suggests that standards of quality have been violated.

A recent comparative analysis of carrying capacity frameworks affirms the similarity of their underlying structures and suggests a number of related themes shared among these frameworks (Nilsen and Taylor 1997):

1. Encouragement of interdisciplinary planning teams.

2. A primary focus on management of recreation-related impacts.

3. A need for sound natural and social science information.

4. Establishment of clear, measurable management objectives.

5. Definition of recreation opportunities as comprised of natural, social, and managerial conditions.

6. A linkage among recreation activities, settings, experiences, and benefits.

7. Recognition that relationships between recreation use and resulting environmental and social impacts can be complex.

Table 4-1. Carrying capacity frameworks.

Limits of Acceptable Change	Visitor Impact Management	Visitor Experience and Resource Protection
Step 1. Identify area concerns and issues	Step 1. Preassessment database reviews	Element 1. Assemble an interdisciplinary project team
Step 2. Define and describe opportunity classes	Step 2. Review of management objectives	Element 2. Develop a public involvement strategy
Step 3. Select indicators of resource and social conditions	Step 3. Selection of key impact indicators	Element 3. Develop statements of primary park purpose, significance, and primary interpretive themes
Step 4. Inventory resource and social conditions	Step 4. Selection of standards for key impact indicators	Element 4. Analyze park resources and existing visitor use
Step 5. Specify standards for resource and social indicators	Step 5. Comparison of standards and existing conditions	Element 5. Describe a potential range of visitor experiences and resource conditions
Step 6. Identify alternative opportunity class allocations	Step 6. Identify probable causes of impacts	Element 6. Allocate potential zones to specific locations
Step 7. Identify management actions for each alternative	Step 7. Identify management strategies	Element 7. Select indicators and specify standards for each zone; develop a monitoring plan
Step 8. Evaluation and selection of an alternative	Step 8. Implementation	Element 8. Monitor resource and social indicators
Step 9. Implement actions and monitor conditions		Element 9. Take management action

8. Recognition of the importance of providing a diversity of recreation opportunities.

9. A focus on elements of recreation opportunities that can be influenced through management.

10. A range of recreation management strategies and tactics.

11. A need for ongoing monitoring and evaluation.

Several applications and evaluations of the above carrying capacity frameworks and related processes are described in the literature (Ashor et al. 1986, Graefe et al. 1986a, Shelby and Heberlein 1986, Absher 1989, Graefe et al. 1990, Vaske et al. 1992, Kaltenborn and Emmelin 1993, Hof et al. 1994, Manning et al. 1995a, Manning et al. 1995b, Manning et al. 1995c, McCoy et al. 1995, Manning and Lime 1996, Manning et al. 1996b, Manning et al. 1996c, Manning 1997, McCool and Cole 1997b, Ritter 1997, Warren 1997).

The Status of Carrying Capacity

As applied to outdoor recreation, carrying capacity is more complex than its initial applications in other fields of study (Burch 1981, Stankey 1989). Recreation carrying capacity includes natural resource, social and managerial considerations, descriptive and prescriptive components, management objectives and indicators and standards of quality, and management judgment. It seems clear that there can be no *one* carrying capacity for a park or outdoor recreation area. Rather, carrying capacity is dependent upon how the various components of the concept are fashioned together. This complexity and apparent lack of definitiveness have caused some disillusionment. Characterizations such as "slippery" (Alldredge 1973), "elusive" (Graefe et al. 1984), and "illusive" (R. Becker et al. 1984) have been applied to recreation carrying capacity. This difficulty with carrying capacity seems to be borne out in surveys of park and wilderness managers (Washburne 1981, Washburne and Cole 1983, Manning et al. 1996a). Even though many managers suspect that recreational use of their areas has exceeded carrying capacity, they have not yet established such carrying capacities.

The weaknesses and shortcomings of carrying capacity have been noted by a number of writers. Several point out that the term implies a single "magic number" for each recreation area, and that this, of course, is misleading and obscures the role of management judgments (Bury

1976, Washburne 1982). For this reason, a stronger emphasis on management objectives has been suggested by some as an alternative to carrying capacity (Becker and Jubenville 1982, Jubenville and Becker 1983, Stankey et al. 1984). Similarly, it has been noted that analyses of carrying capacity often ignore the ability of management to affect the amount of use that can be accommodated; the term "design capacity" has been suggested as an alternative to carrying capacity (Godin and Leonard 1977b).

Others have argued that the very term "carrying capacity" seems to imply an undue emphasis on use limitations (Washburne 1982, Burch 1984, Stankey et al. 1984). These writers argue that a number of management alternatives might be used to meet management objectives aside from use limitations, which may often be the least-preferred alternative. Moreover, while management objectives for some areas may well set relatively low carrying capacities and thus ultimately require use limits, other areas will properly have relatively high carrying capacities without need for use limits. In a similar vein, it has been noted that recreation-caused change is not inherently undesirable (Stankey 1974). In fact, use of the more neutral word "change" has been suggested as opposed to "impacts," "damage," or other value-laden terms, since judgment about the relative desirability of change can only be made in relationship to management objectives.

Finally, even J. A. Wagar (1974), author of the original conceptual analysis of recreation carrying capacity, has suggested that borrowing the term from range and wildlife management may not have been a wise choice. The close association between carrying capacity and natural resource or biophysical considerations in the historical sense tends to divert attention from the equally important experiential and managerial concerns that must be a part of carrying capacity as applied to outdoor recreation.

All of these points are valid criticisms. However, the term carrying capacity is deeply entrenched in the field of outdoor recreation, and recent legislation and institutional directives have even made carrying capacity a formal part of outdoor recreation management (Manning et al. 1996e). For example, amendments to Public Law 91-383 (84 Stat. 824, 1970) call for general management plans for units of the national park system to include "identification of and implementation commitments for visitor carrying capacities for all areas of the unit." Moreover, amendments to the National Trails System Act (Public Law 90-543, 1968) require development of a comprehensive plan for trails, including "an identified carrying capacity of the trail and a plan for its implementation." In the regulations implementing the National Forest Management Act of 1976, Section 219.18(a) states that the portion of forest plans providing direction for wilderness management will "provide for limiting and distributing visitor use of specific areas in accord with periodic estimates of the maximum levels of use that allow natural processes to operate freely and that do not impair the values for which wilderness areas were created." And the Nationwide Outdoor Recreation Plan (Bureau of Outdoor Recreation 1973) states that "each federal recreation land managing agency will determine the carrying capacity of its recreation lands."

Despite its shortcomings, the term "carrying capacity" is likely to remain a part of the outdoor recreation field for the foreseeable future. Carrying capacity can be useful as an outdoor recreation management concept when viewed in proper perspective—as an organizational framework for determining and managing appropriate outdoor recreation opportunities. The recreation carrying capacity frameworks developed in the literature and their successful application in the field suggest that carrying capacity is a useful concept in outdoor recreation.

Summary and Conclusions

1. Since its adoption from wildlife and range management, outdoor recreation carrying capacity has evolved from a primary emphasis on natural resource impacts to include equal consideration of recreation experience and management considerations.

2. Recreation use can cause change in the recreation environment, including resource conditions, the quality of the experience provided, and/or management actions.

3. Limits should be determined for the amount of change acceptable.

4. Limits of acceptable change should be formulated and expressed in the form of management objectives and associated indicators and standards of quality.

5. Application of carrying capacity ultimately requires some judgment on the part of managers. However, such judgments should be based on natural resource, social, and managerial considerations.

6. There is no single carrying capacity for an outdoor recreation area. Rather, every area has a range of capacities depending upon management objectives and indicators and standards of quality.

7. Several carrying capacity frameworks have been developed, including Limits of Acceptable Change, Visitor Impact Management, and Visitor Experience and Resource Protection. These frameworks have been successfully applied to a variety of park and recreation areas.

8. Carrying capacity does not necessarily imply strict limitation of use. Some recreation areas will have low capacities and may require use limits, while others will have high capacities and may not need use limits. Moreover, use limits are only one of several recreation management alternatives, and are often the least desirable.

9. Carrying capacity can be a useful concept in outdoor recreation management when viewed as an organizational framework.

Notes

1. These important points are discussed more fully in Chapters 5 and 7.
2. Research on indicators and standards of quality is addressed in Chapter 6.

5

Crowding in Outdoor Recreation
Use Level, Perceived Crowding, and Satisfaction

Concern with Crowding

This chapter examines a large genre of research concerned with crowding in outdoor recreation. There is a relatively long history of concern over the effects of increasing use on the quality of the recreation experience, beginning even before the post-World War II boom in recreation participation (e.g., J. Adams 1930, A. Leopold 1934). Shortly after the beginning of the period of rapidly expanding outdoor recreation in the 1950s and 1960s, a number of popular articles began to generate widespread interest in this topic (e.g., DeVoto 1953, Clawson 1959).

Adoption of the concept of carrying capacity, as described in the previous chapter, and particularly the expansion of the concept to include a social carrying capacity component, provided a convenient foundation on which to base theoretical and empirical crowding research. J. A. Wagar's (1964) conceptual analysis of carrying capacity is again an appropriate place to begin discussion. This analysis suggested that, "When too many people use the same area, some traditional wildland values are lost." This was illustrated with a series of hypothetical relationships between crowding and a number of human motivations inherent in outdoor recreation participation.[1] Crowding was shown to have a detrimental effect on most of these motivations, including esteem and prestige, aesthetic enjoyment, understanding, freedom of choice, self-reliance, and solitude.

The notion that there is some level of visitor use beyond which the quality of the outdoor recreation experience diminishes is a recurrent theme in the early outdoor recreation literature. This issue is at the heart of the social carrying capacity concept and has often contributed, along with concerns over environmental impacts, to regulation of the number of people using outdoor recreation areas. This chapter examines both empirical and theoretical studies of crowding in outdoor recreation. These studies are used to construct and test a conceptual model of crowding. This model suggests that crowding is influenced by a number of issues, including coping behaviors of recreationists, normative definitions of crowding, and several methodological issues.

Empirical Studies of Crowding

One of the earliest empirical studies to address social concern with crowding was conducted for the Outdoor Recreation Resources Review Commission (Department of Resource Development 1962). A large-scale survey of visitors to twenty-four outdoor recreation sites around the country found that nearly 20% of respondents said that there were too many people using the area, though nearly an equal number felt they would have been satisfied with more people.

Most early research on crowding focused primarily on wilderness areas, probably because these areas are required by law to provide opportunities for solitude. Visitors to the Boundary Waters Canoe Area, MN, reported substantial concerns about crowding, with 34% of paddling canoeists reporting being bothered "a little" or "quite a bit" by crowding (Lucas 1964b). This declined to 16% and 8% of motor canoeists and motorboaters, respectively. A related study covering four wilderness areas asked visitors the extent to which they agreed with the statement, "It is reasonable to expect that one should be able to visit a wilderness area and see few, if any people" (Stankey 1973). A large majority of visitors to all of these areas agreed with this statement. And in a series of studies conducted from 1970 through 1972 in nine wilderness and related areas, a range of 13% to 49% of visitors reported that they met too many others during their trip (Lucas 1980).

Since these early studies, crowding has become one of the most frequently studied issues in outdoor recreation. A single-item, nine-point crowding measure (Figure 5-1) that allows direct comparisons across studies, areas, and time has been widely adopted.. Findings using this measure of crowding have been compiled from thirty-five studies addressing fifty-nine different areas and more than 17,000 visitors (Shelby et al. 1989a). Table 5-1 shows the percentage of respondents

text continues on page 84

Table 5-1. Percentage of visitors reporting some degree of perceived crowding. (Adapted from Shelby et al. 1989a.)

Sample	Location	% of visitors reporting the experience as crowded
Boaters	Deschutes River, OR	100
Boaters	Deschutes River, OR	97
Fishers	Colorado River, AZ	94
Boaters	Raystown Lake, PA	91
Pheasant hunters	Bong, WI	89
Boaters	Deschutes River, OR	88
Boaters	Deschutes River, OR	88
Riparian landowners	Lake Delavan, WI	87
Goose hunters	Grand River Marsh, WI	86
Pheasant hunters	Public Hunting Area, WI	85
Trout fishers	Gun Powder River, MD	76
Salmon fishers	Waimakiriri River, New Zealand	75
Boaters	Raystown Lake, PA	75
Salmon fishers	Rakaia River, New Zealand	74
Canoers and boaters	Boundary Waters Canoe Area, MN	73
Rafters	Grand Canyon, AZ	72
Fishers	Klamath River, CA	70
Climbers	Mt. McKinley, AK	70
Boaters	Door County, WI	69
Rafters	Rogue River, OR	68
Rock climbers	Seneca Rocks, West VA	68
Boaters	Raystown Lake, PA	66
Boaters	Raystown Lake, PA	63
Deer hunters	Sandhill, WI	62
Goose hunters	Fishing Bay, MD	61
Floaters	Wolf River, WI	61
Salmon fishers	Rakaia River, New Zealand	59
Deer hunters (muzzle)	Statewide, MD	57
Deer hunters (bow)	Statewide, MD	55
Wildlife photographers	Sandhill, WI	55
Recreationists	Lake Delavan, WI	54

Sample	Location	% of visitors reporting the experience as crowded
Deer hunters (gun)	Statewide, MD	53
Fishers	Brule River, WI	53
Rafters	Grand Canyon, AZ	53
Rafters	Snake River, OR	53
Backpackers	Mt. Jefferson Wilderness, OR	53
Canoers	Brule River, WI	52
Deer hunters	Sandhill, WI	50
Backpackers	Eagle Cap Wilderness, OR	49
Pheasant hunters	Bong, WI	48
Deer hunters	Statewide, WI	46
Salmon fishers	Rakaia River, New Zealand	45
Turkey hunters	Statewide, MD	44
Tubers	Brule River, WI	43
Sailboaters	Apostle Islands, WI	42
Tourists and drivers	Stockings Park, MI	41
Backpackers	White Mt. National Forest, NH	39
Floaters	Klamath River, CA	38
Canoers	Brule River, WI	37
Fishers	Colorado River, AZ	32
Hikers	Dolly Sods Wilderness, WV	31
Goose hunters	Tuckahoe State Park, MD	27
Rafters	Illinois River, OR	26
Trout fishers	Savage River, MD	25
Backpackers	Great Gulf Wilderness, NH	24
Deer hunters	Sandhill, WI	24
Trout fishers	Gun Powder River, MD	23
Goose hunters	Grand River Marsh, WI	17
Deer hunters	Sandhill, WI	12

1	2	3	4	5	6	7	8	9
Not at all crowded		Somewhat crowded			Moderately crowded		Extremely crowded	

Figure 5-1. Standardized measure of crowding.

who reported a score of three or higher on the crowding scale, indicating some degree of perceived crowding. This table indicates substantial diversity in crowding judgments with the percentage of respondents reporting some degree of crowding, ranging from 12% to 100%, with a mean of 57%. Clearly, many visitors to outdoor recreation areas experience some degree of crowding. Analysis of the data in Table 5-1 found that perceived crowding tended to be higher at more accessible or convenient locations and during traditional peak use periods. Perceived crowding was lower at areas where management action had been taken to reduce use. No differences in perceived crowding were found among geographic regions or between consumptive and non-consumptive recreation activities.

Concern with crowding is apparently widely shared by managers of recreation areas as well as visitors. A national survey of managers of wilderness and related areas found that two-thirds of all areas were considered to be beyond capacity in at least some places and at some times (Washburne and Cole 1983). In most of these cases (53%), overuse problems were considered to be of a social or crowding nature as opposed to resource damage. A more recent survey of National Park Service backcountry managers reported that capacity is exceeded either "sometimes" or "usually" in the vast majority of areas (Marion et al. 1993, Manning et al. 1996a).

The Satisfaction Model

Early empirical studies of crowding were followed by theoretical development. Several theorists developed a quantitative model of the effects of increasing use on the recreation experience, based on the economic concept of marginal utility (Clawson and Knetch 1966, Fisher and Krutilla 1972, Alldredge 1973). Substituting recreation visits for input and satisfaction for output, the theoretical constructs of production

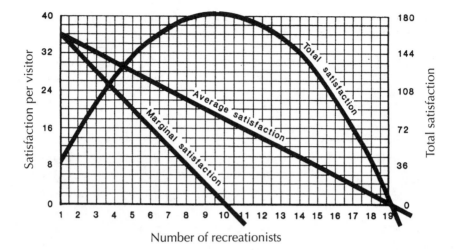

Figure 5-2. Hypothetical relationship between increasing visitor use and satisfaction. (Adapted from Alldredge 1973.)

economics suggest that as visitors are added to a recreation area, the marginal satisfaction of each individual visitor will progressively decline due to crowding, but total or aggregate satisfaction will increase. This process continues until the marginal satisfaction of the nth visitor no longer exceeds the drop in satisfaction of previous visitors. At this point, aggregate satisfaction begins to decline and social carrying capacity has been reached.

Alldredge (1973) illustrated the model with an example of a hypothetical wilderness area. Starting with the area devoid of visitors, no satisfaction is produced (see Table 5-2 and Figure 5-2).[2] As the first visitor enters the area, he or she experiences maximum satisfaction, arbitrarily defined as thirty-six units. As a second visitor is added, the satisfaction of the first visitor is reduced slightly due to very low-level crowding, and the satisfaction of the second visitor is also less than maximum. Even though average satisfaction falls with each additional visitor, total satisfaction continues to rise (though at a declining rate) while marginal satisfaction (the change in total satisfaction) is above zero. As the tenth visitor—in this example—is added, his or her satisfaction just equals the aggregate drop in satisfaction experienced by other visitors and total satisfaction is at its highest. At this point, social carrying capacity has been reached. This is the point at which marginal satisfaction equals zero.

Table 5-2. Hypothetical relationship between increasing visitor use and satisfaction. (Adapted from Alldredge 1973.)

Number of visitors	Average satisfaction per visitor[a]	Total satisfaction	Marginal satisfaction
0	0	0	0
1	36	36	63
2	34	68	62
3	32	96	28
4	30	120	24
5	28	140	20
6	26	156	16
7	24	168	12
8	22	176	8
9	20	180	4
10	18	180	0
11	16	176	-4
12	14	168	-8
13	12	156	-12
14	10	140	-16
15	8	120	-20
16	6	96	-24
17	4	68	-28
18	2	36	-32
19	0	0	-36
20	-2	-40	-40
21	-4	-84	-44

[a] Measured in hypothetical units of satisfaction which Alldredge termed "enjoyils."

The driving force behind this model is an assumed inverse relationship between use level and satisfaction; for the individual, increased use causes decreased satisfaction. This approach to crowding has been called the "satisfaction model" (Heberlein and Shelby 1977).

Testing the Satisfaction Model

Empirical tests of the relationship between use level and satisfaction have taken several forms. An early test was conducted as part of a larger survey of visitors to four wilderness areas (Stankey 1973). Visitors were asked to indicate how they felt about encountering increasing numbers of other parties, reporting their satisfaction on a five-point scale ranging from "very pleasant" to "very unpleasant." "Satisfaction curves" were then constructed showing the effect of increasing numbers of encounters with both backpackers and horseback riders on satisfaction (Figure 5-3). The curves generally support the satisfaction model as satisfaction falls nearly consistently, though not proportionally, through the range of other parties encountered. The data, however, were derived from hypothetical questions, and further empirical testing was warranted.

Two tests of the satisfaction model conducted in the mid-1970s took an economic approach to the issue, closely following Alldredge's (1973) model as described earlier. Visitors to the Spanish Peaks Primitive Area, MT, were given descriptions of five hypothetical wilderness trips in the study area (Cicchetti and Smith 1973, Cicchetti 1976). Trips varied in the number of trail encounters per day and camp encounters per night, and respondents were asked to report the highest price they were willing

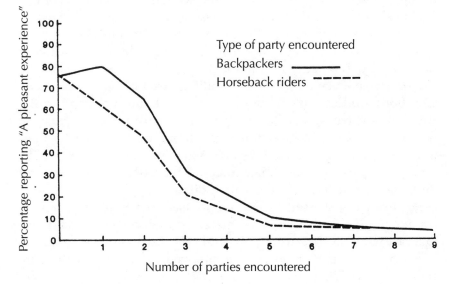

Figure 5-3. Satisfaction curves for encounters with hikers and horseback riders in three western wilderness areas. (From Stankey 1973.)

to pay for each of the hypothetical trips. The survey was conducted by mail and received a relatively low response rate—less than 50%. Moreover, approximately one-third of the visitors who responded did not answer the questions concerning willingness to pay, many indicating they were unable to quantify their willingness to pay for wilderness recreation. Study findings showed no statistically significant relationship between willingness to pay and either trail encounters or camp encounters. By statistically controlling four other independent variables, the two encounter measures could be shown to reduce willingness to pay only slightly.

The second test using willingness to pay as a measure of satisfaction focused on visitors to six Rhode Island ocean beaches (McConnell 1977). Respondents were asked how much they would have been willing to pay to come to the beach they used. Measurements were also taken of site conditions, including number of people per acre on the beach and air temperature. As in the previous study, initial analysis of the findings showed no statistically significant relationship between density (people per acre) and willingness to pay. Statistically controlling for three other independent variables, the correlation between density and willingness to pay was increased to a statistically significant level, but this relationship varied substantially among the six beaches studied.

These studies tended to cast doubt on the assumed inverse relationship between use level and satisfaction. The simple bivariate relationship between these variables assumed in the satisfaction model was not found in either study. Only after statistically controlling several other independent variables, a practice that would not be feasible under field conditions, could a statistically significant relationship be demonstrated. Even under these conditions, the relationship varied by site. Both studies suffer from the potential shortcomings of the willingness to pay approach: it is often difficult to quantify the value of non-market goods such as outdoor recreation, and there may be built-in biases to such questions if respondents think their answers will be used to formulate pricing policy. Finally, both studies were conducted under predominately hypothetical conditions.

Subsequently, the satisfaction model has been tested under field conditions. Satisfaction has been measured under density conditions that vary naturally in recreation areas. The results of a number of studies conducted in this manner are summarized, to the extent they are comparable, in Table 5-3.

text continues on page 92

Table 5-3. Findings from empirical tests of the relationships among use level, perceived crowding, and satisfaction.

Study	Area	Users	Use level / satisfaction	Use level/ crowding	Crowding/ satisfaction
R. Lee 1975,1977	Yosemite National Park, CA	Hikers, campers			None[1]
Heberlein 1977	Brule River, WI	Canoeists, tubers, fishers	R = .009		
Lucas 1980	Desolation Wilderness, CA	Hikers	$\gamma = .17$		
	Selway-Bitterroot Wilderness Area, MT	Hikers, horseback riders	$\gamma = .21$		
	Bob Marshall Wilderness Area, MT	Hikers, horseback riders	$\gamma = .26$		
	Cabinet Mtns. Wilderness, MT	Hikers, horseback riders	$\gamma = -.14$		
	Scapegoat Wilderness, MT	Hikers, horseback riders	$\gamma = .31$		
	Mission Mtns. Wilderness, MT	Hikers, horseback riders	$\gamma = .20$		
	Spanish Peaks Primitive Area, MT	Hikers, horseback riders	$\gamma = .11$		
	Great Bear Wilderness, MT	Hikers, horseback riders	$\gamma = -.08$		
	Jewel Basin Hiking Area, MT	Hikers, horseback riders	$\gamma = .08$		
Manning and Ciali 1980	4 Vermont rivers	Fishers, floaters, swimmers	R = .14		

Study	Area	Users	Use level / satisfaction	Use level/ crowding	Crowding/ satisfaction
Shelby 1980a	Colorado River, Grand Canyon National Park, AZ	Rafters	R = .00[a] R = .05 R = .03 R = .01 R = -.01 R = .02	R = .05[a] R = .05 R = .05 R = .03 R = .12 R = .13	
Absher and Lee 1981	Yosemite National Park, CA	Backpackers		$R^2 = .07$	
R. Becker 1981	Upper Mississippi River	River users	None		
Bultena et al. 1981b	Mt. McKinley National Park, AK	Hikers	R = -.01- (-.06)	R = .33 - .35	R = -.05
Gramann and Burdge 1981	Lake Shelbyville, IL	Reservoir users	R = .06		
Womble and Studebaker 1981	Katmai National Monument, AK	Developed area campers	$R^2 = .09$	$R^2 = .07$	
Ditton et al. 1982	Buffalo River, AR	Floaters	R = .02	R = .09	R = .12
Heberlein et al. 1982	Sandhill Wildlife Management Area, WI	Deer hunters	R = .10	R = .28	
Titre and Mills 1982	Guadalupe River, TX	Floaters	None[2]	Sig.[3]	
Vaske et al. 1982b	Dolly Sods Wilderness, WV	Hikers	R = -.02	R = .31	R = -.18
West 1982b	Ottawa National Forest, MI	Hikers		$R^2 = .05$	

Study	Area	Users	Use level / satisfaction	Use level/ crowding	Crowding/ satisfaction
Shelby et al. 1983	Brule River, WI	Canoers	$R^2 = .21$		
	Wisconsin	Deer hunters	$R^2 = .22$		
	Grand River Marsh, WI	Goose hunters (managed)	$R^2 = .03$		
	Grand River Marsh, WI	Goose hunters (firing line)	$R^2 = .23$		
	Rogue River, OR	Floaters	$R^2 = .02- .06$		
	Colorado River, Grand Canyon National Park, AZ	Floaters	$R^2 = .02$		
Hammitt et al. 1984	Hiawassee River, TN	Tubers	$R = .61$		
Westover and Collins 1987	Urban park, MI	Visitors	$R^2 = .28$		
Andereck and Becker 1990	Fort Sumter National Monument, SC	Visitors	$R^2 = .08$ (at Fort) $R^2 = .14$ (on boat)		
Armistead and Ramthun 1996	Blue Ridge Parkway, VA	Visitors at Visitors Center			$R^2 = .01$
Confer et al. 1996	5 ocean beaches, DE	Beach visitors	$R^2 = .16$		
Tarrant and English 1996	Nantahala River, NC	Rafters, canoeists/ kayakers	$R = .001^4$ $R^2 = .14^5$		
Tarrant et al. 1997	Nantahala River, NC	Rafters, canoeists/ kayakers	Rafters: $R^2 = .23^6$ $R^2 = .27^7$ $R^2 = .32^8$ $R^2 = .05^9$ $R^2 = .09^{10}$ $R^2 = .12^{11}$		

Study	Area	Users	Use level / satisfaction	Use level/ crowding	Crowding/ satisfaction
				Kayakers/ canoeists:	
				$R^2 = .24^6$	
				$R^2 = .24^7$	
				$R^2 = .34^8$	
				$R^2 = .05^9$	
				$R^2 = .04^{10}$	
				$R^2 = .06^{11}$	

R = product moment correlation coefficient; R^2 = multiple correlation coefficient; γ = gamma; a = the correlation coefficients in these columns are for the following six use level/interaction variables: people per week leaving the put-in point; river contacts per day; people per day seen on the river; time in sight of people on the river; percentage of all attraction sites with contacts; and average number of people seen at attraction sites.
1. No relationship between perceived crowding and behavioral measures of satisfaction.
2. No relationship using analysis of variance. 3. Significant relationship using analysis of variance, but only on high use portion of the river. 4. Private users. 5. Commercial users.
6. With rafts on river. 7. With rafts at put-in. 8. With rafts at rapids. 9. With kayaks/canoes at river. 10. With kayaks/canoes at put-in. 11. With kayaks/canoes at rapids

The most striking aspect of the table is the generally low relationships between variables. In many cases, the relationships are not statistically significant. The strength of relationships between use level and satisfaction, for example, are low to moderate for two to four of the wilderness areas studied by Lucas (1980). In all other studies and areas where these variables were tested, relationships were weak or nonexistent. A moderately strong relationship between use level and crowding was found in about half the areas where these variables were measured; other areas found a weak relationship or none. The relationship between crowding and satisfaction was found to be generally weak or nonexistent. R. Lee (1977) found no relationship between perceived crowding and satisfaction as measured by intensity of greeting behavior along trails and extent of search behavior for appropriate campsites. Though the relationship for Colorado River rafters reported by Shelby (1980a) is statistically significant, it is weak; perceived crowding explains only 2% of the variation in reported satisfaction.

Taken together, these studies, covering a variety of areas ranging from rural areas to national parks to wilderness, cast considerable doubt on the satisfaction model. Why are use levels and satisfaction seemingly so unrelated? The answer appears to lie in understanding of several conceptual and methodological issues.

Expanding the Satisfaction Model

Crowding in outdoor recreation is a natural extension of a more general and long-standing interest in crowding and human behavior. Marked increases in population growth over the past several decades have generated concern for potentially detrimental implications of high population density. Exploration of social dysfunctions related to population density has been the focus of a considerable body of social-psychological literature over the past fifty years or more.

Sociological and psychological studies of crowding have resulted in mixed findings. Early correlation studies often found statistically significant, positive relationships between population density and various indicators of social pathology such as criminal activity, mental illness, and marital dissatisfaction (e.g., Lottier 1938, Faris and Dunham 1965, R. Mitchell 1971). Experimental studies have been less consistent in their findings. Subjects exposed to high-density conditions have, in some studies, exhibited more negative reactions than subjects exposed to low-density conditions (e.g., Griffitt and Veitch 1971, Valins and Baum 1973). Other similar studies have found no such effects (e.g., Freedman et al. 1971, S. Smith and Haythorn 1972).

Several theorists have speculated on the reasons for these mixed findings in crowding research. Crowding is often analyzed within social interference and stimulus overload theories (Schmidt and Keating 1979, Baum and Paulis 1987). Social interference theory suggests that crowding occurs when the number of other people present interferes with one's goals or desired activities. Stimulus overload theory suggests that crowding is the result of one being overwhelmed by the presence of others.

A related theoretical approach suggests that a variety of coping mechanisms are evolved by individuals and groups to combat perceived crowding (Altman 1975). When the environment becomes too densely populated, new behaviors are adopted that help relieve associated stress and anxiety. The classic work of Milgram (1970), for instance, has illustrated the ways in which urban residents cope with excessive, unwanted contacts—brusque conversations, unlisted telephones, and disregard of strangers, even when they may be in need.

Finally, normative theory distinguishes between the concepts of use level and crowding (Stokols 1972a, b). Use level is a physical concept relating number of people per unit of space; it is strictly neutral and suggests no psychological or experiential evaluation or interpretation.

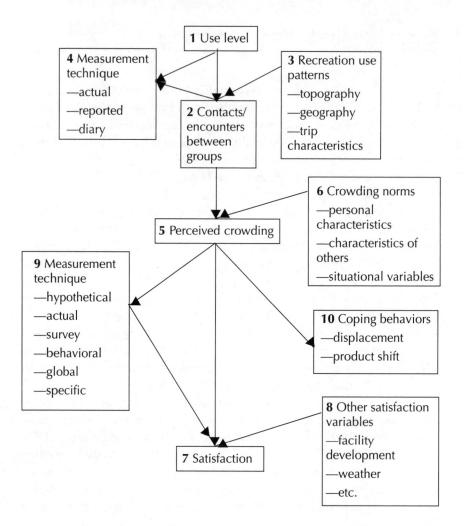

Figure 5-4. An expanded crowding model.

Crowding, on the other hand, has a psychological meaning; it is a negative and subjective evaluation of a use level. Thus, use level may increase to a point where it is perceived to interfere with one's activities or intentions, but only at this point does crowding occur. Several social-psychological studies indicate that crowding judgments are influenced both by the activities being pursued and by the settings in which they occur (e.g., Desor 1972, Cohen et al. 1975). Thus, crowding appears to be a normative concept, dependent upon a variety of circumstances.

These theoretical approaches to crowding have generated a number of hypotheses in outdoor recreation that help illuminate the relationship between use level and satisfaction (Gramann 1982, Manning 1985b, 1986, Stankey 1989, Westover 1989). These hypotheses and their empirical testing, along with some methodological issues introduced later in this chapter, have expanded the simple bivariate satisfaction model to a more comprehensive model as shown in Figure 5-4. The components of this model are described in the remainder of this section.

Coping Behavior

It is widely hypothesized that outdoor recreationists utilize three primary forms of coping behavior: displacement, rationalization, and product shift. Displacement is a behavioral coping mechanism in that it involves spatial or temporal changes in use patterns. Rationalization and product shift are cognitive coping mechanisms involving changes in the ways visitors think about recreation experiences and opportunities.

Displacement. Many writers have suggested that as use levels increase, some recreationists become dissatisfied and alter their patterns of recreation activity to avoid crowding, perhaps ultimately moving on to less used areas. In this manner, they are displaced by users more tolerant of higher use levels. This suggests that the reason for a lack of relationship between use level and perceived crowding is that people who are sensitive to existing use levels at each recreation site have been displaced from these sites. It is important to note that displacement does not have to involve a shift from one recreation area to another— intersite displacement—but can involve shifts within a recreation area— intrasite displacement—and shifts from one time period to another— temporal displacement. The displacement hypothesis was suggested as early as 1971 when it was described as a process of "invasion and succession" (Clark et al. 1971).

A number of studies have addressed this hypothesis empirically. Several have focused on changes in behavior directly associated with use level. Rafters on the Colorado River in Grand Canyon National Park, AZ, for instance, were found to have changed their trip plans as a function of river use level (J. Nielson and Shelby 1977). Changes included limiting the number of attraction sites visited and the time spent at each, both actions designed to limit contact with other rafting parties. Similarly, hikers in two wilderness areas reported changing the length and/or route of their trip because of use levels encountered: 25% in the Spanish Peaks Primitive Area, MT, and 44% in the more heavily used Desolation Wilderness Area, CA (Stankey 1980a).

A slightly different methodology was applied in a study of visitors to the Boundary Waters Canoe Area, MN, and indications of displacement were again found (D. Anderson 1980, 1983, D. Anderson and Brown 1984). Visitors who had made more than four trips to the area were studied to determine changes in trip patterns over time. The vast majority of respondents were found to have changed their pattern of use by selecting different entry points or campsites, or by entering on a different day of the week. Factors related to trip changes included use level, litter, noise, and environmental impacts. In a similar study of boaters using the Apostle Islands National Lake Shore, WI, boaters whose first trip to the area had occurred earlier evaluated existing contact levels more negatively than those whose first trip had occurred more recently; earlier visitors also more frequently avoided more heavily used islands (Vaske et al. 1980).

A study of backcountry campers in Great Smoky Mountains National Park, NC/TN, asked about the extent to which a series of six potential intrasite and temporal displacement behaviors were adopted (Hammitt and Patterson 1991). Between 14% and 44% of visitors reported employing these behaviors either "always" or "usually." Respondents who rated "solitude" as most important to their experience tended to adopt displacement behaviors to a greater degree. A similar study of boaters at Lake Red Rock, IA, found that 17% of respondents had begun using the lake to avoid crowding elsewhere; an additional 14% of respondents reported that they had shifted their use of the lake to weekdays to avoid crowding (Robertson and Regula 1994).

A small group of studies has examined shifts in recreation areas or intersite displacement. Two of these studies have focused on recreation use of two rivers in the same geographic areas. The first studied use of the Lower St. Croix and Upper Missouri Rivers (R. Becker 1981a, R. Becker et al. 1981). A small subsample of respondents was identified who had purposely shifted use from one river to the other, at least partially in response to use levels. The second study examined use of the Rogue and Illinois Rivers, OR (Shelby et al. 1988a). Over a third of respondents (36%) reported that they would shift their use from the Rogue River to the lesser-used Illinois River if Rogue River use increased beyond their expected levels.

In a different approach, J. Nielson and Endo (1977) studied a sample of private (non-commercial) river runners on the Colorado River, Grand Canyon National Park, AZ, from 1959 to 1975. River-running histories were solicited from respondents. Approximately 30% of the sample were found to have shifted their river-running activities to rivers with a lower use level, and might therefore be considered examples of the displacement process, although this is obviously speculative. Moreover, while the rivers to which these persons shifted were indeed less used, they were also closer to home, required less skill, involved shorter trips, and were less wild—which may simply be a function of the fact that there are few remote, wild rivers with low use levels available.

Two other studies are suggestive of the displacement process. One studied visitors to two recreation areas in Pennsylvania (Wohlwill and Heft 1977). One area, the Poconos, was substantially more developed than the other, Pine Creek. Users of the Pine Creek area were found to have traveled significantly longer distances, suggesting that they had been forced to search out lower-use areas. Users of the Poconos were much more supportive of high-convenience facilities and high development levels. The authors suggest that a "positive feedback system" is in operation whereby initial use creates pressure for facilities, which in turn attract more use, and so on. In this system, users who prefer low development and low use levels are easily displaced. This suggestion has been supported by a study of winter visitors to Great Smoky Mountains National Park, NC/TN (Hammitt and Hughes 1984); 78% of respondents reported they avoid backpacking in the park in the summer due to heavy use, and instead visit other less-used areas.

Only one study of displacement has used a panel approach, a more rigorous methodology (Kuentzel and Heberlein 1992a). This study surveyed the same group of boaters at the Apostle Islands National Lakeshore, WI, at a ten-year interval—1975 and 1985. Findings supported intrasite displacement behavior (respondents who had shifted to lower-use portions of the area tended to report higher levels of perceived crowding in 1975), but found no evidence of intersite displacement. A study of visitors to the Sylvania Recreation Area, MI, also found no support of intersite displacement (West 1981a). An on-site survey of visitors, coupled with a telephone survey of past visitors, found that past visitors who no longer used the area did not have greater perceptions of crowding than other categories of visitors. Nor was there any relationship between feeling crowded and intent to visit the area again.

Rationalization. A second coping behavior suggested in outdoor recreation involves a process of rationalization. Since recreation activities are voluntarily selected and sometimes involve a substantial investment of time, money, and effort, some people may rationalize their experience and report high levels of satisfaction, regardless of conditions. This hypothesis is rooted in the theory of cognitive dissonance developed by Festinger (1957) and others, and suggests that people tend to order their thoughts in ways that reduce inconsistencies and associated stress. Therefore, to reduce internal conflict, people may be inclined to rate their recreation experience highly regardless of actual conditions. This, then, may explain why reported satisfaction is often not related to use levels.

This hypothesis appears reasonable when applied, as it originally was, to rafters on the Colorado River in Grand Canyon National Park, AZ (Heberlein and Shelby 1977). For most people, this trip is a substantial undertaking: trips are long, normally requiring at least a week; commercial passengers pay high fees; and private trips may have to wait years to receive a permit. Under these conditions, many people might refuse to be easily disappointed. The hypothesis loses some of its appeal, however, when applied to less extraordinary circumstances. Little support for this hypothesis, for example, was found in a study of river use in Vermont (Manning and Ciali 1980). Most visitors were in-state day users. With such a relatively small investment in their trip, it seems likely that they would admitted they had had an unsatisfactory experience because of crowding or for any other reason. Indeed, many respondents were not hesitant to express dissatisfaction, with reported satisfaction ratings ranging throughout the response scale.

Product Shift. The third coping mechanism suggested in outdoor recreation involves the cognitive behavior of product shift (Heberlein and Shelby 1977, Hendee et al. 1990, Stankey and McCool 1984, Shelby and Heberlein 1986, Stankey 1989). This hypothesis suggests that visitors who experience higher use levels than are expected or preferred may alter their definition of the recreation opportunity in congruence with the conditions experienced.

Several studies have addressed this issue empirically. Studies of users of the Rogue River, OR, suggest that product shift is a relatively common coping strategy (Shelby et al. 1988a). When users were asked how they would react to encountering more visitors on the river than expected, 34% responded that they would change the way they thought about the river, deciding it was less remote than initially believed. A follow-up survey conducted seven years later compared these two samples with respect to the type of recreation opportunity provided by the river. Over this time period, the river experienced a 45% increase in use. In the initial survey, 20% of respondents reported that the river provided a "wilderness" experience, 66% a "semi-wilderness" experience, and 14% an "undeveloped recreation" experience. In the follow-up survey, these percentages had changed to 4, 59, and 37 respectively, suggesting substantial product shift.

A study of visitors to Aravaipa Canyon Wilderness, AZ, is also suggestive of product shift (S. Moore et al. 1990). The number of visitors encountered was related to perceptual definitions of the area. Respondents who encountered larger numbers of visitors reported a lessened sense of solitude, and also reported lessened feelings of freedom, that no one had been there before, and of unspoiled wilderness. In other words, higher use levels led to broader judgments of the study area as something less than pristine wilderness.

Two panel studies have addressed the issue of product shift. The first was focused again on the Rogue River, OR (Shindler and Shelby 1995). Surveys of the same river users were conducted fourteen years apart, a period in which river use increased 70%. In the initial survey, 25% of respondents reported that the river provided a "wilderness" experience. However, this declined to 8% in the follow-up survey, suggesting substantial product shift. However, the second panel study, the study of boaters at Apostle Islands National Lakeshore, WI, described above, found no evidence of product shift (Kuentzel and Heberlein 1992a). ·

Summary. Potential coping behaviors of recreation visitors have been examined in a number of studies. However, findings have been mixed. There is substantial evidence of temporal and intrasite displacement in outdoor recreation. Support for intersite displacement is less definitive. Few studies have addressed rationalization. A small number of studies are generally supportive of product shifts as a cognitive coping mechanism. Based on these findings, a coping behavior component (box 10) encompassing displacement and product shift has been added to the expanded crowding model in Figure 5-4.

Normative Definitions of Crowding

The normative approach to crowding suggests that use level is not interpreted negatively as crowding until it is perceived to interfere with or disrupt one's objectives or values. This approach has proved fertile for theory building and testing in outdoor recreation. A variety of factors have been suggested as influencing normative interpretations of crowding. These factors can be grouped into three basic categories: personal characteristics of visitors, characteristics of others encountered, and situational variables.

Personal Characteristics of Visitors. A variety of personal characteristics of visitors have been found to influence crowding norms. These include motivations for outdoor recreation, preferences and expectations for contacts, experience level, and attitudes toward management.

Motivations, Preferences, and Expectations. Three of the personal characteristics of visitors that seem to be closely interrelated in this context are motivations for recreation and preferences and expectations for use level.[3] These factors have been addressed in several studies, some of which included two or even all three factors. One of the more comprehensive studies surveyed recreationists on the Buffalo National River, AR (Ditton et al. 1983). Wide diversity in perceived crowding was found among the sample of river floaters, and motivations for the trip were found to be significantly related to perceived crowding. Not surprisingly, respondents who felt crowded reported significantly higher ratings on the motivation "to get away from other people," while those whose enjoyment was enhanced by contacts reported significantly higher ratings on the motivations "to be part of the group," "to have thrills and excitement," and "to share what I have learned with others." In addition, respondents who felt crowded reported lower fulfillment ratings for seven of the nine motivations tested. The survey also included questions on expected and preferred number of contacts with others. Mean scores comparing reported with expected contacts were consistently found to be significantly higher for respondents who felt crowded than for groups reporting neutral effect or increased enjoyment. Those who felt crowded were more likely to report having seen more people than expected. The same results were obtained for preferred contacts: those who felt crowded were distinguished from others by the fact that they tended to report experiencing more contacts than they preferred.

These results have been generally corroborated by other studies addressing these factors. Motivations were included in a study of crowding among backcountry hikers in Yosemite National Park, CA (Absher and Lee 1981). While use level alone explained only 7% of the variation in perceived crowding (see Table 5-3), the addition of respondent ratings of seven trip motivations to the model increased the variance explained in perceived crowding to 23%. In particular, hikers who gave a relatively high rating to the motivation of "quietude" were more likely to feel crowded, while those rating "nature involvement" and "shared experiences" high were less likely to feel crowded. Another study relating motivations to perceived crowding found that floaters on the Green and Yampa Rivers in Dinosaur National Monument, CO, who rated the motivations of "stress release / solitude" and "self-awareness" highly were more sensitive to higher use levels (Roggenbuck and Schreyer 1977, Schreyer and Roggenbuck 1978).

Several studies have addressed the role of preferences and expectations in normative interpretations of crowding. A study of Colorado River floaters through Grand Canyon National Park, AZ, found virtually no relationship between various use level / interaction measures and perceived crowding (R ranged from .05 to .13) (Shelby 1980a). However, much higher correlations were found between perceived crowding and both expectations for contacts (R = -.30 and -.39, depending on the measure used), and preferences for contacts (R = -.40). Similarly, only a weak relationship was found between use level and perceived crowding among campers at Katmai National Monument, AK; use level explained only 9% of the variation in perceived crowding (Womble and Studebaker 1981). However, expectations and preferences for use level explained 20% and 37%, respectively, of the variation in perceived crowding. A study of hikers at Mount McKinley National Park, AK, found moderately strong relationships between contacts experienced and measures of perceived crowding (R = .33 to .35, depending upon how contacts were measured) (Bultena et al. 1981b). However, stronger relationships were found between perceived crowding and preference for contacts (R = .45) and expectations for contacts (R = .42). A wide-ranging study of six areas supporting a variety of recreation activities found that by adding expectations and preferences for contacts to actual contacts, the amount of variance in perceived crowding explained was increased by 5% to 19% across all areas studied (Shelby et al. 1983). Similar findings regarding the influence of expectations and preferences on perceived crowding have been reported in studies of hikers in two eastern wilderness areas (Vaske et al. 1982b, Graefe et al. 1986b), canoeists in the Boundary Waters Canoe Area Wilderness, MN (Watson 1995b), and visitors to Fort Sumter National Monument, SC (Andereck and Becker 1993), and the Blue Ridge Parkway, VA (Armistead and Ramthun 1996).

A related issue found in the literature is the suggestion that some visitors who are new to an activity or area have little or no expectation about the conditions they will find, including use levels (J. Nielson and Shelby 1977, J. Nielson et al. 1977). This issue has been called the "floating baseline" effect (Schreyer et al. 1976) and the "uninitiated newcomer" hypothesis (West 1981a) and suggests that first-time users tend to accept what they find as normal, whereas repeat visitors evaluate what they find against past experience. This hypothesis might help explain the lack of relationship between use level and satisfaction, as crowding norms and expectations are likely to be shaped by the use levels found on site. However, like the coping behavior of rationalization discussed in the previous section, this hypothesis appears most reasonable when applied to "once in a lifetime" areas and activities, but seems less broadly applicable to less extraordinary areas and activities where newcomers generally comprise only a small percentage of all visitors. Moreover, the studies described above indicate that most recreationists, regardless of experience, are able to report expectations for use levels.[4] Empirical evidence regarding this issue is mixed. A study of visitors to the Sylvania Recreation Area, MI, found no difference in perceived crowding between first-time and repeat visitors (West 1981a). However, a study of recreation specialization—a multi-faceted concept comprised of experience and related variables—found that expectations for use level were more important in explaining perceived crowding for specialized as opposed to nonspecialized hikers on the White Mountain National Forest, NH (Graefe et al. 1986b).[5] This issue is addressed more directly in the following section on experience.

A second related issue is that areas and activities are self-selected by recreationists to meet preferences and expectations, including those concerning use level. Consequently, it might be expected that visitors would generally be satisfied regardless of use level. The generally high levels of satisfaction found in many outdoor recreation studies are supportive of this hypothesis. More directly supportive are three studies that indicate visitors tend to select recreation sites in line with their preferences and expectations about use level and related conditions (R. Becker 1978, Greenleaf et al. 1984, Stewart and Carpenter 1989). All of these studies found that hikers in lower-use zones tended to be the least tolerant of contact with others or placed greater emphasis on solitude as a motivation for hiking.

This hypothesis begins to break down, however, as opportunities for outdoor recreation, particularly low-use alternatives, become limited. Recreationists may use a particular area even though use level is higher than preferred or expected because there are no reasonable alternatives available. Most of the studies reviewed in this chapter have found some degree of perceived crowding, and this may be indicative of limited alternatives for low-use recreation opportunities. This situation may become more prevalent as participation in outdoor recreation continues to rise.

Experience. While the studies described above have focused considerable attention on motives, preferences, and expectations, perhaps the most widely studied personal characteristic thought to influence crowding norms is experience. Experience level is thought to affect normative definitions of crowding either through refinement of tastes or by virtue of exposure to lower-density conditions as a result of earlier participation (Krutilla 1967, Munley and Smith 1976, Bryan 1977). The bulk of the empirical evidence supports the notion that more experienced users are more sensitive to higher use levels. This appears true regardless of how experience is measured: general experience in the activity, rate of participation, experience on-site, and other dimensions.[6] Four studies previously described found a positive relationship between experience and sensitivity to crowding, two with regard to experience on-site, and the other two across several dimensions of experience (Vaske et al. 1980, Ditton et al. 1983, Graefe et al. 1986b, Armistead and Ramthun 1996). Several other studies corroborate these findings. Backcountry hikers in Grand Canyon National Park, AZ, with more on-site experience were found to have a greater desire to be alone along with other more "purist" views (Towler 1977). More experienced Appalachian Trail hikers expressed stronger preferences for low-use hiking (Murray 1974). A study of visitors to the Bridger Wilderness Area, WY, observed that more experienced campers tended to select campsites farther from other campers (Heberlein and Dunwiddie 1979). More-experienced hikers in the Sandwich Range Wilderness, NH, were found to report higher levels of perceived crowding (Berry et al. 1993). And visitors with more snorkeling experience were found to feel more crowded than other visitors to Buck Island Reef National Monument, U.S. Virgin Islands (Graefe and More 1992).

Two studies do not support the relationship described above between use level/crowding and experience. Stankey (1980a) tested for the effect of general wilderness experience on the "satisfaction curves" described earlier in this chapter. No effects were found except that more experienced visitors to the Spanish Peaks Primitive Area, MT, indicated a greater tolerance for encountering large groups of visitors. And the study of backpackers in Yosemite National Park, CA, described earlier found no statistically significant relationship between general backcountry camping experience and perceived crowding (Absher and Lee 1981).

Attitudes. Attitudes toward wilderness and the extent to which attitudes conform with values suggested in the Wilderness Act (sometimes called "wilderness purism") have also been found to affect normative definitions of crowding. Both studies that have applied a wilderness purism scale to the issue of crowding have found that it distinguishes among respondents with respect to perceived crowding. The "satisfaction curves" derived by Stankey (1973) from wilderness users were found to be distinctly different for strong purists and average visitors. For strong purists, satisfaction dropped off both more quickly and more steeply with increasing number of encounters. And under field conditions, a study of floaters on the Green and Yampa Rivers in Dinosaur National Monument, CO, found that respondents with the most "purist" attitudes consistently reported a higher degree of crowding at each encounter level tested (Schreyer and Roggenbuck 1978).

Demographics. It has been suggested that demographic characteristics might affect crowding norms. Few studies have addressed this issue. However, no studies have reported a statistically significant relationship between perceived crowding and age, sex, or education level of respondents (Absher and Lee 1981, Chavez 1993).

Summary. The bulk of the empirical evidence suggests that motivations for recreation, preferences and expectations for use levels and contacts with others, experience level, and attitudes influence the point at which increasing use level is negatively interpreted as crowding. These factors have therefore been included (box 6) in the expanded crowding model (Figure 5-4).

Characteristics of Those Encountered. There is considerable evidence that the characteristics of those encountered also affect crowding norms. Factors found important include type and size of group, behavior, and the degree to which groups are perceived to be alike.

Type and Size of Group. It seems only reasonable to think that tolerance for meeting another group would depend, at least to some extent, on its characteristics. Several studies support this view empirically, with the type of group most often defined in terms of mode of travel. An early study of the Boundary Waters Canoe Area, MN, found that paddling canoeists distinguished sharply among the three types of area users when asked their reactions to meeting other groups (Lucas 1964b, c). They disliked encountering motorboats, were less resentful of encountering motorized canoes, and were relatively tolerant of encountering at least some other paddled canoes. Motor canoeists made similar distinctions, though not as sharply. Thus, canoeists felt crowded at much lower levels of use where motorboats were present.

Other studies of wilderness visitors have also found differential crowding effects based on mode of travel (Stankey 1973, 1980). The "satisfaction curves" shown in Figure 5-3 demonstrate different tolerances for encountering backpackers and horseback riders along wilderness trails. Similar differences in satisfaction curves were found for paddling canoeists, motor canoeists, and motorboaters in the Boundary Waters Canoe Area, MN, corroborating the findings of Lucas as described above. Compatibility indexes have also been developed for four types of trail users—hikers, horseback riders, bicycle riders, and motorcycle riders—by asking respondents how desirable it would be to encounter other types of trail users (McCay and Moeller 1976). The highest compatibility ratings for three of the four types were for meeting their own kind.[7]

It has also been suggested that party size affects crowding norms (Lime 1972b). Empirical evidence supports this notion. For example, a majority of wilderness visitors reported that they would prefer to see five small groups during the day rather than one large group (Stankey 1973).

Behavior. The behavior of other groups also appears to affect crowding norms. A study of the Au Sable River, MI, found that about half of fishers and streamside residents objected to seeing canoeists; however, they objected primarily because of inconsiderate behavior, such as yelling or shouting, rather than sheer numbers. There was substantial objection to the behavior of groups exceeding ten canoes. A more detailed study of behavior and its relationship to perceived crowding was conducted on hikers in the Ottawa National Forest, MI (West 1982b). This study found that 30.9% of hikers were bothered by other users. However, probing more deeply, it was found that of those bothered by other users, 56.9% were bothered by the behavior of others, 31.4% by the number of others encountered, and 4.1% by different types of users. Specific forms of behavior reported as bothering respondents were, in decreasing order: noise, yelling, and loud behavior; littering and polluting lakes; and noncompliance with rules. Respondents exposed to high perceived use level (those reporting ten or more contacts) and negative behavior felt crowded 47.9% of the time, while residents exposed to high perceived use level but not negative behavior felt crowded only 16.7% of the time. A third study asked floaters on the Guadalupe River, TX, to report both the number of encounters with other groups and whether these encounters were considered disruptive, enhancing, or neutral (Titre and Mills 1982). The number of disruptive encounters was found to be a more consistent predictor of perceived crowding than any other measure, including perceived use level.

Perceptions of Alikeness. The third characteristic of other groups that appears to affect crowding norms is the degree to which groups are perceived as being alike. This factor is probably related to behavior, but is more difficult to measure and study. Consequently, it has been addressed more often on a theoretical than empirical basis.

In Chapter 2, it was noted that the vast majority of people participate in outdoor recreation in family, friendship, or other social groups. This suggests that the notion of solitude often associated with certain types of outdoor recreation may not mean simple isolation from others. In fact, under appropriate conditions, social interaction among recreationists may be expected and enjoyed (Cheek 1972). It also suggests an inward focus on interpersonal relationships within the social group. Both of these notions are ultimately important in the concept of alikeness.

Several studies have developed conceptual analyses of solitude in outdoor recreation (Twight et al. 1981, Hammitt 1982, Hammitt and Brown 1984, Hammitt and Madden 1989, Rutlin and Hammitt 1994, Hammitt and Rutlin 1995). These studies have borrowed on theoretical work in social-psychology which has identified the following dimensions of solitude and the broader notion of privacy (Westin 1967, Pastalan 1970, N. Marshall 1972, 1974):

1. Intimacy: an attempt to achieve interpersonal relationships between or among members of a small group of selected members.

2. Solitude: a desire to be alone at times without interruptions.

3. Anonymity: a desire for freedom from identification in a public setting.

4. Reserve: a preference to avoid self-disclosure, particularly to those other than close friends.

5. Seclusion: the visual and auditory seclusion of one's home (campsite, etc.) from neighbors and traffic.

6. Not neighboring: a feeling that visitation by neighbors and choice of friends should be controlled.

Based on this theoretical work, scales have been developed to empirically test the application of these dimensions of solitude to outdoor recreation.

An initial study surveyed users of a developed campground in Shenandoah National Park, VA, and backpackers in the Allegheny National Forest, PA, asking them to rate the importance of selected dimensions of solitude (Twight et al. 1981). Backpackers were found to score significantly higher than developed-area campers on the dimensions of intimacy, solitude, anonymity, and seclusion, though the differences in general were not great. The differences in scores on intimacy were the largest. This suggests the potential importance of intimacy in more primitive types of outdoor recreation.

A series of laboratory and field studies on solitude and privacy in outdoor recreation have also been conducted. Scales to measure alternative dimensions of solitude/privacy were initially administered to samples of college students (Hammitt 1982, Hammitt and Brown 1984). The context of these studies was a wilderness environment. These studies identified several important functions of solitude/privacy in keeping with social-psychological theory. These functions included emotional release, personal autonomy, reflective thought, personal distance, and intimacy. Scale items receiving the lowest ratings concerned isolation and individual notions of solitude. Field tests conducted on backpackers in Great Smoky Mountains National Park, NC/TN, and visitors to Ellicott Rock Wilderness Area, SC, generally confirmed laboratory findings (Hammitt and Madden 1989, Rutlin and Hammitt 1994, Hammitt and Rutlin 1995). Based on these studies, it was concluded that solitude in outdoor recreation might be broadly defined as "being in a natural, remote environment that offers a sense of tranquility and peacefulness and that involves a freedom of choice in terms of both the information that users must process and the behavior demanded of them by others" (Hammitt and Madden 1989). These findings have been generally corroborated in a similar study of visitors to wilderness areas in Australia (Priest and Bugg 1991).

Based on this research, solitude in outdoor recreation may have more to do with interaction among group members free from disruptions than with physical isolation. This suggests that, as long as contacts with other groups are not considered disturbing, they may not engender feelings of crowding or dissatisfaction. And this in turn suggests the importance of alikeness.

An early conceptual study of the social definition of parks and related areas suggested the potential importance of alikeness among visitors

(R. Lee 1972). In this study, a variety of park environments were observed to be highly ordered social systems that help to ensure predictable forms of behavior. Contrary to their conventional image as free and unregulated spaces, park environments are governed by practical and informal behavioral norms based on regularities in meaning and use assigned by user groups. Deviations from these norms are often viewed with suspicion and anxiety. This study concluded that "individuals seek outdoor areas where they may share a scheme of order with others similar enough to themselves to be able to take for granted many everyday normative constraints." In this context, the number of visitors present may not be as important as a shared system of values and behavioral norms.

A follow-up study of backpackers in Yosemite National Park, CA, elaborates on this line of reasoning (R. Lee 1975, 1977). As reported in Table 5-3, no relationship was found in this study between perceived crowding and behavioral measures of satisfaction. This finding is attributed to the idea that most social interaction between groups in outdoor recreation settings is conducted with little conscious deliberation or, in more technical terms, in non-symbolic modes of communication. This type of communication is defined as "spontaneous and direct responses to the gestures of the other individual, without the intermediation of any interpretation" (Blumer 1936). People are therefore largely unaware of such social interaction, and it has little effect on perceptions of crowding. Lee's studies of backpackers conclude that the quality of recreation experience "appears to be closely linked with the opportunity to take for granted the behavior of other visitors," and that "an essential ingredient for such an experience [is] the assumption that other visitors are much like oneself, and will, therefore, behave in a similar manner." Thus, to the extent that groups are perceived as alike and require little conscious attention, use levels and encounters have limited disruptive effects on intimacy and other dimensions of solitude desired by social groups.

The potential importance of perceptions of alikeness is emphasized in a conceptual study that suggests a lack of well-established behavioral norms within wildland types of outdoor recreation (Cheek and Burch 1976). Few of the physical and institutional screens of everyday life— walls, gates, neighborhoods—are present to segregate groups who wish to limit contact. Well-established behavioral norms may be lacking in wilderness recreation as the following passage suggests:

> Unlike golf and other organized sports, which have
> normative mechanisms for including strangers in the play,

wilderness camping is especially fluid. Wilderness camping has no clear and validated rules regarding roles, goals, and relationships, except those already established within the intimate group. Consequently, strangers are disruptive because there is no context within which they can be fit (Cheek and Burch 1976: 168).

The inward focus of the social group and concerns for alikeness among groups is illustrated in an observational study of fishing and other recreation behavior at high mountain lakes in Washington State (Hendee et al. 1977). It was observed that 80% of anglers carried out most of their fishing activity within about 20 feet of a companion, but 75% remained 100 feet or more from people in other parties. Similarly, all but 10% of anglers engaged in at least some conversation with companions while fishing, but more than 90% did not converse with anyone from another party. Moreover, the limited conversation that did occur between parties was "often probing as if to determine the extent to which parties shared motives, interests, or expertise that might serve as the basis for continuing the contact."

Two other empirically based studies have examined the notion of alikeness among recreation groups. Earlier in this chapter, it was noted that a study of visitors to the Boundary Waters Canoe Area, MN, found that paddling canoeists generally disliked encountering motorboaters, but that the reverse was generally not true (Lucas 1964b). This phenomenon has been termed "asymmetric antipathy" and was reexamined at a later time in the same study area to see whether this conflict pattern persisted over time (Adelman et al. 1982).[8] Similar results were obtained: 71% of paddlers disliked meeting and/or seeing motorboat users, while only 8% of motorboat users disliked meeting and/or seeing paddlers. The study went on to assess the perceived similarity of each group of visitors to the other. The majority of motorboaters perceived paddling canoeists as similar to themselves, while the majority of paddling canoeists perceived motorboaters as dissimilar to themselves. This relationship held over all measures of perceived similarity. Thus, it appears that perceptions of similarity or alikeness between recreation groups may be closely associated with normative definitions of crowding.

A second empirical study related to the issue of perceived alikeness focused on an urban park in Michigan (Westover and Collins 1987). This study found a relatively strong relationship between use level and perceived crowding as reported in Table 5-3. However, respondents who expressed trust that other visitors were willing to help them (an expression of shared norms and behavioral predictability) tended to report lower levels of crowding.

While the potential importance of perceived alikeness to crowding is evident, little is known about how such perceptions are formed. It is likely that initial judgments are made on the basis of outward appearances, such as group structure (e.g., size), behavior (e.g., noise), activities (e.g., mode of travel), and other physical manifestations (e.g., clothing, equipment). From a theoretical standpoint, it has been suggested that "recreation activities often serve as a symbolic identification for a cultural group" (Knopp and Tyger 1973). Moreover, values in outdoor recreation may be expressed and interpreted in shorthand notations, just as they are in society at large:

> Such patterns are not unlike the visual symbols of
> counterculturalists, soul brothers, decal-flagged middle
> Americans who announce a shared value system which
> brings them together by setting them apart from other social
> groups (Burch 1974:96).

Summary. Several characteristics of those encountered in outdoor recreation areas can affect normative definitions of crowding. When others are encountered who are viewed as inappropriate or different in unfavorable ways, crowding is perceived at relatively low levels of use. Pertinent characteristics of those encountered include type and size of group, behavior, and perceptions of alikeness. These factors have been added (box 6) to the expanded crowding model in Figure 5-4.

Situational Variables. The environment in which encounters occur can influence, to some extent, the way in which those encounters are perceived and evaluated. Important variables include the type of recreation area, location within an area, and environmental quality and design.

Type of Area. It was suggested very early in the outdoor recreation literature that there are inter-area differences in crowding norms (Clawson and Knetsch 1966). Hypothetical curves relating the effects of use level to recreation quality were seen as taking dramatically different shapes for three types of recreation areas: wilderness, an unimproved campground, and a highly developed campground. That different use levels are appropriate for different types of recreation areas seems obvious in a conceptual way, though not much is known about the issue in a quantitative sense. Empirical evidence is offered by a study of use level and crowding (measured as willingness to pay) that found different relationships at different types of ocean beaches ranging from a natural area to a highly developed "singles" beach (McConnell 1977). Different patterns of desired use levels have also been found among users of six river types ranging from primitive torrent to urban meander (Manning and Ciali 1981).

Location within an Area. More focus has been placed on intra-area differences in crowding norms. The most consistent finding has been high sensitivity to encounters associated with campsite location. One study found that two-thirds of wilderness visitors preferred a campsite far away from others (Burch and Wenger 1967). Similarly, a series of studies at several western wilderness areas found visitors especially sensitive to campsite encounters (Stankey 1973, 1980). The vast majority of respondents (75%) agreed with the statement, "When staying out overnight in the wilderness, it is most enjoyable not to be near anyone else." Visitors also reported higher sensitivity to encounters at campsites than along trails. A third study conducted in nine wilderness areas reported similar findings: the large majority of visitors preferred to camp alone (Lucas 1980a). The only empirical evidence that varies from this pattern is a study of river users that found that campground encounters had little effect on perceived crowding; however, these were campgrounds occupied before and after a float trip, which may explain their lack of significance (Ditton et al. 1983). A higher sensitivity to use levels at campsites reflects the importance of the campsite in recreation activity patterns. Campers in both developed and backcountry areas spend the majority of their waking hours in and around the campsite (King 1966, Hendee et al. 1977a).

Heightened sensitivity to encounters has also been found in the "interior" of recreation areas as opposed to the "periphery." Given the choice, 68% of wilderness visitors expressed a preference for encounters to occur within the first few miles from the road rather than interior zones (Stankey 1973). An analogous study of boaters found that respondents were more sensitive to crowding on the lake than at access points (Graefe and Drogin 1989).

Environmental Factors. It has been suggested that crowding may also depend to some extent on the physical, non-human environment (Hammitt 1983). The general social-psychological literature suggests, for example, that an office can be perceived as crowded because the amount and configuration of furnishings prohibit one from functioning as desired, even when no one else is present. This notion has been termed "environmental affordances" (Gibson 1977, 1979) and "functional density" (Rapaport 1975). This issue has received little attention in outdoor recreation, though a study of crowding in a national park campground is suggestive (Womble and Studebaker 1981). This study, as reported in Table 5-3, found little relationship between use level and perceived crowding. However, the study went on to explore the open-ended comments section of the questionnaire in an effort to identify other factors that might account for unexplained variance in crowding perceptions. Several factors were identified, the most important of which were proximity of campsites and insufficient facilities. This suggests that design aspects of the recreation environment may be involved in normative definitions of crowding.

A related consideration is the perceived quality of the recreation environment. A study of the Dolly Sods Wilderness Area, WV, developed an index of perceived environmental disturbance (Vaske et al. 1982b). The index was comprised of six items for which respondents rated perceived conditions as worse than, about the same as, or better than expected. In keeping with other studies investigating visitor perceptions of environmental impacts, as reported in Chapter 3, the overall index indicated that visitors generally found environmental conditions about the same as or slightly better than expected. However, some respondents rated conditions worse than expected, and this had a substantive effect on perceived crowding. When the perceived environmental disturbance index was added to measures of reported, preferred, and expected use levels, the amount of variance explained in perceived crowding rose from 23% to 33%. Moreover, the index had the largest effect on perceived crowding of any of the four independent variables. These findings indicate that perceived crowding is influenced not only by the physical presence of others, but also by the environmental impacts left by previous visitors. These findings are consistent with other studies which indicate that visitors are more often disturbed by the presence of litter or other environment degradation than by contacts with other groups of visitors (Stankey 1973, R. Lee 1975, Lucas 1980).

Summary. Situational variables can affect normative definitions of crowding. That is, the environment in which encounters occur, as defined by the type of recreation area, the location within an area, design considerations, and perceived environmental quality help to determine when and where use level is perceived as crowding. These factors have been added (box 6) to the expanded crowding model in Figure 5-4.

Methodological Issues

Investigations of the relationships between use level, crowding, and satisfaction have brought to light several important methodological issues that potentially affect these relationships. These include the distinction between use level and contacts, alternative measures of contacts, the multidimensional nature of satisfaction, consistency of satisfaction measures, and the need for behavioral measures of crowding and satisfaction.

Use Level and Contacts. The first issue concerns the relationship between use level and contacts or encounters. It is often implicitly assumed that increasing use levels result in proportional increases in contacts. But the limited research into this issue indicates otherwise. Use level on the Colorado River in Grand Canyon National Park, AZ, defined as the number of people per week leaving the principal put-in point, was measured simultaneously with contact levels between parties (J. Nielson and Shelby 1977, J. Nielson et al. 1977, Shelby 1980a). These variables were positively related to a high degree, but use level explained only about half of the variation in contacts. A study of backcountry use in Mount McKinley National Park, AK, found an even lower relationship between use level and contacts (Bultena et al. 1981b). The unexplained variance in contact levels may be due to the complexity and randomness of trip patterns, intervening structural elements of topography and geography which limit contacts, deliberate behavior by visitors to avoid contacts as use levels increase, and other unknown factors. It should be remembered from Chapter 2 that recreation use patterns tend to be highly uneven over both space and time. Moreover, it was reported earlier in this chapter that, in several studies, visitors have reported changing the length and route of their trips in response to use levels. Both of these findings may help explain the lower relationship between use level and crowding than intuitively might have been expected. These findings suggest the need for a research and management emphasis on measuring contacts in addition to use levels. While measures of use level are more generally available, it is contacts with other groups that visitors experience most directly and that are likely to affect perceived crowding and satisfaction.

Measuring Contacts. A related issue concerns how contacts are measured. Several techniques are found in the literature: actual contacts—recorded by a participant observer (Cole et al. 1997a, Shelby 1980a); reported contacts—self-reports by respondents after the outing (e.g., Manning and Ciali 1980, Cole et al. 1997a); diary contacts—self-reports by respondents recorded during the outing (McCool et al. 1977, Lewis et al. 1996b), and contacts reported by rangers who are on patrol (Cole et al. 1997a). Two studies have used and compared multiple measures of contacts. A study of river use in Oregon applied and compared three of the above measures (Shelby and Colvin 1982). Users who experienced fewer than six contacts were generally accurate in their self-reports (by comparison with actual contacts), but at higher levels of contact, most users reported only about half as many contacts as actually occurred. Reported and diary contacts were found to be in close agreement. A study of hikers in six heavily used wilderness areas in Washington and Oregon also used three measures of contacts (Cole et al. 1997a). At high use levels, respondents often under-reported trail encounters compared to trained observers and wilderness rangers. At lower use levels, reports of contacts tended to be more comparable across the three measures. These studies suggest that, in low-use recreation areas, self-reported contacts might be relied upon as reasonably accurate and should generally be used because of the administrative difficulties and potential intrusion on the visitors' experience represented by diaries. But in relatively high-use areas, reported and diary contacts must be used with caution. Unfortunately, actual contacts are usually difficult and expensive to measure. However, the potential usefulness of reported and diary contacts should not be overlooked, even when they are known to be inaccurate. Self-reports represent the visitors' perceived reality, and this is important in assessing recreation quality.

Multidimensional Nature of Satisfaction. Perhaps the most important methodological issue concerning the relationships discussed in this chapter is measurement of satisfaction. The bivariate satisfaction model discussed early in this chapter suggests that satisfaction is a direct function of use level. In fact, as was noted in Chapter 1, satisfaction is a complex, multidimensional concept. The earliest attempt at testing the satisfaction model hints at this issue. In none of the "satisfaction curves" developed by Stankey (1973) (such as those in Figure 5-3) does satisfaction reach its theoretical scaled maximum—even when the level of encounters is zero. Similar results have been found elsewhere (Manning and Ciali 1980). Clearly, factors other than use level must contribute to satisfaction.

The studies reported in Table 5-3 suggest this more directly, particularly those of R. Lee (1975) and Shelby (1980a). In these studies, perceived crowding had little or no effect on satisfaction. However, both studies go on to identify a number of diverse variables that are correlated with satisfaction, including absence of litter and other pollution, low level of facility development, pleasant social demeanor of others, and good physical condition of the trail.

The problem of measuring satisfaction solely as a function of use level or perceived crowding is illustrated by a study of river use in Vermont, as shown in Figure 5-5. In this study, the relationship between use level and satisfaction was measured under both hypothetical and field conditions. Under the hypothetical conditions, respondents are implicitly asked to assume away all other factors and focus only on the two variables under consideration—use level and satisfaction. Using

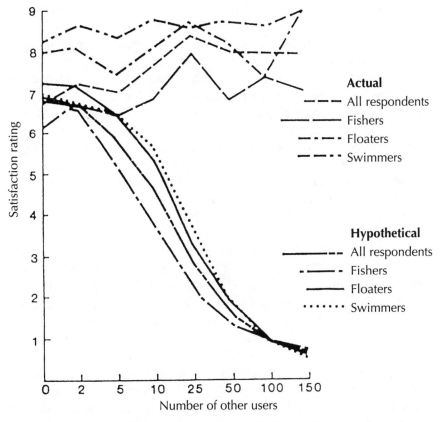

The scale of the X axis is not proportional, and is drawn this way to keep the data points from being too highly skewed toward the origin

Figure 5-5. Relationship between use level and satisfaction under hypothetical and actual conditions. (From Manning and Ciali 1980.)

this approach, a clear negative relationship was found. However, caution should be used in interpreting such findings and incorporating them into management policy. Research results from this idealized and rigorous set of assumptions may not hold under more complex field conditions. Tested under actual field conditions, no relationship was found between use level and satisfaction. But once again, caution must be used in interpreting these results. The absence of relationships may be due to mediating variables such as those discussed in this chapter.

The potentially complex effects of use level on satisfaction have been illustrated in another way in a study of deer hunting (Heberlein et al. 1982). Number of hunters was found to have both positive and negative effects on overall satisfaction. Increased numbers of hunters result in more deer seen per hunter (as more deer are moved through the area), and this has a positive effect on satisfaction. However, increased numbers of hunters also result in more interference among hunters, and this detracts from satisfaction.

A number of studies suggest that a multiple-item approach to measuring satisfaction may help resolve this dilemma. For example, a study of floaters on the Buffalo National River, AR, developed and tested a five-item satisfaction scale (Ditton et al. 1981). Results indicated that a better model of overall satisfaction could be obtained with the multiple-item scale than with any of the individual scale items. Moreover, different independent variables entered the regression models for each of the individual satisfaction scale items, indicating that each item was tapping a somewhat different dimension of satisfaction. Other studies suggest that, in most cases, researchers and managers are interested in evaluating the effects on users of individual attributes such as contact level (Shelby et al. 1980, Shelby and Heberlein 1986). In such cases, global measures of satisfaction are usually too far removed from the individual attributes to be effective measures of satisfaction. Empirical findings tend to support this notion. A detailed study of satisfaction among campers measured satisfaction for individual attributes of the camping experience in addition to overall satisfaction (Dorfman 1979). Though overall satisfaction was correlated with other measures of satisfaction to a statistically significant degree (R generally ranged between .30 and .60), it is clear these variables were not measuring the identical concept.

Consistency of Satisfaction Measures. Closely related to the above issue are questions of timing, content, and context of satisfaction measures. At least two studies have demonstrated that there can be differences in satisfaction, depending upon when such measures are taken—during the activity, at its conclusion, or at some later date (G. Peterson and

Lime 1973, Stewart and Hull 1992). Findings suggest that measures of satisfaction may become more positive over time. This might be explained using the rationalization process described in the section on coping behaviors earlier in this chapter. As time passes, negative evaluations may fade to minimize cognitive dissonance. Differences in reported satisfaction have also been found to be related to questionnaire content and context (Schomaker and Knopf 1982a, b). Alternative wording of questions designed to measure satisfaction has been found to result in significantly different satisfaction scores. And when satisfaction measures were intermixed with questions evaluating specific aspects of the trip, average satisfaction scores were lower than when the satisfaction measures were presented alone. There is little to indicate what approach to either of these issues is "better." Rather, the key seems to be consistency; the approach used should be as consistent as possible, especially when results are to be compared among areas or over time (Knopf and Lime 1981, Lime et al. 1981).

The Need for Behavioral Measures. A final methodological issue concerns the need for behavioral measures of crowding and satisfaction, or more precisely, multiple measurement approaches. Research in outdoor recreation has been dominated by survey methods. A review of methodological approaches employed in studies published in the *Journal of Leisure Research*, for example, found that 94% used survey techniques (Riddick et al. 1984). While survey methods can be exceedingly useful, their potential shortcomings are well documented, particularly the potential weakness of the assumption that attitudes are closely related to behavior (e.g., Deutscher 1966, Wicker 1969, Heberlein 1973, Clark 1977, Manfredo and Shelby 1988). Two studies of crowding highlight this potential weakness. One of these studies found that even though many hikers reported feeling at least somewhat crowded, observations of their behavior indicated little or no effort to achieve additional privacy (R. Lee 1977). This obviously calls into question the validity of self-reports of crowding in this case (and perhaps others as well). A second study also raises questions about self-reports of perceived crowding (West 1981b). This survey of national forest backpackers found 22% of respondents reported some degree of perceived crowding. However, 70% of this subsample did not favor lowering permitted use levels.

These findings suggest a more diversified research approach in outdoor recreation. While behavioral measures of outdoor recreation through techniques such as observation also have potential weaknesses (Burch 1964b, Webb et al. 1966, Campbell 1970, Glancy 1986), these are different from those of the survey approach. The best solution is, therefore, to apply multiple research approaches, using each to validate the other.

Summary. Several methodological issues can affect the relationships among use level, perceived crowding, and satisfaction. These issues involve the ways in which these variables are conceptualized and measured. These factors have been added (boxes 3, 4, 8, and 9) to the expanded crowding model in Figure 5-4.

An Expanded Crowding Model

The issues discussed in this section are incorporated in the expanded crowding model in Figure 5-4. While the relationships among use level, perceived crowding, and satisfaction can be complex, the issues discussed in this section result in a more comprehensive and realistic model of crowding in outdoor recreation. The expanded model recognizes that recreation use level (box 1) results in contacts between groups (box 2), but that other variables affect contacts as well, including topography, geography, and the complexities of trip patterns (box 3). Moreover, the way in which contacts are measured will affect the ultimate number derived (box 4). Second, the model shows that contacts between groups affect perceived crowding (box 5), but so does the way in which these contacts are interpreted (box 6). Crowding norms based on personal characteristics of visitors, the characteristics of those encountered, and situational variables affect the point at which contacts are evaluated negatively. Third, perceived crowding affects overall satisfaction (box 7), but is only one of theoretically many variables to do so (box 8). Moreover, the relationship between perceived crowding and satisfaction depends on measurement techniques (box 9). Finally, feelings of perceived crowding can result in displacement of some users, so their satisfaction is not measured, or some users may simply redefine the type of recreation opportunity they experienced (box 10).

Summary and Conclusions

1. There has been long-standing concern over the effect of increasing use levels on the quality of the recreation experience.

2. This concern over use levels has been based on an assumed inverse relationship between use level and satisfaction, sometimes called the "satisfaction model."

3. Empirical tests have generally found relatively weak, if any, statistical relationships among use level, perceived crowding, and satisfaction.

4. Reasons for this lack of relationship include coping behaviors of recreationists, normative definitions of crowding, and several methodological issues. More specifically, these reasons are:

A. Visitors sensitive to increasing use levels may be displaced by visitors less sensitive to use levels.

B. Personal characteristics of visitors influence when use level is evaluated as crowding. These characteristics include motivations, preferences, expectations, experience, and attitudes.

C. The characteristics of others encountered influence when use level is evaluated as crowding. These characteristics include type and size of group, behavior, and perceptions of alikeness.

D. The situation in which encounters occur influences when use level is evaluated as crowding. These factors include type of recreation area, location within the area, design considerations, and perceived environmental quality.

E. Contacts between recreation groups are not solely a function of use level.

F. Contacts between recreation groups may vary depending upon whether they are measured objectively by observers or self-reported by visitors.

G. Satisfaction is a multi-faceted concept, influenced only partially by use level and perceived crowding.

H. The relationship between crowding and satisfaction depends upon how satisfaction is measured: hypothetically or under field conditions; through survey or behavioral approaches; and globally or specifically.

5. The way in which the above items influence the relationship between use level and satisfaction is shown schematically in Figure 5-4.

6. Satisfaction is not an appropriate criterion for managing use level and crowding in recreation areas. If the process of displacement is operating or if in some other way the population of visitors is changing, satisfaction is likely to remain high despite changing use conditions. The ultimate result will be loss of diversity in outdoor recreation opportunities, particularly low use alternatives.

7. More research is needed into what constitutes perceptions of alikeness between recreation groups. Inherent in this issue is why visitors often don't report all of the contacts they experience.

8. Recreation areas and zones should be managed to encourage relatively homogenous groups in terms of party type and size, behavior, and other factors that contribute to perceptions of alikeness.

9. Management and research attention should be focused on contact levels in addition to more generally available measures of use level. Contacts are more directly related to perceptions of crowding than use level. Moreover, spatial and temporal use patterns might be managed to reduce contacts without affecting overall use levels.

10. Global measures of satisfaction are generally not appropriate for either research or management purposes. More attribute-specific satisfaction measures are needed.

11. Measurement of use level, crowding, and satisfaction-related variables should be as consistent as possible among areas and over time. The single-item, nine-point measure of perceived crowding used in many studies is a good example.

12. Solitude in outdoor recreation has several potential meanings in addition to the traditional concept of physical isolation. In particular, opportunity for intimacy within social groups is important.

Notes

1. The topic of motivations in outdoor recreation is discussed more fully in Chapter 7.
2. It is evident that wilderness and other outdoor recreation areas provide vicarious satisfaction and other values even when unvisited. The focus in this analysis, however, is on direct satisfaction derived by recreation visitors.
3. Motivations for recreation are discussed more fully in Chapter 7.
4. This issue is considered more fully in Chapter 6.
5. Recreation specialization is the subject of Chapter 11.
6. Several studies have developed sophisticated treatments of recreation experience, combining and testing a variety of measures. For example,

Hammitt and McDonald (1983) developed an index combining several measures of recreation experience. Two studies of river recreationists have integrated a variety of experience measures and tested their effect on area and trip evaluations (Schreyer and Lime 1984, Schreyer et al. 1984). All of these studies have found that experience level has statistically significant effects on selected visitor attitudes and perceptions, though none of the studies has addressed perceived crowding directly. Measures of recreation experience are discussed more fully in Chapter 11.

7. The issue of conflict in outdoor recreation is addressed in Chapter 9.

8. Recreation conflict is often asymmetric in nature. This issue is described more fully in Chapter 9.

6

Indicators and Standards of Quality
A Normative Approach

A Normative Approach

Chapter 4 described the way in which indicators and standards of quality have emerged as a central focus of contemporary carrying capacity frameworks. Indicators of quality are measurable variables that help define the quality of the recreation experience. Standards of quality define the minimum acceptable condition of indicator variables. Examples of indicators and standards of quality are offered in Chapter 4. Carrying capacity can be defined and managed by means of monitoring indicators of quality and management activities to ensure that standards of quality are not violated. But how are indicators and standards of quality formulated?

Research on crowding in outdoor recreation, described in Chapter 5, is suggestive of an important approach. Crowding can be understood as a normative process. That is, outdoor recreation visitors often have preferences, expectations, or other standards by which to judge a situation as crowded or not. In fact, research demonstrates that such standards are often more important in crowding judgments than the number of other groups encountered. If such standards can be defined and measured, then they may be useful in formulating indicators and standards of quality.

This chapter describes the application of normative theory and methods to the formulation of indicators and standards of quality. Characteristics of good indicators and standards of quality are outlined, examples of indicators and standards of quality are compiled and presented, and a series of conclusions from this research are developed and discussed. Finally, a series of theoretical and methodological issues are identified regarding application of the normative approach to indicators and standards of quality in outdoor recreation.

Norm Theory and Methods

Developed in the disciplines of sociology and social-psychology, normative theory and related empirical methods have attracted substantial attention as an organizing concept in outdoor recreation research and management (Heberlein 1977, Shelby and Heberlein 1986, Vaske et al. 1986b, 1992, 1993, Shelby et al. 1996). Much of this literature has been organized around the work of J. Jackson (1965), who developed a methodology for measuring norms. Adapting these methods to outdoor recreation, visitors can be asked to evaluate alternative levels of potential impacts caused by increasing recreation use levels. For example, visitors might be asked to rate the acceptability of encountering increasing numbers of recreation groups while hiking along trails. Resulting data would measure the personal crowding norm of each respondent. These data can then be aggregated to test for social crowding norms, or the degree to which norms are shared across groups.

Social norms can be illustrated graphically, as shown in Figure 6-1. Using hypothetical data associated with the example described above, this graph plots average acceptability ratings for encountering increasing numbers of visitor groups along trails. The line plotted in this illustration is sometimes called an "encounter" or "contact preference curve" (when applied to crowding-related variables), or might be called an "impact acceptability curve" more generally, or simply a "norm curve."

Norm curves like that illustrated in Figure 6-1 have several potentially important features or characteristics. First, all points along the curve above the neutral line—the point on the vertical axis where evaluation ratings fall from the acceptable into the unacceptable range—define the "range of acceptable conditions." All of the conditions represented in this range are judged to meet some level of acceptability by about half of all respondents. The "optimum condition" is defined by the highest point on the norm curve. This is the condition that received the highest rating of acceptability from the sample as a whole. The "minimum acceptable condition" is defined as the point at which the norm curve crosses the neutral line. This is the condition that approximately half of the sample finds acceptable and half finds unacceptable. "Norm intensity," or norm "salience"—the strength of respondents' feelings about the importance of a potential indicator of quality—is suggested by the distance of the norm curve above and below the neutral line. The greater this distance, the more strongly respondents feel about the indicator of quality or the condition being measured. High measures of

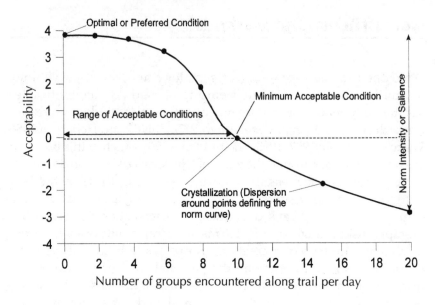

Figure 6-1. Norm curve.

norm intensity or salience suggest that a variable may be a good indicator of quality because respondents feel it is important in defining the quality of the recreation experience. "Crystallization" of the norm concerns the amount of agreement or consensus about the norm. It is usually measured by standard deviations or other measures of variance of the points which describe the norm curve. The less variance or dispersion of data around those points, the more consensus there is about social norms. Norm curves are sometimes constructed with the vertical axis of the graph representing the percentage of respondents who report each level of impact as the maximum acceptable.

Norms can also be measured using a shorter, open ended question format by asking respondents to report the maximum level of impact that is acceptable to them. In the example illustrated in Figure 6-1, respondents would simply be asked to report the maximum number of groups they would find acceptable to meet while hiking along trails during a day's time. This format is designed to be less burdensome to respondents, but it also yields less information. Alternative question formats for measuring norms are addressed more fully later in this chapter.

Indicators of Quality

Indicators of quality are receiving increasing attention in the outdoor recreation literature. Normative theory and methods as described above have been applied less directly to indicators of quality than standards of quality. However, the extent to which visitors agree about the importance of potential indicators of quality is important and reflects a substantive normative component. Moreover, norm intensity or salience as described above is a measure of the importance of potential indicators of quality and can be derived from normative methods. The literature has addressed two important issues regarding indicators of quality: criteria defining good indicators of quality and studies designed to identify potential indicators of quality.

Characteristics of Good Indicators of Quality. Several studies have explored characteristics that define good indicators of quality (Schoemaker 1984, Stankey et al. 1985, Merigliano 1990, Whittaker and Shelby 1992, National Park Service 1997). These characteristics can be used to further understand the role of indicators and standards of quality in outdoor recreation and to assist in evaluation and selection among potential indicator variables. Characteristics of good indicators of quality include the following:

1. Specific. Indicators should define specific rather than general conditions. For example, "solitude" would not be a good indicator of quality because it is too general. "The number of other groups encountered per day along trails" would be a better indicator variable.

2. Objective. Indicators should be objective rather than subjective. That is, indicator variables should be measured in absolute, unequivocal terms. Variables that are subjective, expressed in relative terms, or subject to interpretation make poor indicators. For example, "the number of people at one time at Wild Arch" is an objective indicator because it is an absolute number that can be readily counted and reported. However, "the percentage of visitors who feel crowded at Wild Arch" is a subjective indicator because it is subject to interpretation by visitors—it depends on the types of visitors making the judgment, the behavior of other visitors, and other variables.

3. Reliable and Repeatable. An indicator is reliable and repeatable when measurement yields similar results under similar conditions. This criterion is important because monitoring of indicator variables is often conducted by more than one person.

4. Related to Visitor Use. Indicators should be related to at least one of the following attributes of visitor use: level of use, type of use, location of use, or behavior of visitors. A major role of indicators of quality is to help determine when management action is needed to control the impacts of visitor use. Thus, there should be a strong correlation between visitor use and indicators of quality.

5. Sensitive. Indicators should be sensitive to visitor use over a relatively short period of time. As the level of use changes, an indicator should respond in roughly the same proportional degree. If an indicator changes only after impacts are substantial, it will not serve as an early warning mechanism, allowing managers to react in a timely manner.

6. Manageable. Indicators should be responsive to, and help determine the effectiveness of, management actions. The underlying rationale of indicators is they should be maintained within prescribed standards of quality. This implies that they must be manageable.

7. Efficient and Effective to Measure. Indicators should be relatively easy and cost-effective to measure. Indicators of quality should be monitored on a regular basis. Therefore, the more expertise, time, equipment, and staff needed to take such measurements, the less desirable a potential indicator of quality may be.

8. Significant. Perhaps the most important characteristic of indicators is that they help define the quality of the visitor experience. This is

Potential Indicators of Quality	Criteria for Good Indicators of Quality							
	Specific	Objective	Reliable & repeatable	Related to visitor use	Sensitive	Manageable	Efficient & effective to measure	Significant
Indicator 1								
Indicator 2								
Indicator 3								
Indicator 4								
Indicator 5								
Indicator								

Figure 6-2. Evaluation matrix for selecting indicators of quality.

inherent in the very term "indicator." It does little good to monitor the condition of a variable that is unimportant in defining the quality of the visitor experience.

It may be useful to incorporate these characteristics within a matrix for the purpose of evaluating potential indicators of quality as shown in Figure 6-2. Potential indicator variables can be arrayed along the horizontal axis of the matrix and rated as to how well they meet the characteristics described above.

Potential Indicators of Quality. Research has also focused on identifying potential indicators of quality for a variety of recreation areas and activities. This research has been aimed at determining variables important to visitors in defining the quality of the recreation experience. In a broad sense, much of the research reviewed in this book has some application to this issue. For example, preferences of visitors for site attributes, crowding and encounters with other visitors, motivations for recreation, and conflict with other types of users are all suggestive of potential indicators of quality. However, beyond these broad categories of research, several studies have addressed indicators of quality more directly. Potential indicators of quality identified in these studies are compiled in Table 6-1.

These studies have addressed a variety of recreation areas and activities and utilized several study methods, including open- and closed-ended questions and surveys of visitors, interest groups, managers, and scientists. However, several general conclusions might be derived from these study findings. First, it is apparent that potential indicators of quality can be wide ranging. It may be useful to employ the three-fold framework of outdoor recreation described in earlier chapters when thinking about potential indicators of quality. All of the indicator variables in Table 6-1 can be classified into environmental, social, or managerial components.

Second, study findings suggest that many potential indicators of quality are rated at least somewhat important in defining the quality of the recreation experience. This is generally consistent with the "multiple satisfaction" or behavioral approach to outdoor recreation described in Chapter 7.

Third, most of the studies on indicators of quality have found some variables more important than others. For example, litter and other signs of use impacts appear to be universally important. Management-related impacts (e.g., signs, presence of rangers) appear to be less important.

text continues on page 131

Table 6-1. Potential indicators of quality.

Study/Area/Respondents	Indicator of Quality
Mergliano 1990 Wilderness Wilderness managers and scientists	Number of campsites above an acceptable impact index Percent of visitors who report seeing wildlife Range condition and trend Air visibility—extinction coefficient or visual range Litter quantity—number of pieces of litter per campsite or per trail mile; number of pounds of garbage packed out each season Number of manager-created structures Number of signs per trail mile Trail condition—length of multiple trails or number of trail miles with unacceptable problems to visitors (e.g., depth exceeding 8 inches, year-round muddiness) Length of trail in areas managed as trailless Fecal coliform/fecal streptococci ratio (drinking water quality) Number of occupied campsites within sight or sound of each other or visitor report of number of groups camped within sight or sound Number of violations of no-trace regulations Percent of groups carrying a stove (not using a campfire) Number of occurrences of unburied human feces Number of occurrences of motorized noise per day Percent of season wilderness rangers are out patrolling the area Number of regulations that limit visitor use or restrict travel Number of regulatory signs posted beyond trailhead
Shindler and Shelby 1992 Wilderness campsites Members of five interest groups	Amount of bare ground Size and appearance of fire rings Distance from trail Screening from other sites Out of sight/sound of other sites Evidence of litter View of scenery Available firewood Sheltered from weather Dry and well drained Water for aesthetic reasons Flat place for sleeping Close to good fishing Logs and rocks for seating Close to drinking/cooking water

Whittaker 1992 5 Alaska rivers Floaters, motorboaters	Litter Signs of use Campsite competition Fishing competition Launch congestion River encounters Camp encounters Powerboat use Airboat use Rafting/canoeing use Airplane landings Helicopter landings ORV use Hazard signs Interpretive signs Public-use cabins Private cabins Concessions Long-term camps
Roggenbuck et al. 1993 4 wilderness areas Visitors	Amount of litter I see Number of trees around campsite that have been damaged by people Amount of noise associated with human activities within the wilderness Amount of human-made noise originating from outside the wilderness Number of wild animals I see Amount of vegetation loss and bare ground around a campsite Number of horse groups that camp within sight or sound of my campsite Number of hiker groups that camp within sight or sound of my campsite Number of horse groups that travel past my campsite while I am there Number of campfire rings that people have made Number of hiker groups that walk past my campsite Number of large groups that I see along the trails Number of horse groups I see along the trails in a day Percent of time other people are in sight when I'm on the trail Visibility of lights originating from outside the wilderness Total number of people I see hiking along the trail Number of groups of hikers I see along the trail Amount of time I spend traveling on old roads in the wilderness Number of miles of gravel road I travel to get to the wilderness

C. Shafer and
Hammitt 1994
Cohutta Wilderness, GA
Visitors

The total amount of time that your party has in an area without seeing or hearing anyone else

The amount of restriction management places on where you may travel in the area

The number of permanent structures placed by management in the wilderness

Seeing an unusual type of plant

The amount of restriction management places on where you may camp in an area

The level of difficulty required to obtain an overnight permit

The number of vehicles you see at the trailhead

The number of fire rings found in a campsite

The number of days in a row you are able to stay in the wilderness on a given trip

The number of signs designating locations in the wilderness

The number of groups you pass during the day while traveling

Having signs placed by wilderness managers that state regulations about wilderness

The amount of wilderness which does not have trails in it

The distance of campfires from trailheads

The number of rangers you see in the area

The amount of ranger contact in the backcountry to check your permit and/or explain regulations about use

The amount of litter found in campsites

The amount of litter seen along the trail

The number of trees or other vegetation damaged by previous users

The amount of noise heard in the area that comes from outside the wilderness

The amount of fully mature forest in the wilderness area

Observing a natural ecosystem at work

The amount of solitude your group experiences

The amount of noise heard in the area that comes from other wilderness visitors

The number of different species of wildlife you see

The number of areas in the wilderness that are very remote

The distance between your campsite and the campsite of others

Seeing specific types of wildlife

The amount of light visible at night which comes from outside the wilderness

The level of trail maintenance

	The number of groups that pass within sight of your camp An area in the wilderness that is left completely primitive (no trails, bridges) Having a portion of the wilderness where camping location is unconfined Having trail markers placed by management (blazes, cairns, posts)
Manning et al. 1995b,c, 1996b, Manning and Lime 1996 Arches National Park, UT Visitors	Orientation, information, and interpretive services Number and type of visitor facilities Number of people encountered Visitor behavior and activities Resource impacts Park management activities Quality and condition of natural features
Jacobi et al. 1996 Acadia National Park, ME Carriage road visitors	Number of visitors encountered Type of visitors encountered (hikers or bikers) Behavior of visitors (speed of bikers, keeping to the right, obstructing the roads, traveling off the roads)

Encounters with other visitors are important, but how these encounters are manifested may be even more important. For example, type of visitor encountered (e.g., hikers encountering bikers or stock users, floaters encountering motorboaters) may be very important. This is consistent with the literature on crowding described in Chapter 5 and the literature on recreation conflict described in Chapter 9. Behavior of other visitors and associated noise are also important, as are "competition-related" impacts, such as having to share a campsite.

Fourth, visitors to more primitive areas or sites may be generally more sensitive to a variety of potential indicators of quality than visitors to more highly used and developed areas or sites. However, research may have simply not yet identified and studied indicators of quality that are most important to visitors in more highly used areas.

Fifth, for wilderness campsites, social indicators of quality may be generally more important than ecological indicators. For example, scenic views and screening from other campsites may be more important than amount of bare ground and size of fire rings. This is generally consistent with other research that suggests the importance of camping out of sight and sound of other groups and a general lack of perceptiveness on the part of many visitors for ecological impacts of recreation.

Standards of Quality

Standards of quality have received substantial attention in the outdoor recreation literature. As with the literature on indicators of quality, two important issues have been addressed: characteristics of good standards of quality, and studies designed to identify standards of quality.

Characteristics of Good Standards of Quality. Several studies have explored characteristics that might define good standards of quality (Schoemaker 1984, Brunson et al. 1992, Whittaker and Shelby 1992, National Park Service 1997). To the extent possible, good standards of quality should incorporate the following characteristics:

1. Quantitative. Standards should be expressed in a quantitative manner. Since indicators of quality are specific and measurable variables, standards of quality can and should be expressed in an unequivocal way. For example, if an indicator is "the number of encounters with other groups per day on the river," then the standard might be "an average of no more than three encounters with other groups per day on the river." In contrast, "low numbers of encounters with other groups per day on the river" would be a poor standard of quality because it does not specify the minimum acceptable condition in unambiguous terms.

2. Time- or Space-bounded. Incorporating a time- or space-bounded element into a standard of quality expresses both how much of an impact is acceptable and how often or where such impacts can occur. It is often desirable for standards to have a time period associated with them. This is especially relevant for crowding-related issues. For instance, in the above example, the standard of quality for encounters with other groups on the river was expressed in terms of "per day." Other time-bounded qualifiers might include "per night," "per trip," "per hour," or "at one time," depending upon the circumstances.

3. Expressed as a Probability. In many cases, it will be advantageous to include in the standard of quality a tolerance for some percentage of the time that a particular condition will be unavoidably unacceptable; in other words, the standard would include a probability that conditions will be at standard or better. For example, a standard might specify, "no more than three encounters with other groups per day along trails for 80% of days in the summer use season." The 80% probability of conditions being at or above standard allows for 20% of the time that random or unusual events might prevent management from attaining these conditions. This allows for the complexity and randomness inherent in visitor use patterns. In the example of encounters along a trail, several hiking parties might depart from a trailhead at closely spaced intervals on a given day. These groups are likely to encounter each other on the trail several times during the day. On another day, the same number of groups might depart from the trailhead at widely spaced intervals and thereby rarely encounter each other. Similarly, it might be wise to incorporate a tolerance in standards for peak use days, holiday weekends, or other days of exceptionally high visitation. A standard might be set at "50 people at one time at Wild Arch for 90% of the days of the year." The amount of tolerance needed depends on the unpredictability of each individual situation and the degree to which management can consistently control conditions.

4. Impact-oriented. Standards of quality should focus directly on the impacts that affect the quality of the visitor experience, not the management action used to keep impacts from violating the standards. For example, an appropriate standard might be, "no more than ten encounters with other groups on the river per day." This could be a good standard because it focuses directly on the impact that affects the quality of the visitor experience—the number of other groups encountered. Alternatively, "a maximum of twenty groups per day floating the river" would not be as good a standard of quality because it does not focus as directly on the impact of concern—visitors experience encounters with other groups more directly than they experience total use levels. Basing standards of quality on management techniques rather than on impacts can also limit the potential range of useful management practices.[1] For example, limiting the number of boats to twenty per day might be used to ensure ten or fewer encounters per day, but other actions, such as more tightly scheduling launch times, could also ensure an appropriate encounter rate and could be less restrictive on the level of visitation to the river.

5. Realistic. Standards should generally reflect conditions that are realistically attainable. Standards that limit impacts to extremely low levels may set up unrealistic expectations in the minds of visitors, may be politically infeasible, and may unfairly restrict visitor use to very low levels.

text continues on page 141

Table 6-2. Normative standards of quality.

Study/Area/ Respondents	Indicator of Quality	Normative Standard	
		Mean	Median
Stankey 1973	Encounters with paddling canoeists	3.5	
Boundary Waters Canoe Area, MN Visitors	Encounters with motor canoeists	0.0	
	Encounters with motorboats	0.0	
Three wilderness areas, Visitors	Encounters with backpacking parties	2.5	
	Encounters with horse parties	1.8	
Stankey 1980 Desolation Wilderness, CA Visitors	Encounters with backpacking parties	9.5	
	Encounters with horse parties	4.0	
	Encounters with large parties	2.6	
	Parties camped within sight or sound	2.4	
Spanish Peaks Wilderness, MT Visitors	Encounters with backpacking parties	4.5	
	Encounters with horse parties	3.5	
	Encounters with large parties	1.8	
	Parties camped within sight or sound	1.9	
Shelby 1981a Colorado River, Grand Canyon National Park, AZ Boaters	Encounters per day	.9/2.4/4.0[1]	
	Hours in sight of others each day	.5/.7/1.5	
	Number of stops out of 10 with encounters	.7/2.0/3.8	
	Chances of meeting 10–30 people at popular places on the river	9%/23%/41%	
	Number of nights out of 10 camped near others	0/1.3/3.0	
Rogue River, OR Boaters	Encounters per day	1.5/2.9/4.4	
	Hours in sight of others each day	.5/1.0/1.9	
	Number of stops out of 5 with encounters	.6/1.6/2.3	
	Chances of meeting 5–20 people at popular places on the river	12%/28%/44%	
	Number of nights out of 5 camped near others	0/1.1/2.1	
Illinois River, OR Boaters	Encounters per day	.7/2.0/2.7	
	Hours in sight of others each day	.4/.9/1.6	
	Number of stops out of 5 with encounters	.2/1.3/1.8	

[1]For wilderness, semi-wilderness, and undeveloped recreation, respectively

Study/Area/ Respondents	Indicator of Quality	Normative Standard	
		Mean	Median
	Number of nights out of 3 camped near others		0/.2/.7
Heberlein et al. 1986, Apostle Islands National Lakeshore, WI Boaters	Number of boats moored at Anderson Bay		11.0
	Number of boats moored at Quarry Bay		11.0
Vaske et al. 1986b Brule River, WI Floaters	Encounters with fishers	7.2	
	Encounters with canoers	5.7	
	Encounters with tubers	2.3	
Shelby et al. 1988a Rogue River, OR Boaters	Encounters per day on river	5.7	
	Number of nights out of 5 camped near others	1.4	
Shelby et al. 1988b Mt. Jefferson Wilderness, OR Campers	Maximum size of fire rings		
	- Hunts Lake	20 inches	
	- Russell Lake	34 inches	
	Maximum area of bare ground		
	- Hunts Lake	750 sq. ft.	
	- Bays Lake	750 sq. ft.	
	- Scout Lake	1450 sq. ft.	
Whittaker and Shelby 1988 Deschutes River, OR Boaters	Hours in sight out of four		1.8-2.2[2]
	Incidents of discourteous behavior per day		0.1-0.2
	Number of stops out of 4 where human waste is seen		0.1-0.3
	Jetboats encountered per day		0.3-1.3
	Boats per hour passing anglers		4.0-4.7
	Fishing holes passed up out of 4 due to competition		1.3-1.7
	Minutes waiting to launch		10.3-14.9
	Nights out of 4 camped with other groups		1.4-1.9
	Nights out of 4 camped near other groups		0.4-0.9
	Camps passed up out of 4 due to competition		1.1-1.2
	Camps out of 4 with fire rings present		0.5-1.1
Patterson and Hammitt 1990 Great Smoky Mountains National Park, NC/TN Backpackers	Encounters at trailhead	3.9	3.0
	Encounters on trail	5.5	4.0
	Encounters at campsite	2.7	2.0

[2]Range over three river segments

Study/Area/ Respondents	Indicator of Quality	Normative Standard	
		Mean	Median
Roggenbuck et al. 1991 New River, WV Floaters	Number of boats seen		
	–Wilderness whitewater	10.1	
	–Scenic whitewater	20.4	
	–Social recreation	33.4	
	Percent of time in sight of other boats		
	–Wilderness whitewater	18.3	
	–Scenic whitewater	32.3	
	–Social recreation	48.1	
	Number of rapids having to wait		
	–Wilderness whitewater	1.2	
	–Scenic whitewater	2.4	
	–Social recreation	4.0	
J. Young et al. 1991 Cohutta Wilderness, GA Visitors	Number of people hiking on trail in a day	11.5	
	Number of large groups hiking on trail in a day		3.4
	Number of hiker groups camped in sight or sound of campsite		2.2
	The number of hiker groups walking past campsite in a day		3.7
	Number of horse groups seen on trail in a day		2.4
	Number of horse groups camped in sight or sound of campsite		1.7
	Percent of time other people are in sight while on trail		13.9
	Number of groups of hikers seen on trail in a day		3.9
	Number of horse groups that travel past my campsite		1.2
Martinson and Shelby 1992 3 rivers Salmon fishers	Encounters with bank fishers		
	Preferred		
	- Klamath	—	
	- Waimakariri	3.6	
	- Lower Rakaia	3.5	
	- Upper Rakaia	<1.0	
	Tolerable		
	- Klamath	12.6	
	- Waimakariri	6.9	
	- Lower Rakaia	9.5	
	- Upper Rakaia	3.8	
Shelby et al. 1992b Colorado River, Grand Canyon National Park, AZ, Guides and trip leaders	Minimum stream flow	10,000 cfs	
	Maximum stream flow	45,000—50,000 cfs	

Study/Area/ Respondents	Indicator of Quality	Normative Standard Mean	Median
Williams et al. 1992a 4 wilderness areas Visitors	Encounters with hiking groups along trail	8.7–11.6[3]	
	Encounters with horse groups along trail	5.1–6.4	
	Encounters with large groups along trail	5.8–7.1	
	Hiker groups camped within sight or sound	3.8–6.9	
	Horse groups camped within sight or sound	3.1–3.8	
	Hiker groups passing by camp	5.5–7.9	
	Horse groups passing by camp	5.4–7.4	
Roggenbuck et al. 1993, 4 wilderness areas Visitors	Number of pieces of litter I can see from my campsite		0–2[4]
	Percent of trees around a campsite that have been damaged by people		0–5
	Number of horse groups that camp within sight or sound of my campsite		1-2
	Number of hiker groups that camp within sight or sound of my campsite		3
	Number of large groups (more than 6 people) that I see along the trail		3-5
	Percent of vegetation loss and bare ground around the campsite		10-20
Ewert and Hood 1995,Ewert 1998 San Gorgonio Wilderness,CA; John Muir Wilderness, CA Visitors	Encounters per day		
	- For urban-proximate wilderness	9.0	
	- For urban-distant wilderness	7.7	
Hammitt and Rutlin 1995, Ellicott Rock Wilderness,SC/NC/ GA Visitors	Encounters at trailhead		
	- Ideal		3.8
	- Maximum		8.7
	Encounters on trail		
	- Ideal		3.2
	- Maximum		6.6
	Encounters at destination site		
	- Ideal		1.0
	- Maximum		2.5

[3]Range over four wilderness areas; [4]Range over four wilderness areas

Study/Area/ Respondents	Indicator of Quality	Normative Standard Mean	Median
	Encounters at all three sites combined		
	- Ideal	2.7	
	- Maximum	5.9	
Shelby and Whittaker 1995 Dolores River, CO Boaters	Maximum stream flow		
	- Large rafts	≈ 900 cfs	
	- Small rafts	≈ 750 cfs	
	- Canoes	≈ 300 cfs	
	- Kayaks	≈ 900 cfs	
Shindler and Shelby 1995 Rogue River, OR Boaters	Encounters with float parties		
	- 1977	5.7	
	- 1991	7.4	
	Encounters with jetboats		
	- 1977	1.5	
	- 1991	1.5	
	Hours in sight of other parties		
	- 1977	1.3	
	- 1991	1.4	
	Acceptable number of stops out of five to meet another group		
	- 1977	1.8	
	- 1991	1.8	
	Acceptable number of nights out of five to camp within sight or sound of another party		
	- 1977	1.4	
	- 1991	1.2	
Watson 1995b Boundary Waters Canoe Area, MN Canoers	Encounters with paddling groups	5.8–8.5[5]	
	Number of nearby campers	2.5–5.7	
Hall and Shelby 1996, Eagle Cap Wilderness, OR Visitors	Encounters with other groups	5.6	4.0
Hall et al. 1996 Clackamas River, OR, Floaters	Encounters with other boaters	7.5/10.4[6]	6/8
	Percent of time in sight of other boaters	49.4/46.6	50/50
	Number of minutes waiting at launch	16.1/18.1	15/15
Lewis et al. 1996b Boundary Waters Canoe Area, MN Canoeists	Encounters with canoe parties on periphery lakes and rivers	5.1	3.1
	Encounters with canoe parties on interior lakes and rivers	3.8	2.5

[5]Range over visitors using four entry points; [6]Range over two question formats

Study/Area/ Respondents	Indicator of Quality	Normative Standard	
		Mean	Median
	Encounters with canoe parties on all lakes and rivers	4.2	2.6
Manning et al. 1995 a, b,Manning and Lime 1996, Manning et al. 1996b, c Arches National Park, UT, Visitors	PAOT at Delicate Arch PAOT at North Window	28 20	
Vaske et al. 1995c, 1996, Columbia Ice Field, Jasper National Park, Canada, Snow- coach riders and hikers	PAOT at attraction site for snowcoach riders - Canadian - Anglo-American - Japanese - German - British PAOT at attraction site for hikers - Canadian - Anglo-American - German - British	96.2 100.5 114.6 104.4 84.5 47.3 55.6 42.1 41.3	
Manning et al. 1997 Acadia National Park, ME Carriage road users	Persons per viewscape[7] Visual approach Long form - Hikers only - Bikers only - Even distribution of hikers and bikers Short form - Acceptability - Tolerance - Acceptability for "others" - Management action Numerical approach - Hikers only - Bikers only - Even distribution of hikers and bikers	17 12 14 11 25 15 18 16 13 18	
Tarrant et al. 1997 Nantehala River, NC, Floaters	Maximum encounters tolerable Rafters With rafts - On the river - At put-in - At rapids	28.4 12.3 9.3	

[7]Number of visitors per 100-meter trail segment

Study/Area/ Respondents	Indicator of Quality	Normative Standard Mean	Median
	With kayaks/canoes		
	- On the river	18.4	
	- At put-in	9.2	
	- At rapids	6.8	
	Kayakers/Canoers		
	With rafts		
	- On the river	37.4	
	- At put-in	14.1	
	- At rapids	10.3	
	With kayaks/canoes		
	- On the river	39.9	
	- At put-in	15.5	
	- At rapids	12.1	
Kim and Shelby 1998, 2 national park campgrounds in Korea Campers	Quiet time in evening		
	Baemasagol Campground	10-11	10:00
	Second Campground	11-12	12:00
	Incidences of inconsiderate behavior		
	Baemasagol Campground	0.69	0
	Second Campground	1.76	2
	Number of campers		
	Baemasagol Campground	71.6	60
	Second Campground	158.1	150
	Number of tents		
	Baemasagol Campground	28.9	23
	Second Campground	55.1	50
	Distance between tents (meters)		
	Baemasagol Campground	2.59	2
	Second Campground	2.15	1
	Number of sightings of litter		
	Baemasagol Campground	1.44	0
	Second Campground	2.15	1.5
	Waiting time for restroom (minutes)		
	Baemasagol Campground	2.54	1.75
	Second Campground	2.95	2
	Waiting time for water supply (minutes)		
	Baemasagol Campground	3.14	2.5
	Second Campground	3.67	3

Potential Standards of Quality. A relatively large number of studies have been conducted to help define standards of quality. Most of these studies have adopted the normative methods described earlier in this chapter. Findings from these studies are compiled in Table 6-2.

These studies have addressed a variety of recreation areas and potential indicators of quality. They have also used alternative question formats and wording, different response scales, and other methodological variations. However, several general conclusions can be derived from this growing body of literature.

First, normative standards can be measured for a variety of potential indicators of quality. While many studies have addressed encounter and other crowding-related variables, other studies have measured norms for widely ranging variables. Norms have been measured for a variety of ecological and social variables representing two of the three components of the basic three-fold framework of outdoor recreation.

Second, most respondents are able to report or specify norms for most variables included in most studies. This issue is sometimes referred to as "norm prevalence" (Kim and Shelby 1998). For example, 87% of canoeists in the Boundary Waters Canoe Area Wilderness, MN, reported a norm for the maximum acceptable number of other groups seen each day at the lake or river where they spent the most time (Lewis et al. 1996a). There are some exceptions to this generalization. For example, a study of floaters on the New River, WV, found that between 29% and 66% of respondents reported a norm for several indicator variables under three alternative types of recreation opportunities (Roggenbuck et al. 1991). Other visitors chose one of two other response options, indicating that the potential indicator of quality did not matter to them, or that it did matter, but they couldn't specify a maximum amount of impact acceptable. Reasons as to why visitors may not be able to report norms are discussed below.

Third, visitors tend to report norms more often in wilderness or backcountry situations than in frontcountry or more developed areas. Moreover, such norms tend to be more highly crystallized. For example, standard deviations of encounter norms for floaters on three western rivers were found to increase as the recreation opportunity described moved from "wilderness" to "semi-wilderness" to "undeveloped recreation" (Shelby 1981a). Moreover, the percentage of floaters on the New River, WV, who reported a series of encounter-related norms decreased across a similar spectrum of recreation opportunities (Roggenbuck et al. 1991).

Fourth, norms tend to be lower (or less tolerant) in wilderness or backcountry areas than in frontcountry or more developed areas. This finding is reflected in many studies included in Table 6-2.

Fifth, there is some consistency in norms within similar types of recreation areas or opportunities. For instance, a study of visitor norms for a variety of potential indicators of quality found broad agreement across all four wilderness areas addressed (Roggenbuck et al. 1993). Moreover, a number of studies suggest that norms for encountering other groups during a wilderness experience are quite low (about four or fewer) and that many wilderness visitors prefer to camp out of sight and sound of other groups.

Sixth, norms generally fall into one of three categories or types: no-tolerance, single-tolerance, and multiple-tolerance. For example, a study of boaters on the Deschutes River, OR, measured norms for a number of potential indicators of quality and found all three types of norms as shown in Figure 6-3 (Whittaker and Shelby 1988). The norm curve for human waste represents a no-tolerance norm: the majority of respondents report that it is never acceptable to see signs of human waste along the river. Other indicators of quality for which no-tolerance norms were reported included selected types of discourteous behavior, and jetboat encounters for non-jetboaters. No-tolerance norms tend to be characterized by a mode at zero impact, high intensity, and high crystallization.

The norm curve for time in sight of others represents a single-tolerance norm: the vast majority of respondents were willing to tolerate some time in sight of others, but were unwilling to accept such impact beyond

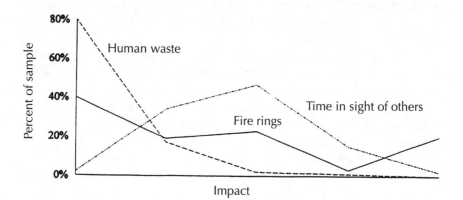

Figure 6-3. Three types of social norms. (From Whittaker and Shelby 1988.)

a certain level (two hours out of four in sight of others). Other indicators of quality for which single-tolerance norms were reported included jetboat encounters for jetboaters, launch waiting times, fishing disturbances, fishing competition, camp sharing, and camp competition. Single-tolerance norms tend to be characterized by a mode at some level of impact greater than zero and a sharp decline in the percentage of respondents reporting tolerances for impacts greater than the modal value.

The norm curve for fire-ring impacts represents a multiple-tolerance norm: multiple "peaks" along the norm curve indicate there are at least two groups of respondents with distinctly different normative standards for this indicator of quality.

Seventh, like perceived crowding discussed in Chapter 5, encounter-related norms often vary with visitor characteristics, characteristics of those encountered, and situational variables. For example, a variety of norms have been found to be related to selected visitor characteristics, including organizational affiliation—activity groups versus environmental organizations—(Shelby and Shindler 1992), level of involvement with wilderness recreation (J. Young et al. 1991), country of origin (Vaske et al. 1995c, 1996), and ethnicity (Heywood 1993a, Heywood and Engelke 1995). Research on the effect of characteristics of those encountered has focused primarily on type of activity. Encounter-related norms have been found to vary depending upon whether those encountered are fishers, canoers, or tubers (Vaske et al. 1986b); boaters or bank fishers (Martinson and Shelby 1992); or hikers or bikers (Manning et al. 1997). Finally, norms have been found to vary in relation to a number of situational or locational variables, including along the river versus campsites (Shelby et al. 1981a), type of recreation area (Shelby 1981a, Vaske et al. 1986b), use level (Hall and Shelby 1996, Lewis et al. 1996b, Shelby et al. 1988b), and periphery versus interior locations (Martin et al. 1989).

Eighth, normative standards of visitors can vary from those of managers. For example, a study of norms for wilderness campsite impacts found that visitors reported more restrictive norms regarding the presence of fire rings and tree damage than did managers (Martin et al. 1989). However, managers reported more restrictive norms for bare ground impacts.

Theoretical and Methodological Issues

The literature on normative standards in outdoor recreation has given rise to a number of theoretical and methodological issues. First, attention has focused on the theoretical foundation of norms and their application to outdoor recreation (Roggenbuck et al. 1991, Shelby and Vaske 1991a, Noe 1992, Heywood 1993a, b, 1996a, b, McDonald 1996, Shelby et al. 1996). As noted in the beginning of this chapter, the concept of norms originated in the fields of sociology and social psychology. In this context, norms traditionally address behaviors that are based on a sense of obligation and have social sanctions associated with them to help ensure broad compliance (Homans 1950, Blake and Davis 1964, Cancian 1975, Rossi and Berk 1985, Biddle 1986). However, as applied in the field of outdoor recreation, norms have been defined more broadly as "standards that individuals use for evaluating behavior, activities, environments, or management proposals as good or bad, better or worse" (Shelby et al. 1996). In this context, recreation-related norms address conditions that are the result of behavior and measure the degree to which selected conditions "ought" to exist. While this may represent an expansion or extension of the traditional concept of norms, the studies in this chapter suggest that normative theory and methods can be useful in formulating standards of quality in outdoor recreation. To avoid confusion and uncertainty in terminology, it may be wise to refer to the types of data described in this chapter as "personal evaluative standards" and "social evaluative standards," rather than personal and social norms. However, the term norms has become widely used in the outdoor recreation literature.

Second, several studies have focused attention on the issue of norm salience. Early in this chapter, salience was defined as the importance of potential indicators of quality in determining the quality of the recreation experience. The issue of salience may help explain why some respondents do not report personal norms (Shelby et al. 1996). When relatively large percentages of respondents do not report norms, it may be that the indicator of quality or impact under study is not important in determining the quality of the recreation experience. Several studies are suggestive of the role of salience in recreation-related norms. As noted earlier, relatively low numbers of floaters on the New River, WV, reported norms for encounter-related indicators of quality when compared to other river recreation studies (Roggenbuck et al. 1991). However, the New River is a relatively high-use area and encounter-related indicators of quality may be less important or salient in this context. This reasoning is supported by other studies, as described earlier, that have found that higher percentages of respondents reported norms for wilderness or backcountry areas than for frontcountry areas. Many of the indicators of quality addressed in these studies are encounter-related and may simply be less important or salient in frontcountry than in backcountry.

A closely related issue concerns how indicators of quality or impacts are perceived and manifested by recreation visitors. Measurement of recreation-related norms should focus as directly as possible on impacts that are relevant to visitors. In this way, visitors are more likely to be able to report norms, norms are likely to be more highly crystallized, and management will be focused more directly on issues of concern to visitors. Data from several studies support the importance of this issue. For example, in the New River study noted above, a higher percentage of respondents reported a norm for waiting time to run rapids (while other boats took their turn) than for number of other boats seen (Roggenbuck et al.1991). Similarly, visitors to the Clackamas River, OR, another relatively high-use area, reported norms more often for percentage of time in sight of other boats than for number of other boats seen (Hall et al. 1996). In relatively high-use areas, use levels may be perceived or manifested differently than in relatively low-use areas. Moreover, in high-use areas, it may simply not be feasible to estimate or evaluate large numbers of encounters with other groups. Several studies have explored alternative expressions of use-related indicators of quality, including physical proximity of fishers along streams (Martinson and Shelby 1992), the number of people at one time (PAOT) at destination or attraction sites (Manning et al. 1995a, b, c, Manning and Lime 1996, Manning et al. 1996b, c, Vaske et al. 1996, Manning et al. 1997), persons per viewscape along trails (Manning et al. 1997), and waiting times for essential services (Kim and Shelby 1998).

Third, visual approaches to measuring standards of quality have been explored in a number of studies (Shelby and Harris 1985, Martin et al. 1989, Shelby et al. 1992a, Heywood 1993a, Hof et al. 1994, Manning et al. 1995a, b, c, Manning and Lime 1996, Manning et al. 1996b, c, Manning 1997, Manning et al. 1998). These have included artistic renderings and photographs. For example, a series of sixteen photographs showing different numbers of visitors at an attraction site was used in a study of crowding-related norms at Arches National Park, UT (Manning et al. 1996c). Respondents rated the acceptability of each photograph and a norm for the maximum PAOT was determined. In certain situations, visual approaches may portray alternative levels of impact more realistically than written descriptions. The study at Arches National Park described above also included a more traditional written measure of norms for the maximum acceptable PAOT. This norm was substantially lower than the one derived from the visual approach. It may be that the written approach to norm measurement draws conscious attention to each person or group encountered, whereas in the visual approach, some persons or groups who are perceived as much "like" the respondent in terms of activity, behavior, and appearance are processed less consciously and do not contribute as heavily to perceived crowding. The potential importance of perceptions of "alikeness" in crowding was described in Chapter 5. In this respect, visual approaches may result in more realistic or "valid" measures of crowding-related norms in certain situations than written or narrative approaches.

Fourth, studies of recreation norms have used a variety of evaluative dimensions. When respondents are asked to evaluate impacts of a range of conditions for potential indicators of quality, the response scale may include terminology specifying "preference," "favorableness," "pleasantness," "acceptability," "tolerance," or some other concept. These alternative evaluative dimensions may have substantially different meanings to respondents and may result in dramatically different norms. Study findings support this assumption. Several studies have included measures of both preferred (or "ideal") conditions and acceptable (or "maximum" or "tolerable") conditions (J. Young et al. 1991, Hammitt and Rutlin 1995, Watson 1995b). In all cases, preferred conditions for encounter-related variables are substantially lower—less than half—than acceptable conditions. The literature on norm theory described above has suggested that norm measurement questions adopt more explicitly normative concepts and terminology (Heywood 1996a). This might include the condition that managers "should" maintain and respondents' beliefs about what "other visitors" feel is acceptable. An initial test of these concepts found that they yielded significantly higher encounter-related norms than acceptability to respondents (Manning et al. 1997, 1999). None of these evaluative dimensions may be more "valid" than any others, but researchers and managers should be conscious of this issue and exercise appropriate care and caution in interpreting and applying study findings. For example, standards of quality based on preference-related norms may result in very high-quality recreation experiences, but may restrict access to a relatively low number of visitors. In contrast, standards of quality based on acceptability or tolerance may result in recreation experiences that are of only marginal quality, but allow access to a larger number of visitors. Studies that employ multiple evaluative dimensions may result in findings that enrich the information base on which standards of quality might be formulated.

Fifth, studies of recreation norms have also used alternative question-and-response formats. Early in this chapter, it was noted that norms are sometimes measured using a repetitive-item (or "long") format whereby respondents are asked to evaluate a range of alternative conditions. An open-ended (or "short") version of this question format has also been employed whereby respondents are asked to specify the maximum acceptable level of impact. Only one study has used both question formats, and this found that the short-question format yielded a lower encounter-related norm (Manning et al. 1997, 1999). Several studies have explored the range of response options that might be included in norm measurement questions (Roggenbuck et al. 1991, Hall et al. 1996, Hall and Shelby 1996). In particular, these studies have addressed the issue of whether respondents should be presented with an option that indicates that the indicator of quality is important to them, but that they cannot specify a maximum number that is acceptable. The principal argument in favor of this option suggests that respondents should not be "forced" into reporting a norm in which they have little confidence. The principal argument against this option is that it may simply present some respondents a convenient way to avoid a potentially difficult question. The only empirical tests directed at this issue found that respondents who chose this option were more like respondents who reported a norm (with respect to reactions to impacts and attitudes toward management) than those who reported that the indicator of quality was not important to them (Hall and Shelby 1996). Moreover, use of this response option did not affect the value of the norm derived, though it did affect the variance or crystallization of the norm (Hall et al. 1996). Thus, use of this response option may not be an important consideration.

Sixth, crystallization of norms is an important research and management issue. As noted earlier in this chapter, crystallization refers to the level of agreement or consensus about recreation norms. The more agreement about norms, the more confidence managers might have in using such data to formulate standards of quality. Most norm-related studies have reported some measure of crystallization. Standard deviations of mean and median values of norms are used most frequently, but coefficients of variation and semi-interquartile ranges have also been recommended to allow comparisons across variables and reduce the effects of extreme values (Roggenbuck et al. 1991, Hall and Shelby 1996). However, there are no statistical guidelines or rules of thumb to indicate what constitutes high or low levels of agreement or consensus, and there is disagreement in the literature concerning how recreation-related norms should be interpreted. Ultimately, some degree of judgment must be rendered by managers. If there appear to be moderate to high levels of agreement over norms, then managers can incorporate study findings into their decisions with confidence. If there does not appear to be much agreement over norms, then managers might focus on resolving conflicts among visitors, consider zoning areas for alternative recreation experiences, or formulate norms based on other considerations.

Seventh, as research on norms has matured, attention has focused on the issue of norm congruence, sometimes called "norm-impact compatibility" (Shelby and Vaske 1991a). This issue concerns the extent to which respondents evaluate relevant aspects of the recreation experience in keeping with their normative standards. If recreation norms are to be used in formulating standards of quality, then research on norm congruence is important to test the internal consistency or "validity" of such norms. A number of studies have addressed this issue across a variety of activities, indicator variables, and areas (Vaske et al. 1986b, Patterson and Hammitt 1990, Hammitt and Patterson 1991, Williams et al. 1991, Ruddell and Gramann 1994, Hammitt and Rutlin 1995, Lewis et al. 1996b, Manning et al. 1996c, d, Vaske et al. 1996). Nearly all have found support for the concept of norm congruence; that is, when conditions are experienced that violate visitor norms, respondents tend to judge such conditions as less acceptable or more crowded and adopt behaviors to avoid such conditions. Only one study has not supported norm congruence (Patterson and Hammitt 1990). However, this study was conducted in a relatively high-use area where encounter norms may not have been salient or highly crystallized.

Eighth, a variety of statistics are available for measuring, analyzing, and interpreting norms (Shelby and Heberlein 1986, Vaske et al. 1986b, Whittaker and Shelby 1988, Shelby et al. 1996). Each has advantages and disadvantages, and these should be considered when selecting appropriate statistical approaches. Norms are generally reported and described in terms of medians and means. Median values have intuitive appeal because they represent the level of impact that half of respondents find acceptable. Mean values are more intuitively straightforward and are easier to calculate, but are easily skewed by outlying or extreme values and may be misleading in the case of multiple-tolerance norms.

Norm curves like those illustrated in Figures 6-1 and 6-3, as well as frequency distributions which show the level of agreement associated with each impact level, are less parsimonious, but offer considerably more information in a graphic and less technical way. Statistical measures of norm crystallization were discussed earlier in this section.

Ninth, research methods used to measure norms have varied widely across the studies reviewed in this chapter. This applies especially to question format and wording. Experimentation in research approaches is clearly warranted to identify and address emerging issues and test the effectiveness of alternative methodological approaches. However, when possible, replication and standardization of research approaches are desirable to enable comparisons across studies and over time. A compendium of frequently used norm-related questions is contained in Donnelly et al. (1992) and may be useful in moving toward more consistent research approaches when advisable.

Tenth, the stability of recreation norms over time has received little research attention, but may become increasingly important. Do norms change or evolve over time? If so, should such changes be incorporated into how recreation areas are managed? The answer to the first question is a technical issue, while the second is more philosophical. Few studies have addressed the variability of norms over time. Those that have have generated mixed or inconclusive results. For example, a 1977 study of encounter norms for boaters on the Rogue River, OR, was replicated in 1984 (Shelby et al. 1988a). No statistically significant difference was found for the number of acceptable river encounters. However, camp encounter norms were found to be significantly higher or more tolerant in the latter study. A similar study conducted in three wilderness areas over a longer interval found few clear, consistent trends in tolerance for inter-group contacts (Cole et al. 1995). Two other studies have found substantial stability of norms over time; however, these studies cover only a two-to-three-year time period (Kim and Shelby 1998, Manning et al. 1999).

Arguments about whether changes in norms should be incorporated into management plans are divided. The underlying rationale of indicators and standards of quality is that they should be set and maintained for some extended period of time, usually defined as the life of the management plan for which they are formulated. Thus, during this time period, standards of quality probably should not be revised substantially. However, management plans are periodically reformulated to reflect the changing conditions of society. It seems reasonable to reassess recreation norms as part of this process and incorporate these findings within long-term planning processes.

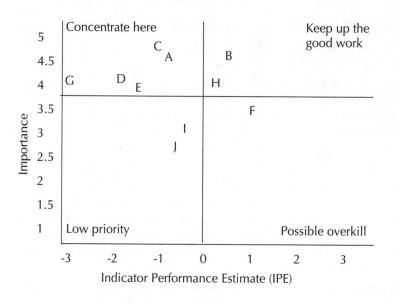

Code Indicators

A = Number of parties of people I see each day. B = Number of large parties (more than 6 people) I see each day. C = Number of parties camped within sight or sound of my campsite. D = Number of parties that walk past my campsite each night. E = Number of visible places I see each day where people have camped. F = Number of horse parties encountered each day. G = Percent of vegetation loss and bare ground seen each day. H = Number of fire rings. I = Number of signs seen each day. J = Number of culverts seen each day.

Figure 6-4. Importance-performance analysis. (From Hollenhorst and Gardner 1994.)

Finally, two organizational frameworks have been suggested to help guide development of indicators and standards of quality and subsequent monitoring and management action. An "importance-performance" framework has been suggested as an aid to formulating indicators and standards of quality (Mengak at al. 1986, Hollenhorst and Stull-Gardner 1992, Hollenhorst et al. 1992b, Hollenhorst and Gardner 1994). Using this framework, visitors are first asked to rate the importance of potential indicator variables, and these results are plotted along a vertical axis as shown in Figure 6-4. Second, visitors are asked a series of normative questions regarding standards of quality for each indicator variable. These data are then related to existing conditions and plotted on a horizontal axis as shown in Figure 6-4. The resulting data provide a graphic representation of the relationship between importance and performance of indicator variables, and where management action should be directed. The data in Figure 6-4, for example, are derived from a survey of visitors to the Cranberry Wilderness, WV, and suggest that indicator variable "A" ("number of parties of people I see each day") is important to visitors, but that visitors currently see more parties of people per day than their standard of quality (Hollenhorst and Gardner 1994). These findings suggest that managers should concentrate their attention on this indicator of quality.

An outdoor recreation "threats matrix" is another framework that might be applied to indicators and standards of quality (L. Leopold et

	Wilderness Threats							
Attributes of wilderness character	Recreation	Livestock	Mining	Fire	Exotic species	Water projects	Atmospheric pollutants	Adjacent lands
Air	1	1	1	2	1	1	4	3
Aquatic systems	4	3	3	4	4	3	4	3
Rock/ landforms	1	2	2	1	1	2	1	1
Soils	3	3	2	5	2	2	4	2
Vegetation	3	3	2	5	4	3	4	2
Animals	4	2	2	4	3	2	2	4
Ecosystems/ landscapes	2	3	2	5	3	2	4	5
Cultural resources	3	2	2	2	1	1	1	1
Wilderness experiences	4	3	2	3	2	2	2	3

Figure 6-5. Wilderness threats matrix. Matrix values are significance ratings for the impacts of each potential threat on each wilderness attribute for all wilderness areas in the U.S. Forest Service's Northern Region. Ratings range from 1 (low) to 5 (high). (From Cole 1994.)

al. 1971, Manning and Moncrief 1979, Cole 1994). A matrix model of outdoor recreation impacts can be created by arraying important attributes of outdoor recreation to form the rows of a matrix, and arraying potential threats to those attributes as the columns of the matrix. Each cell within the resulting matrix represents the various impacts that each threat causes to each attribute. An example of such a matrix is shown in Figure 6-5. This example was developed to determine the significance of threats to wilderness areas within the Northern Region of the U.S. Forest Service (Cole 1994). This example applies to wilderness very broadly, but can be developed more specifically for outdoor recreation. Such a matrix can be useful as a means of identifying potential indicators of quality (important attributes of outdoor recreation that are impacted by potential threats), and the extent to which such indicator variables are threatened and, therefore, need monitoring and management attention.

Summary and Conclusions

1. Indicators and standards of quality have emerged as a central focus of carrying capacity and related recreation management frameworks. As defined in Chapter 4, indicators of quality are measurable variables that help define the quality of the recreation experience. Standards of quality define the minimum acceptable condition of indicator variables.

2. Normative theory and methods have been applied to outdoor recreation as a basis of formulating indicators and standards of quality. As applied to outdoor recreation, personal norms are standards that individuals use to evaluate recreation conditions. Personal norms can be aggregated to test for the existence of broader social norms.

3. Indicators of quality should meet eight characteristics as follows:

   A. Specific

   B. Objective

   C. Reliable and repeatable

   D. Related to visitor use

E. Sensitive

F. Manageable

G. Efficient and effective to measure

H. Significant

These characteristics can be incorporated into a matrix as shown in Figure 6-2 to evaluate potential indicators of quality.

4. Research has identified a variety of potential indicators of quality as shown in Table 6-1. Several broad conclusions can be derived from these studies.

A. Potential indicators of quality can be wide-ranging, representing all three components of the three-fold framework of outdoor recreation: environmental, social, and managerial.

B. Many potential indicators of quality are rated as at least somewhat important in defining the quality of the recreation experience. This is consistent with the multiple satisfaction or behavioral approach to outdoor recreation.

C. There is often a hierarchy of importance among indicators of quality.

D. Visitors to wilderness or backcountry areas may be more sensitive to a variety of indicators of quality than visitors to frontcountry or more developed areas.

E. Social indicators of quality may be more important than ecological indicators for wilderness campsites.

5. Standards of quality should meet five characteristics as follows:

A. Quantitative

B. Time- or space-bounded

C. Expressed as a probability

D. Impact-oriented

E. Realistic

6. Research has measured personal or social norms for a variety of indicators of quality as shown in Table 6-2. Several broad conclusions can be derived from these studies.

A. Normative standards can be measured for a variety of potential indicators of quality.

B. Most respondents are able to report norms for most variables included in most studies.

C. Normative standards are reported more often and are more highly crystallized in wilderness or backcountry areas than in frontcountry or more highly used areas.

D. Norms tend to be lower (or less tolerant) in wilderness or backcountry areas than in frontcountry or more highly used areas.

E. There is some consistency in norms across similar types of recreation areas or opportunities.

F. Norms can generally be categorized as no-tolerance, single-tolerance, or multiple-tolerance.

G. Encounter-related norms tend to vary with visitor characteristics, characteristics of those encountered, and situational variables.

H. Normative standards of quality of visitors may vary from those of managers.

7. A number of theoretical and methodological issues have been identified regarding application of the normative approach to indicators and standards of quality in outdoor recreation:

A. Application of normative theory and methods to outdoor recreation represents an expansion and extension of the normative approach.

B. Measures of recreation norms should be applied to indicators of quality that are salient or important in defining the quality or the recreation experience.

C. Visual approaches may be useful in measuring norms and may result in more realistic or "valid" standards of quality.

D. A variety of evaluative dimensions have been used to measure recreation norms. Appropriate care and caution should be used in interpreting and applying these alternative dimensions. Use of multiple evaluative dimensions may provide an especially rich and useful base of information for formulating standards of quality.

E. A variety of question and response formats have been used to measure recreation norms. The long or repetitive-item question format is more burdensome to respondents than the short or open-ended format, but yields more information. Inclusion of a response option that allows visitors to indicate that an indicator of quality is important, but that they cannot report a maximum acceptable level of impact may not be an important consideration.

F. Norm measurement should include measures of crystallization or consensus. However, the degree of consensus needed to formulate standards of quality is a management judgment and not a statistical or technical issue.

G. Research generally supports the issue of norm congruence, which measures the extent to which visitor evaluations of recreation conditions conform to normative standards. This tends to support the internal consistency or "validity" of recreation norms.

H. A variety of statistics can be used to measure, analyze, and interpret norms. Each has advantages and disadvantages, and all should be applied thoughtfully. Graphic approaches and frequency distributions may also be useful in reporting, interpreting, and applying normative standards.

I. Consistency in norm measurement approaches should be adopted where possible to allow comparisons across studies and over time.

J. Little is known about the stability of recreation norms over time. However, recreation norms should probably be reassessed in accordance with long-term cycles in planning for outdoor recreation areas.

K. Two organizational frameworks—"importance-performance" and an "outdoor recreation threats matrix"—can be useful in formulating indicators and standards of quality and guiding subsequent monitoring and management action.

Notes

1. Recreation management practices are described in Chapter 12.

7

Motivations and Benefits in Recreation
A Behavioral Approach

Early Explorations

Early empirical research in outdoor recreation, like that in all emerging areas of study, was primarily descriptive, focusing on the activities and socioeconomic and cultural characteristics of users, and their attitudes and preferences about management. But even as this descriptive base of information was being built, there were early signs of an analytical interest in recreation, specifically the question of why people participate in outdoor recreation. This interest germinated in the 1960s, blossomed in the 1970s and 1980s, and continues to flourish today, expanding into new areas.

Illustrative of the early interest in motivations for outdoor recreation was a study of fishing in the Quetico-Superior Area, MN (Bultena and Taves 1961). Observing that fishers returning to camp with empty creels were not dissatisfied with their visit to the area, the authors hypothesized that there must be multiple motives involved in outdoor recreation. Tentative support for this hypothesis was found in an exploratory element of this study, which asked visitors to the area to rate the importance of seventeen potential motivations for their visits. Results indicated that visitors to the area tended to think of their trips as a means of escaping familiar routines and the cares associated with living in an urbanized society, along with other diverse motivations. An analogous study of hunting proposed a "multiple satisfaction approach" to this recreation activity, expanding measures of satisfaction from the traditional count of game bagged to include more varied motivations and satisfaction (Hendee 1974). Early studies of camping and wilderness were also suggestive of multiple motivations in outdoor recreation (Stone and Traves 1958, Wildland Research Center 1962, LaPage 1967, Catton 1969, E. Shafer and Mietz 1969).

Two more conceptually based studies were also conducted during this early period (Burch 1965, 1969). Both focused on camping activity in the Pacific Northwest. The first identified six types of play activity symbolic of the various meanings ascribed to camping. The second tested two conventional theories of leisure behavior: the compensatory theory, suggesting that leisure activities are selected to be opposite to and give relief from routine activities; and the familiarity theory, suggesting that leisure activities are selected to be in conformance with routine activities to avoid feelings of uncertainty. Little support was found for either theory.

In a rudimentary sense, studies of recreation and leisure have been suggestive of multiple motivations for several decades. Several classical theories were postulated in the 1950s and 1960s to explain general leisure behavior. Two theories, compensation and familiarity, were noted above. Others included surplus energy (leisure activity burns off excess energy or vitality), relaxation (leisure activity provides respite from intense work or living functions), and catharsis (leisure activity allows purging of emotional tension or anxiety). Several early texts provide standard treatments of this work (Neumeyer and Neumeyer 1949, Larrabee and Meyersohn 1958, Brightbill 1960, Kaplan 1960, DeGrazia 1962).

This chapter examines theoretical and empirical research on motivations and benefits associated with outdoor recreation. This research suggests a "behavioral approach" to recreation, emphasizing why people participate in outdoor recreation activities and the potential benefits gained from such participation. Several conceptual and methodological issues are identified and discussed.

A Behavioral Approach to Recreation

Beginning in the early 1970s, Driver and associates began building a conceptual foundation for the study of motivations in outdoor recreation (Driver and Toucher 1970, Driver 1975, Driver and Brown 1975, Driver 1976, Driver and Bassett 1977, Driver and Brown 1978, Haas et al. 1980a, Driver and Rosenthal 1982, Schreyer and Driver 1989).[1] Empirical approaches to testing these concepts were also developed and have received wide application. The conceptual foundation of this work began with a fundamental look at the nature of recreation, noting that the traditional view of recreation is based on activities—fishing, swimming, camping, etc. (Driver and Toucher 1970). While this activity approach has been useful for a variety of descriptive purposes, it leaves unaddressed a number of potentially important issues:

> Why is the recreationist participating in the activity? What other activities might have been selected if the opportunities existed? What satisfactions or rewards are received from the activity? How can the quality of the experience be enhanced? (Driver and Toucher 1970:10).

To better answer these questions, a behavioral approach was proposed whereby recreation is defined as "an experience that results from recreational engagements" (Driver and Toucher 1970).

This approach is based on psychological theory which suggests that most human behavior is goal-oriented or aimed at some need or satisfaction (Crandall 1980). Perhaps the most widely recognized expression of this theory is Maslow's (1943) hierarchy of human needs

Table 7-1. Four levels or hierarchies of demand for outdoor recreation. (Adapted from Haas et al. 1980.)

Level	Example 1	Example 2
1. Activities	Wilderness hiking	Family picnicking
2. Settings		
A . Environmental setting	Rugged terrain	Grass fields
B. Social setting	Few people	No boisterous teenagers
C. Managerial setting	No restrictions	Picnic tables
3. Motivations	Risk taking	In-group affiliation
	Challenge	Change of pace
	Physical exercise	
4. Benefits		
A. Personal	Enhanced self-esteem	Enhanced personal health
B. Social	Lower crime rate	Family solidarity
C. Economic	Lower health care costs	Increased work production
D. Environmental	Increased commitment to conservation	Higher quality environment

beginning with the most basic requirements for physiological sustenance and ranging through more aesthetic concerns. The work of Driver and associates is based more directly on the expectancy theory developed in social psychology, which suggests that people engage in activities in specific settings to realize a group of psychological outcomes that are known, expected, and valued (e.g., Atkinson and Birch 1972, Lawler 1973, Fishbein and Ajzen 1974). Thus people select and participate in recreation activities to meet certain goals or satisfy certain needs. In this context, recreation activities are more a means to an end than an end in themselves.

The behavioral approach to recreation has been expanded to recognize four levels or hierarchies of demand for outdoor recreation as illustrated in Table 7-1 (Driver and Brown 1978, Haas et al. 1980a). Level 1 represents demands for activities themselves and has been the traditional focus of recreation research and management. Level 2 represents the settings in which activities take place. An activity such as camping, for example, can be undertaken in a variety of environmental, social, and managerial settings, each representing different recreation opportunities. Level 2 demands do not exist in and of themselves; people participate in activities in different settings to fulfill motivations as represented by Level 3 demands. These motivations are desired psychological outcomes. Examples include enjoyment of the out-of-doors, applying and developing skills, strengthening family ties, learning, getting exercise, exploring, reflecting on personal values, temporarily escaping a variety of adverse stimuli at home or at work, taking risks, and so on. Typically, more than one motivation is sought and realized from recreation participation. Finally, Level 4 demands refer to the ultimate or higher-order benefits that can flow from satisfying experiences derived from recreation participation. These benefits may be either personal, social, economic, or environmental. However, these higher order benefits are somewhat abstract and are difficult to measure and associate directly with recreation participation. For this reason, empirical study of the behavioral approach to recreation has focused primarily on Level 3 demands and motivations.

Empirical Tests of the Behavioral Approach

Empirical search for the motivations of general leisure behavior has occupied social scientists for many years and can be traced back as far as the 1920s with the classic Middletown studies of Lynd and Lynd (1929). But the literature is spotty until more recent times. Perhaps the first and best known of the more modern studies are those of Havighurst and associates. Donald and Havighurst (1959), for example, developed a twelve-item checklist of possible meanings of leisure activities, and found systematic relationships between these meanings and the activities in which subjects engaged.

Empirical studies of recreation motivations have become more numerous since the late 1960s. Though these studies share certain characteristics, they tend to fall into one of three general categories: studies of general leisure behavior, explorations of motivations for a specific activity, and the conceptual and empirical studies of Driver and associates.

General Leisure Behavior. The first and largest category of research on motivations is comprised of studies of general leisure behavior. While there are potentially important management implications involved in these studies (for example, the potential substitutability of leisure and recreation activities, addressed in Chapter 10), their popularity has also been influenced by their heuristic value. Social scientists are generally intrigued by such studies, as they allow exploration of why people behave as they do under conditions of few obvious constraints or compelling external forces. Several research approaches have been taken in this general category of studies:

1. Participation rates in various leisure activities have been used to group activities into similar categories (Bishop 1970, Moss and Lamphear 1970, Witt 1971, Hendee and Burdge 1974, Schmitz-Scherzer et al. 1974, Ditton et al. 1975, J. Christensen and Yoesting 1977, London et al. 1977). Various numbers of activity categories that seem to share underlying meanings have been isolated.

2. Lists of potential motivations have been developed and tested for their importance for participation in leisure activities (D. Potter et al. 1973, Hollendar 1977, London et al. 1977, Rossman and Ulehla 1977, Tinsley et al. 1977, Hawes 1978, Tinsley and Kass 1978, S. Adams 1979, Crandall 1979, Tinsley and Kass 1979, Beard and Ragheb 1980, Iso-Ahola and Allen 1982, Beard and Ragheb 1983). Various numbers of basic dimensions of leisure meanings have been isolated.

3. Perceived similarity of leisure activities has been used to group activities into similar categories (Ritchie 1975, B. Becker 1976). As in item 1 above, various numbers of activity categories that seem to share underlying meanings have been isolated.

4. Antecedent or preceding conditions have been related to preferred leisure activity choice (Witt and Bishop 1970). Systematic relationships have been found, indicating that certain leisure activities fulfill certain motivations created by antecedent conditions.

5. Personality traits of subjects have been related to participation in leisure activities (Moss et al. 1969, Moss and Lamphear 1970, Howard 1976) and more directly to motivations for participating in selected leisure activities (Driver and Knopf 1977). Systematic relationships have been found, indicating that certain leisure activities fulfill certain motivations created by selected personality traits.

6. Attitudes toward leisure have been related to participation in leisure activities (Neulinger and Breit 1969, 1971). Systematic relationships have been found, indicating that certain leisure activities fulfill certain motivations created by selected attitudes toward leisure.

7. Reported preferences for leisure activities have been used to group activities into similar categories (Hendee et al. 1971). Several activity categories have been isolated that seem to share underlying meanings.

8. Descriptions and characteristics of leisure activities have been rated and grouped into similar categories (Pierce 1980b, c). Several categories of both descriptions and characteristics of leisure activities that seem to share underlying meanings have been isolated.

9. Participation rates in various leisure activities have been used to group participants into similar categories (Romsa 1973). Several groups of participants have been isolated based on similarity of leisure activities.

Integration of these studies is difficult for several reasons. Leisure and recreation activities and motivations studied have varied widely, as have research approaches and sample populations. Moreover, the statistical methods used are commonly complex, multivariate techniques such as factor analysis, cluster analysis, multidimensional scaling, and discriminant analysis. These techniques are appropriate, but yield results requiring considerable interpretation by the researcher. Nevertheless, these studies as a whole do reveal that leisure activities have underlying meanings to participants, and that these underlying meanings or motivations can be conceptualized and measured.

Specific Recreation Activities. A small and diverse group of studies has followed up on the early explorations described at the beginning of this chapter. All focus on specific outdoor recreation activities and either explore a limited number of potential motivations or use an open-ended technique. Two studies, for example, surveyed fishers, asking them to rank possible reasons for fishing (Moeller and Engelken 1972, Witter et al. 1982). Both studies gained some insight into motivations for fishing, particularly the existence of different motivations for different types of fishing. Management implications of this type of study suggest that different aspects of the fishing environment should be emphasized to enhance satisfaction for different types of fishers. Similar studies of deer hunting found considerable diversity with respect to the importance of various motivations for hunting (Decker et al. 1980) and the extent to which a variety of independent variables contribute to the perceived quality of the hunting experience (Hammitt et al. 1989b). These findings support the "multiple satisfaction approach," demonstrating that hunters clearly ascribe more meaning to hunting than simply bagging game.[2]

Finally, two studies explored motivations of visitors to backcountry areas using an open-ended survey approach. Both studies found a variety of reported motivations. One of these studies found twelve reasons reported for visiting high mountain lakes, with no one reason reported by more than 29% of the sample (Hendee et al. 1977a). Hikers in Grand Canyon National Park, AZ, reported six basic categories of motivations for their activity (Towler 1977). Motivations were found to have a significant effect on visitor expectations for and attitudes about backcountry conditions.

Taken together, the studies in this category suggest that motivations for outdoor recreation—indeed, motivations even within a single outdoor recreation activity—are diverse and can be related to the attitudes, preferences, and expectations of users.

Driver and Associates. A large group of studies of recreation motivations is based directly on the conceptual and empirical work of Driver and associates. To test their conceptual formulations of a behavioral approach to recreation, these researchers have developed and refined a wide-ranging list of potential recreation motivations, along with a series of corresponding scale items representing potential motivations for participating in specific recreation activities. Scale item measurements are usually then reduced through cluster analysis to "domains" representing more generalized categories of motivations. This basic research approach is similar to the studies cited in item 2 in the category of general leisure behavior described earlier in this section. Its potential usefulness for outdoor recreation managers is enhanced, however, because of its direct focus on outdoor recreation activities and its standardization as a result of extensive empirical testing. The motivation scales have been developed and refined through dozens of empirical studies. Tests have generally confirmed both the reliability and validity of the motivation scales (Rosenthal et al. 1982, Manfredo et al. 1996).

The first generation of these studies was applied to a variety of recreation activities, but published results focused primarily on fishing (Knopf et al. 1973, Driver and Knopf 1976, Driver and Cooksey 1977) and river users (Roggenbuck and Schreyer 1977, Schreyer and Roggenbuck 1978, Graefe et al. 1981, Knopf and Lime 1984). Several motivational domains of recreationists have been isolated in these studies, and differences in motivations were found between selected "types" of recreationists. Trout fishers, for instance, were found to rate the motivation of "affiliation" substantially lower than did lake and bank fishers.

Recreation motivation scales were included in a series of nationwide studies investigating a broad spectrum of recreational uses of rivers (Knopf and Lime 1984). Resulting data illustrate the potential management implications of this research approach. Table 7-2 presents two examples. The first compares responses of river floaters on two rivers to seven motivations. Floaters on both rivers rated "view scenery" and "peace and calm" very highly, but differed substantially on other motivations. Floaters on the Delta River, AK, placed much more emphasis on learning, developing skills, exercise, escaping crowds, and being alone than did their counterparts on the Salt River, AZ. Though floaters on both rivers desired "peace and calm," they apparently define it in different ways. These findings are suggestive of the different

Table 7-2. Motivations for river floating (% of respondents). (Adapted from Knopf and Lime 1984.)

	Delta River	Salt River	Rio Grande River	
			First-time visitors	Repeat visitors
View scenery	97	77	88	94
Peace and calm	85	73	62	82
Learn new things	80	50	78	73
Develop skills	78	34	48	76
Escape crowds	76	30	52	82
Exercise	64	48	34	65
Be alone	28	8	6	22

meanings of solitude and privacy in outdoor recreation discussed in Chapter 5. The implications of these findings translate directly into river management objectives, particularly with respect to appropriate use levels.

The second example in Table 7-2 illustrates that even floaters on the same river can differ substantially on motivations. Both first-time and repeat visitors to the Rio Grande River, NM, rated "view scenery," "peace and calm," and "learn new things" highly. But there were substantial differences between the two groups of floaters on the other four motivations, indicating that repeat visitors were substantially more sensitive to use levels. Unless this is taken into account in river management, many repeat visitors are likely to be dissatisfied and perhaps eventually displaced. The study concludes that data of this kind illustrate the advantage of managing for outdoor recreation experiences rather than activities:

> It is clear that repeat visitors on the Rio Grande are looking for different experiences than first-time visitors. It is also clear that Delta River visitors differ in orientation from Salt River visitors. Yet, all four populations are participating in the same recreation activity, river floating. From an activity perspective, they would be viewed as essentially equivalent and not differing in resource requirements. But from an experience perspective, they would be viewed as distinct recreation populations with separate requirements (Knopf and Lime 1984:15).

Another study of floaters on the Green and Yampa Rivers, Dinosaur National Monument, CO, illustrated that motivations for recreation can be related to user attitudes, preferences, and perceptions of crowding (Roggenbuck and Schreyer 1977, Schreyer and Roggenbuck 1978). Selected motive domains were found to be related to attitudes about maximum group size, preferences for campsite development, campsite assignment, trip scheduling, number of acceptable encounters, and perceptions of crowding, though the correlations were not strong. These findings were compared to data from a similar study on the Rio Grande River, Big Bend National Park, TX (Graefe et al. 1981). Remarkable similarity was found between the studies with regard to several motivations. In particular, learning about and experiencing nature and stress release and solitude were the most important motivations across both samples and exhibited highly similar factor domain structures. But, as might be expected from samples drawn from rivers with substantially varying environmental, social, and managerial conditions, other motivational scale items and domains differed substantively. This is further illustrated in Table 7-3, which compares the importance of sixteen motivation domains across three wilderness and three nonwilderness areas.

A second generation of studies has added another methodological step to identify types of recreationists based on motive structure. After appropriate motive domains have been isolated as described above, a further clustering procedure is used to identify groups of respondents

Table 7-3. Comparative ratings of motivation domains. (Adapted from Driver et al. 1987b.)

Motivation	Wilderness Areas			Nonwilderness Areas		
	A	B	C	D	E	F
1. Enjoy nature	1.5 (1)	1.5 (1)	1.6 (1)	2.4 (4)	1.7 (1)	3.1 (2)
2. Physical fitness	2.4 (4)	2.0 (2)	2.2 (2)	2.2 (3)	2.3 (4)	3.1 (2)
3. Reduce tensions	2.1 (2)	2.3 (4)	2.3 (3)	2.7 (5)	2.2 (3)	3.3 (4)
4. Escape noise/crowds	2.2 (3)	2.2 (3)	2.3 (3)	3.1 (9)	2.1 (2)	3.3 (4)
5. Outdoor learning	2.1 (2)	2.4 (5)	2.4 (4)	2.9 (8)	2.3 (4)	3.8 (6)
6. Sharing similar values	2.8 (5)	2.9 (6)	2.9 (5)	1.2 (1)	2.3 (4)	3.1 (2)
7. Independence	3.1 (7)	2.9 (6)	3.0 (6)	2.7 (6)	2.7 (5)	3.7 (5)
8. Family kinship	3.0 (6)	3.0 (7)	3.1 (7)	2.1 (2)	2.1 (2)	3.2 (3)
9. Introspection/spiritual	3.5 (8)	3.1 (8)	2.9 (5)	3.5 (12)	3.5 (8)	4.1 (8)
10. Considerate people	3.6 (9)	3.4 (9)	3.3 (8)	—	—	4.8 (10)
11. Achievement/ stimulation	3.9 (11)	3.1 (8)	3.1 (7)	2.7 (6)	3.1 (6)	4.2 (9)
12. Physical rest	3.8 (10)	4.3 (10)	3.3 (8)	3.2 (10)	2.1 (2)	3.0 (1)
13. Teach/lead others	3.7 (10)	4.3 (10)	3.7 (9)	3.6 (13)	3.1 (6)	5.2 (11)
14. Risk taking	4.7 (12)	4.8 (12)	4.5 (10)	2.2 (3)	2.2 (3)	5.3 (12)
15. Risk reduction	4.8 (13)	4.7 (11)	4.7 (11)	3.3 (11)	3.4 (7)	—
16. Meet new people	5.6 (14)	5.3 (13)	4.5 (10)	3.5 (12)	4.0 (9)	4.0 (7)

A = Weminuche (CO). B = Maroon Bells (CO). C = Shining Rock (NC). D = Little Sahara (UT). E = Arkansas River (CO). F = Lake Shelbyville (IL)
Ratings were made on the following nine-point response format (with numerical codes used to compute means): Adds (to satisfaction) most strongly (1), strongly (2), moderately (3) a little (4); neither adds nor detracts (5); detracts a little (6), moderately (7), strongly (8), most strongly (9).

having relatively similar patterns of response to the motive domains. In this way, groups or "market segments" of recreationists sharing similar motivations are identified. These studies have been conducted on several types of hunters (P. Brown et al. 1977, Hautaluoma and Brown 1978, Hautaluoma et al. 1982); state park visitors (McCool and Reilly 1993), fishers (Dawson 1997), river floaters (Ditton et al. 1982, Floyd and Gramann 1997), wilderness visitors (P. Brown and Haas 1980, S. Allen 1985, Vaske et al. 1986a, Hazel et al. 1990), skiers (Haas et al. 1980b, Mills 1985), heritage tourists (Knopf and Barnes 1980, Prentice 1993), and mountain climbers (Ewert 1994).

All of these studies were able to identify between three and ten groups of respondents with distinctive recreation motivations. Moreover, there were often relationships between the various types of recreationists identified and other characteristics of respondents. For example, motivations of a nationwide sample of river users were found to vary with experience level of respondents (Williams et al. 1990) and by type and size of user group (Heywood 1987). Motivations of state park visitors were related to visitor expenditures (McCool and Reilly 1993) and motivations of mountain climbers were related to experience level of respondents (Ewert 1994).

A study of wilderness visitors is illustrative of these second-generation studies (P. Brown and Haas 1980). This study involved a survey of visitors to the Rawah Wilderness Area, CO. Initial cluster analysis identified eight motivational domains important across the sample as shown in Table 7-4. Respondents were then grouped through a second clustering procedure according to their scores on the eight motivational domains. Five basic "types" of visitors were thus identified. The study describes each visitor type and suggests ways in which this kind of information might be incorporated in wilderness management. For example, visitor types 1 and 2 both place moderate to strong emphasis on seven of the eight motivational domains, but differ on the eighth, Meeting/Observing Other People. Type 1 visitors (19% of the sample) rated this domain as slightly adding to satisfaction, while type 2 visitors (10% of the sample) rated this domain as moderately detracting from satisfaction. These findings suggest that two wilderness zones might be created serving somewhat different objectives and visitors. Both zones would be managed to serve the first seven motivations described (Closeness to Nature, Escape Pressure, etc.), but with different use and contact levels allowed.

text continues on page 171

Table 7-4. Five types of visitors to the Rawah Wilderness Area, CO. (Adapted from Brown and Haas 1980.)

Type	No. of respondents[1]	% of sample[1]	Motivational Domain							
			Relationship with nature	Escape pressures	Autonomy	Achievement	Reflection on personal values	Sharing/recollection	Risk taking	Meeting/observing other people
1	50	19	Most strongly added[2]	Most strongly added	Strongly added	Strongly added	Strongly added	Strongly added	Slightly added	Slightly added
2	27	10	Most strongly added	Strongly added	Strongly added	Strongly added	Strongly added	Moderately added	Slightly added	Moderately detracted
3	44	17	Strongly added	Strongly added	Moderately added	Strongly added	Moderately added	Strongly added	Neither	Slightly added
4	53	20	Strongly added	Strongly added	Strongly added	Moderately added	Moderately added	Slightly added	Slightly added	Neither
5	60	23	Moderately added	Moderately added	Moderately added	Slightly added	Slightly added	Slightly added	Neither	Neither

1. Thirty respondents (11% of the sample) were identified as unique in the sense that they were not grouped with any of the five types. This was primarily a function of missing data for these respondents rather than their true uniqueness.
2. Respondents were asked to state the importance of these motivations to their satisfaction.

Table 7-5. Recreation motivation domains, scales, and scale items*

Domains	Scales/Scale Items**

A. Achievement/ Stimulation	1. Reinforcing self-image
	  a. To gain a sense of self-confidence
	  b. To develop a sense of self-pride
	2. Social recognition
	  a. To have others think highly of you for doing it
	  b. To show others you can do it
	3. Skill development
	  a. To become better at it
	  b. To develop your skills and abilities
	4. Competence testing
	  a. To test your abilities
	  b. To learn what you are capable of
	5. Excitement
	  a. To have thrills
	  b. To experience excitement

B. Autonomy/ Leadership	1. Independence
	  a. To feel my independence
	  b. To be on my own
	2. Autonomy
	  a. To be my own boss
	  b. To be free to make your own choices
	3. Control—Power
	  a. To control things
	  b. To be in control of things that happen

C. Risk Taking	1. Risk taking
	  a. To take risks
	  b. To chance dangerous situations

D. Equipment	1. Equipment
	  a. To use your equipment
	  b. To talk to others about [your/our] equipment

E. Family Togetherness	1. Family togetherness
	  a. To do something with your family
	  b. To bring your family closer together

F. Similar People	1. Being with friends
	  a. To be with members of [your/our]group
	  b. To be with friends
	2. Being with similar people
	  a. To be with [others/people] who enjoy the same things you do
	  b. To be with people having similar values

* Referred to by Driver and associates as Recreation Experience Preference Scales and Domains
**Core scale items

G. New People
1. Meeting new people
   a. To talk to new and varied people
   b. To meet other people in the area
2. Observing other people
   a. To be with and observe other people using the area
   b. To meet other people in the area

H. Learning
1. General learning
   a. To develop [my/your] knowledge of things [here/there]
   b. To learn more about things [here/there]
2. Exploration
   a. To experience new and different things
   b. To discover new things
3. Geography of area
   a. To get to know the lay of the land
   b. To learn about the topography of the land
4. Learn about nature
   a. To study nature
   b. To learn more about nature

I. Enjoy Nature
1. Scenery
   a. To view the scenery
   b. To view the scenic beauty
2. General nature experience
   a. To be close to nature
   b. To enjoy the smells and sounds of nature

J. Introspection
1. Spiritual
   a. To develop personal, spiritual values
   b. To grow and develop spiritually
2. Introspection
   a. To think about your personal values
   b. To think about who you are

K. Creativity
1. Creativity
   a. To be creative
   b. To do something creative such as sketch, paint, take photographs

L. Nostalgia
1. Nostalgia
   a. To think about good times you've had in the past
   b. To bring back pleasant memories

M. Physical Fitness
1. Exercise—physical fitness
   a. To get exercise
   b. To keep physically fit

N. Physical Rest
1. Physical rest
   a. To relax physically
   b. To rest physically

O. Escape Personal/
Social Pressures

1. Tension release
   a. To help get rid of some clutched-up feelings
   b. To help release or reduce some built-up tensions
2. Slow down mentally
   a. To have your mind move at a slower pace
   b. To give your mind a rest
3. Escape role overloads
   a. To get away from the usual demands of life
   b. To avoid everyday responsibilities for a while
4. Escape daily routine
   a. To have a change from your daily routine
   b. To have a change from everyday routine

P. Escape Physical
Pressure

1. Tranquility
   a. To experience tranquility
   b. To experience solitude
2. Privacy
   a. To feel isolated
   b. To be alone
3. Escape crowds
   a. To be away from crowds of people
   b. To experience more elbow room
4. Escape physical stressors
   a. To get away from the clatter and racket back home
   b. To get away from the noise back home

Q. Social Security

1. Social security
   a. To be near considerate people
   b. To get with respectful people

R. Escape Family

1. Escaping family
   a. To be away from the family for a while
   b. To escape the family temporarily

S. Teaching/Leading
Others

1. Teaching—sharing skills
   a. To teach your outdoor skills to others
   b. To share what you have learned with others
2. Leading others
   a. To help direct the activities of others
   b. To lead other people

T. Risk Reduction

1. Risk moderation
   a. To be near others who could help if you need them
   b. To know others are nearby
2. Risk avoidance
   a. To be sure of what will happen to you
   b. To avoid the unexpected

U. Temperature

1. Temperature
   a. To get away from the heat
   b. To experience a nicer temperature

Research on recreation motivations has resulted in a standardized "pool" of items that can be used to measure motivations. These items are shown in Table 7-5 and are organized into twenty-one "domains" or basic categories.

Benefits-Based Management

Early in this chapter, the behavioral approach to understanding recreation was illustrated in Table 7-1. This model identifies four levels or hierarchies of demand for recreation. The empirical research described in this chapter has focused primarily on Level 3 demands and motivations. However, conceptual and empirical work has begun to focus on Level 4 demands, the ultimate or higher-order benefits of recreation that flow to individuals and society at large. This body of work and its application is generally termed "benefits-based management."

Benefits potentially associated with recreation are broadly defined (Driver 1990, 1996). First, the fundamental concept of benefits can include attainment of a desired condition, an improved condition, and prevention of an unwanted condition. Second, benefits can be seen as accruing to individuals, society at large, the economy, and the environment (Driver et al. 1991, Stein and Lee 1995). Personal benefits might include advances in physical and mental health and personal growth and development. Social benefits might include strengthening of family relationships, enhanced community pride, and reduction of social deviance and dysfunction. Economic benefits might include increased productivity, reduced health costs, and local economic growth. Environmental benefits might include reduced pollution levels and protection of endangered species and critical wildlife habitat.

The objective of benefits-based management is to allow managers to more directly measure and facilitate benefits associated with recreation participation (L. Allen 1996, L. Allen and McGovern 1997). Managers are encouraged to specify the benefits they wish to provide, design facilities and services to facilitate these benefits, and measure the extent to which benefits have been realized. Among other things, this requires an understanding of the potential relationships among the four levels of demand for recreation as outlined in Table 7-1. In other words, what benefits are associated with fulfillment of recreation motivations, and how are motivations, in turn, related to recreation activities and the settings in which they occur? Initial empirical studies are suggestive of such relationships (Borrie and Roggenbuck 1995, Stein and Lee 1995, Tarrant et al. 1994, Tarrant 1996). However, this issue is complex and study findings are not definitive. Research on this issue is described more fully in Chapter 8, which addresses the Recreation Opportunity Spectrum, a framework for addressing the structural relationships comprising recreation experience.

Conceptual and Methodological Issues

Several conceptual and methodological issues concerning motivations for recreation have been raised in the literature. Exploration and documentation of relationships among recreation activities, settings, motivations, and benefits was noted above, and this issue is discussed more fully in Chapter 8. A related issue concerns the implied rigor of the structure of such relationships. Traditional interpretations of the behavioral approach to recreation suggest a highly structured "process" by which alternative combinations of recreation activities and settings combine to fulfill selected motivations and produce selected benefits (Driver 1985). Some studies, however, suggest that there may be more emotional and symbolic elements involved in recreation (Williams et al. 1992b). This suggests a more holistic or integrated approach to understanding recreation; recreation activity can be understood as something more than the sum of its attributes or "parts" (P. Brown 1989). The concept of "sense of place" has been suggested as an alternative theoretical construct that may contribute to our understanding of recreation (Williams et al. 1992b). Sense of place concerns the meanings associated with places, including recreation areas, that are formed through personal experience (Tuan 1974, 1977, Relph 1976). Initial empirical studies suggest that sense of place and related concepts can help illuminate recreation behavior (More 1980b, Williams et al. 1992b, R. Moore and Graefe 1994, Ballinger and Manning 1998).

Several methodological issues surround measurement of motivations for recreation. One concerns the basic measurement approach or technique. It was noted in Chapter 5 that the search for relationships between use level and crowding has been partially confounded by the measurement techniques used: attitude surveys and behavioral observations have sometimes yielded conflicting results. Confidence in the findings of social science research can be bolstered when similar results are obtained from divergent study approaches.

It has been noted in the literature that there are three basic approaches to measuring human behavior in general, and motivations for recreation in particular: verbal behavior, overt nonverbal behavior, and physiological response (Driver 1976). Each approach has inherent strengths and weaknesses, and each approach could ideally be used as a check on the others. However, as with crowding research, nearly all studies on motivations for recreation have relied on verbal behavior as manifested in written responses to attitude surveys. Exceptions include a study that relied at least partially on participant observation (Bryan 1977) and studies of pupillary response to natural landscape scenes (G. Peterson and Neumann 1969, Wenger and Videbeck 1969), though these studies had little focus on motivations for recreation. Additional attention to alternative measures of motivations will enhance the confidence with which findings might be applied in the field.

An additional set of methodological issues concerns the time and circumstances under which motivations are measured. A study of the visitor motivation for escaping physical stress was administered to fishers both on-site and four months later by mail (Manfredo 1984). Inconsistencies were found in responses among the same group of subjects. Similar findings have been reported for other types of recreationists (Williams et al. 1988, Stewart 1992). Differences in motivation have also been found to be related to outcome of the recreation experience (Ewert 1993). Motivations reported by mountain climbers after their trips varied as a function of whether or not respondents reached the summit. This suggests that measures of motivations may vary based on when they were administered—before or after the experience. It has been suggested that motivations be measured immediately prior to the recreation activity to determine experience preferences, immediately after the recreation activity to determine attainment of experiences, and some months after the recreation activity to determine enduring experiences (Manfredo et al. 1996).

Summary and Conclusions

1. Interpretation of outdoor recreation has evolved from an "activity approach" to a "behavioral approach" that focuses on why people participate in recreation activities and the benefits gained from such participation.

2. An expanded view of the behavioral approach recognizes four levels of demand for outdoor recreation: activities, settings, motivations, and benefits.

3. Empirical tests of the behavioral approach to outdoor recreation indicate that there are a variety of motivations for participating in outdoor recreation, and these motivations can be measured.

4. Outdoor recreationists can be segmented into relatively homogeneous groups based on their motivations.

5. Benefits-based management has been proposed as a framework for facilitating provision of benefits related to recreation participation. A wide variety of potential benefits have been associated with recreation, but empirical linkages among recreation activities, settings, motivations, and benefits are unclear.

6. Incorporation of emotional and symbolic meanings attached to recreation areas into the behavioral approach or model of recreation may enhance understanding of recreation behavior.

7. Alternative techniques should be applied to measuring recreation motivations to provide methodological checks on the predominant verbal/attitudinal approach.

Notes

1. The experiences derived from participation in recreation activities have been subject to a variety of terminology, including "motivations," "satisfactions," "psychological outcomes," and "experience expectations." The term "motivations" is used generally throughout this chapter and book for the sake of consistency.

2. While such studies clearly suggest that there are multiple motivations and sources of satisfaction in hunting, the importance of bagging game should not be unduly minimized. An open-ended survey conducted by Stankey et al. (1973) asked respondents what big game hunting means. A majority of hunters replied in terms of game bagging outcomes, though a substantial minority gave general outdoor enjoyment and environmental amenity-related responses. The authors conclude from their study:

   > Success [game-bagging] is only one outcome to which hunters aspire; satisfactions derived from esthetic enjoyment, solitude, sociability, challenge, and other aspects of the experience represent significant, and perhaps at times, superior returns to the individual (Stankey et al. 1973:82).

   It seems reasonable to conclude that some minimally acceptable chance of bagging game is a necessary but incomplete element of managing hunting, and other elements will also be necessary to ensure broadly satisfying hunting experiences.

8

The Recreation Opportunity Spectrum
Designs for Diversity

Diversity in Outdoor Recreation

Over the course of this book, numerous studies of visitors to outdoor recreation areas are reviewed. The objectives, scope, and methods of these studies are highly variable, but at least one general finding has been pervasive: outdoor recreation is diverse. This is a recurring theme whether in regard to recreation activities, socioeconomic and cultural characteristics of visitors, attitudes about policy, preferences for services and facilities, sensitivity to crowding and conflict, experience level, and motivations for recreation participation. Diversity in tastes for outdoor recreation is found equally in studies of developed campgrounds and investigations of wilderness hikers. For example, an early study of users of automobile campgrounds concluded that study data:

> . . . illustrate the characteristic heterogeneity of camping as a recreation activity and the multitude of reasons people may have for camping. Diversity in the kinds of facilities provided is an important consideration in recreation planning (King 1966:2).

A study of wilderness hikers concludes similarly:

> Wilderness visitors are not in any sense a uniform or homogeneous population . . . Represented among wilderness visitors are value systems that cover a wide and often conflicting range (Stankey 1972:92).

Research points out that not only are there differences in taste among people, but that people's tastes change over time as well (Burch 1966). A study in the Pacific Northwest found that the type of camping chosen (wilderness camping, automobile camping, or some combination of the two) was strongly related to changes in stage of the family life cycle. A nationwide panel study of campers found similar relationships between camping activity and family life cycle (LaPage 1973, LaPage and Ragain 1974). Based on these relationships, it has been suggested that "The forest camping system is like an omnibus—the seats are often full but often occupied by different persons as they adjust to the flow of time" (Burch 1966).

Diversity is also evident when the "averaging issue" in outdoor recreation is recognized. The example of "the average camper who doesn't exist" was described in Chapter 3 (E. Shafer 1969). The potential problem of relying too heavily on averages has been illustrated as it might apply to camping (J. A. Wagar 1963, 1966, Lime 1974). Studies show that some campers prefer very elaborate facilities for comfort and convenience, while others prefer relatively simple facilities. Moreover, there is a wide range of opinion between these extremes. Providing a single, uniform type of camping opportunity—near the midpoint of the range based on averages, indeed at *any* point along the range—will leave many campers, quite possibly even the majority, less than fully satisfied. However, by offering a range of possibilities, more campers' preferences can be met.

This line of reasoning has been used to develop a definition of quality in outdoor recreation based on diversity (J. A. Wagar 1966). The difficulty in distinguishing between quality and type of recreation opportunities has been a persistent problem for both visitors and managers. It is common to be quite subjective when associating certain types of recreation opportunities with high quality. Those whose recreation tastes are oriented toward the remote and primitive, for example, may consider wilderness recreation to be of high quality and automobile campgrounds as something less. But high quality can and should be found among all types of recreation opportunities. From the perspective of the individual, quality is most appropriately defined as the degree to which a recreation opportunity meets one's needs. From a broader, societal perspective, quality in outdoor recreation can be equated with provision of diverse recreation opportunities.

Diversity in outdoor recreation has also been rationalized in economic terms using an example of a hypothetical undeveloped recreation area (J. A. Wagar 1974). If the area were to be used for wilderness recreation, it might support 3,000 visitor-days of recreation each year. If intensively developed, it might support 300,000 visitor-days of recreation. But the decision between these two alternatives should take into account the issue of scarcity. If developed recreation opportunities are relatively plentiful and wilderness recreation scarce, society may place more value on creating additional wilderness recreation opportunities even though they will accommodate fewer visitor-days. This is in keeping with the economic theory of marginal utility: the more we have of some good or value, the less importance is placed on each additional unit.

This economic rationale has been borne out in an empirical test of Colorado deer hunting that explored public willingness to pay for selected types of hunting opportunities (R. Miller et al. 1977). The value of deer hunting was found to vary among types of hunting opportunities and types of hunting groups. From this, it was demonstrated that total satisfaction of hunters (as measured by willingness to pay) could be increased by providing diversity in hunting opportunities.

Diversity has also been rationalized in political terms (Burch 1974). It can be argued that without broad political support, outdoor recreation areas are not likely to be maintained by society at large, and that this support is not likely to be forthcoming if outdoor recreation areas do not serve the needs of a broad spectrum of the population. Therefore, managers should strive to serve this diversity and not necessarily adhere too closely to the preferences or tastes of any one group or type of visitor.

This chapter outlines several conceptual frameworks designed to encourage diversity in outdoor recreation opportunities. Special emphasis is placed on the Recreation Opportunity Spectrum. Linking the components implicit in these conceptual frameworks—activities, settings, motivations, and benefits—remains a challenge to researchers and managers.

Designs for Diversity

Several studies have noted that a systematic approach to outdoor recreation management is needed if diversity is to be designed appropriately. It would be difficult for a single recreation area, regardless of size, to provide a full spectrum of recreation opportunities. Examining each recreation area in isolation will usually lead to management decisions favoring the majority or plurality of potential visitors. While this is justified in many cases, this process will ultimately result in an entire system of recreation areas designed for the average visitor while neglecting a desirable element of diversity. Instead, each recreation area should be evaluated as part of a larger system of areas, each contributing as best it can to serve the diverse needs of the public. In this way, low density and other minority recreation opportunities can be justified (J. A. Wagar 1974). It has been suggested that this systematic approach be applied on a broad, regional basis; this way management can best ensure "a diverse resource base capable of providing a variety of satisfactions" (Stankey 1974).

Recognition of the need for diversity has led to a number of suggested classification or zoning systems for recreation areas. Very early precursors to recreation opportunity classification systems suggested that different types of forests be planned and managed to meet the needs of alternative recreation activities (R. Marshall 1933, 1938), and that recreation opportunities should range "from the flowerpot at the window to the wilderness" (J. V. Wagar 1951). One of the earliest, more formal suggestions was contained in a handbook on wildland planning which suggested seven zones ranging from "wilderness" to "semi-suburban" (Carhart 1961). Just a year later, the Outdoor Recreation Resources Review Commission included among its major recommendations a proposal for a six-fold classification system for recreation areas, ranging from high-density use to extensive primitive areas, to be applied to all federal recreation lands (ORRRC 1962). A number of other recreation classification systems have been proposed as shown in Table 8-1. Recent attention, however, has focused on a relatively highly developed recreation classification system called the Recreation Opportunity Spectrum (ROS).

Table 8-1. Recreation classification or zoning systems.

Carhart (1961)	Seven wildland zones ranging from wilderness to semi-suburban
ORRRC (1962)	Six area classifications ranging from high-density to historic/cultural
Lloyd and Fischer (1972)	Concentrated and dispersed
Nash (1982)	Paved, pastoral, primeval
National Park Service	Three area classifications: natural, historical, and recreational
US Forest Service	Five recreation experience levels ranging from those emphasizing challenge, solitude, and demanding high skills to those involving extensive facilities and few skills
Wild and Scenic Rivers Act (PL90-542)	Three classes of rivers: wild, scenic, and recreational
National Trails Act (PL90-543)	Three classes of trails: scenic, recreational, and side

The Recreation Opportunity Spectrum

ROS is a conceptual framework for encouraging diversity in outdoor recreation opportunities. A range of factors that define recreation experiences are combined in alternative arrangements to describe diverse recreation opportunities. As noted above, the concept of diversity underlying ROS is not new. In an early conceptualization of satisfaction in camping, it was suggested that selected components of camping were important to satisfaction, and these components were referred to as "continua," a concept that is at the heart of the ROS system (Bultena and Klessig 1969).

The distinguishing characteristic of ROS is the degree to which it has been formalized and translated into management guidelines. The relationships among site factors that combine to define recreation opportunities have been arranged in configurations that suggest relatively standard categories of opportunities. Moreover, the system has been adopted by two major federal recreation agencies, the U.S. Forest Service and the Bureau of Land Management (Buist and Hoots 1982, Driver et al. 1987a). ROS was developed simultaneously by two groups of researchers: Clark and Stankey (1979a) and Brown, Driver, and associates (P. Brown et al. 1978, Driver and Brown 1978, P. Brown et al. 1979). The approaches are quite similar, but some important differences also exist.

Both approaches to ROS recognize a four-fold hierarchical framework of demands for recreation as described in Chapter 7 on recreation motivations—activities, settings, motivations, and ultimate benefits— and the focus of both approaches is on Level 2 demands, settings. Brown, Driver, and associates take a more empirically oriented approach to ROS, seeking to link settings to the motivations or psychological outcomes they fulfill. This is a natural extension of their work on motivations for recreation described in Chapter 7.

Clark and Stankey (1979a) take a more applied approach. They note that as knowledge of linkages between recreation settings and psychological outcomes improves, so will the efficacy of meeting visitor demands. But in the meantime, managers should emphasize the provision of diversity in recreation settings based on the assumption that a corresponding diversity of experiences will be produced.

Both approaches also recognize, as discussed in Chapter 4, that recreation settings are defined by three broad categories of factors: environmental, social, and managerial. By describing ranges of these

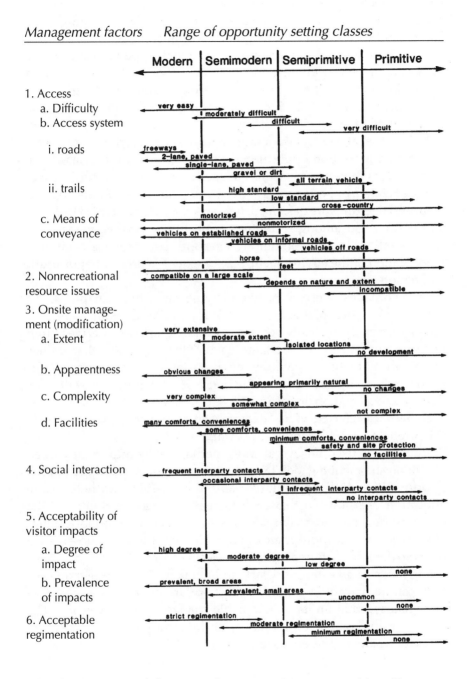

Management factors   Range of opportunity setting classes

Figure 8-1. Factors defining outdoor recreation opportunities. (From Clark and Stankey 1979a.)

factors, selected types of recreation opportunities can be defined quite closely. Clark and Stankey (1979a) are most specific in defining these factors and the resulting recreation opportunity types. They suggest that six basic factors—access, nonrecreational resource uses, on-site management, social interaction, acceptability of visitor impacts, and acceptable regimentation—be used to define the opportunity spectrum as shown in Figure 8-1. Each opportunity type is defined by the combination of factors lying directly beneath it in the figure.

P. Brown et al. (1978) take a more narrative or descriptive approach to defining recreation opportunity types. Six opportunity classes are identified, as shown in Table 8-2. For each recreation opportunity class, the associated experience provided and the physical, social, and managerial settings are described. Five specific factors are used to define and distinguish among recreation opportunity classes: managerial regimentation, interaction among user groups, evidence of human modification of the environment, size or extent of area of opportunity, and remoteness.

In the broadest sense, ROS, like carrying capacity in Chapter 4, is a conceptual or organizing framework for thinking about recreation opportunities. It explicitly recognizes that experiences derived from recreation are related to the settings in which they occur, and that settings in turn are a function of environmental, social, and managerial factors. By describing ranges of these factors, ROS illustrates the potential diversity of recreation opportunities. The underlying rationale for ROS is sometimes referred to as "experience-based setting management" (Manfredo et al. 1983, Floyd and Gramann 1997).

ROS can be used in several ways, perhaps most importantly as an allocation and planning tool. Taking into account demands for recreation opportunities and their relative abundance, ROS can help guide allocation decisions so that each recreation area contributes to the diversity desirable in a complete system of recreation opportunities. Moreover, once an appropriate opportunity type has been chosen, ROS can help define specific management objectives for each setting attribute. Using noise as an example, Clark and Stankey (1979b) illustrate how ROS can be helpful in setting an appropriate management objective and ensuring that limits of acceptable change are not exceeded. The ROS concept has been adopted as an integral part of the carrying capacity frameworks described in Chapter 4.

text continues on page 185

Table 8-2. The Recreation Opportunity Spectrum. (From P. Brown et al. 1978.)

Opportunity class/ Experience opportunity	Physical, social, and managerial setting
Primitive (P) Opportunity for isolation (from the sights and sounds of people), to feel a part of the natural environment, to have a high degree of challenge and risk, and to use outdoor skills.	Area is characterized by essentially unmodified natural environment of fairly large size. Concentration of users is fairly low and evidence of other area users is minimal. The area is managed to be essentially free from evidence of human-induced restrictions and controls. Only essential facilities for resource protection are used and are constructed of on-site materials. No facilities for comfort or convenience of the user are provided. Spacing of groups is informal and dispersed to minimize contacts with other groups or individuals. Motorized use within the area is not permitted.
Semi-primitive, non-motorized (SPNM) Some opportunity for isolation from the sight and sounds of people, but not as important as for primitive opportunities. Opportunity to have a high degree of interaction with the natural environment, to have moderate challenge and risk, and to use outdoor skills.	Area is characterized by a predominantly unmodified natural environment of moderate to large size. Concentration of users is low, but there is often evidence of other area users. The area is managed in such a way that minimum on-site controls and restrictions may be present, but are subtle. Facilities are primarily provided for the protection of resource values and safety of users. On-site materials are used where possible. Spacing of groups may be formalized to disperse use and provide low-to-moderate contacts with other groups or individuals. Motorized use is not permitted.
Semi-primitive, motorized (SPM) Some opportunity for isolation from the sights and sounds of people, but not as important as for primitive opportunities. Opportunity to have a high degree of interaction with the natural environment, to have moderate challenge and risk, and to use outdoor skills. Explicit opportunity to use motorized equipment while in the area.	Area is characterized by a predominantly unmodified natural environment of moderate to large size. Concentration of users is low, but there is often evidence of other area users. The area is managed in such a way that minimum on-site controls and restrictions may be present, but are subtle. Facilities are primarily provided for the protection of resource values and safety of users. On-site materials are used where possible. Spacing of groups may be formalized to disperse use and provide low-to-moderate contacts with other groups or individuals. Motorized use is permitted.

Opportunity class/ *Experience opportunity*	*Physical, social, and managerial setting*

Rustic (R)
About equal opportunities for affiliation with user groups and opportunities for isolation from sights and sounds of people. Opportunity to have a high degree of interaction with the natural environment. Challenge and risk opportunities are not very important. Practice and testing of outdoor skills may be important. Opportunities for both motorized and non-motorized forms of recreation are possible.

Area is characterized by predominantly natural environment with moderate evidences of the sights and sounds of people. Such evidences usually harmonize with the natural environment. Concentration of users may be low to moderate with facilities sometimes provided for group activity. Evidence of other users is prevalent. Controls and regimentation offer a sense of security and are on-site. Rustic facilities are provided for convenience of the user as well as for safety and resource protection. Moderate densities of groups is provided for in developed sites and on roads and trails. Low to moderate densities prevail away from developed sites and facilities. Renewable resource modification and utilization practices are evident, but harmonize with the natural environment. Conventional motorized use is provided for in construction standards and design of facilities.

Concentrated (C)
Opportunities to experience affiliation with individuals and groups are prevalent as is the convenience of sites and opportunities. These factors are generally more important than the setting of the physical environment. Opportunities for wild-land challenges, risk-taking, and testing of outdoor skills are unimportant, except for activities such as down-hill skiing for which challenge and risk-taking are important.

Area is characterized by substantially modified natural environment. Renewable resource modification and utilization practices are primarily to enhance specific recreation activities and to maintain vegetative cover and soil. Sights and sounds of people are readily evident, and the concentration of users is often moderate to high. A considerable number of facilities are designed for use by a large number of people. Facilities are often provided for special activities. Moderate to high densities of groups and individuals are provided for in developed sites, on roads and trails, and water surfaces. Moderate densities are provided for away from developed sites. Facilities for intensified motorized use and parking are available.

Opportunity class/ Experience opportunity	Physical, social, and managerial setting
Modern urbanized (MU) The opportunities to experience affiliation with individuals and groups are prevalent, as is the convenience of sites and opportunities. These factors are more important than the setting of the physical environment. Opportunities for wildland challenges, risk-taking, and testing outdoor skills are unimportant.	Area is characterized by a substantially urbanized environment, although the background may have natural elements. Renewable resource modification and utilization practices are to enhance specific recreation activities. Vegetative cover is often exotic and manicured. Soil protection is usually accomplished with hard surfacing and terracing. Sights and sounds of people, on-site, are predominant. Large numbers of users can be expected both on-site and in nearby areas. A considerable number of facilities are designed for the use and convenience of large numbers of people and include electrical hookups and contemporary sanitation services. Controls and regimentation are obvious and numerous. Facilities for highly intensified uses and parking are available with forms of mass transit often available to carry people throughout the site.

The specific setting attributes of ROS can also be useful in designing and conducting inventories of recreation opportunities (Kliskey 1998). ROS also provides an explicit framework within which consequences of alternative management actions can be evaluated. And finally, ROS provides a means of matching desired visitor experiences with available opportunities. ROS provides relatively specific descriptions of available recreation opportunities, and this can help visitors more readily identify those opportunities most likely to meet their desired experiences. This can also reduce potential conflict between incompatible recreation activities (Daniels and Krannich 1990). If recreation resources are consistently managed for defined types of opportunities that are made known to the public, this is likely to have substantial benefits to both visitors and managers (Jubenville and Becker 1983). Visitors are more likely to be satisfied with the opportunities they select, and managers are less likely to have to resort to regulatory measures designed to control inappropriate visitor use.

Linking Activities, Settings, Motivations, and Benefits

The previous chapter on motivations for recreation suggested that recreation can be understood within the behavioral approach or model. This model outlined a basic structure under which recreationists participate in selected activities in specific settings to fulfill motivations that in turn lead to benefits. Under this model, managers might be able to provide recreation opportunities (comprised of alternative activities and settings) designed to fulfill certain motivations and produce related benefits. ROS, by suggesting a series of relationships among these factors, begins to provide a formal structure within which this model can be made operational.

Relationships among the four components of the behavioral model have received relatively little empirical testing. Some of these linkages appear intuitively obvious. Opportunities for contact with the natural environment, for example, are likely to be enhanced through limited development of the setting. Opportunities for solitude might be enhanced in relatively low use areas. And opportunities for challenge and risk-taking should be greater in areas providing only low-standard trails and other improvements. But these are only generalities, and knowledge about such relationships would be increased by empirical testing.

A number of studies have begun searching for these relationships. An early study of visitors to three western wilderness areas examined both motivations and physical setting preferences (Haas et al. 1979). Respondents reacted to a series of scaled items for both motivations and physical setting attributes, and these response sets were cluster analyzed following the procedures developed by Driver and associates described in Chapter 7. Several domains for both motivations and setting attributes were identified, but no attempt was made to relate the two. A second study of visitors to the Glenwood Springs Resource Area, CO, attempted to go a step further (P. Brown and Ross 1982). Multiple regression analysis was used to explore for relationships between motivations and settings, and a number of such relationships were found. The statistical significance of these relationships was generally enhanced when the sample was grouped according to activity. In other words, people sharing the same activity had more uniform relationships between motivations and setting preferences than all recreationists considered together.

Several studies have included more thorough tests of these relationships. A survey of snowmobilers and cross-country skiers asked respondents to rate motivation scale items and scale items describing selected attributes of the physical, social, and management environments (McLaughlin and Paradice 1980). Cluster analysis revealed four types of visitors based on recreation motivations. A number of statistical relationships were found among these types of users and desired attributes of the recreation environment.

A second study surveyed visitors to three wilderness areas, asking respondents to rate a number of motivation, setting attribute, and management action scale items (Manfredo et al. 1983). Each set of scale items was cluster analyzed, and five of the motivation clusters were selected for further object cluster analysis, isolating three visitor types based on similar motivation ratings. Type 1 visitors were labeled High Risk/Achievement Group, type 2 visitors were labeled Low Risk/Social Interaction Group, and type 3 visitors, who represented the largest proportion of visitors (60% of the sample) and tended to be less distinctive in their motivation ratings, were labeled Norm Group. The three types of visitors were then examined to see whether there were significant differences among them in activities engaged in and preferences for setting attributes and management actions. A number of differences were found. Though there were no differences among the three groups with regard to the four activities having the highest participation rates and the one activity with a very low participation rate, there were differences for the two activities with moderate participation rates. In addition, there were statistically significant differences among the three types of visitors on seven of the setting attribute clusters and four of the management action clusters. Though the magnitude of the differences was generally not large, the sample was relatively homogeneous—all respondents were wilderness visitors. A more diverse respondent group may have yielded greater levels of statistical significance.

A third study examined relationships among recreation activities, settings, and motivations for visitors to the Delaware state park system (Vogelsong et al. 1998). Relationships among all three of these variables were found. For example, visitors to historical parks (defined as a setting attribute) placed more emphasis of "nature/learning" than did visitors to other types of parks. Recreation activities also varied by type of park. For example, swimming/sunbathing was the dominant activity at seashore parks, hiking/walking predominated at suburban parks, and activities were more mixed at lake and pond-based parks.

A fourth study surveyed visitors to the Cohutta Wilderness, GA/ TN, and the Okefenokee Wilderness, GA (C. Shafer and Hammitt 1995b). Visitors were asked to rate the importance of five motivations for wilderness recreation; the importance of selected environmental, social, and managerial conditions in wilderness; and the extent to which visitors adopted selected behaviors to direct or control the recreation experience. A number of significant correlations were found, suggesting that visitors who rated selected motivations as important tended to associate certain wilderness settings with those motivations, and often behaved in ways designed to maximize attainment of those motivations. For example, visitors who rated the "unconfined" nature of wilderness experiences as highly important tended to use wilderness areas where fewer management restrictions were present.

A fifth study surveyed hunters in five states (Floyd and Gramann 1997). Respondents were asked to rate the importance of 30 motivation scale items, and resulting data were used in cluster analysis to group respondents into four "market segments." These four groups were then compared with regard to their preference scores for selected hunting setting characteristics, including access, amount of regimentation, presence of other hunters, traces of other hunters, nonrecreational uses, and on-site management. In many cases, the four market segments of hunters differed significantly in their preferences for specific setting features. For example, the "outdoor enthusiast" market segment of hunters reported the strongest preferences of any group for exclusive use, lack of evidence of previous hunters, and lack of development.

Several other studies have explored the relationships among selected elements of the behavioral model. Most have found what might best be described as "modest" relationships. These include relationships between the activities in which respondents participated and the type of resource selected within an Australian national park (Collins and Hodge 1984), activities and motivations of Delaware state park visitors (Confer et al. 1997), and setting attributes and type of resource selected by fishers in Colorado (Harris et al. 1985). However, a study of visitors to five protected areas in Costa Rica found little relation between motivations of visitors and setting preferences (Wallace and Smith 1997).

Two related studies have used different but less direct approaches to linking motives, settings, and activities. The first approach was an effort to translate motivational scale items directly into management terms (Knopp et al. 1979). Respondents were asked to rate a series of environmental setting elements that were designed to reflect basic motivations, rather than motivation items themselves. The data set was combined with preferences for eleven management actions and reduced through cluster analysis to four rather distinct associations, descriptively labeled "noise and development tolerant," "activity setting," "nature and solitude," and "nature with comfort and security." The second approach studied motivations for river floating across eleven diverse rivers (Knopf et al.1983). The study hypothesized that if motives are related to setting attributes, then significant differences in motives should be found across diverse settings. The results were mixed. While some significant differences in motives were found, there was a striking general similarity of motives across river settings. However, the degree to which similar motives were satisfied in different settings was not addressed.

A final group of studies has focused more directly on relationships among elements of ROS and benefits-based management as described in Chapter 7. A nationwide study of river floaters explored the degree to which motivations for recreation varied across river segments reflecting a primitive-urban continuum (Williams and Knopf 1985). Motivations were found to be more strongly related to other variables including water flow and trip duration. A study of campers in several Australian parks examined the relationships between one biophysical site attribute (naturalness) and one social site attribute (use level) (Heywood 1991, Heywood et al. 1991). Both linear and nonlinear relationships were found. A third study measured motivations of campers in three ROS classes at Land Between the Lakes, KY (Yuan and McEwen 1989). Thirteen motivations were found to vary across at least two ROS classes; however, no differences were found for eighteen motivations across any of the ROS classes. A related study of visitors to a Bureau of Land Management area in Colorado measured activity preferences, motivations associated with these activities, and preferred ROS class (Virden and Knopf 1989). While findings were mixed, the study concluded that "the data clearly suggests that relations among these variables exist, in support of tenets of underlying theoretical principles of the Recreation Opportunity Spectrum." Finally, another study of visitors to a Bureau of Land Management area in Colorado was designed to test relationships suggested by benefits-based management (Stein and Lee 1995). This study concluded that "the benefits visitors desire can be linked to particular recreation activities and to physical, social, and managerial setting characteristics." However, more support was found for the linkage between benefits and setting characteristics than for the linkage between benefits and recreation activities.

The research reviewed in this section offers some support for the conceptual foundation of ROS, benefits-based management, and related frameworks. However, definitive relationships among the elements comprising these frameworks are far from clear (McCool et al. 1985). It may be unrealistic to expect to find such highly structured relationships. It seems reasonable, for example, to expect that some motivations for recreation might be fulfilled through multiple activities and/or settings (McCool 1978). For instance, the motivation to experience nature might be fulfilled through mountain biking as well as hiking, and might be found in a city park as well as a national park. Indeed, some motivations, as well as benefits, may be nearly universal. Moreover, the empirical relationships assumed in ROS and related frameworks may be partially masked by limited choices that often confront recreationists and by peoples' inherent adaptability. Finally, the emotional and symbolic meanings that recreationists may assign to some recreation areas may confound the relationships assumed to underlie ROS.

Extending the Opportunity Spectrum

ROS has received broad and deserved attention from both managers and researchers. However, it can be expected to undergo some refinements in content and interpretation. The need for extended work on ROS has been explicitly noted by one of its original designers:

> It is critical that current and potential users recognize that, although considerable research and management experience underlies the ROS, many judgements have been made in making it operational. . . . The result is a "best guess" tool for planning, management, and research that will improve with experience if, and only if, the underlying assumptions, objectives, and expectations, and documentation of its use are explicitly stated. Changes in the specifications of the ROS details *will be necessary* (Clark 1982: 10, emphasis in original).

One suggestion to extend ROS concerns redefining the relationships among the three basic factors that describe recreation opportunities: environmental, social, and managerial conditions (Manning 1985a). In ROS, the implicit relationship among these factors is linear as illustrated

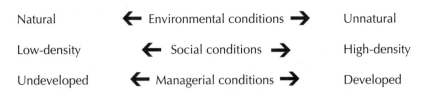

Natural   ← Environmental conditions →   Unnatural

Low-density   ← Social conditions →   High-density

Undeveloped   ← Managerial conditions →   Developed

Figure 8-2. Linear relationship among environmental, social, and managerial conditions as suggested by ROS. (From Manning 1985a.)

in Figure 8-1 and Table 8-2. As environmental conditions change from natural to unnatural, social and managerial conditions are suggested as changing in a corresponding manner. As a result, only certain combinations of factors appear possible. Of course, the linear relationships suggested in ROS are intuitively meaningful in many, perhaps most, cases; but theoretically, at least, there is no reason that natural environments cannot, or should not, support relatively high-density use under intensively managed conditions. Moreover, there is empirical evidence to suggest demand for these and other seemingly unconventional recreation opportunities. The diversity of attitudes, preferences, and motivations of users discussed in earlier chapters is generally suggestive of this, and several studies have addressed this issue directly. For example, an early study conducted in the Quetico-Superior Area, MN, found numerous "inconsistencies" among the response patterns of visitors (Bultena and Traves 1961). Noting that 99% of visitors strongly favored preserving the area in its natural state, the authors go on to point out that ". . . a relatively high proportion of the campers, and a somewhat smaller, although sizable proportion of the canoeists, inconsistently also favor the development of more facilities in the area." The authors refer to this substantial subpopulation of users as "wilderness compromisers." Another study of river users found that motivations of respondents tended to cluster into sets or packages, and that:

> Most of the sets or packages . . . meet the criterion of conventional wisdom, or an intuitive notion of what belongs together. On occasion, however, a grouping may occur which appears incongruous to the manager or planner. This package may have a small but real constituency which deserves attention (Knopp et al. 1979:325).

A study described earlier examined the relationships between campers' preferences for naturalness of campgrounds and their preferences for use level (Heywood 1991, Heywood et al. 1991). Both linear and nonlinear relationships were found. Finally, a study of backpackers at Grand Canyon National Park, AZ, suggests that greater variation in setting attributes, particularly those regarding management restrictions on campsite selection, may increase the degree to which motivations for solitude are fulfilled (Stewart and Carpenter 1989).

Potential users of ROS should be explicitly aware of the wide-ranging ways in which environmental, social, and managerial factors can be combined to produce diverse recreation opportunities. This seems in keeping with the intentions of the designers of ROS; publications describing the concept emphasize the need for diversity and caution that the guidelines offered to illustrate ROS, such as those contained in Figure 8-1 and Table 8-2, not be interpreted too strictly. Along these lines, several studies have suggested modifications to ROS in an effort to adapt it to regional variations (Lichtkoppler and Clonts 1990, Kaltenborn and Emmelin 1993, Lynch and Nelson 1997).

Potential limitations of ROS have been noted by pointing out that, in the most fundamental sense, it is visitors who produce recreation experiences, not managers (Driver and Brown 1984). Managers contribute to this process by providing what they believe to be appropriate settings and opportunities. In view of these limitations, ROS might best be considered an organizing or conceptual framework like carrying capacity as described in Chapter 4. And as with carrying capacity, a considerable amount of management judgment will be needed in applying ROS.

Summary and Conclusions

1. Outdoor recreation is highly diverse. Diversity is found in many elements of outdoor recreation, including recreation activities, socioeconomic and cultural characteristics of visitors, attitudes about policy, preferences for services and facilities, sensitivity to crowding and conflict, experience level, and motivations for recreation participation.
2. Corresponding diversity is needed in outdoor recreation opportunities.
3. High quality can and should be found among all types of outdoor recreation opportunities.

4. From the perspective of the individual recreationist, quality can be defined as the degree to which a recreation opportunity meets one's needs. From a broader, societal perspective, quality can be equated with provision of diverse recreation opportunities.

5. Several conceptual frameworks have been developed to encourage and guide provision and management of diverse outdoor recreation opportunities. The Recreation Opportunity Spectrum (ROS) is the most widely known and applied such framework. ROS is based on the following propositions:

   A. Recreation experiences are influenced by the settings in which recreation activities occur.

   B. Recreation settings are defined by environmental, social, and managerial conditions.

   C. Alternative combinations of environmental, social, and managerial conditions can be used to create a diversity of recreation opportunities.

6. Research has yet to establish definitive linkages among recreation activities, settings, motivations, and benefits. However, highly structured or rigid relationships among these variables may be an unrealistic expectation.

7. ROS and related conceptual frameworks should be extended to explicitly incorporate a wider variety of recreation opportunities based on alternative, nonlinear combinations of environmental, social, and managerial conditions.

8. ROS is a conceptual framework that can be useful in guiding recreation research and management. However, additional research is warranted on potential linkages among recreation activities, settings, motivations, and benefits. Moreover, a considerable amount of management judgment is needed in applying ROS.

9

Recreation Conflict
Goal Interference

Conflict in Outdoor Recreation

Early descriptive studies of outdoor recreation often found substantial conflict among participants in alternative recreation activities. Canoeists in the Boundary Waters Canoe Area, MN, for example, were found to be relatively tolerant of meeting other canoeists, but to dislike meeting motorboaters (Lucas 1964b, c). Similarly, visitors to several Western wilderness areas were found to be more tolerant of meeting backpackers than stock users (Stankey 1973, 1980a). And a study of four types of trail users in Ohio—hikers, horseback riders, bike riders, and motorcycle riders—developed "compatibility indexes" among these activities by asking participants how desirable it would be to encounter other types of trail users (McCay and Moeller 1976). The highest compatibility ratings for three of the four types of trail users were meeting their own kind.

Research has continued to identify and study many types of conflict in outdoor recreation, and conflict appears to be expanding as technology contributes to development of new recreation equipment and activities and as contemporary lifestyles become increasingly diverse (Williams 1993, W. Hendricks 1995, Watson 1995a). Examples include mountain bikes, helicopters for access to backcountry skiing, and use of llamas for backcountry hiking. Types of conflict identified in this body of research are summarized in Table 9-1. A distinctive finding among many of these studies is the asymmetric or "one way" nature of such conflict. That is, participants in one activity may object to the presence or behavior of participants in another activity, but the reverse is not true, at least not to the same degree.

Table 9-1. Examples of recreation conflict.

Study	Conflicting groups
Lucas 1964b, c	Canoeists and motorboaters
Brewer and Fulton 1973	Hikers and motorcyclists
Knopf et al. 1973	Canoeists and fishers
Knopp and Tyger 1973	Snowmobilers and cross-country skiers
Stankey 1973	Canoeists and motorboaters Hikers and stock users
Driver and Bassett 1975	Canoeists and fishers
McCay and Moeller 1976	Hikers, horseback riders, bikers, motorcyclists
Lime 1977b	Canoeists and motorboaters
Shelby 1980b	Motorized rafters and oar-powered rafters
Stankey 1980a	Hikers and stock users
Gramann and Burdge 1981	Fishers and water skiers
Noe et al. 1981, 1982	ORV users and nonusers
Adelman et al. 1982	Canoeists and motorboaters
E. Jackson and Wong 1982	Cross-country skiers and snowmobilers
McAvoy et al. 1986	Private boaters and commercial boaters
S. Moore and McClaran 1991	Hikers and pack stock users
Watson et al. 1991a, b	Hikers and mountain bikers
Ivy et al. 1992	Canoeists and motorboaters
Watson et al. 1994; Watson and Niccolucci 1992a	Hikers and stock users
Blahna et al. 1995	Hikers and horse users; horse users and llama users
Gibbons and Ruddell 1995	Backcountry skiers and helicopter skiers
Ramthun 1995	Hikers and mountain bikers
Vaske et al. 1995a	Hunters and nonhunters
Jacobi et al. 1996	Hikers and bikers

This chapter presents a theoretical model of the types of conflict described above. Following that, a series of empirical studies of conflict are reviewed. Based on this literature, an expanded model of recreation conflict is constructed and described. Finally, management implications of conflict research are discussed.

A Theoretical Model

Research and experience have documented many manifestations of crowding in outdoor recreation. However, this descriptive approach focuses primarily on what can be viewed as the symptoms of this issue—the apparent discord between different types of visitors. A more theoretical approach is needed to begin to understand why such conflicts exist and, ultimately, how they might be resolved or managed.

An initial theoretical model focused on potential origins of conflict (Jacob and Schreyer 1980). Conflict was defined as "goal interference attributed to another's behavior." This definition is based on both expectancy theory as described in Chapter 7 on recreation motivations and discrepancy theory (Fishbein and Ajzen 1975). Expectancy theory suggests that human behavior, including outdoor recreation, is goal-oriented. That is, people participate in recreation activities because they expect to achieve certain goals. Discrepancy theory defines satisfaction in outdoor recreation as the difference between desired and achieved goals. Conflict is a special application of discrepancy theory where dissatisfaction is attributed to another individual's or group's behavior. In this way, conflict tends to be differentiated from crowding or sheer competition for resources.

Jacob and Schreyer's theoretical model suggests that conflict can be linked to or caused by four major factors. The first of these factors is activity style and refers to the various personal meanings assigned to a recreation activity. Components of activity style can include intensity of participation, status as defined by equipment and expertise, and range of experience and definition of quality.

The second factor influencing conflict is resource specificity and refers to the significance attached to using a specific recreation resource for a given recreation experience. Components of resource specificity include evaluation of resource quality, sense of possession, and status based on intimate knowledge of a recreation area.

The third factor influencing conflict is mode of experience and refers to varying expectations of how the natural environment will be perceived. The primary component of this factor concerns the extent to which the recreation participant is focused or unfocused on the environment.

The final factor influencing conflict is lifestyle tolerance and refers to the tendency to accept or reject lifestyles different from one's own.

Components of lifestyle tolerance include level of technology and resource consumption and prejudice.

These four factors give rise to a set of ten propositions as shown in Table 9-2. These propositions suggest the conditions under which recreation conflict is most likely to occur. The four factors that can cause conflict as described above, along with their corresponding propositions, suggest that conflict is not necessarily an objective state, but can be an interpretation based on experience, beliefs, and attitudes. Moreover, conflict does not necessarily have to be a function of direct contact between individuals or groups. This theoretical model has been influential in guiding empirical conflict research.

A second theoretical model of conflict suggests that it is derived primarily by the interaction of two factors—dependence on technology and dominance over nature (Bury et al. 1983). However, these variables can be seen as part of recreation "activity style," and therefore incorporated within the more comprehensive model of conflict described above.

Table 9-2. Propositions of conflict. (From Jacob and Schreyer 1980.)

1. The more intense the activity style, the greater the likelihood of a social interaction with less intense participants will result in conflict.

2. When the private activity style confronts the status-conscious activity style, conflict results because the private activity style's disregard for status symbols negates the relevance of the other participant's status heirarchy.

3. Status-based interactivity conflict occurs when a participant desiring high status must interact with another viewed as lower status.

4. Conflict occurs between participants who do not share the same status hierarchies.

5. The more specific the expectations of what constitutes a quality experience, the greater the potential for conflict.

6. When a person who views the place's qualities as unequaled confronts behaviors indicating a lower evaluation, conflict results.

7. Conflict results when users with a possessive attitude toward the resource confront users perceived as disrupting traditional uses and behavioral norms.

8. Conflict occurs for high status users when they must interact with the lower status users who symbolize devaluation of a heretofore exclusive, intimate relationship with the place.

9. When a person in the focused mode interacts with a person in the unfocused mode, conflict results.

10. If group differences are evaluated as undesirable or a potential threat to recreation goals, conflict results when members of these two groups confront one another.

Empirical Studies of Conflict

A number of studies have addressed conflict empirically. Many of these studies are included in Table 9-1 and have documented the existence of conflict in outdoor recreation. However, many of these studies have gone on to explore underlying reasons for conflict using the theoretical model outlined above. In keeping with the goal interference definition of conflict, several studies have examined the role of motives in explaining recreation conflict. An early exploration of camping was suggestive of the potential importance of motives, at least from a conceptual basis (Clark et al. 1971a). Differences in recreation motivations on the part of "traditional" versus "modern" campers was theorized as causing conflict between different groups of campers. Early empirical studies of canoeists and fishers on the Au Sable River, MI, supported this notion empirically (Knopf et al. 1973, Driver and Bassett 1975). Fishers scored substantially lower on the motivation of affiliation, and this was thought to contribute to the conflict experienced between participants in these activities.

Additional evidence of the role of motivations in recreation conflict was found in a study of fishers and water skiers on Lake Shelbyville, IL (Gramann and Burdge 1981). Anglers were divided into two groups: those considered to have experienced conflict (defined as reporting having observed reckless boating), and those considered not to have experienced conflict. Significant differences were found between the two groups on several intuitively meaningful motivations, including escape, enjoying the smells and sounds of nature, using and discussing equipment, feeling their independence, doing things with family, and chancing dangerous situations. The differences, however, were not strong statistically, though this may have been due to the indirect measure of conflict.

A study of conflict between snowmobilers and cross-country skiers is also supportive of the role of motivations (E. Jackson and Wong 1982). Participants in both activities in Alberta, Canada, were surveyed as to their recreational orientation (as expressed by their participation in other recreation activities) and motivations for participation. Significant differences were found between the two groups on both aspects. The characteristics of the two activities studied were found to carry over into other recreational activities. Snowmobilers tended to participate in more extractive, active, and mechanized activities, while cross-country skiers tended to participate in passive, self-propelled, and low-impact activities. Moreover, there were statistically significant differences between the two groups on eleven of the sixteen motivation items studied. The study concluded that:

> Perceived conflicts are best understood not simply as an outcome of the choice of activity, but rather as stemming from a fundamental orientation of recreational preferences, expressed conceptually in terms of participation in other activities, and motivations for participation (E. Jackson and Wong 1982:59).

Three other studies also suggest that motives or goals are important in explaining and understanding recreation conflict. Visitors experiencing conflict related to off-road vehicles at Cape Hatteras National Seashore, NC, reported they were unable to fully attain goals associated with their visit and that this was attributed to other types of visitors (Noe et al. 1981). Similarly, conflict between nonmotorized backcountry skiers and those using helicopters for access to the backcountry was found to be related to differences in goal orientation between participants in the activities (Gibbons and Ruddell 1995). Finally, visitors to Padre Island National Seashore, TX, whose recreation goals were more dependent on the behavior of others were more likely to experience conflict (Ruddell and Gramann 1994).

A second issue addressed in several conflict studies concerns broad social values. Such social values may include beliefs, attitudes, and more global worldviews. For example, an early study of conflict between snowmobilers and cross-country skiers in Minnesota found significant differences between participants in these activities with regard to attitudes toward environmental issues and management of outdoor recreation areas (Knopp and Tyger 1973). Two studies addressing conflict between hikers and pack stock users have suggested the importance of "symbolic values" or broad philosophical considerations (S. Moore and McClaran 1991, Blahna et al. 1995). These considerations include beliefs about the meaning and importance of wilderness and the "appropriateness" of selected recreation activities.

Two other studies address the role of social values in recreation conflict. A study of visitors to the Rattlesnake National Recreation Area, MT, found that hikers often objected to the use of the area by mountain bikers (Watson et al. 1991a). However, many hikers could not specify behavior of bikers that was objectionable, suggesting that biking was considered inappropriate on the basis of broad philosophical grounds. A second study found conflict between hunters and nonhunters at

Mount Evans, CO, even though these activities were physically separated by zoning and vegetative screening (Vaske et al. 1995a, b). Lack of direct physical interaction between participants in these two types of activities suggests that conflict may be associated with contrasting attitudes and worldviews.

A related issue concerns perceived similarity between groups, or perceptions of alikeness. The degree to which groups perceive themselves as like or different from other groups has been found to be related to measures of recreation conflict. For example, motorboat users in the Boundary Waters Canoe Area, MN, considered themselves to be much like canoeists (Adelman et al. 1982). However, canoeists perceived themselves as very different than motorboaters. These differences in perceived alikeness are consistent with asymmetric conflict between participants in these two activities. Similarly, the study of visitors to the Rattlesnake National Recreation Area, MT, described above, found that mountain bikers considered themselves to be much like hikers, but hikers considered mountain bikers to be very different (Watson et al. 1991a). Again, this finding is in keeping with the asymmetric conflict between these groups. Interestingly, this study also found that hikers and mountain bikers, at least those who used the wilderness portion of the area, were quite similar on objective measures of their interest in wilderness and their attachment to wilderness as a recreation resource.

The studies described above, along with several others, have found a variety of other variables to be related to some form of recreation conflict. Most of these variables arise from the theoretical model of conflict described earlier. For example, an early study of conflict among visitors to reservoirs in Oregon suggests that the type and level of technology employed by visitors contributes to perceived conflict (Devall and Harvey 1981). Level of experience or commitment to a recreation activity has also been found to influence conflict for canoeists on the Delaware River, DE (Todd and Graefe 1989) and in the study of hunters and nonhunters to Mount Evans, CO, described above (Vaske et al. 1995a).

The degree to which visitors report symbolic attachment to recreation areas—often called "place attachment"—has been suggested as important in defining recreation conflict in three studies (Watson et al. 1991a, Williams et al. 1992b, Gibbons and Ruddell 1995). All of these studies address wilderness or related backcountry settings and span a variety of recreation activities.

A study of conflict between canoeists and motorboaters in Everglades National Park, FL, found two variables related to perceived conflict (Ivy et al. 1992). Tolerance of respondents for sharing resources with members of other activity groups and the degree to which expectations for encountering other types of activity groups were accurate were found to explain 40% of the variance in reported conflict for canoeists.

Two other variables have been found to be related to recreation conflict. A study of pack stock-related conflicts found safety concerns to influence reports of conflict (Blahna et al. 1995). And the study of visitors to Padre Island National Seashore, TX, described above found that visitor norms are related to perceived conflict (Ruddell and Gramann 1994). Visitors whose noise-related norms were relatively low tended to report conflict more often than those whose norms were less sensitive.

Finally, two recent studies have taken a more comprehensive approach to studying recreation conflict. The first focused on conflicts between hikers and stock users in three western wilderness areas (Watson et al. 1993, 1994). Seventeen variables hypothesized to be related to conflict were included in the study. These variables represented all four of the factors or categories of variables included in Jacob and Schreyer's (1980) theoretical model of conflict described earlier in this chapter. Several statistical models were developed that could predict perceived conflict based on these variables. Variables representing all four of the theoretical factors were useful in predicting conflict.

The other broad study of recreation conflict focused on hikers and mountain bikers on the Big Water Trail System, UT (Ramthun 1995). This study included four variables representing two of the basic factors thought to influence recreation conflict. Two of these variables—outgroup bias (unfavorable evaluation of groups to which one does not belong) and years of participation were found to have statistically significant effects on sensitivity to conflict.

An Expanded Conflict Model

Theoretical and empirical work can be synthesized to outline an expanded conceptual model of recreation conflict. The model proposed by Jacob and Schreyer (1980) continues to provide the basic outline for this expanded model as the empirical studies described above have supported inclusion of the four factors or categories of variables originally thought to influence recreation conflict. However, these

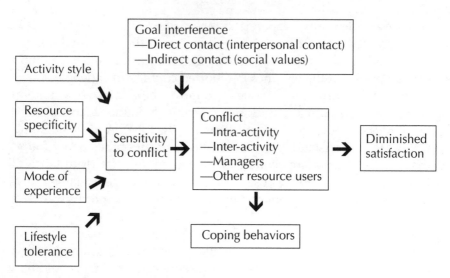

Figure 9-1. Expanded conflict model.

empirical studies and other conceptual treatments of conflict have suggested several additional components to a more comprehensive conflict model.

An expanded conflict model can be described schematically and narratively. Figure 9-1 outlines several basic components of an expanded model of recreation conflict. The four factors or categories of variables related to conflict as suggested by Jacob and Schreyer (1980) are shown. Interpreted broadly, these factors can be seen to encompass all of the variables found to be statistically related to conflict as described in the previous section on empirical research. For example, motivations for recreation can be interpreted as part of one's recreation activity style, social values as contributing to lifestyle tolerance, and place attachment as a subset of resource specificity.

However, the expanded model suggests that these variables determine sensitivity to conflict rather than conflict as it is experienced and attributed directly to others. In other words, they establish preconditions that are more likely to lead to conflict given certain behaviors or other stimuli. These variables have been suggested as creating a "catalyzing situation" for conflict (Blahna et al. 1995). The distinction between conflict and sensitivity to conflict is suggested in empirical studies of conflict that have identified and measured both of these elements (Watson et al. 1993, 1994, Ramthun 1995). Sensitivity to conflict is often measured generally and indirectly by asking respondents the extent to which they like or dislike meeting participants in other recreation activities. Conflict, on the other hand, is measured more specifically and directly by asking respondents if and how participants in other recreation activities interfered with their goals or enjoyment. This latter concept is more in keeping with the definition of conflict as "goal interference attributed to others." Empirical evidence suggests that sensitivity to conflict and conflict are related but separate concepts.

Research also suggests that conflict is not limited to that which occurs between recreation activities or groups (intra-activity conflict) (Hammitt 1989, Schreyer 1990). Conflict can occur within recreation groups (inter-activity conflict) (Todd and Graefe 1989), between recreation visitors and managers (Clark et al. 1971a), and between recreationists and other types of resource uses (McAvoy et al. 1986).

There is also a visitor response component to recreation conflict that has received only limited theoretical attention (Owens 1985, Schneider and Hammitt 1995). Recreationists who experience conflict may engage in coping behaviors that allow them to adapt to conflict stimuli. A variety of coping behaviors have been identified in crowding research as described in Chapter 5, but little is known about such behaviors with respect to conflict. Recreationists who are unable to cope experience diminished satisfaction or a lower-quality experience.

Finally, it is apparent that conflict can result from both direct and indirect contact between recreation participants. Direct contact refers to the overt behavior of others that is seen to interfere with one's goals. Indirect contact can refer to the simple presence (seen or unseen) of undesirable outgroups or artifacts of such groups, including associated environmental impacts.

Managing Conflict

Research on conflict suggests several insights for managing this issue. In particular, these insights are based on an understanding of conflict as something more than simple incompatibility among recreation activities. The traditional definition of conflict is "goal interference attributed to others," and its elaboration in the conflict model in Figure 9-1 suggests that conflict among groups is often the manifestation of underlying causes. Therefore, management action may not be effective if it does not address these underlying causes.

Zoning or separation of conflicting recreation activities is probably the most common management approach to conflict. The Recreation Opportunity Spectrum framework described in Chapter 8 is an example of this approach (Daniels and Krannich 1990). As the names suggest, the primary difference between the "semi-primitive non-motorized" and "semi-primitive motorized" opportunity classes or zones of ROS is the presence or absence of motorized vehicles. This serves to zone or separate potentially conflicting motorized and non-motorized activities. Research suggests that where direct or interpersonal conflict is present (i.e., the behavior of participants in one activity interferes with the attainment of goals for participants in another activity), zoning may be an effective management strategy.

However, educational programs may also be an effective management approach to conflict. This is particularly the case where conflict is related to indirect causes such as alternative social values. Educational programs can be effective in two ways. First, they can help establish a basic etiquette, or code of conduct or other behavioral norms that might lessen both direct and indirect conflict. Second, they can help address indirect or social values-related conflict by increasing tolerance of recreation visitors for other types of groups and activities (Ivy et al. 1992, Ramthun 1995) This might be accomplished by explaining the reasons behind certain behaviors that might be viewed as objectionable and by emphasizing similarities that are shared by recreation groups and activities. The potential of such management approaches is suggested by research that has found potentially important similarities between conflicting groups (Watson et al. 1991a), a general concern on the part of recreation visitors for the impacts they may have on others (Hollenhorst et al. 1995), a willingness to adopt modifications in behavior or restrictions on use to lessen such impacts (Hammitt et al. 1982, Noe et al. 1982), and the fact that some recreationists participate in multiple activities, some of which may be seen to conflict, suggesting that these individuals should have some empathy and tolerance for other types of visitors (Watson et al. 1996b).

Finally, the asymmetric or one-way nature of much recreation conflict suggests that management is needed to maintain the quality of recreation for visitors who are sensitive to conflicting uses. Without active management, visitors who are sensitive to conflict are likely to be dissatisfied or ultimately displaced.

Summary and Conclusions

1. Substantial conflict between groups and activities has been found in outdoor recreation. Examples of such conflict are summarized in Table 9-1.

2. Recreation conflict may be increasing, due at least partially to technology, which creates new recreation equipment and activities.

3. Recreation conflict tends to be characterized by an asymmetric or "one way" direction.

4. Conflict in recreation has been conceptualized on the basis of discrepancy theory and has been traditionally defined as "goal interference attributed to others."

5. Empirical studies have found that recreation conflict is related to a number of variables, including motivations for recreation, broad social values, perceived similarity of groups or activities, type and level of technology employed, level of experience or commitment, attachment to place, tolerance for sharing resources, expectation for encountering other types of activity groups, safety concerns, and recreation-related norms.

6. Theoretical and empirical research suggests that recreation conflict can be understood according to the schematic model outlined in Figure 9-1. Basic components of the model include the following:

   A. Four broad factors or categories of variables can lead to heightened sensitivity to conflict. These factors include activity style, resource specificity, mode of experience, and lifestyle tolerance.

   B. Both direct (or interpersonal) and indirect (or social values) contact can lead to goal interference and conflict.

   C. Conflict can occur among recreation activities, within recreation groups, between recreationists and managers, and between recreationists and other resource users.

   D. Some recreationists may adopt coping behaviors to reduce or eliminate conflict.

   E. Conflict can lead to diminished satisfaction on the part of some recreation visitors.

7. Research suggests several insights on managing recreation conflict. Zoning or separating recreation groups or activities can be effective where goal interference is related to direct or interpersonal contact.

However, educational programs are more likely to be effective where goal interference is related to indirect contact or differences in social values. The asymmetric or one-way nature of much recreation conflict suggests that management is needed to maintain the quality of recreation for visitors who are sensitive to conflict.

10

Substitutability
Alternative Recreation Opportunities

The Concept of Substitutability

The issue of substitutability—the extent to which one recreation activity might be a satisfactory substitute for another—has intrigued recreation researchers and managers for a long time. Early interest focused on the similarities of selected leisure and recreation activities and identification of groups of activities that seemed to be related. This early interest was primarily academic and was related to the issue of classification, which is an inherent part of all developing fields of scientific study. Early critiques of recreation research explicitly called for more research in this area (Meyersohn 1969, Burdge et al. 1981).

However, the extent to which recreation activities within such categories or types might be substituted for one another quickly developed a number of potentially important and practical implications. For example, if lower-cost recreation activities (e.g., pool swimming) could be substituted for higher-cost activities (e.g., swimming at ocean beaches), then management agencies might be able to provide recreation opportunities more efficiently. Moreover, dramatic increases in recreation activity, particularly in the 1960s and 1970s, suggested that the supply of certain types of recreation opportunities might not be sufficient to meet demand. Could alternative types of recreation substitute for those in short supply? Increasing demand also suggested that limits might have to be placed on the use of certain outdoor recreation areas and that some visitors may ultimately be displaced from recreation areas due to crowding and/or conflicting use. To what extent might substitutability of recreation activities help mitigate these issues?

This chapter reviews research on the potential substitutability of recreation activities. Initial research focused on identifying basic recreation "activity types," while more recent research has employed more direct measures of substitutability. Theoretical and methodological issues associated with substitutability are identified and described.

Activity Types

As noted above, initial interest in this area of research focused on identifying broad patterns of leisure and recreation behavior in the general population. In particular, attention was placed on defining clusters or types of activities that share certain characteristics (J. Christensen and Yoesting 1977, Vaske et al. 1990). Resulting clusters of activities are generally referred to as activity types.

The earliest explorations of activity types were primarily conceptual and qualitative. Two early texts on leisure suggested that general leisure activities might be classified in two ways. The first classified broad leisure patterns into five basic types: social, games and sports, art, movement, and immobility (Kaplan 1960). The second suggested that general leisure activities might be classified into a series of polar types, such as indoor and outdoor, active and passive, and solitary and social (DeGrazia 1962). A third example, based on more direct observation of visitors to twelve national forest campgrounds, identified six basic types of recreation activity, defined as symbolic labor, expressive play, subsistence play, unstructured play, structured play, and sociability (Burch 1965).

This conceptual approach was followed by a series of empirical studies that defined recreation activity types based on statistical correlations (Moss and Lamphear 1970, Bishop 1971, Burton 1971, Hendee et al. 1971, Neulinger and Breit 1971, Tatham and Dornoff 1971, Witt 1971, Field and O'Leary 1973, Romsa 1973, Hendee and Burdge 1974, O'Leary et al. 1974, Ritchie 1975, B. Becker 1976, Howard 1976, J. Christensen and Yoesting 1977, London et al. 1977, Duncan 1978, Hawes 1978, Chace and Check 1979, Tinsley and Johnson 1984). Using multivariate statistical techniques such as factor and cluster analysis and multidimensional scaling, data on one or more dimensions of leisure and recreation activities were analyzed to identify categories of activities that shared such dimensions. The most commonly used dimension was frequency of participation, but other dimensions included preferences for activities, attitudes toward activities, type of social group in which participation occurs, reported satisfaction, motivations for activities, and perceived similarity of activities.

Three studies can be used to illustrate this genre of research. One study asked a sample of college students to report their frequency of participation in twenty-five leisure and recreation activities (Moss and Lamphear 1970). Factor analysis was used to identify eight clusters of activities that were statistically related and appeared to have face validity. Two of these clusters of activities were then examined through results of a standardized, personal-needs test administered to respondents. Findings suggest that the leisure and recreation activities within each cluster tend to fulfill the same personal needs.

A second study explored activity types based on preferences for leisure and recreation activities (Hendee et al. 1971). A sample of campers at national parks and national forests in Washington State were asked to indicate their preferred camping-related recreation activities from a list of twenty-six activities. Five categories of similar activities were identified. Statistically significant relationships were found between selected categories of activities and basic demographic and socioeconomic variables such as age and education.

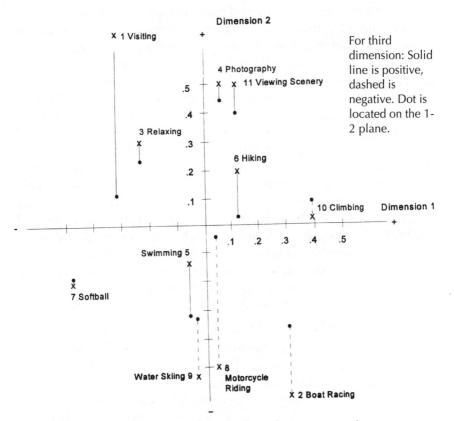

Figure 10-1. Three-dimensional map of similarity across eleven recreational activities. (From B. Becker 1976.)

A third study allowed respondents to directly assess perceived similarity among recreation activities (B. Becker 1976). A sample of college students was asked to rate the similarity of eleven pairs of leisure and recreation activities. Using multi-dimensional scaling, a three-dimensional "solution" to perceived similarity was derived. Similarity of activities was "mapped" as shown in Figure 10-1. This map suggests several clusters of activity types.

Activity type research has generally reported several clusters of activities that are considered similar based on the dimension under study. However, several potential shortcomings of this research are apparent, especially when these studies are linked to the concept of substitutability (Moss and Lamphear 1970, Beaman 1975, J. Christensen and Yoesting 1977, Baumgartner and Heberlein 1981, Burdge et al. 1981, Vaske et al. 1983, G. Peterson et al. 1985, Williams 1988a, Vaske et al. 1990). First, these studies are highly variable with regard to the leisure and recreation activities addressed and, perhaps more importantly, the activity types identified. It is difficult to generalize relatively standard activity types that might be used to classify or categorize broad patterns of leisure and recreation activity. Second, this research tends to treat general types of recreation activities (e.g., "hunting") as though they are homogeneous or monolithic. However, research demonstrates that certain types of hunting (e.g., deer and goose hunting) are dissimilar, particularly with respect to their substitutability (Baumgartner and Heberlein 1981, Vaske et al. 1990). (This issue is discussed more fully in the following section.) Finally, and most importantly, the assumption that substitutability of recreation activities necessarily follows from the fact that two or more recreation activities are related in terms of dimensions such as frequency of participation or even perceived similarity is generally unfounded. Such activities might be more appropriately considered to be complements, not substitutes. To be fair, activity type research did not necessarily evolve out of interest in substitutability. However, implications of activity type research were discussed in many of the studies noted above. For example, one important study observed that:

> A major implication of the [activity types identified] is the
> potential substitutability of activities within and between the
> five activity clusters. Since participation in activities within
> the five clusters is highly intercorrelated, it may be that, at
> least at a high generalized level, activities in the same cluster
> provide similar satisfactions. Thus, for many people, some of

these activities may be substitutable with little loss of satisfaction (Hendee and Burdge 1974:106).

This assumption was first tested explicitly in a study that asked respondents the degree to which they could substitute activities within the same activity type while obtaining a similar level of satisfaction (J. Christensen and Yoesting 1977). The study was administered to a representative sample of households in northeastern Iowa and used five activity types derived from a previous statewide general population study. The percentage of respondents who reported they could substitute activities within activity types with similar satisfaction ranged from 45 to 67 across the four activity types. The large percentage of respondents who reported they could not substitute activities without diminished satisfaction suggests that the issue of substitutability is more complex than initially thought and that activity-type research is not a sufficient approach to understanding and guiding substitutability. This issue has led to a second generation of research that has focused more directly on substitutability.

Direct Measures of Substitutability

A second generation of research has adopted more direct measures of substitutability. Two basic approaches have been developed. The first and most common measure is often called the direct-question method and asks respondents to report alternative recreation activities they consider to be substitutes for an activity under study (O'Leary et al. 1974, Baumgartner and Heberlein 1981, Manfredo and Anderson 1987, Vaske et al. 1990, Shelby and Vaske 1991b, Choi et al. 1994). The second basic research approach is behavioral and documents the activities that are substituted by respondents who are unable to participate in their chosen recreation activity (McCool and Utter 1982, Vaske et al. 1983).

One study has tested the direct question method in conjunction with the activity type approach described in the preceding section (Vaske et al. 1990). This study focused on potential substitutes for turkey hunting in Maryland. This issue had particular relevance because the state had closed the annual turkey-hunting season due to resource considerations. Using the activity type approach, a sample of previous turkey hunters were asked to report their frequency of participation in fifty-five recreation activities. Using factor analysis, twenty-five clusters of activities were identified. Turkey hunting was grouped with grouse, squirrel, and rabbit hunting, suggesting these four activities may be substitutable. Using the direct question method, respondents were also asked to report what recreation activities they considered to be good substitutes for turkey hunting. Twenty-one percent of the sample reported that they considered turkey hunting to have no good substitute activity. The remainder of the sample reported a total of 460 recreation activities they considered to be good substitutes. However, grouse, squirrel, and rabbit hunting were reported only sixty-seven times, suggesting that, from the respondents' point of view, these activities are generally not viewed as good substitutes for turkey hunting. These findings suggest that the direct question method may be a more valid measure of substitutability.

Other studies using the direct question method have developed several insights into the issue of substitutability. For example, a study of substitutes for salmon fishing on two New Zealand rivers suggests that substitutability may have potentially important spatial and temporal, as well as activity, dimensions (Shelby 1985, Shelby and Vaske 1991b). Study findings suggest that, while some fishers may be able to substitute other recreation activities, others, given the chance, would substitute the same activity on a different river or would substitute the same activity on the same river at a different time. These multiple dimensions of substitutability are illustrated in Figure 10-2. The upper left cell in the matrix represents the situations in which recreationists may choose to participate in the same activity at the same location, but substitute a different time period. The upper right cell represents situations in which recreationists may choose the same activity, but substitute a different location. The lower left cell represents situations in which recreationists may choose to participate in a different activity at the originally intended location. And the lower right cell represents situations in which recreationists may choose to substitute both the intended activity and location. This typology of substitution alternatives suggests that the issue of substitutability is considerably broader than originally envisioned.

This study also asked respondents why other regional rivers were not considered to be substitutes for the river under study. A number of issues were cited, including longer driving distance, increased expense, poor quality fishing, crowding, and lack of scenery.

While they are not based on the direct question method, economic models of recreation demand have also suggested the substitutability

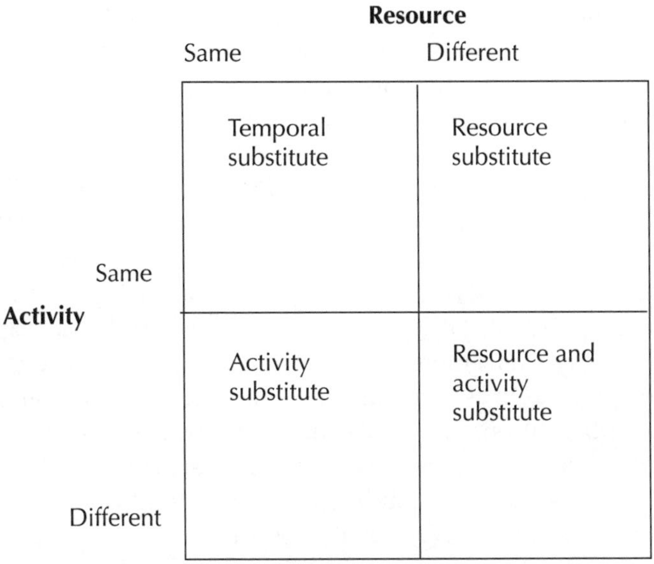

Resource

	Same	Different
Same	Temporal substitute	Resource substitute
Different	Activity substitute	Resource and activity substitute

Activity (labeled on left side: Same, Different)

Figure 10-2. A typology of substitution alternatives. (From Shelby and Vaske 1991b.)

of recreation sites (Burt and Brewer 1971, Cheung 1972, Cesario 1973, Cesario and Knetsch 1976, Cordell 1976, Knetsch 1977, Ewing 1980, S. Smith 1980, Rosenthal et al. 1984, G. Peterson et al. 1985). These models tend to focus on travel distance and associated costs of travel from population centers to alternative recreation sites. They also use aggregate population data rather than modeling the specific site choices made by individual recreationists.

Other studies using the direct question method have suggested several factors that are important in determining substitutability, and these factors can apply to both the originally intended activity and/or resource being considered as a substitute. For example, a study of deer and goose hunters in Wisconsin asked respondents to report activities that they could substitute and "enjoy doing just as much" (Baumgartner and Heberlein 1981). Most deer hunters (59%) reported few or no substitutes, while only 18% of goose hunters reported few or no substitutes. Respondents also rated the importance of selected motivations for hunting and other aspects of the hunting experience. Deer hunters reported significantly higher ratings than goose hunters on a number of motivations, including interaction among group members and bagging game. Deer hunters were also introduced to their sport at an earlier age than goose hunters and reported a higher participation rate. These findings suggest that the social meaning of a recreation activity can influence the degree to which it is substitutable, and that the more important such elements are, the fewer substitutes there are likely to be.

A survey of fly-fishers on the Metolius River, OR, also found that attributes of the recreation activity and its setting can affect substitutability (Manfredo and Anderson 1987). First, fishers were asked what they would do if the river were no longer available for fly-fishing. Nearly all the respondents (95%) reported that they would participate in the same activity in a different but similar location. This suggests that resource substitution as noted in Figure 10-2 may be more common than activity substitution. Respondents were also asked to rate the importance of a variety of the resource, social, and managerial attributes of fly-fishing on the study river. Findings show that the more important such attributes are, the fewer substitutes there are and that such substitutes tend to be rated lower in quality. This suggests that more "specialized" recreationists may have fewer substitute activities available.[1]

A similar study of statewide saltwater fishers in Texas found weaker support for the effect of recreational specialization on substitutability, but found that the probability of substituting alternative activities was significantly affected by type of social group. In Chapter 2, it was noted that most people participate in outdoor recreation in social groups and that type of social group can influence the choice of recreation activities and related behavior. In this study, respondents were presented with a scenario in which they could not participate in the fishing activity they originally intended. Respondents were more likely to substitute visiting a beach park, touring a nearby waterfront shopping and historic district, and going to a nearby theme park if they were participating in family-oriented groups. Respondents who were by themselves or with friends were more likely to substitute going fishing on a commercial party boat. The influence of social group on substitutability has been corroborated in a study of substitution of water-based recreation activities (O'Leary et al. 1974).

Behavioral measures offer a potentially powerful methodology for studying substitutability, but few such studies have been conduced. The most direct study was conducted as part of the research on turkey hunting in Maryland described earlier in this section (Vaske et al. 1983). Since the turkey-hunting season had been closed, hunters were forced to find a substitute activity. Respondents were asked whether the activity in which they engaged was judged to be "a good substitute for fall turkey hunting" (the dependent variable). Most respondents (68%) replied "yes." Three independent variables were measured as well. Two of these independent variables were considered "researcher-defined" judgments of similarity among activities: whether the substitute activity was hunting related, and whether participation occurred in the same social group. The third independent variable was a "respondent-defined" judgment of similarity among activities: respondents were asked directly whether the substitute activity was considered to be similar to turkey hunting. Only the latter independent variable was significantly related to the dependent variable. This suggests that researcher-defined measures of similarity may lack validity and that substitutability research should focus primarily on similarity judgments of recreationists.

The other behaviorally based study of substitutability focused on recreationists who did not obtain a permit to float the Middle Fork of the Salmon River, ID (McCool and Utter 1982). The number of permits granted to float this river is well below demand and available permits are allocated by means of a lottery system. Respondents who did not receive a permit were asked to report their substitute activity. Surprisingly, nearly 40% of respondents floated the river anyway by joining with a group that did receive a permit. This may indicate a flaw in administration of the lottery system whereby multiple members of the same group can apply for a permit. However, it also suggests that some relatively unique recreation opportunities, such as floating a nationally prominent river, may have few equivalent substitutes. The literature on place attachment described in Chapter 7 is also suggestive of the emotional ties to certain recreation areas or types of areas, and the implications this may have for substitutability (Williams et al. 1992b, Ballinger and Manning 1997).

Theory and Methods of Substitutability

Research on substitutability has facilitated development of a broad theory of substitution among recreation activities and has explored a variety of methodological issues. The definition of substitutability has evolved along with this literature. As originally conceived, substitutability focused on the potential interchangeability among recreation activities within defined activity types. Definitions of substitutability have since evolved to include an element of experiential quality and to recognize that substitutability includes consideration not only of recreation activities, but of location, time, and strategic means of access. The more comprehensive definition of substitutability suggests that it is

> . . . the interchangeability of recreation experiences such that acceptably equivalent outcomes can be achieved by varying one or more of the following: the timing of the experience, the means of gaining access, the setting, and the activity (Brunson and Shelby 1993).

A related statement of substitutability theory has also been developed in the literature (Iso-Ahola 1986b). While this theoretical framework was originally applied to substitution of recreation activities, its constructs would appear to be equally applicable to substitution over time and space as well. This theoretical framework is developed in a series of postulations, derivations, and corollaries as shown in Figure 10-3. The theory suggests that substitutability is influenced by two fundamental considerations: reasons why a substitution is necessary and perceptions about substitute activities. With regard to the former, successful substitution is theorized as less likely as a function of the following factors:

1. Freedom of choice is perceived to be limited.
2. Substitution is forced externally and arbitrarily.
3. Actions requiring substitutions are perceived to be directed at the individual or referent group.
4. The reason for substitution is judged to be unfair or unjustified.
5. Requirement for substitution is unexpected.
6. Psychological investment is high in the originally intended activity.

With regard to the latter, successful substitution is theorized as less likely as a function of the following factors:

1. Psychological qualities of substitute activities are not judged to be similar.

2. The activity to be replaced is specialized.

3. There are few substitute activities available.

4. The attractiveness/pleasantness of substitute activities are judged to be dissimilar.

5. The psychological motivations underlying substitute activities are judged to be dissimilar.

6. The activity to be replaced is driven by relatively specialized motivation.

7. Substitute activities are perceived to be relatively high in cost with respect to time, money, or effort.

Several elements of this theoretical framework have been supported empirically in the research described in this chapter. For example, motivations and level of recreation specialization have been shown to be related to substitutability. However, many elements of this theoretical framework have not yet been tested. A research agenda has recently been proposed to examine several high priority issues related to substitutability (Brunson and Shelby 1993). These issues include:

1. How should equivalence among potential activities be determined and measured?

2. What is the pattern of recreational preferences across the typology of substitution alternatives illustrated in Figure 10-2?

3. What is the relationship between intended substitute activities as reported in the direct question method and subsequent behavior?

4. What are the tradeoffs among temporal substitutes and strategic substitutes (such as joining with another group if a required use permit is not available)?

5. How does recreation activity specialization affect resource or site substitutability?

6. How does place attachment affect substitutability?

7. Why do some recreationists choose to substitute activities that are not perceived to be equivalent to the originally intended activity?

8. When temporal substitutes are chosen, how does this affect behavior during the time associated with the originally intended activity?

9. What are the relationships between substitutability and research on longer-term constraints on or barriers to leisure and recreation activity?

text continues on page 220

Postulate 1: When faced with the possible substitution, a person's feeling of choice or freedom mediates his or her willingness to substitute.

> **Derivation 1:** External forcing of or pressure for substitution of leisure behaviors gives rise to psychological reactance or arousal that reduces one's willingness to substitute.

>> **Corollary 1 (to Derivation 1):** the stronger and the more explicit the perceived threat for a person to substitute a leisure activity, the less willing he or she is to substitute.

>> **Corollary 2 (to Derivation 1):** If a person perceives his or her interests and those of an agent of freedom-reduction to be similar, then his or her psychological reactance is lower and willingness to substitute is greater than when no correspondence of interests is perceived.

>> **Corollary 3 (to Derivation 1):** If the factors that force substitution are perceived to be directed at oneself (person-specific) or one's reference group, then one's willingness to substitute is lower than when such factors are perceived as general and not person-specific.

> **Derivation 2:** If the reason(s) for substitution are understandable, justifiable, or fair, one's willingness and tendency to substitute is greater than if the reason(s) are not perceived as understandable, justifiable, or fair.

> **Derivation 3:** When the need for substitution of a leisure activity arises unexpectedly, an individual's willingness to substitute is lower than when the substitution is expected.

>> **Corollary 1 (to Derivation 3):** The higher the psychological investment in the initiation of leisure participation (and consequently the more surprising and unexpected the need for substitution), the lower the willingness to substitute.

> **Derivation 4:** Leisure satisfaction associated with participation in an activity that represents a forced substitution is lower than leisure satisfaction flowing from participation in an activity that is not perceived as a forced substitution.

Postulate 2: If the psychological qualities of the available alternative activity(ies) are comparable to those of the substitutable activity, the individual experiences less reduction in perceived choice (due to the need for substitution) than when those qualities are not comparable; therefore, the individual's willingness to substitute is greater when the qualities are comparable than when they are not.

> **Derivation 5:** A person's willingness to substitute is greater if the leisure activity to be replaced is part of a broad leisure repertoire than when it is part of a narrow leisure repertoire.

>> **Corollary 1 (to Derivation 5):** A person's willingness to substitute is greater when the number of available leisure alternatives is perceived to be great than when it is perceived to be non-existent or small.

Derivation 6: A person's willingness to substitute is greater when his or her leisure alternative(s) are similar in attractiveness or pleasantness to the activity to be replaced.

Derivation 7: A person's willingness to substitute is greater if the psychological motives and rewards of the original leisure activity are perceived substitutable than if they are not.

Corollary 1 (to Derivation 7): The more unique or the more activity-specific the psychological motives and rewards that a person attaches to or expects to derive from the current activity (the one required to be replaced), the less willing he or she is to substitute that activity.

Corollary 2 (to Derivation 7): A person's willingness to replace a current activity is greater if the most important psychological motive(s) and reward(s) are perceived to be substitutable than if they are not perceived to be substitutable or if only the least important psychological motives and rewards are perceived to be substitutable.

Corollary 3 (to Derivation 7): A person's willingness to substitute is positively related to the number and quality of psychological rewards or benefits he or she expects to gain from participation in a leisure activity.

Corollary 4 (to Derivation 7): A person's willingness to substitute is greater when a leisure alternative is expected to bring about feeling of competence than when it is not.

Corollary 5 (to Derivation 7): A person's willingness to substitute is lower if he or she believes that a leisure alternative will not offer the same quality of social interaction as does the present activity.

Derivation 8: A person's willingness to substitute is inversely related to the perceived costs (in terms of money, time, and effort) of participation in the initially desired activity and in the alternative leisure activities.

Figure 10-3 . A theory of substitutability. (Adapted from Iso-Ahola 1986b.)

At least two methodological issues associated with substitutability research have been identified in the literature. The first concerns the hypothetical nature of the direct question method (G. Peterson et al. 1985). As described in the preceding section, this method asks respondents to report substitute activities, locations, or times they would adopt if the originally intended activity, location, or time were unavailable. The validity of such reports is unknown. More behavioral research seems warranted on what recreationists actually do when confronted with the need to substitute an activity, location, or time.

The second methodological issue concerns verbal versus visual stimuli in substitutability research. Research on the perceived similarity of recreation activities is normally conducted through verbal descriptions of activities and/or areas. However, such information might also be presented visually. A comparative study of verbal and visual descriptions suggests that each research approach has advantages and disadvantages (Williams 1988a). However, an important potential advantage of the visual approach is that choice of relevant information about the activity or location may be determined more by the respondent and less by the researcher.

Summary and Conclusions

1. Initial interest in the potential substitutability of recreation opportunities focused on identifying categories of similar leisure and recreation activities. This interest was based on scientific classification of leisure and recreation behavior.

2. Practical implications of substitutability of recreation activities include economic efficiency in providing recreation opportunities, meeting growing demand for recreation, and dealing with the potential effects of crowding and displacement.

3. A number of studies have used multivariate statistical procedures to identify clusters or groups of recreation activities (activity types) that share certain characteristics. These studies have been based on frequency of participation, attitudes and preferences related to recreation activities, type of social group, motivation for recreation activities, and perceived similarity among recreation activities.

4. The assumption (implicit or explicit) that recreation activities within the same activity type are substitutes is generally unsupported. Such activities might be more appropriately considered to be complements than substitutes.

5. A second generation of substitutability research has adopted a direct-question method whereby respondents are asked to identify alternative activities they consider to be substitutes for the recreation activity under study. An important element of this approach is that substitute activities are considered by respondents to have outcomes (e.g., satisfaction, benefits) generally equivalent to the originally intended activity.

6. Studies using the direct-question method have developed several insights into the issue of substitutability, including identification of spatial, temporal, and strategic substitutability alternatives; the potential role of social meaning, including motivations; the potential effect of recreation specialization; and the role of social groups in substitutability.

7. Little research has been conducted using behavioral measures of substitutability. More research in this area is warranted given the hypothetical nature of the direct-question method. Initial behavioral research emphasizes the potential importance of using respondent-defined judgments of similarity or substitutability as opposed to researcher-defined judgments, and the potential importance of place attachment on substitutability.

8. Research on substitutability has led to an expanded definition of substitutability and facilitates a broad theoretical framework as outlined in Figure 10-3. However, considerably more research is needed to test the multiple components of this theoretical framework and to allow the concept of substitutability to be incorporated directly into recreation management.

Notes

1. The issue of recreation specialization is considered more fully in Chapter 11.

11

Specialization in Recreation
Experience and Related Concepts

Experience and Related Concepts

Experience in recreation—measured through frequency of participation, years of participation, or a variety of other ways—has been a focus of early and continuing research. Research has been driven by the notion that experience may be an important variable or concept for differentiating among recreationists. A recreationist who is a beginner or novice may have little knowledge of the recreation activity undertaken and the setting in which it occurs. On the other hand, it is likely that an advanced or expert recreationist has a substantially greater knowledge base. Such differences in knowledge may lead to differences in attitudes, preferences, and behavior.

Early theoretical work emphasized the potential importance of experience in recreation and broadened its scope as well. An initial conceptual base hypothesized that recreationists evolve through recreation or leisure "careers" (Kelly 1974, 1977). Through a process of socialization, recreationists may acquire specialized knowledge, skills, attitudes, and norms that define their development from beginner to expert. This theoretical base was used to propose the concept of recreation specialization, which was defined as "a continuum of behavior from the general to the particular, reflected by equipment and skills used in the sport and activity setting preferences" (Bryan 1977). Four dimensions were used to define the recreation specialization framework: technique preferences, setting preferences, experience in the activity, and the relationship of the activity to other areas of life. These dimensions were used to propose and test a typology of fishing that was seen to range across four categories: occasional fishers, generalists, technique specialists, and technique/setting specialists. Similarly, a study of sailing at Apostle Island National Lakeshore, WI, has identified a seven-stage "trajectory" of specialization that begins with boating with friends, moves through yacht club membership, and ultimately ends with abandonment of the activity (Kuentzel and Heberlein 1997).

The concept of recreation specialization expands on the notion of experience to include cognitive, behavioral, and psychological components in an effort to distinguish and define among types of recreationists. Subsequent research has addressed both experience and specialization and their potential relationships to the attitudes, preferences, and behavior of recreationists.

This chapter reviews the literature on recreation specialization. Experience level of recreationists and the more robust concept of specialization are examined to determine their potential influence on recreation-related attitudes, preferences, and behavior. Several theoretical and methodological issues are identified and discussed.

Measures of Recreation Experience

Measures of experience have been included in a relatively large number of recreation studies. Many such studies have found experience to be related to a variety of variables, including perceived crowding (J. Nielson et al. 1977, Vaske et al. 1980); conflict (Driver and Bassett 1975); perceptions of recreation-related impacts (D. Anderson 1980), campsite selection (Heberlein and Dunwiddie 1979), route selection (McFarlane et al. 1998), and willingness to pay for recreation (Munley and Smith 1976).

More recent studies have tended to focus more directly on experience and its potential to discriminate among recreation visitors. Some of these studies have employed relatively straightforward measures of experience while others have adopted more complex, multifaceted measures. A relatively early study of floaters on the Green River through Desolation Canyon, UT, were simply asked how many times they had run this stretch of river (Schreyer 1982). Respondents were then divided into three experience categories—first-time floaters, moderate-experience floaters, and high-experience floaters. A number of differences were found among the three experience categories. For example, more experienced floaters were more likely to be on a private rather than commercial trip, and were more specific in reporting motivations associated with the trip.

		Total number of river trips			
		High		Low	
		Number of rivers run		Number of rivers run	
		High	Low	High	Low
Number of trips	High	Veterans	Locals		
on the study river	Low	Visitors		Collectors	Beginners and Novices

Novices = First trip on any river

Beginners = 2–5 trips total on 5 or fewer rivers or 6–10 trips total on 4 or fewer rivers

Locals = 6 or more trips on 1 river only (study river) or 6 or more trips on up to 4 rivers, but 5 or more of these trips must be on the study river

Collectors = 6–10 trips total on 5–10 rivers

Visitors = Over 10 trips total, but no more than 4 on the study river

Veterans = Over 10 trips total on at least 5 rivers, with at least 5 trips on the study river

Figure 11-1. Experience Use History (EUH). (From Schreyer et al. 1984.)

A more recent study of fishers in Texas also used frequency of participation as a measure of experience (Ditton et al. 1992, Choi et al. 1994). Based on number of days fished during the previous twelve months, respondents were grouped into four experience-based categories. Several differences among respondents were found based on experience. For example, more experienced fishers were more interested in catching "trophy" fish and were more interested in fishing-related publications and media.

Several studies have noted that there are multiple dimensions of experience that might be included in recreation research. While the studies described above focus on amount of experience, *type* of experience may also be important in influencing recreation-related attitudes, preferences, and behavior. To incorporate this additional dimension of experience, an index comprised of three experience-related variables was created in a study of river-based recreation to form a composite measure termed Experience Use History (EUH) (Schreyer et al. 1984). Variables included were (1) the number of times the respondent floated the study river, (2) number of rivers the respondent had floated, and (3) total number of river trips the respondent had made. This composite variable used data from a series of national river recreation studies. Based on alternative combinations of the three experience-related variables, six types of respondents were identified as shown in Figure 11-1. Moreover, significant differences were found among these types of respondents across a variety of variables, including motivations, perceived conflict, and attitudes toward management practices. A follow-up study corroborated differences among EUH categories, suggesting that the motivations of respondents grow increasingly complex with higher levels of experience (Williams et al. 1990).

Several other studies have employed multidimensional indexes of experience, though these have not adopted the EUH measure described above. The first study surveyed floaters on three rivers in the Southeast (Hammitt and McDonald 1983). An overall index of experience was comprised of measures of four dimensions of river recreation experience: (1) number of years of river floating, (2) frequency of river floating, (3) frequency of floating on the study river, and (4) total number of floating trips on the study river. Using the resulting overall index, level of experience was found to influence several attitudinal variables. For example, more experienced visitors were more perceptive of environmental disturbance to the river environment and were more supportive of management controls on river use.

A related study examined four similar measures of experience among a sample of horseback riders along the Big South Fork National River and Recreation Area, TN (Hammitt et al. 1989a). This study also employed a self-assessment of experience/skill level by respondents by asking respondents to classify themselves in one of four categories ranging from beginner to expert. Significant differences in respondent preferences for equestrian-related facilities and services were found using both measures of experience. However, the more objective index of experience was more strongly related to most of the dependent variables.

A third study addressed winter backpacking in Great Smoky Mountains National Park, NC/TN (Hammitt et al. 1986). Several dimensions of experience were measured, including overall experience in the park, winter experience, and overall experience. These dimensions of experience were tested for their relationships to motivations for winter backpacking. Only one statistically significant relationship was found: respondents with more overall experience and more experience in winter tended to rate the motivation of solitude more highly.

One other study has compared alternative measures of experience (Schreyer and Lime 1984). As with two of the studies described above, this study also used data from a national series of river recreation studies. Visitors were classified as to whether they had floated the study river and whether they had floated other rivers. Visitors who were novices on the study river but who had floated other rivers were found to have motivations similar to those of visitors who had floated the study river. However, those with experience on other rivers, but no experience on the study river were found to be similar to true novices with regard to subjective evaluations of the recreation experience, including perceived crowding and conflict.

Differential effects of alternative measures of experience suggest that the concept of experience is more complex than originally envisioned. Based on this complexity, it has been recommended that multivariate statistical methods such as factor analysis and principal-components analysis be used to create indexes of experience from multiple experience-related variables (Watson and Niccolucci 1992b). These statistical procedures test the correlations among experience-related variables and allow for creation of statistically based multidimensional indexes as opposed to unidimensional researcher-created indexes.

This approach to measuring and analyzing experience was used in a study of visitors to Nopiming Provincial Park, Manitoba, Canada (McFarlane et al. 1998). Eight measures of experience at the study park and general wilderness experience were included in factor analysis to create standardized indexes of experience. Resulting indexes were found to be significantly related to routes of travel through the study area. For example, the most experienced visitors tended to choose the more remote, difficult routes with the least management intervention.

Complexity surrounding the concept of experience is further illustrated by a laboratory study of the relationship between experience level and preferences for wilderness attributes (Watson et al. 1991b). Contrary to expectations, respondents with greater levels of experience did not report more narrowly defined preferred attribute categories than respondents with lower levels of experience. Study findings suggest that while greater experience may lead to cognitive distinctions among wilderness attributes (i.e., the ability to distinguish among wilderness settings), it may also lead to broader and more generalized judgments concerning the acceptability of such settings.

From Experience to Specialization

As described earlier, the concept of recreation specialization broadens interest in experience to include cognitive, behavioral, and psychological components. Experience may contribute to shaping each of these components. For example, the more experienced a recreationist is in a given activity, the more skilled he or she may be, thus contributing to a cognitive component of specialization. Experience can also be used as a direct measure of the behavioral component of specialization. For example, frequency of participation is sometimes used to help define degrees of specialization. However, there are other potential behavioral measures of specialization, including the type of recreation activity. For example, fly-fishing is generally considered to be a more specialized type of fishing than fishing with bait. Finally, the psychological component of specialization concerns the meaning of the activity to the participant and its relationship to other areas of the participant's life. This is often measured in terms of "involvement" in the activity, "commitment" to the activity, or "centrality" of the activity to the participant's lifestyle.

A growing number of studies have addressed recreation specialization. However, these studies have used a variety of methods to explore selected components of specialization. Moreover, these studies have examined the relationship between specialization and a variety of recreation-related attitudes, preferences, and behaviors.

Aside from experience, the psychological elements of involvement in an activity, commitment to an activity, and related concepts have received the most conceptual and empirical attention (Van Doren and Lentnek 1969, Manfredo and Anderson 1982, Wellman et al. 1982a, Buchanan 1985, Williams 1985, Schreyer and Beaulieu 1986, Williams and Huffman 1986, Chapman and Helfrich 1988, Selin and Howard 1988, Virden and Schreyer 1988, Bloch et al. 1989, McIntyre 1989, J. Young et al. 1991, T. Brown and Siemer 1992, Kuentzel and Heberlein 1992b, Kuentzel and McDonald 1992, McIntire and Pigram 1992, Mowen et al. 1997, Merrill and Graefe 1998). For example, a survey of canoeists on nine rivers in Virginia included a series of questions addressing the degree of involvement of participants in this activity (Wellman et al. 1982a). These questions included measures of financial investment in canoeing-related equipment and how important or central the activity was to the respondent. These latter measures included membership in canoeing-oriented organizations, subscriptions to canoeing-oriented periodicals, ownership of canoeing-oriented books, and a self-assessment of respondent involvement in canoeing. These measures were combined with several measures of participation in canoeing (similar to those described in the previous section) to form an overall index of specialization. Specialization index scores were then statistically related to respondent judgments of the seriousness of sixty-eight potentially depreciative behaviors that can occur in river-based recreation. Specialization was found to be significantly related to only eleven of the depreciative behaviors. However, this study was conducted on rivers that are not technically demanding, and this may have limited the amount of variation in specialization needed to adequately test for such differences. A follow-up study used the same measures of specialization, but applied them in a laboratory experiment in which subjects were asked to judge the similarity of pairs of photographs of recreation activity based on the type of activity, the setting, and social context (Williams 1985). Some significant relationships between specialization and respondent judgments were found, but the study was considered to be primarily exploratory and suggestive.

Stronger relationships were found in a study of specialization and importance ratings of a series of physical, social, and managerial setting attributes for backcountry recreation opportunities (Virden and Schreyer 1988). This study constructed an overall index of specialization for hikers in three western wilderness areas using several measures of experience, commitment, and centrality to lifestyle. Statistically significant differences were found between specialization and twenty-one of the thirty-eight setting attributes studied. For example, as specialization increased, tolerance for seeing other visitors along trails decreased. The authors conclude that study findings "offer support for [the] premise that specialization, or stage of development within an activity, reflects the value and preference for certain types of environments." A related study of experience and commitment also found significant relationships between specialization and the importance of setting attributes for wilderness recreation (Schreyer and Beaulieu 1986).

A different research design was employed in a study of floaters on the Ocoee River, TN (Kuentzel and McDonald 1992). This study incorporated measures of experience, commitment, and centrality to lifestyle, but did not combine these measures into an overall index of specialization. Rather, each of these measures was related to three dependent variables—motivations for participation, perceived crowding, and preferences for management actions—to assess the relative influence of these three elements of specialization. A number of statistically significant relationships were found, but the three elements of specialization studied were found to have differential effects on visitor attitudes and preferences. For example, measures of commitment correlated positively with motivations related to taking risks and seeking thrills, while measures of past experience correlated negatively with these motives.

Other studies of specialization that have focused on involvement and commitment as elements of specialization have found significant relationships with several dependent variables, including the perceived quality of management (McIntyre and Pigram 1992), standards of quality for social conditions in wilderness (J. Young et al. 1991), the amount of information used in making decisions concerning competing recreation opportunities (Williams and Huffman 1986), and evaluation of hunting opportunities (Kuentzel and Heberlein 1992b).

The cognitive variable of skill has also received empirical attention in a number of studies (Donnelly et al. 1986, Graefe et al. 1986b, Hollenhorst 1990, Steele et al. 1990, Ewert 1994, Dawson 1995, Hopkins and Moore 1995, Tarrant et al. 1997, Merrill and Graefe 1998). For example, hikers on the White Mountain National Forest, NH, were classified into three levels of specialization based on measures of experience and self-reported skill level (ranging from beginner to expert) (Graefe et al. 1986b). More highly specialized visitors reported significantly higher levels of crowding. Moreover, the number of other hikers encountered and preferences for meeting other hikers explained substantially more of the variance in perceived crowding for highly specialized visitors than for less specialized visitors. This suggests that more highly specialized visitors tend to have more highly developed preferences. Three other studies of specialization and crowding tend to corroborate these findings (Hammitt et al. 1984, Hollenhorst 1990, Tarrant et al. 1994). Other studies incorporating skill into measures of specialization have found statistically significant relationships with several dependent variables, including motivations (Ewert 1994), setting preferences (Hopkins and Moore 1995, Merrill and Graefe 1998), and socialization (Steele et al. 1990).

A related study of fishing on the Salmon River, NY, is suggestive of a cognitive element of specialization (Dawson et al. 1992 a, b). This study classified fishers by fishing technique and found statistically significant differences among these groups with regard to attitudes toward fishing regulations. For example, support for a ban on snagging fish (considered a low specialized technique) increased with increasingly specialized groups of fishers.

A final issue that may be related to specialization is "wilderness purism." Wilderness purism is an aggregate measure of attitudes toward wilderness that is intended as an indication of the degree to which respondents view wilderness as a reflection of the ways in which it is defined within relevant legislation (Hendee et al. 1968, Stankey 1972, Shin and Jaakson 1997). Wilderness purism may comprise an attitudinal dimension of specialization to the extent that it is a reflection of experience in wilderness or other components of specialization. A multiple-item measure of wilderness purism was administered to a sample of hikers in the Cohutta Wilderness, GA (C. Shafer and Hammitt 1995a). Purism was found to be related to wilderness experience (a behavioral dimension of specialization) and concern for the natural, social, and managerial elements of wilderness conditions.

Theory and Methods of Specialization

Much of the theoretical basis of recreation specialization was outlined in Bryan's (1977) original explication of the concept as described earlier in this chapter. However, this theoretical basis has been expanded, clarified, and critiqued as a result of the empirical studies reviewed in the previous two sections, along with additional conceptual studies. This section describes several elements of the theoretical basis of specialization and then outlines several methodological issues.

An element of the original concept of specialization suggested the role of what were called "leisure social worlds." These are reference groups of recreationists who share a common level of specialization and help to define the meanings, preferences, and norms of behaviors that are associated with such levels of specialization. Communication within leisure social worlds can be informal, but is often codified in various mass media such as guide books, specialty magazines, and equipment catalogues. Individuals evolve along the specialization continuum at least partly as a function of assimilating the specialized world view outlined by leisure social worlds.

Based on this social-worlds construct, a series of eight propositions have been developed that elaborate on the concept of specialization (Ditton et al. 1992). These propositions are shown in Table 11-1. The empirical studies reviewed in the previous two sections have provided support for several of these propositions. For example, a number of studies have demonstrated a positive correlation between level of experience in a recreation activity and measures of specialization, including involvement, commitment, and centrality to lifestyle. Moreover, specialization has been linked to a number of recreation-related attitudes and preferences.

Empirical research has also documented that specialization can be comprised of a number of elements, such as experience level, skill/expertise, involvement/commitment, and centrality to lifestyle. Elements of specialization can be classified into three basic components—behavioral, cognitive, and psychological—and linked as suggested in Figure 11-2. This conceptual model of specialization is generally seen as self-reinforcing. For example, increasing experience in a recreation activity might lead to enhanced skills, which in turn contribute to one's psychological involvement in the activity.

The circularity of the conceptual model illustrated in Figure 11-2 has been subject to some criticism. This is because specialization is defined in terms of behavioral, cognitive, and psychological components, and its antecedent conditions are often defined in similar terms (Ditton et

Table 11-1. Propositions of specialization. (Adapted from Ditton et al. 1992.)

1. Persons participating in a given recreation activity are more likely to become more specialized in that activity over time.

2. As level of specialization in a given recreation activity increases, the value of side bets (the financial, social, and other costs associated with participation) will likely increase.

3. As level of specialization in a given recreation activity increases, the centrality of that activity in a person's life will likely increase.

4. As level of specialization in a given recreation activity increases, acceptance and support for the rules, norms, and procedures associated with the activity will likely increase.

5. As level of specialization in a given recreation activity increases, the importance attached to the equipment and the skillful use of that equipment will likely increase.

6. As level of specialization in a given recreation activity increases, dependency on a specific resource will likely increase.

7. As level of specialization in a given recreation activity increases, level of mediated interaction (involvement with mass media related to that activity) relative to that activity will likely increase.

8. As level of specialization in a given recreation activity increases, the importance of activity-specific elements of the experience will decrease relative to non-activity-specific elements of the experience.

al. 1992, Kuentzel and Heberlein 1992b). Thus, some studies of specialization might be seen as representing a tautology. For example, if specialization is measured through level of involvement with a recreation activity, then it is not useful to also test the influence of specialization on recreation involvement or a similar concept.

A second criticism of specialization focuses on the issue of congruence between two of its underlying concepts (Kuentzel and McDonald 1992). Specialization is generally defined as a continuum as one evolves from beginner to expert. However, specialization is also generally acknowledged as a multidimensional concept, comprised of behavioral, cognitive, and psychological components. The assumption that underlies this conceptual model is that the various components of specialization are positively correlated. That is, as behavioral measures of specialization increase, so do cognitive and psychological measures, and in this way specialization rises and falls in a predictable linear fashion. However, it is not difficult to imagine circumstances in which this assumption might be violated. For example, a rock climber who is highly specialized might reduce participation in this activity because

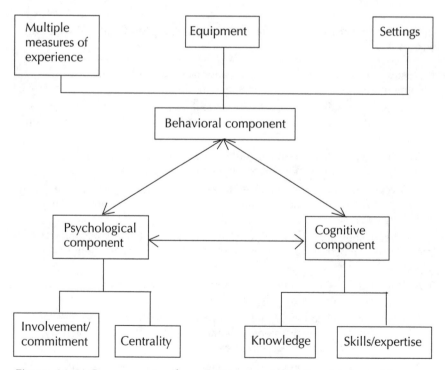

Figure 11-2. Components of recreation specialization.(Adapted from Little 1976 and McIntyre and Pigram 1992.)

of growing family obligations. This person may remain highly committed to climbing as measured by attitudes and equipment, but would not be judged as highly specialized by virtue of frequency of participation. This suggests that, while overall indexes of specialization may be useful in research, it might also be wise to examine the influence of individual measures that comprise such indexes.

A third criticism of specialization suggests that it may be too simplistic, or that it may have been interpreted and applied in too literal a manner (T. Brown and Siemer 1992). While recreationists may often progress in a generalized manner along a specialization continuum as defined by technique, skill, involvement, or other measures, it may be misleading to monolithically classify individuals as occupying a single point along such a continuum. In fact, recreationists may move along this continuum in both directions depending upon circumstances. The same individual, for example, may exhibit highly specialized fishing behavior on a weekend outing with other anglers, but may adopt considerably less specialized behavior when introducing children to fishing.

Research has also suggested two additional dimensions of specialization. Most research on specialization has centered on recreation activities. However, research on place attachment suggests that recreationists might also become "place specialists" with respect to either a specific geographic location or type of place such as designated wilderness (Williams et al. 1992b). Initial empirical research suggests that recreation activity specialization and place attachment may be related (Mowen et al. 1998). A study of visitors to Mount Rogers National Recreation Area, VA, measured both activity involvement (activity specialization) and place attachment. Respondents who were classified as "high" in both measures tended to rate both the setting and the overall recreation experience more positively.

A second dimension of specialization concerns comparisons of specialization across activities or subactivities (Donnelly et al. 1986). Nearly all research on specialization has focused on *degree* of specialization within a single activity. However, alternative recreation activities or subactivities are likely to have different *ranges* of specialization. Degree of specialization refers to the location of an individual on a specialization continuum, while range of specialization refers to the length of the specialization continuum for any recreation activity or subactivity. It has been hypothesized that degree and range of specialization are inversely related as illustrated in Figure 11-3 (Donnelly et al. 1986). This figure suggests that as motorboaters and

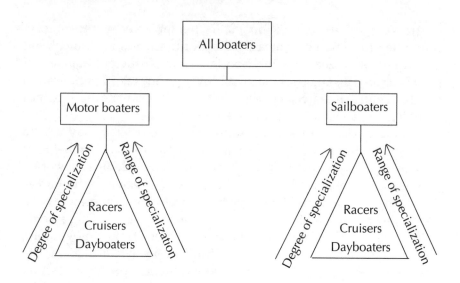

Figure 11-3. Degree and range of specialization. (From Donnelly et al. 1986.)

sailboaters increase their degree of specialization from day boaters to cruisers to racers, the range of specialization within these subactivities becomes narrower. Empirical measures of specialization support the notion that degree of specialization increases as one moves up through these subactivities. Degree of specialization was also found to be higher for sailboaters than for motorboaters. However, no differences in range of specialization were found among subactivities as measured by the standard deviations of specialization index scores. Differences in specialization among recreation activities and subactivities may be a useful concept and warrants further investigation.

Several methodological issues are also apparent in specialization research. First, there is considerable disparity in the ways in which various components of specialization are measured. For example, the cognitive variable skill is sometimes measured by researchers based on demonstrated expertise (e.g., Ewert 1994) and sometimes through respondent self-assessment (e.g., Tarrant et al. 1997).

Second, there are inconsistencies among studies regarding what variables constitute measures of what components of specialization (Kuentzel and McDonald 1992). For example, number of magazine subscriptions related to a given recreation activity has been defined as a measure of the behavioral component of specialization in some studies (e.g., Block et al. 1989) and as a measure of the psychological component of specialization in other studies (e.g., Chipman and Helfrich 1988).

Third, nearly all studies of specialization have tested its influence on attitudinal rather than behavioral measures of recreation. An empirical test of the relationship between specialization and the type of hunting in which respondents engaged found no significant relationship (Kuentzel and Heberlein 1992b). While this study suggests several theoretical and methodological reasons for this finding, it also signifies the potential importance of extending specialization research to include behaviorally based measures.

Finally, research on specialization can be confounded by the fact that multiple dimensions of specialization may not necessarily be positively related. As noted earlier, this suggests that when overall indexes of specialization are used, the multiple measures comprising such indexes should be examined individually as well. As noted earlier, the same issue applies to research on experience. Alternative measures of experience (e.g., years of participation, frequency of participation, participation at selected areas) may provide quite different insights into the concept of specialization (Schreyer and Lime 1984, Schreyer et al. 1984, Watson and Niccolucci 1992b).

Summary and Conclusions

1. There has been longstanding interest in experience and related concepts as a way to differentiate among recreationists and their attitudes, preferences, and behaviors.

2. Measures of recreation experience have varied from single-item variables focused on frequency of participation to composite indexes comprised of multiple dimensions of experience that measure both amount and type of experience.

3. Measures of recreation experience have been found to be related to a number of attitudes, preferences, and behavior, including perceived crowding, conflict, perception of recreation-related impacts, campsite selection, willingness to pay for recreation, motivations for recreation, attitudes toward management practices, and preferences for facilities and services.

4. Initial interest in experience has been broadened to encompass the concept of recreation specialization. Recreation specialization has been defined as "a continuum of behavior from the general to the

particular, reflected by equipment and skills used in the sport and activity setting preferences."

5. Recreation specialization can be seen to include three basic components—behavioral, cognitive, and psychological—as shown in Figure 11-2.

6. Measures of recreation specialization often use a composite index of specialization comprised of multiple dimensions, including experience, involvement in an activity, commitment to an activity, skill or expertise, and the centrality of the activity to one's lifestyle.

7. Measures of specialization have been found to be related to a number of attitudes, preferences, and behaviors, including perception of recreation-related impacts, importance of recreation setting attributes, perceived quality of recreation management, standards of quality for social conditions, evaluation of recreation opportunities, motivations for recreation, perceived crowding, and preferences for management actions.

8. Wilderness purism—the degree to which a person views wilderness as a reflection of the ways in which it is defined by relevant legislation—may constitute an attitudinal dimension of recreation specialization.

9. Recreation specialization involves "leisure social worlds" and the formal and informal role that such reference groups play in defining the world views of highly specialized recreationists. Based on this social-worlds perspective, a series of eight propositions underlying recreation specialization have been defined as shown in Table 11-1.

10. Research on recreation specialization must be careful to avoid a potential tautology represented by measuring specialization in terms that are similar to the variables it is hypothesized to influence.

11. Studies that use composite indexes of experience and specialization should also examine the effects of individual measures that comprise such indexes.

12. The concept of recreation specialization should not be interpreted and applied too literally. Recreationists may adopt a variety of recreation behaviors depending upon circumstances.

13. Recreation specialization may apply to places as well as activities.

14. Recreation specialization may have both "degree" and "range" dimensions. These dimensions suggest that certain recreation activities or subactivities may be more specialized than others.

15. Methodological issues in recreation specialization that warrant more research attention include: (1) disparity in which specialization-related variables are measured, (2) inconsistencies in measures used to represent the primary conceptual components of specialization, (3) lack of behaviorally oriented research, and (4) the potential differential effects of alternative measures of experience and specialization.

12

Managing Outdoor Recreation
Alternative Management Practices

Outdoor Recreation Management

The preceding chapters have explored a variety of issues in outdoor recreation. The underlying purpose of the studies reviewed has been to gain a better understanding of these issues with the ultimate goal of enhancing the satisfaction of visitors to parks and outdoor recreation areas. These studies suggest that management of outdoor recreation is needed.

The group of studies examined in this chapter focus more directly on managing outdoor recreation. These studies outline a series of alternative management practices and have begun to evaluate their effectiveness. Based on these studies, a number of guidelines and related insights are developed. The last section of this chapter describes the current status of and trends in outdoor recreation management.

Alternative Management Practices

Many writers have suggested a variety of management practices that might be applied to outdoor recreation problems such as crowding, conflict, and environmental impacts. It is useful to organize these practices into classification systems to illustrate the broad spectrum of alternatives available to outdoor recreation managers.

One classification system defines alternatives on the basis of management strategies (Manning 1979b). Management strategies are basic conceptual approaches to management that relate to achievement of desirable objectives. Four basic strategies can be identified for managing outdoor recreation as illustrated in Figure 12-1. Two strategies

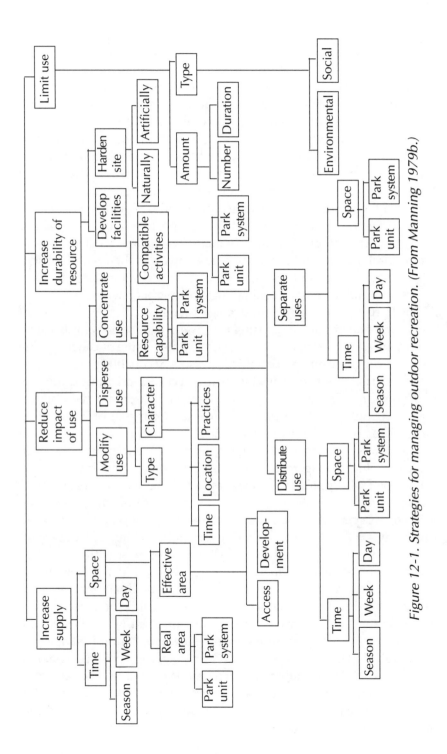

Figure 12-1. Strategies for managing outdoor recreation. (From Manning 1979b.)

deal with supply and demand: the supply of recreation opportunities may be increased to accommodate more use, or the demand for recreation may be limited through restrictions or other approaches. The other two basic strategies treat supply and demand as fixed, and focus on modifying either the character of recreation to reduce its adverse impacts or the resource base to increase its durability.

There are a number of sub-strategies within each of these basic management strategies. The supply of outdoor recreation areas, for example, can be increased in terms of both space and time. With respect to space, new areas may be added or existing areas might be used more effectively through additional access or facilities. With respect to time, some recreation use might be shifted to off-peak periods.

Within the strategy of limiting demand, restrictions might be placed on the total number of visitors that are allowed or their length of stay. Alternatively, certain types of use that can be demonstrated to have high social and/or environmental impacts might be restricted.

The third basic management strategy suggests reducing the social or environmental impacts of existing use. This might be accomplished by modifying the type or character of use or by dispersing or concentrating use according to user compatibility or resource capability.

A final basic management strategy involves increasing the durability of the resource. This might be accomplished by hardening the resource itself (through intensive maintenance, for example) or developing facilities to accommodate use more directly.

A second system of classifying management alternatives focuses on tactics or actual management practices. Management practices are direct actions or tools applied by managers to accomplish the management strategies described above. Restrictions on length of stay, differential fees, and use permits, for example, are management practices designed to accomplish the strategy of limiting recreation demand. Management practices are often classified according to the directness with which they act on visitor behavior (Gilbert et al. 1972, Lime 1977c, G. Peterson and Lime 1979, Chavez 1996). As the term suggests, direct management practices act directly on visitor behavior, leaving little or no freedom of choice. Indirect management practices attempt to influence the decision factors upon which visitors base their behavior. A conceptual diagram illustrating direct and indirect recreation management practices is shown in Figure 12-2. As an example, a direct management practice aimed at reducing campfires in a wilderness environment would be a regulation barring campfires and enforcement of this regulation. An indirect management practice would be an education program designed to

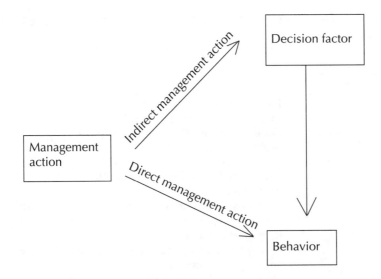

Figure 12-2. Diagram of direct versus indirect management tactics. (Adapted from G. Peterson and Lime 1979.)

inform visitors of the undesirable ecological and aesthetic impacts of campfires and encourage them to carry and use portable stoves instead. A series of direct and indirect management practices is shown in Table 12-1.

The relative advantages and disadvantages of direct and indirect recreation management practices have received substantial attention in the recreation literature. Generally, indirect management practices are favored when and where they are believed to be effective (G. Peterson and Lime 1979, McCool and Christensen 1996). This is particularly true for wilderness and related types of outdoor recreation opportunities (Clark and Stankey 1979a, Lucas 1982, Hendee et al. 1990). Indirect management practices are favored for several reasons (McCool and Christensen 1996). First, legislation and management agency policies applied to wilderness and related areas often emphasize provision of recreation opportunities that are "unconfined." Thus, direct regulation of visitor behavior may be inconsistent with such management objectives. Second, recreation is a form of leisure activity connoting freedom of choice in thought and actions. Regulations designed to control visitor behavior can be seen as antithetical to the very nature of recreation. Especially in the context of wilderness and related areas, recreation and visitor regulation have been described as "inherently contradictory" (Lucas 1982). Third, many studies indicate that, given the choice, visitors prefer indirect over direct management

Table 12-1. Direct and indirect management practices. (Adapted from Lime 1977c, 1979.)

Type	Example
Direct (Emphasis on regulation of behavior; individual choice restricted; high degree of control.)	Impose fines
	Increase surveillance of area
	Zone incompatible uses spatially (hiker only zones, prohibit motor use, etc.)
	Zone uses over time
	Limit camping in some campsites to one night, or some other limit
	Rotate use (open or close roads, access points, trails, campsites, etc.)
	Require reservations
	Assign campsites and/or travel routes to each camper group in backcountry
	Limit usage via access point
	Limit size of groups, number of horses, vehicles, etc.
	Limit camping to designated campsites only
	Limit length of stay in area (maximum/minimum)
	Restrict building of campfires
	Restrict fishing or hunting
Indirect (Emphasis on influencing or modifying behavior; individual retains freedom to choose; control less complete, more variation in use possible.)	Improve (or not) access roads, trails
	Improve (or not) campsites and other concentrated use areas
	Improve (or not) fish and wildlife populations (stock, allow to die out, etc.)
	Advertise specific attributes of the area
	Identify the range of recreation opportunities in surrounding area
	Educate users to basic concepts of ecology
	Advertise underused areas and general patterns of use
	Charge consistent entrance fee
	Charge differential fees by trail, zone, season, etc.
	Require proof of ecological knowledge and recreational activity skills

practices (Lucas 1983). Finally, indirect management practices may be more efficient because they do not entail the costs associated with enforcement of rules and regulations.

Emphasis on indirect management practices, however, has not been uniformly endorsed (McAvoy and Dustin 1983, Cole 1993, Shindler and Shelby 1993). It has been argued that indirect practices may be ineffective. There will always be some visitors, for example, who will ignore management efforts to influence the decision factors that lead to behavior. The action of a few may, therefore, hamper attainment of management objectives. It has been argued, in fact, that a direct, regulatory approach to management can ultimately lead to more freedom rather than less (Dustin and McAvoy 1984). When all visitors are required to conform to mutually agreed-upon behavior, management objectives are more likely to be attained and a diversity of recreation opportunities preserved. There is empirical evidence to suggest that, under certain circumstances, direct management practices can enhance the quality of the recreation experience (Frost and McCool 1988, Swearingen and Johnson 1995). Moreover, research suggests that visitors are surprisingly supportive of direct management practices when they are needed to control the impacts of recreation use (D. Anderson and Manfredo 1986, Shindler and Shelby 1993).

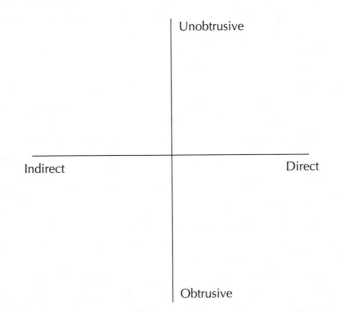

Figure 12-3. Two dimensions of recreation management practices. (Adapted from McCool and Christensen 1996.)

An analysis of management problems caused by visitors suggests that both direct and indirect management practices can be applicable depending upon the context (Gramann and Vander Stoep 1987, Alder 1996). There are several basic reasons why visitors may not conform to desired standards of behavior. These reasons range from lack of knowledge about appropriate behavior to willful rule violations. Indirect management practices, such as information and education programs, seem most appropriate in the case of the former, while direct management practices, such as enforcement of rules and regulations, may be needed in the case of the latter.

It has been suggested that there is really a continuum of management practices that range from indirect to direct (B. Hendricks et al. 1993, McCool and Christensen 1996). As an example, an educational program on the ecological and aesthetic impacts of campfires would be found toward the indirect end of a continuum of management practices. A regulation requiring campers to use portable stoves instead of campfires would be a more direct management practice. Finally, aggressive enforcement of this regulation with uniformed rangers would clearly be a very direct management practice. This suggests that management practices might also be viewed as ranging along two dimensions as illustrated in Figure 12-3 (McCool and Christensen 1996). Not only can management practices be direct or indirect, they can also be implemented in an obtrusive or unobtrusive manner. It has also been suggested that direct and indirect management practices are not mutually exclusive and that, in fact, they can often complement each other (Alder 1996, Cole et al. 1997a). For example, a regulation banning campfires (a direct management practice) should be implemented in conjunction with an educational program explaining the need for such a regulation (an indirect management practice).

A relatively comprehensive outline of recreation management practices is shown in the matrix in Figure 12-4. The vertical axis of the matrix outlines recreation management practices based on both strategies and tactics. Eight basic strategies are identified and several tactics are included under each strategy. The horizontal axis outlines a series of basic problems or issues in outdoor recreation. Cells within the matrix indicate the management practices that are most applicable to each type of problem or issue.

Classification of management practices might be based on many factors or concepts. The approaches described above simply illustrate the array of alternatives available for outdoor recreation management. For any given problem, there are likely several potential solutions.

Explicit consideration should be given to this variety of approaches rather than relying on those that are familiar or administratively expedient.

Evaluating Management Practices

A growing body of literature has focused on the potential effectiveness of selected recreation management practices. This literature can be organized into several broad categories of management issues, including visitor information and education programs, use rationing and allocation, and other recreation management practices.

Information and Education. Substantial research and management attention has focused on information and education programs as a recreation management practice. This practice is generally seen as an indirect and "light-handed" management approach. As a recreation management practice, information and education programs are

text continues on page 248

Table 12-2. Application of information and education to recreation management problems. (Adapted from Hendee et al. 1990, Roggenbuck 1992, and Vander Stoep and Roggenbuck 1996.)

Type of Problem	Example	Potential effectiveness of information and education
Illegal	Theft of Indian artifacts. Invasion of wilderness by motorized off-road vehicles	Low
Careless actions	Littering. Nuisance activity (e.g., shouting)	Moderate
Unskilled actions	Selecting improper camping spot. Building improper campfire	High
Uninformed actions	Selecting a lightly used campsite in the wilderness. Using dead snags for firewood. Camping in sight or sound of another party	Very high
Unavoidable actions	Human body waste. Loss of ground cover vegetation in the campsite	Low

Recreation management problems

Recreation management strategies and tactics	A	B	C	D	E	F	G	H	I	J	K	L	M
I. Reduce use of the entire area													
1. Limit number of visitors in the entire area													
2. Limit length of stay in the entire area													
3. Encourage use of other areas													
4. Require certain skills and/or equipment													
5. Charge a flat visitor fee													
6. Make access more difficult throughout the entire area													
II. Reduce use of problem areas													
7. Inform potential visitors of the disadvantages of problem areas and/or advantages of alternative areas						X		X	X	X	X		
8. Discourage or prohibit use of problem areas						X	X	X	X	X	X	X	
9. Limit number of visitors in problem areas						X	X	X	X	X	X	X	
10. Encourage or require a length-of- stay permit in problem areas						X	X	X	X	X	X	X	
11. Make access to problem areas more difficult and/or improve access to alternative areas						X	X	X	X	X	X	X	
12. Eliminate facilities or attractions in problem areas and/or improve facilities or attractions in alternative areas									X				
13. Encourage off-trail travel						X	X	X	X	X	X		
14. Establish differential skill and/or equipment requirements						X	X	X	X	X	X		
15. Charge differential visitor fees						X	X	X	X	X	X		
III. Modify the location of use within problem areas													
16. Discourage or prohibit camping and/or stock use on certain campsites and/or locations	X	X	X	X			X	X	X	X	X	X	X
17. Encourage or permit camping and/ or stock use only on certain campsites and/or locations	X	X	X	X			X	X	X	X	X	X	X
18. Locate facilities on durable sites	X												
19. Concentrate use on sites through facility design and/or information		X							X		X	X	X
20. Discourage or prohibit off-trail travel										X	X		
21. Segregate different types of visitors		X					X						
IV. Modify the timing of use													
22. Encourage use outside of peak use periods						X							
23. Discourage or prohibit use when impact potential is high	X	X				X		X	X	X	X	X	
24. Charge fees during periods of high use and/or high-impact potential	X	X				X		X	X	X	X		X

Recreation management problems

Recreation management strategies and tactics	A	B	C	D	E	F	G	H	I	J	K	L	M
V. Modify type of use and visitor behavior													
25. Discourage or prohibit particularly damaging practices and/or equipment		X	X	X	X	X	X	X	X	X	X	X	X
26. Encourage or require certain behavior, skills, and/or equipment		X	X	X	X	X		X	X	X	X	X	X
27. Teach a recreation use ethic		X	X	X	X	X	X	X	X	X			
28. Encourage or require a party size and/or stock limit	X						X						
29. Discourage or prohibit stock			X				X	X			X		
30. Discourage or prohibit pets									X		X		
31. Discourage or prohibit overnight use			X					X		X			
VI. Modify visitor expectations													
32. Inform visitors about recreation uses							X						
33. Inform visitors about conditions they may encounter in the area							X						
VII. Increase the resistance of the resource													
34. Shield the site from impact	X								X			X	
35. Strengthen the site	X				X								
VIII. Maintain or rehabilitate the resource													
36. Remove problems	X	X	X	X									
37. Maintain or rehabilitate impacted locations	X	X	X										

A. Deterioration of managed trails; B. Development of undesired trails; C. Excessive deterioration of campsites; D. Proliferation of campsites; E. Litter; F. Too many encounters; G. Visitor conflict; H. Deterioration of grazing areas; I. Human waste; J. Harassment of wildlife; K. Competition with wildlife; L. Attraction and feeding of wildlife; M. Contamination of water bodies

Figure 12-4 Matrix of recreation management strategies and tactics and their application to recreation management problems. (Adapted from Cole et al. 1987.)

designed to persuade visitors to adopt behaviors that are compatible with recreation management objectives. Research suggests that this approach tends to be viewed very favorably by recreation visitors (Roggenbuck and Ham 1986, Stankey and Schreyer 1987, McCool and Lime 1989, Roggenbuck 1992, Vander Stoep and Roggenbuck 1996).

A conceptual application of information and education to recreation management problems is illustrated in Table 12-2. This table classifies problem behaviors in outdoor recreation into five basic types and suggests the potential effectiveness of information and education on each. At the two ends of the spectrum, problem behaviors can be seen as either deliberately illegal (e.g., theft of Indian artifacts) or unavoidable (e.g., disposal of human waste). In these instances, information and education may have little or no effectiveness. However, the other three types of problem behaviors—careless actions (e.g., littering), unskilled actions (e.g., selecting an improper campsite), and uninformed actions (e.g., using dead snags for firewood)—may be considerably more amenable to information and education programs.

Table 12-3. Stages of moral development. (From H. Christenson and Dustin 1989.)

Kohlberg's six stages of moral development		Gilligan's perspectives on moral development	
Stage	Overriding concern	Perspective	Overriding concern
Preconventional morality			
1	Fear of punishment	1	Reference and relation to self; survival; self-oriented; similar to Kohlberg's 1 and 2
2	Maximizing pain/ minimizing pleasure		
Conventional morality			
3	What significant others think	2	Reference and relation to others; pleasing others is important; somewhat similar to Kohlberg's 3 and 4
4	What society thinks		
Postconventional morality			
5	Justice and fairness	3	Reference and relation to self and others; integration of 1 and 2 above; caring is the highest value; departs from Kohlberg at this point.
6	Self-respect		

A second conceptual approach to the application of information and education is based on theories of moral development and is illustrated in Table 12-3 (H. Christensen and Dustin 1989). This approach builds on two prominent theories of moral development as suggested by Kohlberg (1976) and Gilligan (1982). Both theories suggest that people tend to evolve through a series of stages of moral development ranging from those that are very self-centered to those that are highly altruistic and are based on principles of justice, fairness, and self-respect. Individual visitors to parks and recreation areas may be found at any of the stages of moral development shown in Table 12-3. Management implications of this conceptual approach suggest that information and education programs should be designed to reach visitors at each of these stages of moral development. For example, to reach visitors at lower levels of moral development, managers might emphasize extrinsic rewards and punishments for selected types of behavior. However, communicating with visitors at higher levels of moral development might be more effective by means of emphasizing the rationale for selected behaviors and appealing to one's sense of altruism, justice, and fairness.

Application of communication theory to outdoor recreation suggests that the potential effectiveness of information and education is dependent upon a number of variables associated with visitors and the content and delivery of messages (Roggenbuck and Ham 1986, Stankey and Schreyer 1987, Manfredo 1989, Vaske et al. 1990a, Manfredo and Bright 1991, Manfredo 1992, Roggenbuck 1992, Bright et al. 1993, Bright and Manfredo 1995, Basman et al. 1996, Vander Stoep and Roggenbuck 1996). For example, visitor behavior is at least partially driven by attitudes, beliefs, and normative standards. Information and education programs aimed at "connecting" with or modifying relevant attitudes, beliefs, or norms may be successful in guiding or changing visitor behavior. Moreover, the substance of messages and the media by which they are delivered may also influence the effectiveness of information and education programs.

From a theoretical standpoint, information and education can be seen to operate through three basic models (Roggenbuck 1992). The first model is applied behavior analysis. This approach to management focuses directly on visitor behavior rather than antecedent variables such as attitudes, beliefs, and norms. For example, visitors can be informed of rewards or punishments that will be administered dependent upon visitor behavior. Applied behavior analysis is the simplest and most direct theoretical model of information and education.

However, since it does not address underlying behavioral variables such as attitudes, beliefs, and norms, its effectiveness may be short term and dependent upon continued management action.

A second theoretical model of information and education is the central route to persuasion. In this model, relevant beliefs of visitors are modified through delivery of substantive messages. New or modified beliefs then lead to desired changes in behavior. While this is a less direct and more complex model, it may result in more lasting behavioral modification.

A third theoretical model of information and education is the peripheral route to persuasion. This model emphasizes non-substantive elements of information and education messages, such as message source and medium. For example, messages from sources considered by visitors to be authoritative or powerful may influence behavior while other messages may be ignored. This model may be especially useful in situations where it is difficult to attract and maintain the attention of visitors, such as at visitor centers, entrance stations, and bulletin boards, all of which may offer multiple and competing information and education messages. However, like applied behavior analysis, the peripheral route to persuasion may not influence antecedent conditions of behavior and, therefore, may not have lasting effects.

A relatively large number of empirical studies have examined the effectiveness of a variety of information and education programs. These studies fall into several categories, including (1) those designed to influence recreation use patterns, (2) studies focused on enhancing visitor knowledge, especially knowledge related to minimizing ecological and social impacts, (3) studies aimed at influencing visitor attitudes toward management policies, and (4) studies that address depreciative behavior such as littering and vandalism.

Recreation Use Patterns. As noted in Chapter 2, recreation use patterns are often characterized by their uneven spatial and temporal nature. Problems such as crowding may be reduced if use patterns could be redistributed to some degree. Using computer-based simulation models, a number of studies have documented the effectiveness of spatial and temporal use redistribution in reducing contacts among recreation groups (Gilbert et al. 1972, Romesburg 1974, V. Smith and Krutilla 1974, V. Smith and Headly 1975, V. Smith and Krutilla 1976, McCool et al. 1977, G. Peterson et al. 1977, deBettencourt et al. 1978, Schecter and Lucas 1978, Manning and Ciali 1979, G. Peterson and deBettencourt 1979, G. Peterson and Lime 1980, Manning and Potter 1982, 1984, F. Potter and Manning 1984, Rowell 1986, Underhill et al. 1986, Van

Wagtendonk and Coho 1986, Wang and Manning 1999). It has been shown, for example, that a nearly 20% cut in total use would be required to achieve the same reduction in contacts obtainable through use redistributions (Potter and Manning 1984).

Several studies have explored the potential effectiveness of information and education programs as a means of redistributing recreation use. An early study examined the use of roadside signs to redistribute use and found them effective (P. Brown and Hunt 1969). Similarly, the use of positively and negatively oriented trail signs were found to redistribute use at Rocky Mountain National Park, CO (Ormrod and Trahan 1977). Even simple designation of a site as an "official" park or recreation area can lead to increased use (R. Becker 1981b). Another early study explored the effectiveness of providing visitors with information on current use patterns as a way to alter future use patterns (Lime and Lucas 1977). Visitors who had permits for the most heavily used entry points in the Boundary Waters Canoe Area, MN, were mailed an information packet including a description of use patterns, noting in particular heavily used areas and times. A survey of a sample of this group who again visited the study area the following year found that three-fourths of respondents felt that this information was useful, and about one-third were influenced in their choice of entry point, route, or time of subsequent visits.

A study in the Shining Rock Wilderness Area, NC, experimented with two types of information programs designed to disperse camping away from a heavily used meadow (Roggenbuck and Berrier 1981, 1982). Two treatment groups were created. A brochure explaining resource impacts associated with concentrated camping and showing the location of other nearby camping areas was given to one treatment group, while the other was given the brochure in addition to personal contact with a wilderness ranger. Both groups dispersed their camping activity to a greater degree than a control group, but there was no statistically significant difference between the two treatment groups.

A similar experiment was conducted on trail use in the backcountry of Yellowstone National Park, MT/WY/ID (Krumpe and Brown 1982). A sample group of hikers was given a guidebook that described the attributes of lesser-used trails prior to obtaining a backcountry permit. Through a later survey and examination of permits, it was found that 37% of this group had selected one of the lesser-used trails compared to 14% of a control group. Results also indicated that the earlier the information was received, the more influence it had on behavior. Studies employing user-friendly microcomputer-based information approaches have also been found to be effective in influencing recreation use patterns (Huffman and Williams 1986, 1987, Hultsman 1988, D. Harmon 1992, Alpert and Herrington 1998).

Hikers in the Pemigewasset Wilderness, NH, were studied to determine the influence of wilderness rangers as a source of information and education (C. Brown et al. 1992). Only about 20% of visitors reported that the information received from wilderness rangers influenced their destination within the study area. However, visitors who were less experienced and who reported that they were more likely to return to the study area were more likely to be influenced by the information provided, suggesting that the information program may be more effective over time.

Potential problems in using information and education programs to influence recreation use were illustrated in a study in the Selway-Bitterroot Wilderness, MT (Lucas 1981). Brochures describing current recreation use patterns were distributed to visitors. Follow-up measurements indicated little effect on subsequent use patterns. Evaluation of this program suggested three limitations on its potential effectiveness: (1) many visitors did not receive the brochure, (2) most of those who did receive the brochure received it too late to affect their decision-making, and (3) some visitors doubted the accuracy of the information contained in the brochure.

Visitor Knowledge. A second category of studies has focused primarily on enhancing visitor knowledge through information and education programs. Most of these studies have examined knowledge associated with reducing the potential ecological and social impacts caused by recreation. Two early studies focused on distinct types of users— backpackers in Rocky Mountain National Park, CO (Fazio 1979b) and motorists in a New York state park (Feldman 1978). The study of backpackers provided information on low-impact camping practices through a series of media: a brochure, a trailhead sign, a slide and sound exhibit, a television program, and a newspaper feature article. Not enough visitors were exposed to the latter two media to evaluate their effectiveness. However, exposure to the slide/sound exhibit, the slide/ sound exhibit plus the brochure, and the slide/sound exhibit plus the trailhead sign resulted in significant increases in visitor knowledge. Exposure to the trailhead sign and brochure were not found to be very effective. The study of motorists also found that exposure to two types of information/education media—a brochure and a cassette tape—both increased the knowledge level of respondents.

More recent studies have also found significant effects of information and education programs on visitor knowledge and subsequent behavior. For example, a sample of day hikers to subalpine meadows in Mt. Rainier National Park, WA, was given a short, personal interpretive program on reasons for and importance of complying with guidelines for off-trail hiking (Kernan and Drogin 1995). Visitors who received this program and those who did not were later observed as they hiked. Most visitors (64%) who did not receive the interpretive program did not comply with off-trail hiking guidelines, while most visitors (58%) who did receive the interpretive program complied with the guidelines.

Bulletin boards at trailheads have also been found to be effective in enhancing visitor knowledge about low-impact hiking and camping practices (Cole et al. 1997b). Visitors exposed to low-impact messages at a trailhead bulletin board were found to be more knowledgeable about such practices than visitors who were not. However, increasing the number of messages posted beyond two did not result in increased knowledge levels.

Workshops and special programs delivered to organizations can also be effective in enhancing knowledge levels as well as intentions to follow recommended low-impact practices. The effectiveness of these types of information and education programs have been demonstrated in two studies aimed at Boy Scouts (Dowell and McCool 1986) and a volunteer group associated with the Boundary Waters Canoe Area Wilderness, MN (Jones and McAvoy 1988). In both cases, treatment groups scored higher than control groups on tests of knowledge and behavioral intentions administered immediately after the programs and at a later date. Research also suggests that commercial guides and outfitters can be trained to deliver information and education programs to clients that are effective in enhancing visitor knowledge (Sieg et al. 1988, Roggenbuck et al. 1992) and that trail guide booklets can also be effective (Echelberger et al. 1978).

Not all research has found information and education programs to be as effective as indicated in the above studies. A study of the effectiveness of interpretive programs at Great Smoky Mountains National Park, NC/TN found mixed results (Burde et al. 1988). There was no difference in knowledge about general backcountry policies between backcountry visitors exposed to the park's interpretive services and those who were not exposed. However, the former group did score higher on knowledge of park-related hazards. A test of visitor compliance rates with campground regulations in Acadia National Park, ME, found no difference between time periods when a special brochure was and was not used (W. Dwyer et al. 1989). Finally, a test of a special brochure on appropriate behavior relating to bears found only limited change in actual or intended behavior of visitors (Manfredo and Bright 1991). Visitors requesting information on wilderness permits for the Boundary Waters Canoe Area Wilderness, MN, were mailed the special brochures. In a follow-up survey, only 18% of respondents reported that they had received any new information from the brochure, and only 7.5% reported that they had altered their actual or intended behavior.

Visitor Attitudes. A third category of studies on the potential effectiveness of information and education programs has examined their influence on visitor attitudes toward a variety of management agency policies (Robertson 1982, Olson et al. 1984, C. Nielson and Buchanan 1986, Cable et al. 1987, Manfredo et al. 1992, Bright et al. 1993, Ramthun 1996). These studies have found that information and education programs can be effective in modifying visitor attitudes so they are more supportive of recreation and related land management policies. For example, visitors to Yellowstone National Park, MT/WY/ID, were exposed to interpretive messages designed to influence their beliefs about fire ecology and the effects of controlled-burn policies (Bright et al. 1993). These messages were found to influence both beliefs about fire ecology and attitudes based on those beliefs.

Depreciative Behavior. A fourth category of studies on the potential effectiveness of information and education as a management practice has focused on depreciative behavior, especially littering. A number of studies have found that a variety of information and education messages and related programs can be effective in reducing littering behavior and even cleaning up littered areas (Burgess et al. 1971, Clark et al 1971b, Marler 1971, Clark et al. 1972a, b, Powers et al. 1973, Lahart and Bailey 1975, Muth and Clark 1978, H. Christensen 1981, H. Christensen and Clark 1983, Oliver et al. 1985, H. Christensen 1986, Roggenbuck and Passineau 1986, Vander Stoep and Gramman 1987, Horsley 1988, Wagstaff and Wilson 1988, H. Christensen et al. 1992, Taylor and Winter 1995). For example, samples of visitors to a developed campground were given three different treatments: a brochure describing the costs and impacts of littering and vandalism, the brochure plus a personal contact with a park ranger, and these two treatments plus a request for assistance in reporting depreciative behaviors to park rangers (Oliver et al., 1985). The brochure plus the personal contact was the most effective treatment; this reduced the number of groups who littered their campsite from 67% to 41% and reduced the number of groups who damaged trees at their campsite from 20% to 4%. Types of messages and related purposes found to be effective in a number of studies include incentives to visitors to assist with clean-up efforts and the use of rangers and trip leaders as role models for cleaning up litter.

Several other types of studies, while not directly evaluating the effectiveness of information and education, are also suggestive of the potential of information and education as a recreation management practice. First, studies of visitor knowledge indicate that marked improvements are possible that could lead to improved visitor behavior. For example, campers on the Allegheny National Forest, PA, were tested for their knowledge of rules and regulations that applied to the area (Ross and Moeller 1974). Only 48% of respondents answered six or more of the ten questions correctly. A similar study of visitors to the Selway-Bitterroot Wilderness Area, ID, tested knowledge about wilderness use and management (Fazio 1979a). Only about half of the twenty questions were answered correctly by the average respondent. However, there were significant differences among types of respondents, type of knowledge, and the accuracy of various sources of information, providing indications of where and how information and education programs might be channeled most effectively.

Second, several studies indicate that current information and education programs could be substantially improved (Hunt and Brown 1971, Fazio 1979b, Cockrell and McLaughlin 1982, Fazio and Ratcliffe 1989). Evaluation of literature mailed in response to visitor requests has found several areas of needed improvements, including more timely response, more direct focus on management problems and issues, greater personalization, more visual appeal, and reduction of superfluous materials.

Third, a survey of wilderness managers has identified the extent to which twenty-five visitor education techniques are used (Doucette and Cole 1993). Study findings are shown in Table 12-4. Only six of these education techniques—brochures, personnel at agency offices, maps, signs, personnel in the backcountry, and displays at trailheads—are used in a majority of wilderness areas. Managers were also asked to rate the perceived effectiveness of education techniques. It is clear from Table 12-4 that personnel-based techniques are generally considered to be more effective than media-based techniques.

Related studies have examined the sources of information used by outdoor recreation visitors for trip planning (Uysal et al. 1990, Schuett 1993). Many respondents report using sources of information that are not directly produced by management agencies, such as outdoor clubs, professional outfitters, outdoor stores, guidebooks, newspaper and magazine articles, and travel agents. This suggests that management agency linkages with selected private and commercial organizations may be an especially effective approach to information and education.

Studies on information and education as a recreation management practice are relatively numerous, but highly diverse, employing a variety of message types and media and addressing a variety of issues and target audiences. Generally, these studies suggest that information and education can be an effective recreation management practice. Moreover, a number of guidelines for using information and education can be developed from this literature (Roggenbuck and Ham 1986, P. Brown et al. 1987, Manfredo 1989, 1992, Roggenbuck 1992, Doucette and Cole 1993, Bright 1994, Basman et al. 1996, Vander Stoep and Roggenbuck 1996):

1. Use of multiple media to deliver messages is often more effective than use of a single medium.

2. Information and education programs are generally more effective with visitors who are less experienced and who are less knowledgeable. Young visitors may be an especially attractive target audience.

3. Brochures, personal messages, and audio-visual programs may be more effective than signs.

4. Messages may be more effective when delivered early in the recreation experience, such as during trip planning.

5. Messages from sources judged highly credible may be most effective.

6. Computer-based information systems can be an effective means of delivering information and education.

7. Training of volunteers, outfitters, and commercial guides can be an effective and efficient means of communicating information and education to visitors.

8. Information on the impacts, costs, and consequences of problem behaviors can be an effective information and education strategy.

9. Role modeling by park rangers and volunteers can be an effective information and education strategy.

10. Personal contact with visitors by rangers or other employees can be effective in communicating information and education.

11. Messages should be targeted at specific audiences to the extent possible. Target audiences that might be especially effective include those who request information in advance and those who are least knowledgeable.

Table 12-4. Use and perceived effectiveness of 25 education techniques in wilderness areas. (Adapted from Doucette and Cole 1993.)

Technique	Percentage used	Mean perceived effectiveness rating
Brochures	74	2.5
Personnel at agency offices	70	2.7
Maps	68	2.1
Signs	67	2.3
Personnel in backcountry	65	3.8
Displays at trailheads	55	2.6
Displays at agency offices	48	2.7
Posters	48	2.3
Personnel at school programs	47	2.9
Slide shows	36	2.9
Personnel at campgrounds	35	2.9
Personnel at public meetings	34	2.8
Personnel at trailheads	29	3.3
Personnel at visitor centers	26	3.0
Videos	21	2.6
Agency periodicals	18	2.3
Displays at visitor centers	18	2.5
Guidebooks	13	2.5
Interpreters	11	3.6
Computers	11	1.9
Commercial radio	9	1.9
Commercial periodicals	8	2.4
Movies	7	2.6
Commercial television	4	2.3
Agency radio	1	2.4
Mean of personnel-based techniques		3.1
Mean of media-based techniques		2.4
Mean of all techniques		2.6

Effectiveness scale: 1 = "not effective"; 5 = "highly effective"

Use Rationing and Allocation. Substantial attention has been focused on the management practice of limiting the amount of use that park and recreation areas receive. Use rationing is controversial and is generally considered to be a management practice of "last resort" because it runs counter to the basic objective of providing public access to parks and recreation areas (Hendee and Lucas 1973, Behan 1974, Hendee and Lucas 1974, Behan 1976, Dustin and McAvoy 1980). However, limits on use may be needed to maintain the quality of the recreation experience and to protect the integrity of critical park resources.

Rationing and Allocation Practices. Five basic management practices have been identified in the literature to ration and allocate recreation use (Stankey and Baden 1977, Fractor 1982, Shelby et al. 1989c, McLean and Johnson 1997). These include reservation systems; lotteries; first-come, first-served or queuing; pricing; and merit. A reservation system requires potential visitors to reserve a space or permit in advance of their visit. A lottery also requires potential visitors to request a permit in advance, but allocates permits on a purely random basis. A first-come, first-served or queuing system requires potential visitors to "wait in line" for available permits. A pricing system requires visitors to pay a fee for a permit which may "filter out" those who are unable or unwilling to pay. A merit system requires potential visitors to "earn" the right to a permit by virtue of demonstrated knowledge or skill.

Each of these management practices has potential advantages and disadvantages, which are summarized in Table 12-5. For example, reservation systems may tend to favor visitors who are willing and able to plan ahead, but these systems may be difficult and costly to administer. Lotteries are often viewed as eminently "fair," but can also be difficult and costly to administer. Although relatively easy to administer, first-come, first-served systems may favor visitors who have more leisure time or who live relatively close to a park or recreation area. Pricing is a commonly used practice in society to allocate scarce resources, but may discriminate against potential visitors with low incomes. Merit systems are rarely used, but may lessen the environmental and social impacts of use.

Several principles or guidelines have been suggested for considering and applying use rationing and allocation practices (Stankey and Baden 1977). First, emphasis should be placed on the environmental and social

text continues on page 262

Table 12-5. Evaluation of five recreation use rationing practices. (From Stanley and Baden 1977.)

	Reservation	Lottery	First come, first served	Pricing	Merit
Clientele group benefited by system	Those able and/or willing to plan ahead; i.e., persons with structured lifestyles.	No one identifiable group benefited. Those who examine probabilities of success at different areas have better chance.	Those with low opportunity cost for their time (e.g., unemployed). Also favors users who live nearby.	Those able or willing to pay entry costs.	Those able or willing to invest time and effort to meet requirements.
Clientele group adversely affected by system	Those unable or unwilling to plan ahead; e.g., persons with occupations that do not permit long-range planning, such as many professionals.	No one identifiable group discriminated against. Can discriminate against the unsuccessful applicant to whom the outcome is important.	Those persons with high opportunity cost of time. Also those persons who live some distance from areas. The cost of time is not recovered by anyone.	Those unwilling or unable to pay entry costs.	Those unable or unwilling to invest time and effort to meet requirements.
Experience to date with use of system	Main type of rationing system used in both National Forests and National Parks.	Limited. However, it is a common method for allocating big-game hunting permits.	Used in conjunction with reservation system in San Jacinto Wilderness. Also used in some National Park Wildernesses.	Little. Entrance fees sometimes charged, but not to limit use.	Little. Merit is used to allocate use for some specialized activities such as river running.

	Reservation	Lottery	First come, first served	Pricing	Merit
Acceptability of system to users[1]	Generally high. Good acceptance in areas where used. Seen as best way to ration by users in areas not currently rationed.	Low.	Low to moderate.	Low to moderate.	Not clearly known. Could vary considerably depending on level of training required to attain necessary proficiency and knowledge level.
Difficulty for administrators	Moderately difficult. Requires extra staffing, expanded hours. Record keeping can be substantial.	Difficult to moderately difficult. Allocating permits over an entire use season could be very cumbersome.	Low difficulty to moderately difficult. Could require development of facilities to support visitors waiting in line.	Moderate difficulty. Possibly some legal questions about imposing a fee for wilderness entry.	Difficult to moderately difficult. Initial investments to establish licensing program could be substantial.
Efficiency—extent to which system can minimize problems of suboptimization	Low to moderate. Underutilization can occur because of "no shows," denying entry to others. Allocation of permits has little relationship to value of the experience as judged by the applicant.	Low. Because permits are assigned randomly, persons who place little value on an opportunity stand as good a chance of gaining entry as those who place high value on it.	Moderate. Because system rations primarily through a cost of time, it requires some measure of worth by participants.	Moderate to high. Imposing a fee requires user to judge worth of experience against costs. Uncertain as to how well use could be "fine-tuned" with price.	Moderate to high. Requires user to make expenditures of time and effort (and maybe dollars) to gain entry.

	Reservation	Lottery	First come, first served	Pricing	Merit
Principal way in which use impact is controlled	Reducing visitor numbers. Controlling distribution of use in space and time by varying number of permits available at different trailheads or at different times.	Reducing visitor numbers. Controlling distribution of use in space and time by number of permits available at different places or times, thus varying probability of success.	Reducing visitor numbers. Controlling distribution of use in space and time by number of persons permitted to enter at different places or times.	Reducing visitor numbers. Controlling distribution of use in space and time by using differential prices.	Some reduction in numbers as well as shifts in time and space. Major reduction in per capita impact.
How system affects user behavior[2]	Affects both spatial and temporal behavior.	Affects both spatial and temporal behavior.	Affects both spatial and temporal behavior. User must consider cost of time of waiting in line.	Affects both spatial and temporal behavior. User must consider cost in dollars.	Affects style of user's behavior.

1. Based upon actual field experience as well as upon evidence reported in visitor studies (Stanley 1973).
2. This criterion is designed to measure how the different rationing systems would directly impact the behavior of users (e.g., where they go, when they go, how they behave, etc.).

impacts of recreation use rather than the amount of use *per se.* Some types of recreation use may cause more impacts than others. To the extent that such impacts can be reduced, rationing use of recreation areas can be avoided or at least postponed. Second, as noted above, rationing use should probably be considered a management practice of last resort. Less direct or "heavy-handed" management practices would seem more desirable where they can be demonstrated to be effective. Third, good information is needed to implement use rationing and allocation. Managers must be certain that social and/or environmental problems dictate use rationing and that visitors are understood well enough to predict the effects of alternative allocation systems. Fourth, combinations of use rationing systems should be considered. Given the advantages and disadvantages of each use-allocation practice, hybrid systems may have special application. For example, half of all permits might be allocated on the basis of a reservation system and half on a first-come, first-served basis. This would serve the needs of potential visitors who can and do plan vacations in advance as well as those whose jobs or lifestyles do not allow for this. Fifth, use rationing should establish a linkage between the probability of obtaining a permit and the value of the recreation opportunity to potential visitors. In other words, visitors who value the opportunity highly should have a chance to "earn" a permit through pricing, advance planning, waiting time, or merit. Finally, use-rationing practices should be monitored and evaluated to assess their effectiveness and fairness. Use rationing for recreation is relatively new and is likely to be controversial. Special efforts should be made to ensure that use-rationing practices accomplish their objectives.

Fairness. A critical element of use-rationing and allocation practices is "fairness" (Dustin and Knopf 1989). Parks and outdoor recreation areas administered by federal, state, and local agencies are public resources. Use-rationing and allocation practices must be seen as both efficient and equitable. But how are equity, fairness, and related concepts defined? Several studies have begun to develop important insights into this issue. These studies have outlined several alternative dimensions of equity and measured their support among the public.

One study identified four dimensions of an overall theory of "distributive justice" (Shelby et al. 1989c). Distributive justice is defined as an ideal whereby individuals obtain what they "ought" to have based on criteria of fairness. A first dimension is "equality" and suggests that all individuals have an equal right to a benefit such as access to parks and outdoor recreation. A second dimension is "equity" and suggests that benefits be distributed to those who "earn" them through some investment of time, money, or effort. A third dimension is "need" and suggests that benefits be distributed on the basis of unmet needs or competitive disadvantage. A final dimension is "efficiency" and suggests that benefits be distributed to those who place the highest value upon them.

Insights into these dimensions of distributive justice were developed through a survey of river runners on the Snake River in Hell's Canyon, ID (Shelby et al. 1989b). Visitors were asked to rate the five use allocation practices described above—reservation; lottery; first-come, first-served; pricing; and merit—on the basis of four criteria: perceived chance of obtaining a permit, perceived fairness of the practice, acceptability of the practice, and willingness to try the practice. Results suggest that visitors use concepts of both fairness and pragmatism in evaluating use-rationing practices. However, pragmatism—the perceived ability on the part of the respondent to obtain a permit—had the strongest effect on willingness to try each of the allocation practices. These findings suggest that managers have to convince potential visitors that proposed use allocation practices are not only "fair," but that they will provide them with a reasonable chance to obtain a permit.

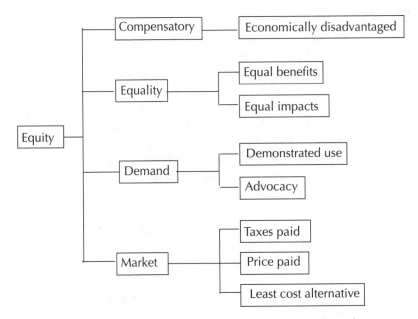

Figure 12-5. Dimensions of equity for allocating park and recreation benefits. (Adapted from Crompton and Lue 1992.)

A second series of studies has examined a more extended taxonomy of equity dimensions that might be applied to provision of a broad spectrum of park and recreation services (Wicks and Crompton 1986, Wicks 1987, Wicks and Crompton 1987, Crompton and Wicks 1988, Wicks and Crompton 1989, 1990, Crompton and Lue 1992). Eight potential dimensions of equity are identified as shown in Figure 12-5. A first dimension is compensatory and allocates benefits on the basis of economic disadvantage. The second two dimensions are variations of equality and allocate benefits to all individuals equally or ensure that all individuals ultimately receive equal total benefits. The fourth and fifth dimensions are based on demand and allocate benefits to those who make greatest use of them or those who advocate most effectively for them. The final three dimensions of equity are market-driven and distribute benefits based on amount of taxes paid, the price charged for services, or the least-cost alternative for providing recreation services.

These dimensions of equity were described to a sample of California residents, and respondents were asked to indicate the extent to which they agreed or disagreed with each dimension of equity as a principle for allocating public park and recreation services (Crompton and Lue 1992). A majority of the sample agreed with only three of the dimensions. These dimensions were, in decreasing order, demonstrated use, price paid, and equal benefits.

Visitor Attitudes and Preferences. Despite the complex and controversial nature of use rationing and allocation, there is considerable support for a variety of such management practices among visitors (Stankey 1973, Fazio and Gilbert 1974, Stankey 1979, Lucas 1980, McCool and Utter 1981, Utter et al. 1981, McCool and Utter 1982, Shelby et al. 1982, Schomaker and Leatherberry 1983, Lucas 1985, Shelby et al. 1989b, Glass and More 1992, Watson 1993, Watson and Niccolucci 1995). Support for the general principle of use restrictions was noted in Chapter 2. Research suggests that even most individuals who have been unsuccessful at obtaining a permit continue to support the need for use rationing (Fazio and Gilbert 1974, Stankey 1979, McCool and Utter 1982). A study of visitors to three wilderness areas in Oregon found that support for use restrictions was based on concerns for protecting both resource quality and the quality of the visitor experience (Watson and Niccolucci 1995). Support by day hikers was influenced most strongly by concerns with crowding, while support by overnight visitors was influenced by concern for both crowding and environmental impacts.

Preferences among alternative use rationing practices have been found to be highly variable, based on both location and type of user

(Magill 1976, McCool and Utter 1981, Shelby et al. 1982, Shelby et al. 1989b, Glass and More 1992). Support for a particular use-allocation practice appears to be related primarily to which practices respondents are familiar with and the extent to which they believe they can obtain a permit. A study of river managers found that first-come, first-served and reservation systems were judged the two most administratively feasible allocation practices and were also the most commonly used practices (Wikle 1991).

In keeping with the generally favorable attitude toward use limitation described above, most studies have found visitor compliance rates for mandatory permits to be high, ranging from 68% to 97% with most areas in the 90% range (Lime and Lorence 1974, Godin and Leonard 1977a, Van Wagtendonk and Benedict 1980, Plager and Womble 1981, Parsons et al. 1982). Moreover, permit systems that have incorporated trailhead quotas have been found to be effective in redistributing use both spatially and temporally (Hulbert and Higgins 1977, Van Wagtendonk 1981, Van Wagtendonk and Coho 1986).

A common precursor to mandatory permit systems in wilderness and related areas is voluntary self-registration. Visitors are asked to register themselves at trailheads as a measure of use for management purposes. Compliance with this management practice has been found to be considerably less uniform than with mandatory permits: registration rates have been found to vary from 21% to 89%, with most in the 65% to 80% range (Wenger 1964, Wenger and Gregerson 1964, James and Schreuder 1971, Lucas et al. 1971, James and Schreuder 1972, Lucas 1975, Leatherberry and Lime 1981, Scotter 1981, Lucas and Kovalicky 1981). Several types of visitors have especially low registration rates, including day users, horseback riders, and single-person parties.

Pricing. Among the use-rationing and allocation practices described above, pricing has received special attention in the literature. Pricing is the primary means of allocating scarce resources in a free-market economy. Economic theory generally suggests that higher prices will result in less consumption of a given good or service. Thus, pricing may be an effective approach to limiting use of parks and outdoor recreation areas. However, park and recreation services in the public sector have traditionally been priced at a nominal level or have been provided free of charge. The basic philosophy underlying this policy is that access to park and recreation services is important to all people and no one should be "priced out of the market." Interest in instituting or increasing fees at parks and outdoor recreation areas has generated a considerable body of literature that ranges from philosophical to theoretical to empirical (F. Anderson and Bonsor 1974, Gibbs 1977, Manning and Baker 1981, Driver 1984, Manning et al. 1984, Rosenthal et al. 1984, Schreyer and Knopf 1984, M. Anderson et al. 1985, R. Becker et al. 1985, Cockrell and Wellman 1985a, b, Dustin 1986, Manning and Koenemann 1986, Martin 1986, Walsh 1986, Binkley and Mendelsohn 1987, Daniels 1987, Dustin et al. 1987, Harris and Driver 1987, Leuschner et al. 1987, McCarville and Crompton 1987, C. McDonald et al. 1987, Bamford et al. 1988, Reiling et al. 1988, Schultz et al. 1988, Fedler and Miles 1989, Stevenson 1989, Manning and Zwick 1990, Kerr and Manfredo 1991, G. Peterson 1992, Reiling et al. 1992, N. Christensen et al. 1993, Reiling and Cheng 1994, Scott and Munson 1994, Emmett et al. 1996, Lundgren 1996, Manning et al. 1996f, McCarville 1996, McCarville et al. 1996, Reiling and Kotchen 1996, Reiling et al. 1996, Bowker and Leeworthy 1998).

Studies of pricing have tended to focus on several issues related to its potential as a recreation management practice. First, to what extent does pricing influence use of parks and related areas? Findings have been mixed. For example, a study of day users at six recreation areas administered by the Army Corps of Engineers found that 40% of respondents reported they would no longer use these areas if a fee was instituted (Reiling et al. 1996). However, other studies have shown little or no effects of pricing on recreation use levels (Manning and Baker 1981, R. Becker et al. 1985, Leuschner et al. 1987, Rechisky and Williamson 1992). The literature suggests that the influence of fees on recreation use is dependent upon several factors, including:

1. The "elasticity of demand" for a park or recreation area. Elasticity refers to the slope of the demand curve that defines the relationship between price and quantity consumed. This issue is illustrated in Figure 12-6. The demand for some recreation areas is relatively elastic, meaning that a change in price has a comparatively large effect on the quantity consumed (or visitation). The demand for other recreation areas is relatively inelastic, meaning that a change in price has a comparatively small effect on the quantity consumed (or visitation).

2. The significance of the recreation area. Parks of national significance, such as Yellowstone National Park, are likely to have a relatively inelastic demand, suggesting that pricing is not likely to be effective in limiting use unless price increases are quite dramatic. Parks that are less significant are likely to be characterized by more elastic demand, and pricing may be an effective use-allocation practice.

3. The percentage of total cost represented by the fee. In cases where the fee charged represents a relatively high percentage of the total cost

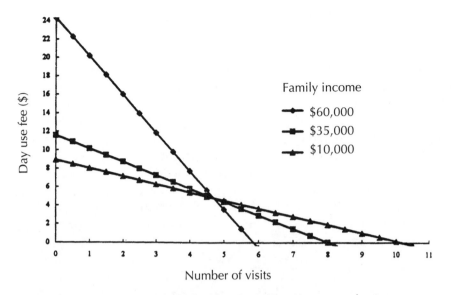

Figure 12-6. Demand curves for day use recreation areas by income level. (From Reiling et al. 1996.)

of visiting a recreation area, pricing is likely to be a more effective use-limiting approach. However, where the fee charged represents only a small percentage of the total cost, pricing is not likely to be an effective use-limiting approach.

4. The type of fee instituted. Pricing structure can be a potentially important element in determining the effectiveness of fees as management practice. For example, a daily use fee might be more effective in limiting total use than an annual pass that allows unlimited use opportunities for a flat fee.

A second issue addressed in the literature is the acceptability of fees to potential visitors. Again, study findings are mixed, though they often suggest that there is a substantial willingness to pay for park and recreation services. However, research suggests that the acceptability of fees is at least partially dependent on several factors, including:

1. Dispensation of resulting revenues. If revenues derived from fee programs are retained by the collecting agency and reinvested in recreation facilities and services, then fees are often judged to be more acceptable to park visitors.

2. Initiation of fee or increase in existing fee. Public acceptance of new fees where none were charged before tends to be relatively low compared to increases in existing fees.

3. Local or non-local visitors. Local visitors tend to be more resistant to new fees or increased fees than non-local visitors. As described above, this is probably because fees represent a larger percentage of the total cost of visiting a recreation area for local visitors. Moreover, local residents are likely to visit a given recreation area more often than non-local residents.

4. Provision of comparative information. Visitor acceptance of fees is likely to be greater when information is provided on the costs of competing or substitute recreation opportunities and when visitors are made aware of the costs of providing recreation opportunities.

A third issue concerns the potential for pricing to discriminate against certain groups in society, particularly those with low incomes. Once again, research on this issue is mixed. For example, one study examined the socioeconomic characteristics of visitors to two similar outdoor recreation areas in Virginia, one of which charged an entrance fee, and the other did not (Leuscher et al. 1987). No differences were found in income levels, suggesting the fee had no discriminatory effect. However, two studies of willingness to pay recreation fees at state parks and Army Corps of Engineers day-use areas found that lower-income visitors had a more elastic demand curve than did high-income users as illustrated in Figure 12-6 (Reiling et al. 1992, 1994). This suggests that pricing may discriminate against lower-income visitors.

A final issue concerns the use of differential pricing to influence recreation use patterns. Differential pricing consists of charging higher or lower fees at selected times and locations. In Chapter 2, it was noted that outdoor recreation tends to be characterized by relatively extreme "peaking." That is, certain areas or times are used very heavily while other times or areas are relatively lightly used. Can pricing be used to even out such recreation use patterns? Research is suggestive of this potential use of pricing (LaPage et al. 1975, Willis et al. 1975, Manning et al. 1982). For example, studies of experimental differential campsite pricing at Vermont state parks documented significant shifts in campsite occupancy patterns (Manning et al. 1984, Bamford et al. 1988).

Other Recreation Management Practices. As suggested earlier in this chapter, a number of other practices are available to manage outdoor recreation. Most of these tend to be direct management practices. Beyond information/education programs and limiting use, four broad categories of management practices addressed in the literature include rules and regulations, law enforcement, zoning, and site design and management.

Rules and Regulations. Rules and regulations are a commonly used recreation management practice, though their use can sometimes be controversial (Lucas 1982, 1983). Common applications of rules and regulations in outdoor recreation include group size limitations, assigned campsites and/or travel itineraries, area closures, length of stay limitations, and restrictions on and/or prohibition of campfires. The importance of encouraging visitors to comply with rules and regulations is emphasized in a study of the national park system that found that visitors who did not comply with rules and regulations caused extensive damage (D. Johnson and Vande Kamp 1996).

As noted earlier in this chapter, research indicates that visitors are often unaware of rules and regulations (Ross and Moeller 1974). This suggests that managers must effectively communicate rules and regulations to visitors using the principles and guidelines described in the section on information and education programs. In particular, visitors should be informed of the reasons why applicable rules and regulations are necessary, sanctions associated with failure to comply with rules and regulations, and alternative activities and behaviors that can be substituted for those not allowed.

Only limited research has addressed the effectiveness of rules and regulations as a recreation management practice. The literature suggests most visitors support limitations on group size, but that group types should also be considered when promulgating such regulations (Roggenbuck and Schreyer 1977, Heywood 1985). Group size limits should not be set so low that they affect primary social groups of visitors who may have strong motivations for social interaction. However, research indicates that social groups in outdoor recreation tend to be small.

Research suggests that regulations requiring the use of assigned campsites in wilderness or backcountry are generally not supported by visitors (Lucas 1985, D. Anderson and Manfredo 1986). An extreme version of this regulation requires backpackers to follow a fixed travel itinerary. Studies of the effectiveness of this regulation have found that visitor compliance rates are relatively low (Van Wagtendonk and Benedict 1980, Parsons et al. 1981, 1982, Stewart 1989, 1991). For example, 44% to 77% of backcountry campers were found not to be in full compliance with their permit itinerary across four zones of Grand Canyon National Park, AZ (Stewart 1989). Noncompliance was primarily caused by visitors using campsites other than those specified or staying in the backcountry more or fewer nights than originally specified.

Research on regulations closing selected areas to public use suggest they are supported by visitors if the underlying reason is clear and justified (Frost and McCool 1988). Most visitors were found to obey a regulation closing selected backcountry campsites for ecological reasons (Cole and Ranz 1983). Regulations closing areas to camping in selected natural areas in Norway have also been found to be effective, although the effects of such regulations can substantially threaten traditional use and users (Vorkinn 1998). This suggests that regulations should be used cautiously.

Law Enforcement. Little research has been conducted on law enforcement in outdoor recreation. Most of the literature in this area discusses the controversial nature of law enforcement in this context (F. Campbell et al. 1968, Bowman 1971, Hadley 1971, Hope 1971, Schwartz 1973, Connors 1976, Shanks 1976, Wicker and Kirmeyer 1976, L. Harmon 1979, Morehead 1979, Wade 1979, Westover et al. 1980, Philley and McCool 1981, Heinrichs 1982, Perry 1983, Manning 1987). However, one study focused on the use of uniformed rangers to deter off-trail hiking at Mt. Rainier National Park, WA (Swearingen and Johnson 1995). The presence of a uniformed ranger was found to significantly reduce off-trail hiking. Moreover, visitors tended to react positively to this management practice when they understood that the presence of a ranger was needed for information dissemination, visitor safety, and resource protection.

Zoning. Zoning is another basic category of recreation management practices. In its most generic sense, zoning simply means assigning certain recreation activities to selected areas (or restricting activities from areas as the case may be). Zoning can also be applied in a temporal dimension as well as in a spatial sense. Finally, zoning can be applied to alternative management prescriptions as a way of creating different types of outdoor recreation opportunities (Greist 1975, Haas et al. 1987). For example, "rescue" and "no-rescue" zones have been proposed for wilderness areas, though this is controversial (McAvoy and Dustin 1981, McAvoy et al. 1985, Dustin et al. 1986, Harwell 1987, D. Peterson 1987, McAvoy 1990).

In its most fundamental form, zoning is widely used to create and manage a diversity of recreation opportunities. The basic concept of zoning is at the heart of the Recreation Opportunity Spectrum described in Chapter 8. Zoning is also used in outdoor recreation to restrict selected recreation activities from environmentally sensitive areas and to separate conflicting recreation uses. No primary research has been conducted on the potential effectiveness of zoning.

Site Design and Management. A final category of recreation management practices is site design and management. Recreation areas can be designed and manipulated to "harden" them against recreation impacts and manage the use made of them. For example, boardwalks can be built to concentrate use in developed areas and facilities can be constructed along trails to channel use in appropriate areas (Hultsman and Hultsman 1989, Doucette and Kimball 1990). Moreover, campsites can be designated and designed in ways to minimize social and ecological impacts (Godin and Leonard 1976, McEwen and Tocher 1976, Echelberger et al. 1983b). However, most of these management practices involve resource management activities that are beyond the scope of this book. Hammitt and Cole (1998) provide an excellent review of the outdoor recreation literature addressing site and resource management.

Status and Trends in Recreation Management

What recreation management practices are used most often and how effective are they? What are the trends in recreation management? Several studies conducted over the past two decades offer insights into these questions (Godin and Leonard 1979, Bury and Fish 1980, Fish and Bury 1981, Washburne 1981, Washburne and Cole 1983, Marion et al. 1993, Manning et al. 1996a). These studies have focused on wilderness and backcountry areas and have involved periodic surveys of recreation managers. The most recent study explored current recreation management practices in the national park system (Marion et al. 1993, Manning et al. 1996a). Managers of all national park backcountry areas were asked to indicate which of more than 100 recreation management practices were currently used and which were judged most effective. Management practices used in over half of all areas are shown in Table 12-6, along with all management practices judged to be "highly effective."

Comparisons across the studies noted above can provide some insights into trends in recreation management problems and practices, at least in the context of wilderness and backcountry areas. Although the areas, management agencies, and research methods varied among these studies, their primary objectives were similar—to assess recreation management problems and/or practices in resource-based recreation areas. These studies provide benchmarks at four points in time—1979,

1981, 1983, and 1993—and suggest several basic trends in recreation management problems and practices.

First, environmental impacts, primarily on trails and campsites, are the dominant recreation-related problems perceived by managers throughout these studies. In all four studies, managers tended to report site deterioration, including soil erosion and loss of vegetation, as the most frequently occurring recreation management problem.

Second, social problems of crowding and conflicting uses appear to have increased over time. The initial study in 1979 revealed no crowding problems. The study reported that user conflict was cited as a problem by 29% of wilderness managers, but this conflict was associated primarily with non-conforming uses of wilderness, such as grazing and off-road vehicles. More recent studies report substantial and increasing levels of crowding and conflict among recreation users. For example, crowding was reported as a problem "in many places" in 1983 at 10% of all areas studied, including 2% of National Park Service areas. By 1993, between 10% and 27% (depending upon location—campsite, trail, attraction site—within the area) of National Park Service areas reported crowding "in many or most areas." Moreover, conflict between different types of users was reported as widespread in 2% of areas in 1983, but was reported as a problem "in many or most areas" in 1993 by as many as 9% of areas.

Third, carrying capacity has become a pervasive but largely unresolved issue. The initial study in 1979 did not report carrying capacity as a significant issue. However, by 1983 recreation use was judged to exceed carrying capacity "sometimes" or "usually" in at least some areas by over half of all managers. Carrying capacity problems in National Park Service areas were reported as equally extensive in 1983 and 1993, with 70% of managers reporting that carrying capacity is exceeded either "sometimes" or "usually" in at least some areas. Despite the apparent seriousness of the carrying capacity issue, most managers have not yet addressed it adequately. Nearly half of all areas studied in 1983 reported that they were unable to estimate carrying capacity for any portions of their areas. Moreover, the percentage of National Park Service areas unable to estimate carrying capacity rose from 36% in 1983 to 57% in 1993. Finally, despite the fact that 43% of National Park Service areas currently are able to estimate carrying capacity in at least some portions of their areas, considerably less than half of these areas make such estimates based on scientific studies.

Fourth, implementation of both direct and indirect recreation management practices have tended to increase over time. For example,

Table 12-6. Most commonly used and effective recreation management practices. (Adapted from Manning et al. 1996a.)

Most commonly used (% of areas using)

Most effective

Educate visitors about "pack-it-in, pack-it-out" policy (91)

Prohibit visitors from cutting standing dead wood for fires (83)

Educate visitors about how to minimize their impacts (77)

Remove litter left by visitors (74)

Instruct visitors not to feed wildlife (74)

Require backcountry overnight visitors to obtain permits (68)

Instruct visitors to bury human wastes (66)

Require groups to limit their length of stay at campsites (64)

Give verbal warnings to visitors who violate regulations (63)

Require groups to limit their size (62)

Prohibit pets from the backcountry (61)

Prohibit use of horses in selected areas (59)

Instruct visitors to bury human wastes away from all water sources (57)

Inform visitors about potential crowding they may encounter in selected areas (56)

Discourage use of environmentally sensitive areas (54)

Inform visitors about managers' concerns with visitor use impacts at attraction areas (54)

Instruct visitors to view wildlife from a distance (53)

Perform regular trail maintenance (52)

Require groups to limit their length of stay in the backcountry (51)

Campsite impacts
designate campsites
prohibit campfires
provide campsite facilities
restore campsites
limit group sizes
implement campsite reservation system

Trail impacts
maintain and rehabilitate trails
use impact monitoring system
use formal trail system and plan
implement quotas on amount of use

Wildlife impacts
temporarily close sensitive areas
regulate food storage and facilities
provide user education programs
restrict pets
provide information workshops for commercial outfitters and guides

Water impacts
provide primitive toilets at high-use sites

Visitor crowding and conflicts
implement quotas on amount of visitor use
control access to backcountry with visitor transportation system

overnight permits for backcountry camping were required by 41% of areas in 1983, but were required by 68% of areas in 1993. Party size limits are imposed in increasing numbers of areas, up from 43% in 1981 to 62% in 1993. Length-of-stay limits are also imposed in increasing numbers of areas, up from 16% in 1981 to 51% in 1993. Finally, minimum-impact education programs were employed in 77% of areas in 1993, up from 35% reported in 1981. Although some of these differences may be the result of differences among management agencies, the magnitude of the differences suggests a shift in management practices.

Fifth, day use is an emerging issue that warrants more management attention. The study in 1983 was the first to report that a very large percentage of all wilderness-related recreation use was accounted for by day users. The average percentage of all visitor groups that are day users ranged from 44% in Bureau of Land Management areas to 83% for Fish and Wildlife Service areas. In National Park Service areas, the percentage of day users has remained relatively constant over the past decade: 62% in 1983 and 64% in 1993. The issue of day use is exacerbated by two factors (Roggenbuck et al. 1994). First, many management problems are attributed by managers to day users. In fact, in the judgment of managers, day users are more responsible than overnight visitors for most types of management problems. Second, day users often are not targeted for management actions. For example, only 8% of National Park Service areas require a permit for day use.

Finally, management of outdoor recreation is becoming more complex and more sophisticated. This trend is reflected in the nature of the four studies examined in this section. The original study in 1979 was primarily an exploratory study asking managers to describe their primary problems. The basic concept of wilderness areas emerged as a primary issue while managers struggled with the legal and operational definitions of wilderness and related areas. The second study, reported in 1981, focused primarily on recreation management practices across several land management agencies. The third study in 1983 adopted several objectives, including determining recreation use patterns, recreation-related problems, and recreation management practices. The fourth and most recent study incorporated the preceding objectives and added others, including investigating the perceived causes of management problems, the effectiveness of management practices, and the degree to which management actions are based on scientific study. The progression of these four studies illustrates that awareness and knowledge about recreation-related problems and management practices are expanding.

Studies on alternative recreation management practices are beginning to be marshaled into handbooks and other types of guidelines that can be used by recreation managers. For example, the matrix illustrated in Figure 12-4 is adapted from a handbook developed for wilderness managers (Cole et la. 1987). In addition to suggesting which recreation management practices might be applied to a series of recreation-related problems, the handbook offers basic information on understanding and applying each of the thirty-seven recreation management practices identified. A similar handbook has been developed for use by managers of national parks and related areas (D. Anderson et al. 1998). Prototypes of computer-based "expert systems" are also being developed to provide recreation managers with guidance based on the scientific literature (Flekke et al. 1996).

However, research suggests that recreation management is influenced by managers and the agencies they represent, as well as the expertise available to them (Kaufman 1960, Holland and Beazley 1971, Driver and Brown 1983, Kennedy 1985, 1987a, b, Magill 1988, Van Meter 1988, Twight and Lyden 1988, Bullis and Tompkins 1989, Twight and Lyden 1989, Dennis and Magill 1991). For example, a survey of recreation managers on several national forests in California found that most were educated in the natural resources fields of study that have traditionally emphasized commodity production rather than the social sciences (Dennis and Magill 1991). Moreover, most managers reported that their training in recreation management had occurred "on the job," suggesting that traditional professional orientations and management practices were being perpetuated. Finally, the administrative structure of the management agency was found to provide relatively few opportunities for professional advancement for managers educated in the social sciences. These findings suggest that many of the social science-based issues in outdoor recreation may be difficult to address under traditional administrative structures.

Finally, recreation management can be influenced by personal philosophy as well. A study of wilderness managers in the Southwest found that the personal wilderness philosophy of managers influenced the types of wilderness management practices undertaken (Virden and Brooks 1991). For example, managers who favor a stronger biocentric orientation to wilderness may be more likely to adopt direct recreation management practices such as regulating visitor behavior. A study of wilderness visitors has found similar types of relationships between environmental values and philosophy and support for wilderness management practices (Valliere and Manning 1995, Manning and

Valliere 1996). These findings suggest that managers and others concerned with recreation management and related matters should be encouraged to develop thoughtful professional philosophies through academic and professional education.

Summary and Conclusions

1. A variety of practices are available to manage outdoor recreation.

2. Recreation management practices can be classified based on their strategic purpose. Basic strategies for outdoor recreation management include increasing the supply of recreation opportunities, limiting recreation use, reducing the impacts of existing use, and increasing the durability of the resource. Management practices can also be classified on the basis of whether they act directly or indirectly on visitor behavior.

3. Indirect management practices are generally favored where they are believed to be effective. However, direct management practices are justified when needed to attain recreation management objectives. A combination of indirect and direct management practices may be needed to achieve maximum effectiveness.

4. Explicit consideration should be given to all applicable recreation management practices rather than relying on those that are familiar or expedient.

5. Information and education programs are indirect recreation management practices and are generally supported by visitors. The potential effectiveness of information and education programs may depend upon a number of variables, including: the type of problem addressed; the attitudes, beliefs, and norms of visitors; the substance of the message delivered; the medium by which the message is delivered; and the source of the message. Information and education programs have been found to be effective in influencing recreation use patterns, enhancing visitor knowledge of low-impact behaviors, influencing visitor attitudes about management policies, and reducing depreciative behaviors such as littering and vandalism.

6. Use rationing and allocation are direct recreation practices and are often controversial. However, visitors tend to support these management practices when they are needed to protect the quality

of the visitor experience and park resources. Five basic rationing and allocation practices are available, including: reservation system; lottery; first-come, first-served or queuing; pricing; and merit. Potential advantages and disadvantages of each of these practices are summarized in Table 12-5. Use rationing and allocation must be based on consideration of both efficiency and equity.

7. Pricing has received special research attention as a recreation management practice. The effect of pricing on recreation use is dependent upon several variables, including elasticity of demand, significance of the recreation area, percentage of total cost represented by the fee charged, and the type of fee charged. Acceptability of fees to visitors is dependent upon several factors, including dispensation of resulting revenues, whether the fee is newly instituted or an increase in an existing fee, local or non-local residence of visitors, and provision of comparative information. When using pricing as a recreation management practice, special care should be exercised in testing for potential discriminatory effects.

8. Other categories of recreation management practices include rules and regulations, law enforcement, zoning, and site design and management. Only limited research has assessed the potential effectiveness of these practices.

9. Periodic studies of the four major federal outdoor recreation agencies outline the status and trends of outdoor recreation management, especially as they apply to wilderness and backcountry areas. Commonly used management practices and those judged most effective are shown in Table 12-6.

10. Recreation management can be influenced by selected characteristics of managers and the agencies they represent. Recreation managers may need more social science incorporated into their academic and professional education and should give explicit and careful attention to developing personal and professional philosophies of outdoor recreation.

13

Principles and Practices of Outdoor Recreation
Knowledge into Action

Knowledge into Action

At the beginning of this book, it was suggested that management implications of outdoor recreation research become evident after the findings from a number of studies have been reviewed, synthesized, and integrated. The purpose of this final chapter is to examine the body of knowledge presented in the book and to develop a series of management implications based on this knowledge. This task is approached in two stages. First, a series of basic "principles of outdoor recreation" is suggested. These principles are necessarily broad and are drawn from findings that recur throughout the preceding chapters. Second, a framework is developed to guide management of outdoor recreation. This framework provides a basic structure for planning and managing outdoor recreation and incorporates the principles of outdoor recreation noted above. Finally, several observations are offered on the relationship between outdoor recreation research and management.

Principles of Outdoor Recreation

Principle 1. Outdoor recreation should be considered within a three-fold framework of concerns: the natural environment, the social environment, and the management environment. The multi- disciplinary nature of outdoor recreation noted at the beginning of the book was evident in the review and discussion of a number of outdoor recreation issues. This basic three-fold framework of outdoor recreation was found to be useful in the analysis of a number of outdoor recreation issues, including carrying capacity, diversity of outdoor recreation opportunities, and indicators and standards of quality. Each component holds potentially important implications for defining outdoor recreation opportunities and experiences, and failure to give explicit consideration to each component may leave outdoor recreation unmanaged in important ways. This three-fold framework is a useful way to consider and analyze outdoor recreation in a comprehensive, multidisciplinary fashion.

Principle 2. There is substantial diversity in outdoor recreation. Diversity is found in many aspects of outdoor recreation, including recreation activities, socioeconomic and cultural characteristics of participants, visitor attitudes and preferences, experience level, sensitivity to crowding and conflict, and motivations for outdoor recreation. Simple averages or majority opinions sometimes used to report or summarize outdoor recreation research tend to obscure this inherent diversity. Recreation research and management should be careful to acknowledge this diversity.

Principle 3. Diversity is needed in outdoor recreation opportunities. Recognition of diversity in outdoor recreation as suggested in Principle 2 leads logically to the need for diversity in outdoor recreation opportunities. The natural, social, and management environments that define outdoor recreation opportunities should be combined in a variety of alternative arrangements to produce diversity in the greater system of parks and outdoor recreation areas. Each recreation area should be considered as part of a larger system of recreation opportunities. In this way, satisfaction in outdoor recreation might be maximized.

Principle 4. Explicit objectives are needed to guide management of outdoor recreation. If a diversity of outdoor recreation opportunities is to be provided, such opportunities must be explicitly designed and managed. Management objectives ultimately should be expressed in terms of indicators and standards of quality. Indicators and standards of quality define management objectives in quantitative and measurable terms. This allows managers to clearly describe recreation opportunities and to monitor the degree to which such opportunities are achieved.

Principle 5. Recreation management should be applied thoughtfully, but deliberately. Research indicates that there can be significant social problems associated with outdoor recreation, including crowding and conflicting uses. Without management intervention, these problems are likely to be exacerbated. For example, visitors who are sensitive to crowding and conflict ultimately may be displaced or dissatisfied. While recreation management often may involve difficult value judgments, management should be applied by design, not by default.

Principle 6. Outdoor recreation is most appropriately defined in terms of motivations and benefits rather than participation in activities. Though participation in activities is the outward manifestation of outdoor recreation, it is motivations and benefits that ultimately drive participation. Consideration of motivations and benefits in outdoor recreation will lead to a more fundamental understanding of visitors and more successful management.

Principle 7. Quality in outdoor recreation can be defined as the degree to which recreation opportunities provide the experiences for which they are designed and managed. Principles 2 and 3 addressed diversity in outdoor recreation and the corresponding need for diversity in opportunities. This principle suggests that correspondence between experience and opportunities is the most appropriate criterion for determining quality in outdoor recreation. Implicit in this principle is the notion that type and quality of outdoor recreation are distinct concepts. Many types of outdoor recreation opportunities exist and each can and should be of high quality.

Principle 8. Satisfaction of visitors to outdoor recreation areas is a multifaceted concept. Visitors are perceptive of and sensitive to many aspects of the natural, social, and management environments that comprise outdoor recreation areas and opportunities. Though some aspects are more important than others, many considerations may affect visitor satisfaction. Management of outdoor recreation should be broad-based, providing explicit attention to as many of these aspects as are known and manageable. Consideration should be given to a wide range of potential indicators of quality.

Principle 9. There is a high degree of interrelationship among outdoor recreation issues and variables. The outdoor recreation literature can be divided into a number of issues and themes as suggested by the chapters used to organize this book. However, many of these issues are linked by a series of common variables. For example, motivations for outdoor recreation are important in understanding a number of recreation issues, including crowding, conflict, and substitutability. Similarly, experience can be seen to affect several aspects of outdoor recreation, such as attitudes and preferences, indicators and standards of quality, and specialization. While outdoor recreation is a complex social phenomenon, some of this complexity can be reduced by focusing on variables that influence multiple aspects of recreation quality and behavior.

Principle 10. A concerted effort is needed to obtain systematic and objective information about and from visitors. Research indicates that managers' perceptions of outdoor recreation may differ from those of visitors. If a basic purpose of managing outdoor recreation is to provide satisfying experiences to visitors, then objective and systematically collected information is needed from visitors about what defines satisfying recreation experiences.

Principle 11. Outdoor recreation opportunities should be managed for identifiable segments of the visitor population. Research suggests that outdoor recreation visitors can be segmented into relatively homogeneous groups based on a variety of variables such as experience, motivations, attitudes and preferences, sensitivity to crowding and conflict, and normative standards. To the extent feasible, recreation opportunities should be designed and managed for identifiable segments of visitors. This approach can help maximize visitor satisfaction by reducing crowding and conflict and can increase the social carrying capacity of parks and outdoor recreation areas.

Principle 12. A variety of practices are available for managing outdoor recreation. Outdoor recreation managers should give explicit consideration to a variety of management practices rather than relying on those that are familiar or administratively expedient. Alternative management practices should be considered in the context of the strategic objectives to be accomplished. In general, indirect management practices should be favored over direct practices where they can be demonstrated to be effective. Rationing use should be implemented only when other management practices are ineffective or not feasible.

A Recreation Management Framework

The complex and multidisciplinary nature of outdoor recreation suggests that management should be considered within a structured framework. This section outlines such a process. It should be emphasized that what is suggested is a process not a prescription. As the above principles suggest, there is too much diversity in outdoor recreation for standardized management approaches to be appropriate. What is needed is a logical and thoughtful process by which rational and defensible management approaches can be formulated and implemented.

The management framework outlined in this section borrows and builds upon the carrying capacity processes described in Chapter 4. In particular, it relies on Limits of Acceptable Change (Stankey et al. 1985), Visitor Impact Management (Graefe et al. 1990), and Visitor Experience and Resource Protection (National Park Service 1997). In a broad sense, these processes can be seen as comprehensive guides to outdoor recreation management. The management framework outlined in this section also incorporates the principles of outdoor recreation described above. This outdoor recreation management framework is illustrated in Figure 13-1 and is described below.

Step 1. Inventory existing recreation conditions. Management of outdoor recreation begins with an inventory and assessment of recreation conditions. The three-fold framework of outdoor recreation suggested in Principle 1 should guide this inventory and assessment process. Baseline data should be gathered for each of the three major components of outdoor recreation: the natural, social, and management environments.

Substep 1-A. Inventory and assess the natural environment of the area. The natural resources of an outdoor recreation area often are a principal focus of visitors, and outdoor recreation agencies often are charged with maintaining some degree of protection for natural resource values and processes. Information on the extent, location, and quality of the natural resource base therefore is important in outdoor recreation management. Pertinent questions to be answered in the natural resources inventory and assessment process include:

1. Does the area contain unique or outstanding ecological, scientific, educational, historic, or cultural resources that warrant special management attention?

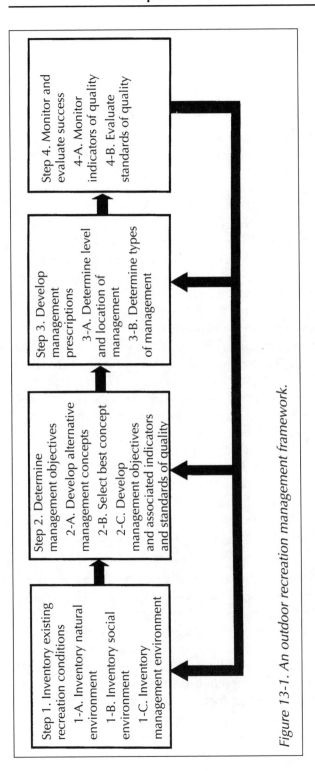

Figure 13-1. An outdoor recreation management framework.

2. Does the area contain critical habitat for threatened or endangered species?

3. How fragile are the area's resources, and what changes are likely to occur as a result of recreation use?

4. In what condition—how natural—are the area's resources?

Substep 1-B. Inventory and assess the social environment of the area. The social environment is an important element of outdoor recreation opportunities. Inventory and assessment of the social environment involves a determination of what types of experiences are desired by the public from the area under study. As suggested in Principle 6, it would be most appropriate to conduct this assessment in terms of visitor motivations and benefits. However, since research methods for this type of assessment are complex and still evolving, surrogates for motivations and benefits also may be useful, such as visitor attitudes and preferences, desired activities, personal characteristics of visitors, and indicators and standards of quality. Recognizing the differences between visitors and non-visitors to outdoor recreation areas, some effort should be made to include interested non-visitors in this process. While survey research commonly is used to gather such information, behavioral or observational measures of visitor use patterns should supplement the survey approach when and where feasible. The major emphasis of this effort, as suggested in Principle 10, is to obtain systematic and objective information from and about visitors. Pertinent questions to be answered in the social inventory and assessment process include:

1. What kinds of recreation does the area now support?

2. What are the recreation motivations of people attracted to the area?

3. What are the attitudes and preferences of potential visitors toward management policies, facilities, and services?

4. What are the socioeconomic and cultural characteristics of people attracted to the area?

Substep 1-C. Inventory and assess the management environment of the area. The way in which an outdoor recreation area is managed affects both the condition of the natural resource base and the types of recreation experiences provided. In addition, management often is constrained by various institutional dictates. The management inventory and assessment process should determine both potentials and constraints. Pertinent questions to be answered in this process include:

1. What management practices currently are applied to the area?

2. What legislative and policy dictates apply to the area?

3. What personnel and financial resources are available for area management?

The description of current recreation conditions collected in Step 1 will provide input for Step 2 of the management framework.

Step 2. Determine management objectives. The process of formulating management objectives as suggested in Principle 4 begins with broad management concepts and works toward specific indicators and standards of quality. It starts with consideration of the baseline data collected in Step 1 and incorporates public involvement and management judgments.

Substep 2-A. Develop alternative management concepts. The three-fold framework of outdoor recreation suggested in Principle 1 again is instructive in this context. Theoretically, the three factors involved in outdoor recreation—the natural environment, social conditions, and the type of management applied—can be combined in widely ranging configurations. The underlying concept of the Recreation Opportunity Spectrum can provide guidance in this process, but broad management directions need to be established for each of the three basic factors.

Initial assessment of the inventory data gathered in Step 1 normally suggests general management directions. Legislative or agency policy directives, for example, often describe, at least in a general fashion, the type of recreation experiences to be provided and the emphasis to be placed on maintaining natural resource conditions. The Wilderness Act, for instance, states that areas included in the National Wilderness Preservation System should be managed to emphasize solitude and naturalness. The financial and budgetary resources available for management also can influence management direction; high use levels generally are not feasible without concomitant budgets and personnel to accommodate them. Natural resource factors also can pose important constraints on general management direction. Unique or fragile resources, for example, suggest relatively low use levels and low-impact activities. Finally, the outdoor recreation experiences desired by the public influence management directions. Public preferences should be accommodated to the extent possible, given the constraints of natural resource and management conditions.

Normally, there will be several, perhaps many, management concepts feasible for an area. This is a reflection of the diversity of natural resource, social, and management conditions found and the variety of configurations in which they may be arranged. The situation is made even more complex in large areas that might appropriately be divided into two or more use areas or zones, each reflecting a different combination of conditions and providing a different type of recreation opportunity. But to encourage realistic and efficient public input and evaluation, management concepts must be limited to a few that reflect, in the initial judgment of planners and managers, the most realistic and reasonable alternatives.

Development of alternative management concepts is not a simple task, though several circumstances may reduce its complexity. First, the constraints imposed by natural resource, social, or management factors may limit realistic management alternatives. Second, some measure of public opinion already should have been gained through the social inventory process (Step 1-B) to suggest what types of management alternatives ultimately might be found acceptable by the public. Third, planning in general, particularly in the public sector, tends to be incremental in nature, seldom making changes that differ drastically from current conditions. Thus, realistic management alternatives often will reflect, at least to some degree, current conditions. Fourth, as suggested in Principles 2 and 3, tastes in outdoor recreation are diverse, and opportunities for recreation also should be diverse. Part of the process of designing for diversity should involve comparison of the area under consideration with similar areas on a local, regional, or even national basis. It then may be appropriate to focus on opportunities which currently are in short supply and for which there seems to be an additional demand. The desirability of diversity in outdoor recreation also suggests that, if the area is extensive enough, management concepts might provide a range of uses, particularly if the area is unique or outstanding in some way. Fifth, Principle 11 suggests that outdoor recreation opportunities should be managed for identifiable segments of the visitor population. Thus, the management concepts developed should reflect combinations of environmental, social, and managerial conditions that are compatible in the minds of the public.

Though these guidelines may help with the development of management concepts, the process still depends on the considered judgment of outdoor recreation planners and managers. It should be remembered from Principles 4 and 5 that recreation management in general, and formulation of management objectives in particular— though they should be based on objective data—ultimately involve some management judgment.

Substep 2-B. Select the best management concept. Selection of a management concept involves systematic evaluation of the alternative concepts developed in the previous step. This evaluation can be facilitated by systematically examining and describing the effects of each concept. Pertinent considerations include (1) the contribution of each concept to diversity in the total outdoor recreation system, (2) potential effects of each concept on visitor use of the area, (3) the natural resource and social values that are enhanced or diminished by each concept, and (4) the management feasibility of accomplishing each concept.

There are no precise methods for weighing these effects and determining the best management concept. A considerable amount of management judgment is again involved. But a program of public involvement also is essential. Interested members of the public should be informed of the management concepts under consideration and have the opportunity to comment on them. This process of public input may produce new concepts for consideration or, more likely, combinations or modifications of the original concepts. After an appropriate period of public involvement, a decision must be made by managers to provide broad management direction for the area.

Substep 2-C. Develop management objectives and associated indicators and standards of quality.[1] The general prescriptions of Step 2-B need to be made more specific so they can guide day-to-day management and be used to evaluate management success. These specific descriptors are management objectives and associated indicators and standards of quality, and should be expressed in as explicit and quantifiable terms as possible.

As in the preceding two steps, some degree of judgment is needed in translating management concepts into management objectives and indicators and standards of quality. However, several factors can help guide this process. First, the management concepts themselves indicate which elements in the total recreation environment are to be emphasized and may suggest a general range of conditions for these elements. A management concept emphasizing solitude as an important element of the area, for example, logically would lead to an emphasis on managing contacts between groups and would suggest that contacts be kept to a relatively small number.

Second, research can indicate which factors of the total recreation environment should be the subject of management objectives. As noted in Principle 8, satisfaction of visitors is a multifaceted concept; thus, there often will be a relatively large number of factors for which management objectives might be developed. Public input and the research-based literature reviewed in this book provide an indication of management factors important to a variety of recreation visitors.

Third, a program of research can help identify potential indicators and standards of quality as described in Chapter 6. Indicators of quality are variables that define the quality of the visitor experience. Standards of quality define the minimum acceptable condition of indicator variables. Following the example described above, research on solitude suggests that the number of other groups encountered may be an important indicator of quality. Moreover, research has found that visitors may have normative standards about the acceptable number of such encounters and that this may help identify standards of quality.

Fourth, if a program of primary research is not possible, the outdoor recreation literature may be suggestive of potential indicators and standards of quality. Chapter 6 outlines a number of potential indicators and standards of quality that have been identified in a variety of park and outdoor recreation areas. Moreover, the interrelatedness of many variables and issues in outdoor recreation, as suggested in Principle 9, may offer insights into potential indicators and standards of quality. For example, information about selected characteristics of visitors, such as their experience level, type of social group, and motivations for recreation may be suggestive of their attitudes and preferences and their sensitivity to issues such as crowding and conflict.

Fifth, management objectives should reflect a range of conditions for factors important to visitors to incorporate a desirable element of diversity. Thus, each recreation area should be considered as an integrated component of the total outdoor recreation system rather than as a separate and isolated entity.

At the conclusion of Step 2, explicit management objectives and associated indicators and standards of quality should be formulated.

Step 3. Develop management prescriptions. The process now turns to determining how to get from the current to the desired situation. This involves deciding what level and type of management actions are to be applied to the area.

Substep 3-A. Determine the level and location of management needed. This will be determined by the congruence between current conditions as determined in the initial inventory and desired conditions as specified by management objectives. Obviously, the wider the difference between existing and desired conditions, the greater will be the management efforts needed to meet management objectives.

Substep 3-B. Determine the type of management needed. If desired conditions currently are unmet, then some management action is needed. As suggested in Principle 12, a variety of practices are available for managing outdoor recreation. Examining the range of management alternatives can be helpful in developing an appropriate management program. Indirect management practices generally should be favored over direct practices where they can be shown to be effective. The evaluation research described in Chapter 12 outlines several types of management practices shown to be effective.

Step 4. Monitor and evaluate success. This is a critical but sometimes neglected step in any management framework. Once a management program has been developed and implemented, it is necessary to periodically assess whether desired conditions are being achieved and maintained. In outdoor recreation management, this involves monitoring indicator variables to determine if standards of quality are being met. As suggested in Principle 7, this is in keeping with the basic definition of quality in outdoor recreation—the degree to which recreation opportunities provide the experiences for which they are designed and managed.

Substep 4-A. Monitor indicators of quality. Indicators of quality should be monitored periodically to determine whether standards of quality are being met (Stynes 1994). An important issue to be addressed in designing the monitoring program concerns how frequently indicator variables should be measured. There are no precise guidelines for making this determination, as site conditions and budgetary circumstances often will be pivotal considerations. However, several circumstances may dictate more frequent monitoring than normal: (1) when the condition of indicator variables is close to those specified by standards of quality, (2) when rates of environmental, social, or managerial change are thought to be high, (3) when the initial inventory and data base for the area are incomplete or of questionable quality, (4) when the potential effectiveness of management actions is not well known or predictable, and (5) where there have been unanticipated changes to the area such as additional access or changes in adjacent land uses.

Substep 4-B. Evaluate standards of quality. Evaluation involves comparing the conditions found in monitoring to those specified by standards of quality and determining whether success has been attained and whether changes in management are needed. As noted in Principle 7, quality in outdoor recreation is most appropriately defined as the degree to which recreation opportunities provide the experiences for which they are designed and managed. If monitoring indicates that standards of quality are being met, then no change in management is needed. However, if monitoring indicates that standards of quality are violated, or are in danger of being violated, then additional management is required.

A final evaluation issue involves the cyclic aspects of the management framework described above and illustrated in Figure 13-1. Under normal circumstances, evaluation focuses on Step 3, analyzing what, if any, changes in management are needed to achieve management objectives. At some point, however, it may be appropriate to reevaluate management objectives. In this case, evaluation focuses on Step 2. Changes in management objectives and associated indicators and standards of quality should only be made consciously and explicitly, following the procedures outlined in Step 2. Evaluations of this scope normally will need to be done only infrequently, perhaps every ten years or so. Finally, there will come a time when baseline data for the area are outdated or no longer adequate, and then evaluation must focus on Step 1. An evaluation of this scope, however, likely will be very infrequent, perhaps only every twenty years or so.

Observations on Recreation Management

The framework described above provides a process by which outdoor recreation can be managed in a logical and thoughtful way. Research can be helpful in applying this framework. However, a certain degree of management judgment will be required in every application of this framework, and these judgments can be difficult and daunting. It should be remembered, however, that such decisions nearly always are subject to change or revision should the need arise. Indeed, the monitoring and evaluation process builds in such opportunities on a periodic basis. Thus, while management judgments should be approached with all due care and consideration, they are not immutable and should not forestall the recreation management process.

As suggested in Principle 5, recreation management should be approached and applied deliberately. Much of the emphasis of this book, developed directly out of the research literature, has been on the need for diversity in outdoor recreation. The evidence suggests that if outdoor recreation is not planned and managed explicitly for a variety of types of opportunities, then recreation experiences are likely to become increasingly similar with the result that visitors who are sensitive or nondominant are likely to be displaced or dissatisfied (Dustin and McAvoy 1982, Schreyer and Knopf 1984). Unfortunately, there is evidence to suggest that recreation management is not moving ahead aggressively, and that the predominant management approach is reactive rather than proactive. For example, surveys of managers of wilderness, backcountry, and related areas have found that many areas have yet to begin to come to grips with the broad issue of carrying capacity (Washburne and Cole 1983, Manning et al. 1996a).

Creativity in management is a closely related issue. The current emphasis of recreation management seems to be placed at the extremes of the opportunity spectrum—wilderness and developed areas (Lucas 1973). More emphasis on creative opportunities between these extremes is needed to more fully accomplish the objective of diversity.

Recreation management is an iterative process involving feedback loops. The first two steps of the management process described above, for example—inventory of existing conditions and formulation of management objectives—are not necessarily discrete activities that can be conducted in isolation from one another. It is difficult to determine what specific factors to inventory from existing conditions without some notion of what management objectives and potential indicators of quality might be. Conversely, it may be unrealistic to set management objectives without some notion of existing recreation conditions. In reality, recreation management may involve several cycles through the management framework described above.

Good information is needed for recreation management. Management decisions will be rational and creditable only if they are based on adequate, objective information. This need is made more pressing by the inherent diversity in outdoor recreation. This diversity among visitors already has been emphasized, but there is diversity as well in natural environments and management systems. Outdoor recreation areas can vary dramatically in their resiliency, location, and uniqueness. Chapter 12 illustrated the variety of management practices available, and several studies have documented their widespread application by outdoor recreation agencies (Schoenfeld 1976, Bury and Fish 1980, Fish and Bury 1981, Marion et al. 1993, Washburne and Cole 1983, Manning et al. 1996). Good information with regard to all of these matters, much of it site-specific, will be needed to make recreation management work as well as it can.

A primary source of information is represented by visitors, potential visitors, and other stakeholders. Visitor surveys and other research approaches, as illustrated by the studies reviewed in this book, can be effective sources of such information. Other forms of public involvement can be useful as well. Experience suggests that transactive planning—collaborative involvement of primary stakeholders—can be effective, especially when compromise must be reached among competing values (Krumpe and McCool 1997, Stankey 1997).

Information also is needed from management. Quality in outdoor recreation is defined as the degree to which recreation opportunities provide the experiences for which they are designed and managed. Unless managers can help guide visitors to the types of opportunities sought, quality is not likely to be maximized.

Managers of parks and related areas should not necessarily let the condition of indicators of quality deteriorate to the minimum acceptable standard of quality before they consider or invoke management actions. Standards of quality are not necessarily goals or objectives; they define the *minimum* acceptable condition of indicator variables (Cole and McCool 1997). Managers should strive for the highest possible quality of indicator variables. Indirect management practices would seem to be especially appropriate as a means of maintaining high standards of quality. However, once monitoring suggests that standards of quality are threatened or violated, management action, employing either indirect or direct management practices, is required.

Standards of quality often can be seen to define a range of visitor opportunities across the zones of a park or related area. Standards of quality for resource and social conditions, for example, will often allow only low levels of impact in wilderness or backcountry-related zones and allow progressively more impact through developed or frontcountry zones. However, there may be standards of quality that are uniform or consistent across zones. Impacts to threatened or endangered species and impacts to nonrenewable cultural resources may be examples of indicator variables that require uniformly strict standards of quality.

In formulating indicators and standards of quality, it may be advisable to consider the local, regional, or even national context of the area under study. Parks and related areas often are viewed by the public as part of a larger destination area. Each park or related area should contribute as appropriate to a greater spectrum of visitor opportunities as defined by resource, social, and management conditions. Moreover, some types of visitor opportunities, especially those that may conflict with park purpose and significance, can be more easily excluded from a park if such opportunities are provided elsewhere. In these ways, consideration of geographical context can contribute to the rationale for formulating indicators and standards of quality.

Finally, it seems appropriate to return to the issue of value judgments and the necessary burden they place on recreation managers. An early study in outdoor recreation concluded that, "As much as public officials might wish to shift the burden to impersonal equations, the formulas devised by researchers can guide but not supplant human judgment" (J. A. Wagar 1964). Over the ensuing years, researchers have devised and tested numerous equations, formulas, relationships, concepts, hypotheses, and theories that can be incorporated into recreation management, but the burden of some element of management judgment remains inescapable.

Relating Research and Management

It was noted at the beginning of this book that outdoor recreation research might be criticized because individual studies may lack broad management implications. One of the purposes of this book is to illustrate that research, when viewed collectively and comprehensively, has a number of important implications for outdoor recreation management.

But criticism of outdoor recreation research by managers, and equally disparaging views of management expressed occasionally by researchers, stem from a number of misunderstandings and misconceptions about the research and management processes and the relationships between them. Part of the problem arises from the distinctions between basic and applied research (D. Johnson and Field 1981, Field and Johnson 1983). Traditionally, research within the academic environment has tended to be more basic than applied. That is, it is oriented toward enhancing knowledge or testing theory within a conventional academic discipline, and hence has a closely defined social context: a relatively small group of peers, narrowly defined limits on subject matter, and a reward system driven largely by scholarly publications. Managers often view this traditional model of research with frustration and impatience; they complain that research problems are defined too narrowly and abstractly to have much application, and that research reports are overly technical and obtuse.

Applied research, on the other hand, is oriented toward gaining immediately useful empirical knowledge and often involves interdisciplinary concerns. Research must be done quickly, irrespective of academic schedules, and primary focus must be placed on variables which are manageable and not just those which enhance understanding.

But this model of research is often frustrating to academics; problems are not defined so as to be amenable to research, management issues frequently involve concerns outside the researcher's discipline, and the academic reward system traditionally does not emphasize successful application of research results.

Communication and compromise between researchers and managers clearly is needed to derive a model of research that is both rewarding and effective (Ewert 1986). Managers and researchers must realize the need for both basic and applied research. The ultimate goal of any research program is to provide useable knowledge, but research results will be most useful when considered within a theoretical framework. Without a theoretical framework, study findings remain isolated facts rather than being integrated into a body of knowledge. Traditionally, recreation research has been criticized for lack of an adequate theoretical foundation (S. Smith 1975, Groves and Wolensky 1977, Driver and Knopf 1981, Burch 1984, Riddick et al. 1984, Tinsley 1984, Heywood 1986). However, as recreation research has matured, it has adopted a stronger theoretical and conceptual foundation (Henderson 1994a).

Perhaps the most important element of cooperation between managers and researchers concerns communication at the time the research problem is defined (Schweitzer and Randall 1974, Stankey 1980c). Applied research suggests that managers provide the initiative for research so they can ensure that their problems will be addressed as directly as possible. But researchers also need to be involved in the process of problem definition to ensure that the problems identified by managers lend themselves to scientific study. The relationship between recreation use and changes in the recreation environment, for example, has both researchable and non-researchable elements. Researchers often can determine the nature of these relationships, and this can suggest appropriate limits of acceptable change. However, setting such limits inevitably will involve some element of management judgment. Managers and researchers must work together to define the problem so that the outcome of research will be satisfying and rewarding to both parties.

Communication of research results also is critical. When reporting applied aspects of research, a different audience must be addressed than when writing for scientific journals:

> . . . academic diction is frequently riddled with jargon, fashionable intellectual clichés, and even occasional foreign phrases. Applied research findings, however, must be communicated in clear, concise, and understandable

composition. The intent is not to impress readers with the writer's intellect, but to convey in a straightforward manner the practical significance of the research results for which the client has paid (D. Johnson and Field 1981:275–276).

It has been suggested that "go-betweens" sometimes may be needed to bridge the communication gap between researchers and managers (McCool and Schreyer 1977, Flekke et al. 1996). Extension agents fill this role in other fields and may be an appropriate model for outdoor recreation (Groves and Wolensky 1977). Pilot and demonstration projects also may be an effective way to communicate research results (Stankey 1980c). The research function might be administratively located within a management agency, and this can enhance communication between researchers and managers (Chilman et al. 1977).

Literature review and synthesis also should be recognized as a potentially valuable form of research. Individual research studies may have few management implications beyond the study location, but broader implications become clearer when a number of studies are integrated and synthesized (e.g., Hendee and Potter 1975, Lime 1976). This would seem an especially efficient and productive type of research for managers to encourage and researchers to pursue.

The management process also is the source of misunderstandings and misconceptions that divide managers and researchers. Researchers undertaking applied studies must realize that their findings are but one input into the decision-making process. A host of other considerations, loosely labeled "political factors," legitimately affect the final outcome of a management issue, regardless of how scientifically sound the research (Shelby 1981b).

Of course, managers too must realize that research is but one input into the decision-making process. Expectations from research must be realistic; research may not solve problems directly. For example, research often can determine and describe the probable consequences of alternative courses of action; however, managers may have to render judgments about which consequences are most desirable.

The timing of research also has implications for its effectiveness (Schreyer 1980). Too often, research is not begun until a problem has reached crisis proportions. At this point, little time is left to conduct an appropriate study, and results must be considered within an atmosphere of highly polarized feelings. Cooperative, long-range research planning can help minimize this problem (G. Peterson and Lime 1978, E. Shafer and Lucas 1979).

Unfortunately, evidence indicates that communication between managers and researchers is limited. A study of federal and state outdoor recreation managers, for example, found that only 6% had regular contact with university researchers, and 16% had regular contact with government agency scientists (McCool and Schreyer 1977). Applied research problems are not likely to be defined appropriately, nor are results likely to be communicated effectively under these circumstances. The same study, however, offers hope that communication and cooperation between managers and researchers can be effective. Contact between managers and researchers was positively and strongly related to managers' judgment of the quality of outdoor recreation research. As noted in Chapter 1, more recent studies suggest that outdoor recreation research generally is judged as efficient and effective (D. Anderson and Schneider 1993, Bengston and Xu 1993, Machlis and Harvey 1993, Schneider et al. 1993).

The last several decades of social science research in outdoor recreation have enhanced understanding of this social phenomenon and offered a number of implications that might help guide management more effectively. The success of future research will be determined, to a large degree, by the extent to which researchers and managers understand and appreciate each other's roles and processes.

Summary and Conclusions

1. The implications of outdoor recreation research begin to emerge after review and synthesis of the broad body of scientific literature in this interdisciplinary field of study.

2. Twelve major principles of outdoor recreation can be abstracted from the outdoor recreation literature reviewed in this book:

   A. Outdoor recreation should be considered within a three-fold framework of concerns: the natural environment, the social environment, and the management environment.

   B. There is substantial diversity in outdoor recreation.

   C. Diversity is needed in outdoor recreation opportunities.

   D. Explicit objectives are needed to guide outdoor recreation management.

E. Recreation management should be applied thoughtfully, but deliberately.

F. Outdoor recreation is most appropriately defined in terms of motivations and benefits rather than participation in activities.

G. Quality in outdoor recreation can be defined as the degree to which recreation opportunities provide the experiences for which they are designed and managed.

H. Satisfaction of visitors to outdoor recreation areas is a multifaceted concept.

I. There is a high degree of interrelationship among outdoor recreation issues and variables.

J. A concerted effort is needed to obtain systematic and objective information about and from visitors.

K. Outdoor recreation opportunities should be managed for identifiable segments of the visitor population.

L. A variety of practices are available for managing outdoor recreation.

3. The principles of outdoor recreation noted above are incorporated in a recreation management framework illustrated in Figure 13-1. This framework outlines a logical and thoughtful process by which rational and defensible management approaches can be formulated and implemented.

4. The effectiveness of outdoor recreation research will be enhanced by the extent to which managers and researchers communicate, and the degree to which they understand and appreciate each other's roles and processes.

Notes

1. As indicated throughout this discussion, management objectives should be developed for important elements of the natural, social, and management environments. However, in keeping with the social science emphasis of this book, management objectives are considered primarily in terms of visitor perceptions, and discussion is limited to elements of these environments that research indicates visitors are aware of and which potentially affect visitor satisfaction. There likely will be other elements, particularly of the natural and management environments, of which visitors are unaware, but which still require explicit management attention and objectives.

Notes on Sources
A Guide to the Social Science Literature in Outdoor Recreation

As noted at the beginning of this book, the field of outdoor recreation is inherently diverse and multidisciplinary, and the scientific literature on outdoor recreation reflects this diversity. Even within the social sciences, outdoor recreation may be studied from a variety of disciplines, including sociology, psychology, geography, political science, and economics. The resulting scientific literature is spread widely across the academic and scholarly landscape.

However, as research on outdoor recreation has matured, a specialized scientific literature has emerged. This literature is found primarily in scholarly and professional journals, conference and symposium proceedings, government reports, and books. A brief description of this literature may be useful to readers who wish to follow up on issues described in this book. In keeping with the emphasis of the book, this description focuses on the primary source material for this book—published, peer-reviewed literature that is generally available through academic libraries.

Journals

The most important source of scientific information on outdoor recreation is scholarly and academic journals. Very early papers on outdoor recreation were published primarily in disciplinary journals. Examples include *American Journal of Sociology, American Sociological Review, Rural Sociology, Journal of Applied Social Psychology, Land Economics,* and *Professional Geographer.* These and other discipline-based journals still publish periodic papers on outdoor recreation.

Several new journals devoted specifically to outdoor recreation, leisure, parks, wilderness and related issues have appeared over the past thirty years, and these journals now constitute the most important source of scholarly work on outdoor recreation. All of these journals maintain strong foundations of peer-review, thereby enhancing confidence in study findings. The *Journal of Leisure Research,* published by the National Recreation and Park Association, was founded in 1969. The purposes of the journal were "to define in multidisciplinary terms the challenges of leisure facing us today and in the future, to stimulate appropriate solutions for these challenges through serious scientific investigation, to disseminate these research findings, and to describe the practical application and testing of research results." A second journal, *Leisure Sciences,* published by Taylor and Francis, Inc., was created in 1977 to stimulate and accommodate a growing number of "scholarly and substantive articles in the fields of leisure, recreation, natural resources, and related environments." The *Journal of Park and Recreation Administration*, published by the American Academy for Park and Recreation Administration, began publication in 1983 as "a practitioner-oriented, research journal for the park and recreation field." All three of these journals are published quarterly, and constitute the major scholarly journals in the field of outdoor recreation. Papers published in these journals are the most frequently cited materials in this book.

A variety of other outdoor recreation-related academic and professional journals are also important sources of information on outdoor recreation. These include *Leisure Studies*, published by the Leisure Studies Association of the United Kingdom; *Leisure and Society*, published by the International Sociological Association; *Parks* and *Park Science*, published by the U.S. National Park Service; *Parks and Recreation* and *Trends*, published by the National Recreation and Park Association; *Journal of Applied Recreation Research*, published by Wilfrid Laurier University Press, Canada; and *World Leisure and Recreation*, published by the World Leisure and Recreation Association, Canada.

A related group of journals focus on travel and tourism. Tourists to national parks and related areas are also outdoor recreation visitors. Tourism-related journals include *Annals of Tourism Research, Journal of Travel Research, Tourism Management, Journal of Sustainable Tourism, Tourism Analysis,* and *Tourism Recreation Research*.

Papers on outdoor recreation are published in a variety of topical journals as well. Several journals on natural resources and the environment often address issues of parks, outdoor recreation, and related matters. Examples of these journals include *Environmental Management, Society and Natural Resources, Environment and Behavior, Journal of Environmental Management, Journal of Soil and Water Conservation, International Journal of Wilderness, Journal of Environmental Education, Natural Resources Journal, Human Ecology Review, Journal of Environmental Systems, Natural Areas Journal,* and *The George Wright Forum*.

Another group of journals addresses applied fields of study within natural resources and the environment, and publishes occasional papers on outdoor recreation. These journals include *Journal of Forestry, Forest Science, Western Journal of Applied Forestry, Northern Journal of Applied Forestry, Wildlife Society Bulletin, Human Dimensions of Wildlife, Journal of Wildlife Management, Fisheries, North American Journal of Fisheries Management, Water Resources Bulletin, Rivers,* and *Coastal Zone Management*.

Proceedings

A second major source of outdoor recreation literature is conference and symposium proceedings. Proceedings of two types of meetings are to be found, serial meetings and topical meetings. Several important series of meetings on research in outdoor recreation are held throughout the United States. The annual Southeastern Recreation Research Conference began in 1979, and its proceedings have been published by Georgia Southern College, the University of Georgia, and, most recently, the Southeastern and Northeastern Forest Experiment Stations of the U.S. Forest Service. The annual Northeastern Recreation Research Symposium began in 1989, and its proceedings are published by the Northeastern Forest Experiment Station of the U.S. Forest Service. The Social Aspects and Recreation Research Symposium began in 1992, and its proceedings are published by the Pacific Southwest Forest Experiment Station of the U.S. Forest Service.

A series of national and international conferences on trends in outdoor recreation was initiated in 1980, and has met every five years. Proceedings have been published for the 1980, 1985, and 1995 conferences as follows:

LaPage, W. (Compiler) 1980. *National Outdoor Recreation Trends Symposium*. USDA Forest Service General Technical Report NE-57 (two volumes).

Wood, J., Jr. (Editor). 1985. *Proceedings of the 1985 National Outdoor Recreation Trends Symposium II*. Atlanta, GA: U.S. Department of the Interior, National Park Service, Southeast Regional Office (two volumes).

Thompson, J., D. Lime, B. Gartner, and W. Sames (Compilers). 1995. *Proceedings of the Fourth International Outdoor Recreation and Tourism Trends Symposium and 1995 National Recreation Resource Planning Conference*. St. Paul, MN: University of Minnesota Extension Service.

The trends conference for the year 2000 will be held in Michigan, and is being organized by Michigan State University.

A variety of topical meetings on outdoor recreation have produced useful proceedings over the past several decades. Two important meetings have focused on wilderness research and management. The National Wilderness Research Conference was held in 1985, and its proceedings were published in two volumes as follows:

Lucas, R. (Compiler) 1986. *Proceedings — National Wilderness Research Conference: Current Research*. USDA Forest Service General Technical Report INT-212.

Lucas, R. (Compiler) 1987. *Proceedings — National Wilderness Research Conference: Issues, State-of-Knowledge, Future Directions*. USDA Forest Service General Technical Report INT-220.

The latter volume contains a series of important state-of-knowledge papers on selected wilderness issues. A second conference on wilderness was held in 1989, and its proceedings were published as:

Lime, D. (Editor). 1990. *Managing America's Enduring Wilderness Resource*. St. Paul, MN: University of Minnesota Extension Service.

A third wilderness conference, Wilderness Science in a Time of Change, will be held in 1999 and its proceedings will include both state-of-knowledge papers and current research.

Several national assessments of outdoor recreation have published substantive scientific studies. As noted at the beginning of this book, most observers date the beginning of serious social scientific study of outdoor recreation to publication of the Outdoor Recreation Resources Review Commission (ORRRC) reports. The ORRRC was a national commission established in 1958 to assess the status of outdoor recreation in America. Its summary report, *Outdoor Recreation for America*, was published by the U.S. Government Printing Office in 1962, along with 29 special studies. A second national assessment of outdoor recreation was conducted in the mid-1980s under the auspices of the President's Commission on Americans Outdoors. While not conducted as a conference, a series of important review papers on a variety of outdoor recreation issues were commissioned and published in 1986 as *A Literature Review: The President's Commission on Americans Outdoors*, Washington, D.C.: U.S. Government Printing Office. A related conference entitled Benchmark 1988 was sponsored by the U.S. Forest Service as part of its ten year assessment of wilderness and outdoor recreation resources. The proceedings were published in two volumes as follows:

Freilich, H. (Compiler) 1989. *Wilderness Benchmark 1988: Proceedings of the National Wilderness Colloquium*. USDA Forest Service General Technical Report SE-51.

Watson, A. (Compiler) 1989. *Outdoor Recreation Benchmark 1988: Proceedings of the National Outdoor Recreation Forum*. USDA Forest Service General Technical Report SE-52.

A variety of specialized conferences, symposia, and workshops on outdoor recreation have been conducted over the past several decades, and these have resulted in a number of proceedings that have proven especially useful in preparing this book. These proceedings include:

Larson, E. (Editor) 1971. *Recreation Symposium Proceedings*. Upper Darby, PA: USDA Forest Service Northeastern Forest Experiment Station.

U.S. Forest Service. 1974. *Outdoor Recreation Research: Applying the Results*. USDA Forest Service General Technical Report NC-9.

U.S. Forest Service. 1977. *Proceedings: River Recreation Management and Research Symposium*. USDA Forest Service General Technical Report NC-28.

Stankey, G. and S. McCool (Compilers) 1985. *Proceedings — Symposium on Recreation Choice Behavior*. USDA Forest Service General Technical Report INT-184.

Shelby, B., G. Stankey, and B. Shindler (Technical Editors) 1992. *Defining Wilderness Quality: The Role of Standards in Wilderness Management — A Workshop Proceedings*. USDA Forest Service General Technical Report PNW-305.

Lime, D. (Editor) 1996. *Congestion and Crowding in the National Park System*. St. Paul, MN: University of Minnesota Agricultural Experiment Station Miscellaneous Publication 86-1996.

Lundgren, A. (Editor) 1996. *Recreation Fees in the National Park System: Issues, Policies, and Guidelines for Future Action*. St. Paul, MN: University of Minnesota Cooperative Park Studies Unit.

McCool, S. and D. Cole. (Compilers) 1997. *Proceedings — Limits of Acceptable Change and Related Planning Processes: Progress and Future Directions*. USDA Forest Service General Technical Report INT-371.

Occasionally, proceedings are compiled from selected papers on outdoor recreation presented at larger meetings. Examples include:

Lime, D. and D. Field (Technical Coordinators) 1981. *Some Recent Products of River Recreation Research*. USDA Forest Service General Technical Report NC-63 (selected papers from the Second Conference on Scientific Research in the National Parks).

Lime, D. (Technical Coordinator) 1982. *Forest and River Recreation: Research Update*. St. Paul, MN: University of Minnesota Agricultural Experiment Station (selected papers from the 1981 Leisure Research Symposium).

Gobster, P. (Editor) 1993. *Managing Urban and High-Use Recreation Settings*. USDA Forest Service General Technical Report NC-163 (selected papers from the Fourth North American Symposium on Society and Resource Management).

Government Documents

A third major source of research on outdoor recreation is government documents. While most federal park and recreation-related agencies publish occasional documents addressing some aspects of outdoor recreation research, only the U.S. Forest Service maintains a strong series of scientific and professional publications. Each regional Forest Experiment Station publishes a series of documents as Research Notes, Research Papers, and General Technical Reports. Many of the proceedings noted above are published as General Technical Reports.

Books

Finally, books are starting to become an important source of scientific information on outdoor recreation. Many scholarly or academic books on outdoor recreation are primarily descriptive and lack a strong research base. These books are primarily designed to serve as introductory texts in park, recreation, and related academic programs. However, a number of edited books contain useful collections of research-based papers, and several authors have prepared books that synthesize selected elements of the outdoor recreation literature. Early books which should not be overlooked include:

Clawson, M. and J. Knetsch. 1966. *Economics of Outdoor Recreation*. Baltimore, MD: The Johns Hopkins Press.

Driver, B. (Editor) 1970. *Elements of Outdoor Recreation Planning*. Ann Arbor, MI: University Microfilms.

Burch, W., N. Cheek, and L. Taylor (Editors) 1972. *Social Behavior, Natural Resources, and the Environment*. New York, NY: Harper and Row.

Cheek, N. and W. Burch. 1976. *The Social Organization of Leisure in Human Society*. New York, NY: Harper and Row.

Cheek, N., D. Field, and W. Burch. 1976. *Leisure and Recreation Places*. Ann Arbor, MI: Ann Arbor Science.

Van Doren, C., G. Priddle, and J. Lewis. 1979. *Land and Leisure: Concepts and Methods in Outdoor Recreation*. Chicago, IL: Maaroufa Press.

More recent books that can be recommended include:

Iso-Ahola, S. 1980. *The Social Psychology of Leisure and Recreation*. Dubuque, IA: Wm. C. Brown Company.

Leiber, S. and D. Fesenmaier (Editors). 1983. *Recreation Planning and Management*. State College, PA: Venture Publishing.

Clawson, M. and C. Van Doren. 1984. *Statistics on Outdoor Recreation*. Washington, D.C.: Resources for the Future.

Walsh, R. 1986. *Recreation Economic Decisions: Comparing Benefits and Costs*. State College, PA: Venture Publishing.

Shelby, B. and T. Heberlein. 1986. *Carrying Capacity in Recreation Settings*. Corvallis, OR: Oregon State University Press.

Graefe, A. and S. Parker. 1987. *Recreation and Leisure: An Introductory Handbook*. State College, PA: Venture Publishing.

Peterson, G., B. Driver, and R. Gregory (Editors). 1988. *Amenity Resource Valuation: Integrating Economics with Other Disciplines*. State College, PA: Venture Publishing.

Jackson, E. and T. Burton (Editors). 1989. *Understanding Leisure and Recreation: Mapping the Past, Charting the Future*. State College, PA: Venture Publishing.

Hendee, J., G. Stankey, and R. Lucas. 1990. *Wilderness Management*. Golden, CO: North American Press.

Vining, J. (Editor). 1990. *Social Science and Outdoor Recreation Management*. Boulder, CO: Westview Press.

Driver, B., P. Brown, and G. Peterson (Editors). 1991. *Benefits of Leisure*. State College, PA: Venture Publishing.

Machlis, G. and D. Field. 1992. *On Interpretation: Sociology for Interpreters of Natural and Cultural History*. Corvallis, OR: Oregon State University Press.

Manfredo, M. (Editor). 1992. *Influencing Human Behavior: Theory and Applications in Recreation, Tourism, and Natural Resources Management*. Champaign, IL: Sagamore Publishing.

Cordell, H. (Principal Investigator). 1999. *Outdoor Recreation in American Life: A National Assessment of Demand and Supply Trends*. Champaign, IL: Sagamore Publishing.

New editions of Wilderness Management and the edited volume by Jackson and Burton (to be published under the title, Leisure Studies: Prospects for the Twenty-First Century) are in press and will be valuable additions to the literature.

Two other types of literature are valuable supplements to social science research on outdoor recreation. Substantial research has been conducted on natural science and ecological aspects of outdoor recreation. The definitive source on this body of work is:

Hammitt, W. and D. Cole. 1998. *Wildland Recreation: Ecology and Management.* New York, NY: John Wiley and Sons.

An expanding body of literature is evolving in social science aspects of natural resources and environmental management, which often includes applications to outdoor recreation. Representative texts include:

Miller, M., R. Gale, and R. Brown (Editors). 1987. *Social Science in Natural Resource Management Systems.* Boulder, CO: Westview Press.
Ewert, A., D. Chavez, and A. Magill (Editors). 1993. *Culture, Conflict, and Communication in the Wildland-Urban Interface.* Boulder, CO: Westview Press.
Ewert, A. (Editor). 1996. *Natural Resource Management: The Human Dimension.* Boulder, CO: Westview Press.

Bibliographic Services

The diverse, multidisciplinary nature of the outdoor recreation literature demands strong bibliographic resources. Reference librarians are invaluable aids in the literature search process, and should be consulted. Fortunately, there are an increasing number of powerful online bibliographic sources to consult as well. All research libraries, of course, have their own electronic catalogs that access their collections, and these should be used. In addition, there are a number of national and international commercial bibliographic services available. These services can index a wide variety of literature, including scholarly journals, conference and symposium proceedings, government documents, books, and popular literature, and some include full text retrieval. Bibliographic services are available to academic libraries on a subscription basis, and some have publicly accessible versions. Generally available bibliographic services that access the literature on outdoor recreation include:

Agricola indexes literature in agriculture and related areas, including forestry, natural resources, water resources, agricultural economics, and rural sociology.
Article1st is a general multidisciplinary index that describes items listed in the table of contents of about 13,000 journals, including many of the recreation-related journals noted above.
Contents1st lists the complete table of contents of the journals included in *Article1st*.
CAB Abstracts indexes and abstracts the worldwide literature in the agricultural sciences and related areas. *Leisure, Recreation, and Tourism Abstracts*, the premier finding tool for journal literature in the broad recreation field, comprises part of this database.

EconLit indexes and abstracts the broad range of literature in economics, including literature that focuses on economic issues in outdoor recreation.

Environment Abtracts indexes and abstracts literature that covers a broad range of topics related to the environment and the management and use of natural resources.

Geobase indexes and abstracts the literature in geography, ecology, natural resources, the environment, planning, and related topics.

GPO Monthly Catalog is a basic index to U.S. government information from all U.S. government agencies, including Congress. U.S Forest Service publications are included in this service, and are also indexed in several other bibliographic services, including *Agricola*, *CAB Abstracts*, and *Social Sciences in Forestry*.

Infotrac SearchBank is a broad, multidisciplinary index to both academic and popular journals, and includes full text retrieval for many citations.

PsycLit is the largest index of journal articles, book chapters, technical reports, and dissertations in psychology, and includes outdoor recreation literature based in the discipline of psychology.

Social Sciences in Forestry is an internet resource produced at the University of Minnesota, and provides strong coverage of forestry and related journal literature for a wide range of topics that have a social science orientation.

Sociofile indexes and abstracts the literature of sociology, social policy, and related disciplines, and is an important resource for locating literature on sociological aspects of outdoor recreation.

SPORTDiscus indexes and abstracts the literature on sport, fitness, recreation, and related fields.

UnCover contains over five million citations to articles taken from the table of contents of nearly 17,000 journals, including many of the recreation journals noted above. For a fee, this service enables the user to receive faxed copies of the text of articles within 24 hours.

References

Absher, J., and Lee, R. (1981). Density as an incomplete cause of crowding in backcountry settings. *Leisure Sciences, 4*, 231-47.

Absher, J., McAvoy, L., Burdge, R., and Gramann, J.. (1988). Public and commercial managers predicting recreationist opinions. *Journal of Park and Recreation Administration, 6*, 66-77.

Absher, J. (1989). Applying the Limits of Acceptable Change model to National Park Service wilderness: An example from Cumberland Island National Seashore. *Proceedings of the 1988 Southeastern Recreation Research Conference.* Athens, GA: University of Georgia, 143-52.

Adams, J. (1930). Diminishing returns in modern life. *Harpers, 160*, 529-37.

Adams, S. (1979). Segmentation of a recreational fishing market: A canonical analysis of fishing attributes and party composition. *Journal of Leisure Research, 11*, 82-91

Adelman, B., Heberlein, T., and Bonnickson, T. (1982). Social psychological explanations for the persistence of a conflict between paddling canoeists and motorcraft users in the Boundary Waters Canoe Area. *Leisure Sciences, 5*, 45-61.

Alder, J. (1996). Effectiveness of education and enforcement, Cairns Section of the Great Barrier Reef Marine Park. *Environmental Management, 20*, 541-51.

Aldrich, R. (1979). *Remote Sensing of Wildland Resources: A State-of-the -Art Review.* USDA Forest Service General Technical Report RM-71.

Alldredge, R. (1973). Some capacity theory for parks and recreation areas. *Trends, 10*, 20-29.

Allen, L. (1996). Benefits-Based Management of recreation services. *Parks and Recreation, 31*, 64-76.

Allen, L., and McGovern, J. (1997). BBM: It's Working. *Parks and Recreation, 32*, 48-55.

Allen, S. (1985). Predicting the impacts of a high-voltage transmission line on big game hunting opportunities in western Montana. *Proceedings—Symposium on Recreation Choice Behavior.* USDA Forest Service General Technical Report INT-184, 86-100.

Allison, M., and Duncan, M. (1987). Women, work, and leisure: The days of our lives. *Leisure Sciences, 9*, 143-62.

Allison, M. (1988). Breaking boundaries: Future directions in cross-cultural research. *Leisure Sciences, 10*, 247-59.

Allison, M. (1992). Fostering cultural diversity: Problems of access and ethnic boundary maintenance. *Proceedings of the Symposium on Social Aspects and Recreation Research.* USDA Forest Service General Technical Report PSW-132, 22-24.

Allison, M. (1993). Access and boundary maintenance: Serving culturally diverse populations. *Culture, Conflict, and Communication in the Wildland-Urban Interface.* Boulder, CO: Westview Press, 99-107.

Alpert, L., and L. Herrington. (1998). An interactive information kiosk for the Adirondack Park visitor interpretive center, Newcomb, NY. *Proceedings of the 1997 Northeastern Recreation Research Symposium.* USDA Forest Service General Technical Report NE-241, 265-67.

Altman, I. (1975). *The Environment and Social Behavior: Privacy, Personal Space, Territory, Crowding*. Monterey, CA: Brooks/Cole Publishing Company.

Andereck, K., and Becker, R. (1990). Density and perceived crowding in a high use built environment. *Proceedings of the 1989 Southeastern Recreation Research Conference*. Athens, GA: University of Georgia, 45-52.

Andereck, K., and Becker, R. (1993). Perceptions of carry-over crowding in recreation environments. *Leisure Sciences, 15*, 25-35.

Anderson, D., Leatherberry, E., and Lime, D. (1978). *An Annotated Bibliography on River Recreation*. USDA Forest Service General Technical Report NC-41.

Anderson, D. (1980). Long-time Boundary Waters' visitors change use patterns. *Naturalist 31*, 2-5.

Anderson, D. (1983). Displacement: One consequence of not meeting people's needs. *Research in Forest Productivity, Use, and Pest Control*. USDA Forest Service General Technical Report NE-90, 31-37.

Anderson, D., and Brown, P. (1984). The displacement process in recreation. *Journal of Leisure Research 16*, 61-73.

Anderson, D., and Manfredo, M. (1986). Visitor preferences for management actions. *Proceedings–National Wilderness Research Conference: Current Research*. USDA Forest Service General Technical Report INT-212, 314-19.

Anderson, D., and Schneider, I. (1993). Using the Delphi Process to identify significant recreation research-based innovations. *Journal of Park and Recreation Administration, 11*, 25-36.

Anderson, D., Lime, D., and Wang, T. (1998). *Maintaining the Quality of Park Resources and Visitor Experiences: A Handbook for Managers*. St. Paul, MN: University of Minnesota Cooperative Park Studies Unit.

Anderson, F., and Bonsor, N. (1974). Allocation, congestion, and the valuation of recreational resources. *Land Economics, 50*, 51-57.

Anderson, M., Reiling, S., and Criner, G. (1985). Consumer demand theory and wildlife agency revenue structure. *Wildlife Society Bulletin, 13*, 375-84.

Applegate, J., and Clark, K. (1987). Satisfaction levels of birdwatchers: An observation on the consumptive-nonconsumptive continuum. *Leisure Sciences, 9*, 129-34.

Armistead, J., and Ramthun, R. (1996). Influences on perceived crowding and satisfaction on the Blue Ridge Parkway. *Proceedings of the 1995 Northeastern Recreation Research Symposium*. USDA Forest Service General Technical Report NE-218, 93-95.

Ashor, J., McCool, S., and Stokes, G. (1986). Improving wilderness planning efforts: Application of the transactive planning approach. *Proceedings—National Wilderness Research Conference: Current Research*. USDA Forest Service General Technical Report INT-212, 424-31.

Atkinson, J., and Birch, D. (1972). *Motivation: The Dynamics of Action*. New York: John Wiley and Sons.

Baas, J. (1992). Identifying service delivery strategies for ethnically diverse users of a wildland-urban recreation site. *Proceedings of the Symposium on Social Aspects and Recreation Research*, USDA Forest Service General Technical Report PSW-132, 40-41.

Baas, J., Ewert, A., and Chavez, D. (1993). Influence of ethnicity on recreation and natural environment use patterns: Managing recreation sites for ethnic and racial diversity. *Environmental Management, 17*, 523-29.

Ballinger, N., and Manning, R. (1998). Sense of place: Mount Desert Island residents and Acadia National Park. *Proceedings of the 1997 Northeastern Recreation Research Symposium*. USDA Forest Service General Technical Report NE-241, 85-88.

Bamford, T., Manning, R., Forcier, L., and Koenemann, E. (1988). Differential campsite pricing: An experiment. *Journal of Leisure Research, 20*, 324-42.

Basman, C., Manfredo, M., Barro, S., Vaske, J., and Watson, A. (1996). Norm accessibility: An exploratory study of backcountry and frontcountry recreational norms. *Leisure Sciences 18*, 177-91.

Bates, G. (1935). The vegetation of footpaths, sidewalks, cart-tracks, and gateways. *Journal of Ecology 23*, 470-87.

Baum, A., and Paulus, P. (1987). Crowding. *Handbook of Environmental Psychology*. New York: John Wiley and Sons.

Baumgartner, R., and Heberlein, T. (1981). Process, goal, and social interaction in recreation: What makes an activity substitutable. *Leisure Sciences 4*, 443-57.

Beaman, J. (1975). Comments on the paper "The substitutability concept: Implications for recreation research and management," by Hendee and Burdge. *Journal of Leisure Research 7*, 146-52.

Beaman, J., Kim, Y., and Smith, S. (1979). The effect of recreation supply on participation. *Leisure Sciences, 2*, 71-87.

Beaman, J., and Stanley, D. (1992). Counting visitors at national parks: Concepts and issues. *Proceedings of the 1991 Northeastern Recreation Research Symposium*. USDA Forest Service General Technical Report NE-160, 111-15.

Beaman, J. (1997). Recreation research past, future and critical relationships with management that influence the direction and success of research: Views from "outside" after more than two decades in a federal agency. *Proceedings of the 1996 Northeastern Recreation Research Symposium*. USDA Forest Service General Technical Report NE-272, 117-24.

Beard, J., and Ragheb, M. (1980). Measuring leisure satisfaction. *Journal of Leisure Research, 12*, 20-33.

Beard, J., and Ragheb, M. (1983). Measuring leisure motivation. *Journal of Leisure Research, 15*, 219-28.

Beardsley, W. (1967). *Cost Implications of Camper and Campground Characteristics in Central Colorado*. USDA Forest Service Research Note RM-86.

Becker, B. (1976). Perceived similarities among recreational activities. *Journal of Leisure Research, 8*, 112-22.

Becker, R. (1978). Social carrying capacity and user satisfaction: An experiential function. *Leisure Sciences, 1*, 241-57.

Becker, R., Gates, W., and Neumann, B. (1980). Establishing representative sample designs with aerial photographic observations. *Leisure Sciences, 3*, 277-300.

Becker, R. (1981a). Displacement of recreational users between the lower St. Croix and upper Mississippi rivers. *Journal of Environmental Management, 13*, 259-267.

Becker, R. (1981b). User reaction to wild and scenic river designation. *Water Resources Bulletin, 17*, 623-26.

Becker, R., Niemann, B., and Gates, W. (1981). Displacement of users within a river system: Social and environmental tradeoffs. *Some Recent Products of River Recreation Research*. USDA Forest Service General Technical Report NC-63, 33-38.

Becker, R., and Jubenville, A. (1982). Forest recreation management. *Forest Science,* New York: John Wiley and Sons, 335-55.

Becker, R., Jubenville, A., and Burnett, G. (1984). Fact and judgment in the search for a social carrying capacity. *Leisure Sciences, 6,* 475-86.

Becker, R., Berrier, D., and Barker, G. (1985). Entrance fees and visitation levels. *Journal of Park and Recreation Administration, 3,* 28-32.

Behan, R. (1972). Wilderness purism—Here we go again. *American Forests, 73,* 8-11.

Behan, R. (1974). Police state wilderness: A comment on mandatory wilderness permits. *Journal of Forestry, 72,* 98-99.

Behan, R. (1976). Rationing wilderness use: An example from Grand Canyon. *Western Wildlands, 3,* 23-26.

Bella, L. (1990). Women and leisure: Beyond androcentricism. *Understanding Leisure and Recreation: Mapping the Past, Charting the Future.* State College, PA: Venture Publishing Company, 151-79.

Bengston, D., and Xu, Z. (1993). Impact of research and technical change in wildland recreation: Evaluation issues and approaches. *Leisure Sciences, 15,* 251-72.

Berger, B. (1962). The sociology of leisure: Some suggestions. *Industrial Relations, 1,* 31-45.

Berry, J., Hals, H., Schriever, J., and Auchley, B. (1993). Hiker characteristics as an indicator of perceived congestion levels in the Sandwich Range Wilderness Area. *Proceedings of the 1992 Northeastern Recreation Research Symposium.* USDA Forest Service General Technical Report NE-176, 51-54.

Bevins, M., and Wilcox, D. (1979). *Evaluation of Nationwide Outdoor Recreation Participation Surveys 1959-1978.* Burlington, VT: University of Vermont Agricultural Experiment Station.

Bevins, M. (1992). Dissatisfied State Park Campers? *Proceedings of the 1991 Northeastern Recreation Research Symposium.* USDA Forest Service General Technical Report NE-160, 91-93.

Biddle, B. (1986). Recent developments in role theory. *Annual Review of Sociology, 12,* 67-92.

Bishop, D., and Ikeda, M. (1970). Status and role factors in the leisure behavior of different occupations. *Sociology and Social Research, 54,* 190-208.

Bishop, D. (1972). Stability of the factor structure of leisure behavior: Analysis of four communities. *Journal of Leisure Research, 2,* 160-70.

Bixler, R., and Morris, B. (1998). The role of "outdoor capital" in the socialization of wildland recreationists. *Proceedings of the 1997 Northeastern Recreation Research Symposium.* USDA Forest Service General Technical Report NE-241, 237-42.

Blahna, D. (1992). Comparing the preferences of black, Asian, Hispanic, and white fishermen at Moraine Hills State Park, Illinois. *Proceedings of the Symposium on Social Aspects and Recreation Research.* USDA Forest Service General Technical Report PSW-132, 42-44.

Blahna, D. and Black, K. (1993). Racism: A concern for recreation resource managers? *Managing Urban and High-Use Recreation Settings.* USDA Forest Service General Technical Report NC-163, 111-18.

Blahna, D., Smith, K., and Anderson, J. (1995). Backcountry llama packing: Visitor perceptions of acceptability and conflict. *Leisure Sciences, 17,* 185-204.

Blake, J., and Davis, K. (1964). Norms, values, and sanctions. *Handbook of Modern Sociology*. Chicago: Rand McNally.

Block, P., Black, W., and Lichstenstein, D. (1989). Involvement with the equipment component of sport: Links to recreational commitment. *Leisure Sciences, 11,* 187-200.

Blumer, H. (1936). Social attitudes and nonsymbolic interaction. *Journal of Educational Sociology, 9,* 515-23.

Borgstrom, G. (1965).*The Hungry Planet: The Modern World at the Edge of Famine*. New York: Macmillan Co.

Borrie, W., and Roggenbuck, J. (1995). Community-based research for an urban recreation application of benefits-based management. *Proceedings of the Second Symposium on Social Aspects and Recreation Research*. USDA Forest Service General Technical Report PSW-156, 159-63.

Boster, M.., Gum, L., and Monachi, D. (1973). A socio-economic analysis of Colorado River trips with policy implications. *Journal of Travel Research, 12,* 7-10.

Boteler, F. (1984). Carrying capacity as a framework for managing whitewater use. *Journal of Park and Recreation Administration, 2,* 26-36.

Bowker, J., and Leeworthy, V. (1998). Accounting for ethnicity in recreation demand: A flexible count data approach. *Journal of Leisure Research, 30,* 64-78.

Bowman, E. (1971). The cop image. *Parks and Recreation, 6,* 35-36.

Brewer, D., and Gillespie, G. (1967). Estimating satisfaction levels of outdoor recreationists. *Journal of Soil and Water Conservation, 22,* 248-49.

Brewer, J., and Fulton, D. (1973). A review of recreation land allocation on the Mark Twain National Forest. *Outdoor Recreation Research: Applying the Results*. USDA Forest General Technical Report NC-9, 1-6.

Bright, A., Manfredo, M., Fishbein, M., and Bath, A. (1993). Application of the theory of learned action to the National Park Service's controlled burn policy. *Journal of Leisure Research, 25,* 263-80.

Bright, A. (1994). Information campaigns that enlighten and influence the public. *Parks and Recreation, 29,* 49-54.

Bright, A., and Manfredo, M. (1995). Moderating effects of personal importance on the accessibility of attitudes toward recreation participation. *Leisure Sciences, 17,* 281-94.

Brightbill, C. (1960). *The Challenge of Leisure*. Englewood Cliffs, NJ: Prentice-Hall, Inc.

Brown, C., Halstead, J., and Luloff, A. (1992). Information as a management tool: An evaluation of the Pemigewasset Wilderness Management Plan. *Environmental Management, 16,* 143-48.

Brown, M. (1994). Ethnic differences in outdoor participation patterns among older adults. *Proceedings of the 1993 Southeastern Recreation Research Conference*. USDA Forest Service General Technical Report SE-90, 1-5.

Brown, P., and Hunt, J. (1969). The influence of information signs on visitor distribution and use. *Journal of Leisure Research, 1,* 79-83.

Brown, P. (1970). Sentiment changes and recreation participation. *Journal of Leisure Research, 2,* 264-68.

Brown, P., Dyer, A., and Whaley, R. (1973). Recreation research—so what? *Journal of Leisure Research, 5,* 16-24.

Brown, P. (1977). Information needs for river recreation planning and management. *Proceedings: River Recreation Management and Research Symposium*. USDA Forest Service General Technical Report NC-28, 193-201.

Brown, P., Hautaluoma, J. and McPhail, S. (1977). Colorado deer hunting experiences. *Transactions of the North American Wildlife and Natural Resources Conference*, Washington, D.C.: Wildlife Management Institute, 216-25.

Brown, P., Driver, B., and McConnell, C. (1978). The opportunity spectrum concept in outdoor recreation supply inventories: Background and application. *Proceedings of the Integrated Renewable Resource Inventories Workshop*. USDA Forest Service General Technical Report RM-55, 73-84.

Brown, P., Driver, B., Burns, D., and McConnell, C. (1979). The outdoor recreation opportunity spectrum in wildland recreation planning: Development and application. *First Annual National Conference on Recreation Planning and Development: Proceedings of the Specialty Conference* (Vol. 2), Washington, D.C.: Society of Civil Engineers, 1-12.

Brown, P., and Haas, G. (1980). Wilderness recreation experiences: The Rawah case. *Journal of Leisure Research, 12*, 229-41.

Brown, P., and Ross, D. (1982). Using desired recreation experiences to predict setting preferences. *Forest and River Recreation: Research Update*. St. Paul, MN: University of Minnesota Agricultural Experiment Station Miscellaneous Report 18, 105-10.

Brown, P., McCool, S., and Manfredo, M. (1987). Evolving concepts and tools for recreation user management in wilderness. *Proceedings—National Wilderness Research Conference: Issues, State-of-Knowledge, Future Directions*. USDA Forest Service General Technical Report INT-220, 320-46.

Brown, P. (1989). Quality in recreation experience. *Outdoor Recreation Benchmark 1988: Proceedings of the National Outdoor Recreation Forum*. USDA Forest Service General Technical Report SE-52, 412-21.

Brown, T., and Siemer, W. (1992). Toward a comprehensive understanding of angler involvement. *Proceedings of the 1991 Northeastern Recreation Research Symposium*. USDA Forest Service General Technical Report NE-160, 149-152.

Brunson, M., and Shelby, B. (1990). A hierarchy of campsite attributes in dispersed recreation. *Leisure Sciences, 12*, 197-209.

Brunson, M., Shelby, B., and Goodwin, J. (1992). Matching impacts with standards in the design of wilderness permit systems. *Defining Wilderness Quality: The Role of Standards in Wilderness Management—A Workshop Proceedings*. USDA Forest Service General Technical Report PNW-305, 101-6.

Brunson, M., and Shelby, B. (1993). Recreation substitutability: A research agenda. *Leisure Sciences, 15*, 67-74.

Bryan, H. (1977). Leisure value systems and recreational specialization: The case of trout fishermen. *Journal of Leisure Research, 9*, 174-87.

Buchanan, T., Christensen, J., and Burdge, R. (1981). Social groups and the meanings of outdoor recreation activities. *Journal of Leisure Research, 13*, 254-66.

Buchanan, T. (1985). Commitment and leisure behavior: A theoretical perspective. *Leisure Sciences, 7*, 401-20.

Buckley, C., and Mendelsohn, R. (1987). Recreation user fees II: An economic analysis. *Journal of Forestry, 85*, 31-35.

Buist, L., and Hoots, T. (1982). Recreation opportunity spectrum approach to resource planning. *Journal of Forestry, 80,* 84-86.

Bullis, C., and Tompkins, P. (1989). The forest ranger revisited: A study of control practices and identification. *Communication Monographs, 56,* 287-306.

Bultena, G., and Taves, M. (1961). Changing wilderness images and forest policy. *Journal of Forestry, 59,* 167-71.

Bultena, G., and Klessig, L. (1969). Satisfaction in camping: A conceptualization and guide to social research. *Journal of Leisure Research, 1,* 348-64.

Bultena, G., and Field, D. (1978). Visitors to national parks: A test of the elitism argument. *Leisure Sciences, 1,* 395-409.

Bultena, G., and Field, D. (1980). Structural effects in national park-going. *Leisure Sciences, 3,* 221-40.

Bultena, G., Albrecht, D., and Womble, P. (1981a). Freedom versus control: A study of backpackers' preferences for wilderness management. *Leisure Sciences, 4,* 297-310.

Bultena, G., Field, D., Womble, P., and Albrecht, D. (1981b). Closing the gates: A study of backcountry use-limitation at Mount McKinley National Park. *Leisure Sciences, 4,* 249-67.

Bumgardner, W., Waring, M., Legg, M., and Goetz, L. (1988). Key indicators of campsite selection at Corps of Engineers lakes. *Journal of Park and Recreation Administration, 6,* 62-78.

Burch, W., Jr. (1964a). Two concepts for guiding recreation decisions. *Journal of Forestry, 62,* 707-12.

Burch, W., Jr. (1964b). *A New Look at an Old Friend–Observation as a Technique for Recreation Research.* Portland, OR: USDA Forest Service, Pacific Northwest Forest and Range Experiment Station.

Burch, W., Jr. (1965). The play world of camping: Research into the social meaning of outdoor recreation. *American Journal of Sociology, 70,* 604-12.

Burch, W., Jr. (1966). Wilderness—the life cycle and forest recreational choice. *Journal of Forestry, 64,* 606-10.

Burch, W., Jr., and Wenger, W., Jr. (1967). *The Social Characteristics of Participants in Three Styles of Family Camping.* USDA Forest Service Research Paper PNW-48.

Burch, W., Jr. (1969). The social circles of leisure: competing explanations. *Journal of Leisure Research, 1,* 125-47.

Burch, W., Jr. (1970). Recreation preferences as culturally determined phenomena. *Elements of Outdoor Recreation Planning.* Ann Arbor: University of Michigan, 61-87.

Burch, W., Jr. (1974). In democracy is the preservation of wilderness. *Appalachia, 40,* 90-101.

Burch, W., Jr. (1981). The ecology of metaphor—Spacing regularities for humans and other primates in urban and wildland habitats. *Leisure Sciences, 4,* 213-31.

Burch, W., Jr. (1984). Much ado about nothing—Some reflections on the wider and wilder implications of social carrying capacity. *Leisure Sciences, 6,* 487-96.

Burde, J., Peine, J., Renfro, J., and Curran, K. (1988). Communicating with park visitors: Some successes and failures at Great Smoky Mountains National Park. *National Association of Interpretation 1988 Research Monograph,* 7-12.

Burdge, R. (1969). Levels of occupational prestige and leisure activity. *Journal of Leisure Research, 9,* 262-74.

Burdge, R., and Field, D. (1972). Methodological perspectives for the study of outdoor recreation. *Journal of Leisure Research, 4,* 63-72.

Burdge, R., and Hendee, J. (1972). The demand survey dilemma: Assessing the credibility of state outdoor recreation plans. *Guideline, 3,* 11-18.

Burdge, R. (1974). The state of leisure research. *Journal of Leisure Research, 6,* 312-19.

Burdge, R., Buchanan, T., and Christensen, J. (1981). A critical assessment of the state of outdoor recreation research. *Outdoor Recreation Planning, Perspectives, and Research.* Dubuque, IA: Kendall-Hunt, 3-10.

Burdge, R. (1983). Making leisure and recreation research a scholarly topic: Views of a journal editor, 1972-1982. *Leisure Sciences, 6,* 99-126.

Bureau of Outdoor Recreation. (1972). *The 1965 Survey of Outdoor Recreation Activities.* Washington, D.C.: U.S. Government Printing Office.

Bureau of Outdoor Recreation. (1973). *Outdoor Recreation: A Legacy for America.* Washington D.C.: U.S. Government Printing Office.

Burgess, R., Clark, R., and Hendee, J. (1971). An experimental analysis of anti-litter procedures. *Journal of Applied Behavior Analysis, 4,* 71-75.

Burns, R., Graefe, A., and Titre, J. (1998). Customer Satisfaction at U.S. Army Corps of Engineers-administered lakes: A compilation of two years of performance data. *Proceedings of the 1997 Northeastern Recreation Research Symposium.* USDA Forest Service General Technical Report NE-241, 12-13.

Burt, O., and Brewer, D. (1971). Evaluation of net social benefits from outdoor recreation. *Econometrica, 39,* 812-27.

Burton, T. (1971). *Experiments in Recreation Research.* London: George Allen and Unwin, Ltd.

Bury, R., and Hall, J. (1963). *Estimating Past and Current Attendance at Winter Sports Areas.* USDA Forest Service Research Note PSW-33.

Bury, R. (1964). *Information on Campground Use and Visitor Characteristics.* USDA Forest Service Research Note PSW-43.

Bury, R., and Margolis, R. (1964). *A Method for Estimating Current Attendance on Sets of Campgrounds.* USDA Forest Service Research Note PSW-42.

Bury, R. (1976). Recreation carrying capacity—Hypothesis or reality? *Parks and Recreation, 11,* 23-25, 56-58.

Bury, R., and Fish, C. (1980). Controlling wilderness recreation: What managers think and do. *Journal of Soil and Water Conservation, 35,* 90-93.

Bury, R., Holland, S., and McEwen, D. (1983). Analyzing recreational conflict. *Journal of Soil and Water Conservation, 38,* 401-3.

Cable, T., Knudson, D., Udd, E., and Stewart, D. (1987). Attitude changes as a result of exposure to interpretive messages. *Journal of Park and Recreation Administration, 5,* 47-60.

Campbell, F., Hendee, J., and Clark, R. (1968). Law and order in public parks. *Parks and Recreation, 3,* 51-55.

Campbell, F. (1970). Participant observation in outdoor recreation. *Journal of Leisure Research 2,* 226-36.

Campbell, M. (1989). Fishing lore: The construction of the "sportsman". *Annals of Tourism Research, 16,* 76-88.

Cancian, F. (1975). *What are Norms? A Study of Beliefs and Actions in a Maya Community.* New York: Cambridge University Press.

Canon, L., Adler, S., and Leonard, R. (1979). *Factors Affecting Backcountry Campsite Dispersion.* USDA Forest Service Research Note NE-276.

Carhart, A. (1961). *Planning for America's Wildlands.* Harrisburg, PA: The Telegraph Press.

Carls, E. (1974). The effects of people and man-induced conditions on preferences for outdoor recreation landscapes. *Journal of Leisure Research, 6,* 113-24.

Carr, D., and Williams, D. (1992). Social structural characteristics of Hispanic recreationists on the Angeles and San Bernardino National Forests. *Proceedings of the Symposium on Social Aspects and Recreation Research.* USDA Forest Service General Technical Report PSW-132, 30-31.

Carr, D., and Williams, D. (1993a). Understanding diverse recreationists: Beyond quantitative analysis. *Managing Urban and High-use Recreation Settings.* USDA Forest Service General Technical Report NC-163, 101-6.

Carr, D., and Williams, D. (1993b). Understanding the role of ethnicity in outdoor recreation experiences. *Journal of Leisure Research 25,* 22-38.

Catton, W., Jr. (1969). Motivations of wilderness users. *Pulp and Paper Magazine of Canada (Woodlands Section),* Dec. 19, 121-26.

Catton, W., Jr. (1971). The wildland recreation boom and sociology. *Pacific Sociological Review 14,* 330-57.

Cesario, F. (1973). A generalized trip distribution model. *Journal of Regional Science, 13,* 233-47.

Cesario, F., and Knetsch, J. (1976). A recreation site demand and benefits estimation model. *Regional Studies, 10,* 97-104.

Chace, D., and Cheek, N. (1979). Activity preferences and participation: Conclusions from a factor analytic study. *Journal of Leisure Research, 11,* 92-101.

Chambers, D. (1986). Constraints of work and domestic schedules on women's leisure. *Leisure Studies, 5,* 309-25.

Chappelle, D. (1973). The need for outdoor recreation: An economic conundrum? *Journal of Leisure Research, 5,* 47-53.

Chavez, D. (1993). *Visitor Perceptions of Crowding and Discrimination at Two National Forests in Southern California.* USDA Forest Service Research Paper PSW-216.

Chavez, D., Larson, J., and Winter, P. (1995). To be or not to be a park: That is the question. *Proceedings of the Second Symposium on Social Aspects and Recreation Research.* USDA Forest Service General Technical Report PSW-156, 29-33.

Chavez, D. (1996). Mountain biking: Direct, indirect, and bridge building management styles. *Journal of Park and Recreation Administration, 14,* 21-35.

Cheek, N., Jr. (1971). Toward a sociology of not-work. *Pacific Sociological Review, 14,* 245-58.

Cheek, N., Jr. (1972). Variations in patterns of leisure behavior: An analysis of sociological aggregates. *Social Behavior, Natural Resources, and the Environment.* New York: Harper and Row Publishers, 29-43.

Cheek, N., Jr., and Burch, W., Jr. (1976). *The Social Organization of Leisure in Human Society.* New York: Harper and Row.

Cheek, N., Jr., Field, D., and Burdge, R. (1976). *Leisure and Recreation Places.* Ann Arbor, MI: Ann Arbor Science.

Cheung, H. (1972). A day-use visitation model. *Journal of Leisure Research, 4,* 139-56.

Chilman, K., Marnell, L., and Pope, R. (1977). Developing a research capacity in field organizations to aid in management decision-making. *Proceedings: River Recreation Management and Research Symposium*. USDA Forest Service General Technical Report NC-28, 163-67.

Chilman, K., Marnell, L., and Foster, D. (1981). Putting river research to work: A carrying capacity strategy. *Some Recent Products of River Recreation Research*. USDA Forest Service General Technical Report NC-63, 56-61.

Chilman, K., Ladley, J., and Wikle, T. (1989). Refining existing recreational carrying capacity systems: Emphasis on recreational quality. *Proceedings of the 1988 Southeastern Recreation Research Conference*. Athens, GA: University of Georgia, 118-23.

Chilman, K., Foster, D., and Everson, A. (1990). Updating the recreational carrying capacity process: recent refinements. *Managing America's Enduring Wilderness Resource*. St. Paul, MN: University of Minnesota, 234-38.

Chilman, K., Lane, D., Foster, D., Everson, A., and Lannog, M. (1990). Monitoring Social conditions on wildlands: designing low-cost systems. *Managing America's Enduring Wilderness Resource*. St. Paul, MN: Minnesota Agricultural Experiment Station, 163-69.

Chipman, B., and Helfrich, L. (1988). Recreational specialization and motivation of Virginia river anglers. *North American Journal of Fisheries Management, 8*, 390-98.

Choi, S., Loomis, D., and Ditton, R. (1994). Effect of social group, activity, and specialization on recreation substitution decisions. *Leisure Sciences, 16*, 143-59.

Christensen, H. (1981). *Bystander Intervention and Litter Control: An Experimental Analysis of an Appeal to Help Program*. USDA Forest Service Research Paper PNW-287.

Christensen, H., and Clark, R. (1983). Increasing public involvement to reduce depreciative behavior in recreation settings. *Leisure Sciences, 5*, 359-78.

Christensen, H., and Davis, N. (1985). Evaluating user impacts and management controls: Implications for recreation choice behavior. *Proceedings—Symposium on Recreation Choice Behavior*. USDA Forest Service General Technical Report INT-184, 71-78.

Christensen, H. (1986). Vandalism and depreciative behavior. *A Literature Review: The President's Commission on Americans Outdoors*. Washington, DC: US Government Printing Office, M-73 - M-87.

Christensen, H., Williams, P., and Clark, R. (1986). *Values and Choices in Outdoor Recreation by Male and Female Campers in Dispersed Recreation Areas*. USDA Forest Service General Technical Research Paper PNW-377.

Christensen, H., and Dustin, D. (1989). Reaching recreationists at different levels of moral development. *Journal of Park and Recreation Administration, 7*, 72-80.

Christensen, H., Johnson, D., and Brookes, M. (1992). *Vandalism: Research, Prevention, and Social Policy*. USDA Forest Service General Technical Report PNW-293.

Christensen, J., and Yoesting, D. (1973). Social and attitudinal variants in high and low use of outdoor recreational facilities. *Journal of Leisure Research, 5*, 6-15.

Christensen, J., and Yoesting, D. (1977). The substitutability concept: A need for further development. *Journal of Leisure Research, 9*, 188-207.

Christensen, J., and Dwyer, J. (1995). Examining African American and white participation after demographic standardization on selected characteristics.

Proceedings of the 1994 Northeastern Recreation Research Symposium. USDA Forest Service General Technical Report NE-198, 159-61.

Christensen, N., Stewart, W., and King, D. (1993). National forest campgrounds: Users willing to pay more. *Journal of Forestry, 91*, 43-47.

Cicchetti, C., Seneca, J., and Davidson, P. (1969). *The Demand and Supply of Outdoor Recreation*. New Brunswick, NJ: Rutgers Bureau of Economic Research.

Cicchetti, C., and Smith, V. (1973). Congestion, quality deterioration, and optimal use: Wilderness recreation in the Spanish Peaks Primitive Area. *Social Sciences Research, 2*, 15-30.

Cicchetti, C. (1976). *The Costs of Congestion*. Cambridge, MA: Ballinger Publishing Company.

Clark, R., Hendee, J., and Campbell, F. (1971a). Values, behavior, and conflict in modern camping culture. *Journal of Leisure Research, 3*, 145-49.

Clark, R., Hendee, J., and Campbell, F. (1971b). *Depreciative Behavior in Forest Campgrounds: An Exploratory Study*. USDA Forest Service Research Paper PNW-161.

Clark, R., Burgess, R., and Hendee, J. (1972a). The development of anti-litter behavior in a forest campground. *Journal of Applied Behavior Analysis, 5*, 1-5.

Clark, R., Hendee, J., and Burgess, R. (1972b). The experimental control of littering. *Journal of Environmental Education, 4*, 22-28.

Clark, R., and Stankey, G. (1976). Analyzing public input to resource decisions. *Natural Resources Journal, 16*, 213-36.

Clark, R. (1977). Alternative strategies for studying river recreationists. *Proceedings: River Recreation Management and Research Symposium*. USDA Forest Service General Technical Report NC-28, 91-100.

Clark, R., and Stankey, G. (1979a). *The Recreation Opportunity Spectrum: A Framework for Planning, Management, and Research*. USDA Forest Service Research Paper PNW-98.

Clark, R., and Stankey, G. (1979b). Determining the acceptability of recreational impacts: An application of the outdoor recreation opportunity spectrum. *Recreation Impact on Wildlands*. USDA Forest Service, Pacific Northwest Region R-6-001-1979, 32-42.

Clark, R. (1982). Promises and pitfalls of the ROS in resource management. *Australian Parks and Recreation*, May, 9-13.

Clarke, A., (1956). The use of leisure and its relation to levels of occupational prestige. *American Sociological Review, 21*, 301-7.

Clawson, M. (1959). The crisis in outdoor recreation. *American Forests, 65*, 22-31, 40-41.

Clawson, M., and Knetsch, J. (1963). Outdoor recreation research: Some concepts and suggested areas of study. *Natural Resources Journal, 3*, 250-75.

Clawson, M., and Knetsch, J. (1966). *Economics of Outdoor Recreation*. Baltimore: Johns Hopkins University Press.

Clawson, M. (1985). Outdoor recreation: twenty-five years of history, twenty-five years of projection. *Leisure Sciences, 7*, 78-99.

Cockrell, D and McLaughlin, W. (1982). Social influences on wild river recreationists. *Forest and River Recreation: Research Update*. St. Paul, MN: University of Minnesota Agricultural Experiment Station, Miscellaneous Publication 18, 140-45.

Cockrell, D., and Wellman, J. (1985a). Democracy and leisure: Reflections on pay-as-you-go outdoor recreation. *Journal of Park and Recreation Administration, 3*, 1-10.

Cockrell, D., and Wellman, J. (1985b). Against the running tide: Democracy and outdoor recreation user fees. *Proceedings of the 1985 National Outdoor Recreation Trends Symposium, Volume II.* Atlanta, GA: U. S. National Park Service, 193-205.

Cohen, J., Sladen, B., and Bennett, B. (1975). The effects of situational variables on judgments of crowding. *Sociometry, 38,* 278-81.

Cole, D. (1982). Controlling the spread of campsites at popular wilderness destinations. *Journal of Soil and Water Conservation, 37,* 291-95.

Cole, D., and Rang, B. (1983). Temporary campsite closure in the Selway-Bitterroot Wilderness. *Journal of Forestry, 81,* 729-32.

Cole, D. (1987). Research on soil and vegetation in wilderness: A state-of-knowledge review. *Proceedings–National Wilderness Research Conference: Issues, State-of-Knowledge, Future Directions.* USDA Forest Service General Technical Report INT-220, 135-77.

Cole, D., Peterson, M., and Lucas, R. (1987). *Managing Wilderness Recreation Use.* USDA Forest Service General Technical Report INT-230.

Cole, D. (1993). Wilderness recreation management. *Journal of Forestry, 91,* 22-24.

Cole, D. (1994). *The Wilderness Threats Matrix: A Framework for Assessing Impacts.* USDA Forest Service General Technical Report INT-475.

Cole, D., Watson, A., and Roggenbuck, J. (1995). *Trends in Wilderness Visitors and Visits: Boundary Waters Canoe Area, Shining Rock, and Desolation Wilderness.* USDA Forest Service Research Paper INT-483.

Cole, D. (1996). *Wilderness Recreation Use Trends, 1965 Through 1994.* USDA Forest Service Research Paper INT-488.

Cole, D., and McCool, S. (1997). The Limits of Acceptable Change process: Modifications and clarifications. *Proceedings–Limits of Acceptable Change and Related Planning Processes: Progress and Future Directions.* USDA Forest Service General Technical Report INT-371, 61-68.

Cole, D., Watson, A., Hall, T., and Spildie, D. (1997a). *High-Use Destinations in Wilderness: Social and Bio-Physical Impacts, Visitor Responses, and Management Options.* USDA Forest Service Research Paper INT-496.

Cole, D., Hammond, T., and McCool, S. (1997b). Information quality and communication effectiveness: Low-impact messages on wilderness trailhead bulletin boards. *Leisure Sciences, 19,* 59-72.

Collins, R., and Hodge, I. (1984). Clustering visitors for recreation management. *Journal of Environmental Management, 19,* 147-58.

Confer, J., Jr., Graefe, A., and Falk, J. (1996). Crowding on the beach: Examining the phenomena of over- and under-manning in alternative environments. *Proceedings of the 1995 Northeastern Recreation Research Symposium.* USDA Forest Service General Technical Report NE-218, 65-72.

Confer, J., Jr., Vogelsong, H., Graefe, A., and Solan, D. (1997). Relationships between motivations and recreation activity preferences among Delaware State Park visitors: An exploratory analysis. *Proceedings of the 1996 Northeastern Recreation Research Symposium.* USDA Forest Service General Technical Report NE-232, 146-53.

Connelly, N. (1987). Critical factors and their threshold for camper satisfaction at two campgrounds. *Journal of Leisure Research, 19,* 159-73.

Connors, E. (1976). Public safety in park and recreation settings. *Parks and Recreation, 11*, 20-21, 55-56.

Cordell, H., and Sykes, C. (1969). *User Preferences for Developed-Site Camping.* USDA Forest Service Research Note SE-122.

Cordell, H., James, G., and Griffith, R. (1970). *Estimating Recreation Use at Visitor Information Centers.* USDA Forest Service Research Paper SE-69.

Cordell, H., and James, G. (1972). *Visitors' Preferences for Certain Physical Characteristics of Developed Campsites.* USDA Forest Service Research Paper SE-100.

Cordell, H. (1976). Substitutions between privately and publicly supplied urban recreational open space. *Journal of Leisure Research, 8*, 160-74.

Cordell, H., McDonald, B., Lewis, B., Miles, M., Martin, J., and Bason, J. (1996). United States of America. *World Leisure Participation.* CAB International, 215-35.

Cordell, H., Lewis, B., McDonald, B., and Miles, M. (1997). National survey on recreation and the environment: Biasing effects of including a participation screening question. *Proceedings of the 1996 Northeastern Recreation Research Symposium.* USDA Forest Service General Technical Report NE-232, 296-300.

Craig, W. (1972). Recreational activity patterns in a small Negro urban community: The role of the cultural base. *Economic Geography, 48*, 107-14.

Crandall, R., and Lewko, J. (1976). Leisure research, present and future: Who, what, where. *Journal of Leisure Research, 8*, 150-59.

Crandall, R. (1979). Social interaction, affect, and leisure. *Journal of Leisure Research, 11*, 165-81.

Crandall, R. (1980). Motivations for leisure. *Journal of Leisure Research, 12*, 45-54.

Crompton, J. and Wicks, B. (1988). Implementing a preferred equity model for the delivery of leisure services in the U.S. context. *Leisure Studies, 7*, 287-304.

Crompton, J., and Lue, C. (1992). Patterns of equity preferences among Californians for allocating park and recreation resources. *Leisure Sciences, 14*, 227-46.

Culp, R. (1998). Adolescent girls and outdoor recreation: A case study examining constraints and effective programming. *Journal of Leisure Research, 30*, 356-79.

Daigle, J. (1993). *Bibliography of Forest Service Recreation Research: 1983-1992.* USDA Forest Service General Technical Report NE-180.

Dana, S. (1957). *Problem analysis: Research in forest recreation.* Washington, D.C.: US Department of Agriculture.

Daniels, S. (1987). Marginal cost pricing and the efficient provision of public recreation. *Journal of Leisure Research, 19*, 22-34.

Daniels, S., and Krannich, R. (1990). The Recreation Opportunity Spectrum as a conflict management tool. *Social Science and Natural Resource Recreation Management.* Boulder CO: Westview Press, 165-79.

Darling, F., and Eichhorn, N. (1967). *Man and Nature in the National Parks: Reflections on Policy.* Washington, DC: The Conservation Foundation.

Dasmann, R. (1964). *Wildlife Biology.* New York: John Wiley and Sons.

Dawson, C., Brown, T., and Connelly, N. (1992a). The angler specialization concept applied: New York's Salmon River anglers. *Proceedings of the 1991 Northeastern Recreation Research Symposium.* USDA Forest Service General Technical Report NE-160, 153-55.

Dawson, C., Buerger, R., and Gratzer, M. (1992b). A reassessment of the angler specialization concept. *Proceedings of the 1991 Northeastern Recreation Research Symposium.* USDA Forest Service General Technical Report NE-160, 156-59.

Dawson, C. (1995). Angler specialization among salmon and trout anglers on Lake Ontario. *Proceedings of the 1994 Northeastern Recreation Research Symposium.* USDA Forest Service General Technical Report NE-198, 39-43.

Dawson, C. (1997). Angler segmentation based on motivational scale scores. *Proceedings of the 1996 Northeastern Recreation Research Symposium.* USDA Forest Service General Technical Report NE-232, 127-30.

deBettencourt, J., Peterson, G., and Wang, P. (1978). Managing wilderness travel: A Markov-based linear programming model. *Environment and Planning, 10,* 71-79.

Decker, D., Brown, T., and Gutierrez, R. (1980). Further insights into the multiple satisfactions approach for hunter management. *Wildlife Society Bulletin, 8,* 323-31.

Deem, R. (1986). *All Work and No Play? The Sociology of Women and Leisure.* Milton Keynes, England: Open University Press.

DeGrazia, S. (1962). *Of Time, Work, and Leisure.* New York: Twentieth Century Fund, Inc.

Dennis, S., and Magill, A. (1991). Professional disposition of wildland-urban interface recreation managers in southern California: Policy implications for the USDA Forest Service. *Journal of Park and Recreation Administration, 9,* 31-41.

Department of Resource Development, Michigan State University. (1962). *The Quality of Outdoor Recreation as Evidenced by User Satisfaction: Outdoor Recreation Resources Review Commission Study Report 5.* Washington, DC: US Government Printing Office.

Desor, J. (1972). Toward a psychological theory of crowding. *Journal of Personality and Social Psychology, 21,* 79-83.

Deutscher, I. (1966). Words and deeds: Social science and social policy. *Social Problems, 13,* 235-54.

Devall, B., and Harry, J. (1981). Who hates whom in the great outdoors: The impact of recreational specialization and technologies of play. *Leisure Sciences, 4,* 399-418.

DeVoto, B. (1953). Let's close the national parks. *Harpers, 207,* 49-52.

Ditton, R., Goodale, T., and Johnson, P. (1975). A cluster analysis of activity frequency and environmental variables to identify water-based recreation types. *Journal of Leisure Research, 7,* 282-95.

Ditton, R., Graefe, A., and Fedler, A. (1981). Recreational satisfaction at Buffalo National River: Some measurement concerns. *Some Recent Products of River Recreation Research.* USDA Forest Service General Technical Report NC-63, 9-17.

Ditton, R., Fedler, A., and Graefe, A. (1982). Assessing recreational satisfaction among diverse participant groups. *Forest and River Recreation: Research Update.* St. Paul, MN: University of Minnesota Agricultural Experiment Station Miscellaneous Publication 18, 134-39.

Ditton, R., Fedler, A., and Graefe, A. (1983). Factors contributing to perceptions of recreational crowding. *Leisure Sciences, 5,* 273-88.

Ditton, R., Loomis, D., and Choi, S. (1992). Recreation specialization: Re-conceptualization from a social worlds perspective. *Journal of Leisure Research, 24,* 33-51.

Donald, M., and Havighurst, R. (1959). The meanings of leisure. *Social Forces, 37,* 355-60.

Donnelly, M., Vaske, J., and Graefe, A. (1986). Degree and range of recreation specialization: Toward a typology of boating-related activities. *Journal of Leisure Research, 18,* 81-95.

Donnelly, M., Vaske, J., and Shelby, B. (1992). Measuring backcountry standards in visitor surveys. *Defining Wilderness Quality: The Role of Standards in Wilderness Management—A Workshop Proceedings.* USDA Forest Service General Technical Report PNW-305, 38-52.

Dorfman, P. (1979). Measurement and meaning of recreation satisfaction: A case study of camping. *Environment and Behavior, 11,* 483-510.

Dottavio, F., O'Leary, J., and Koth, B. (1980). The social group variable in recreation participation studies. *Journal of Leisure Research, 12,* 357-67.

Doucette, J., and Kimball, K. (1990). Passive trail management in northeastern alpine zones: A case study. *Proceedings of the 1990 Northeastern Recreation Research Symposium.* USDA Forest Service General Technical Report NE-145, 195-201.

Doucette, J., and Cole, D. (1993). *Wilderness Visitor Education: Information About Alternative Techniques.* USDA Forest Service General Technical Report INT-295.

Dowell, D., and McCool, S. (1986). Evaluation of a wilderness information dissemination program. *Proceedings–National Wilderness Research Conference: Current Research.* USDA Forest Service General Technical Report INT-212, 494-500.

Dowell, L. (1967). Recreational pursuits of selected occupational groups. *The Research Quarterly, 38,* 719-22.

Downing, K., and Clark, R. (1979). User=s and manager=s perceptions of dispersed recreation impacts: A focus on roaded forest lands. *Proceedings of the Wildland Recreation Impacts Conference.* USDA Forest Service, Pacific Northwest Region, R-6-001-1979, 18-23.

Downing, K., and Clark, R. (1985). Methodology for studying recreation choice behavior with emphasis on grounded inquiry. *Proceedings–Symposium on Recreation Choice Behavior.* USDA Forest Service General Technical Report INT-184, 101-6.

Driver, B., and Brown, P. (1983). Contributions of behavioral scientists to recreation resource management. *Behavior and the Natural Environment.* New York: Plenum Press.

Driver, B., and Toucher, R. (1970). Toward a behavioral interpretation of recreational engagements, with implications for planning. *Elements of Outdoor Recreation Planning.* Ann Arbor, MI: University Microfilms, 9-31.

Driver, B. (1972). Potential contributions of psychology to recreation resources management. *Environment and the Social Sciences: Perspectives and Applications.* Washington, DC: American Psychological Association, 233-48.

Driver, B. (1975). Quantification of outdoor recreationists' preferences. *Research, Camping, and Environmental Education.* University Park, PA: Pennsylvania State University HPER Series 11, 165-87.

Driver, B., and Bassett, J. (1975). Defining conflicts among river users: A case study of Michigan's Au Sable River. *Naturalist, 26,* 19-23.

Driver, B., and Brown, P. (1975). A socio-psychological definition of recreation demand, with implications for recreation resource planning. *Assessing Demand for Outdoor Recreation.* Washington, DC: National Academy of Sciences, 62-88.

Driver, B. (1976). Toward a better understanding of the social benefits of outdoor recreation participation. *Proceedings of the Southern States Recreation Research Applications Workshop.* USDA Forest Service General Technical Report SE-9, 163-89.

Driver, B., and Knopf, R. (1976). Temporary escape: One product of sport fisheries management. *Fisheries, 1,* 21-29.

Driver, B., and Bassett, J. (1977). Problems of defining and measuring the preferences of river recreationists. *Proceedings C River Recreation Management and Research Symposium.* USDA Forest Service General Technical Report NC-28, 267-72.

Driver, B., and Cooksey, R. (1977). Preferred psychological outcomes of recreational fishing. *Proceedings of the National Sport Fishing Symposium.* Arcata, CA: Humboldt State University, 27-39.

Driver, B., and Knopf, R. (1977). Personality, outdoor recreation, and expected consequences. *Environment and Behavior, 9,* 169-93.

Driver, B., and Brown, P. (1978). The opportunity spectrum concept in outdoor recreation supply inventories: A rationale. *Proceedings of the Integrated Renewable Resource Inventories Workshop.* USDA Forest Service General Technical Report RM-55, 24-31.

Driver, B., and Knopf, R. (1981). Some thoughts on the quality of outdoor recreation research and other constraints on its application. *Social Research in National Parks and Wilderness Areas.* Atlanta, GA: National Park Service, 85-99.

Driver, B., and Rosenthal, D. (1982). *Measuring and Improving Effectiveness of Public Outdoor Recreation Programs.* Washington, D.C.: USDA Forest Service, USDI Bureau of Land Management, and George Washington University.

Driver, B. (1984). Public responses to user fees at public recreation areas. *Proceedings: Fees for Outdoor Recreation on Lands Open to the Public.* Gorham, NH: Appalachian Mountain Club, 47-51.

Driver, B., and Brown, P. (1984). Contributions of behavioral scientists to recreation resource management. *Behavior and the Natural Environment.* New York: Plenum Press, 307-39.

Driver, B. (1985). What is produced by management of wildlife by public agencies. *Leisure Sciences, 7,* 281-95.

Driver, B., Brown, P., Stankey, G., and Gregoire, T. (1987a). The ROS planning system: Evolution, basic concepts, and research needed. *Leisure Sciences, 9,* 201-12.

Driver, B., Nash, R., and Haas, G. (1987b). Wilderness benefits: A state-of-knowledge review. *Proceedings–National Wilderness Research Conference: Issues, State-of-Knowledge, Future Directions.* USDA Forest Service General Technical Report INT-220, 294-319.

Driver, B. (1990). Focusing research on the benefits of leisure: Special issue introduction. *Journal of Leisure Research, 22,* 93-98.

Driver, B., Brown, P., and Peterson, G., (Eds.). (1991). *Benefits of Leisure.* State College, PA: Venture Publishing.

Driver, B. (1996). Benefits-driven management of natural areas. *Natural Areas Journal, 16,* 94-99.

Drogin, E., Graefe, A., and Titre, J. (1990). Factors affecting boating satisfaction: A replication and comparative analysis. *Proceedings of the 1990 Northeastern Recreation Research Symposium.* USDA Forest Service General Technical Report NE-145, 167-73.

Duncan, D. (1978). Leisure types: Factor analysis of leisure profiles. *Journal of Leisure Research, 10,* 113-25.

Dustin, D., and McAvoy, L. (1980). "Hardening" national parks. *Environmental Ethics, 2,* 29-44.

Dustin, D., and McAvoy, L. (1982). The decline and fall of quality recreation opportunities and environments. *Environmental Ethics, 4,* 49-57.

Dustin, D., and McAvoy, L. (1984). The limitation of the traffic light. *Journal of Park and Recreation Administration, 2,* 8-32.

Dustin, D. (1986). Outdoor recreation: A question of equity. *Forum for Applied Research and Public Policy, 1,* 62-67.

Dustin, D., McAvoy, L., and Beck, L. (1986). Promoting recreationist self-sufficiency. *Journal of Park and Recreation Administration, 4,* 43-52.

Dustin, D., McAvoy, L., and Schultz, J. (1987). Beware of the merchant mentality. *Trends, 24,* 44-46.

Dustin, D., and Knopf, R. (1989). Equity issues in outdoor recreation. *Outdoor Recreation Benchmark 1988: Proceedings of the National Outdoor Recreation Forum.* USDA Forest Service General Technical Report SE-52, 467-71.

Dwyer, J., and Hutchison, R. (1990). Outdoor recreation participation and preferences by black and white Chicago households. *Social Science and Natural Resource Recreation Management.* Boulder, CO: Westview Press, 49-67.

Dwyer, J. (1992). Outdoor recreation participation: Blacks, whites, Hispanics, and Asians in Illinois. *Proceedings of the Symposium on Social Aspects and Recreation Research.* USDA Forest Service General Technical Report PSW-132, 80-81.

Dwyer, J., and Gobster, P. (1992). Black/white outdoor recreation preferences and participation: Illinois state parks. *Proceedings of the 1991 Northeastern Recreation Research Symposium.* USDA Forest Service General Technical Report NE-160, 20-24.

Dwyer, J. (1993a). Customer evaluation of campground management: Huron-Manistee National Forests. *Proceedings of the 1992 Northeastern Recreation Research Symposium.* USDA Forest Service General Technical Report NE-176, 87-89.

Dwyer, J. (1993b). Outdoor recreation participation: An update on blacks, whites, Hispanics, and Asians in Illinois. *Managing Urban and High-Use Recreation Settings.* USDA Forest Service General Technical Report NC-163, 119-21.

Dwyer, J., and Gobster, P. (1997). The implications of increased racial and ethnic diversity for recreation resource management, planning and research. *Proceedings of the 1996 Northeastern Recreation Research Symposium.* USDA Forest Service General Technical Report NE-232, 3-7.

Dwyer, W., Huffman, M, and Jarratt, L. (1989). A comparison of strategies for gaining compliance with campground regulations. *Journal of Park and Recreation Administration, 7,* 21-30.

Echelberger, H, Deiss, D., and Morrison, D. (1974). Overuse of unique recreation areas: A look at the social problems. *Journal of Soil and Water Conservation, 29,* 173-76.

Echelberger, H., and Moeller, G. (1977). *Use and Users of the Cranberry Backcountry in West Virginia: Insights for Eastern Backcountry Management.* USDA Forest Service Research Paper NE-363.

Echelberger, H., Leonard, R., and Hamblin, M. (1978). *The Trail Guide System as a Backcountry Management Tool.* USDA Forest Service Research Note NE-266.

Echelberger, H., Leonard, R., and Plumley, H. (1981). Validation of trailside registration boxes. *Journal of Soil and Water Conservation, 36,* 53-54.

Echelberger, H., Gilroy, D., and Moeller, G. (Compilers). (1983a). *Recreation Research Publications Bibliography, 1961-1982.* Washington, D. C.: U.S. Forest Service.

Echelberger, H., Leonard, R., and Adler, S. (1983b). Designated-dispersed tentsites. *Journal of Forestry, 81,* 90-91, 105.

Elsner, G. (1970). Camping use-axle count relationship: Estimation with desirable properties. *Forest Science, 16,* 493-95.

Emmett, J., Havitz, M., and McCarville, R. (1996). A price subsidy policy for socio-economically disadvantaged recreation participants. *Journal of Park and Recreation Administration, 14,* 63-80.

Environment Canada and Park Service. (1991). *Selected Readings on the Visitor Activity Management Process.* Ottawa, Ontario: Environment Canada.

Etzkorn, K. (1964). Leisure and camping: The social meaning of a form of public recreation. *Sociology and Social Research, 49,* 76-89.

Ewert, A. (1986). What research doesn't tell the practitioner. *Parks and Recreation, 21,* 46-49.

Ewert, A. (1993). Differences in the level of motive importance based on trip outcome, experience level, and group type. *Journal of Leisure Research, 25,* 335-49.

Ewert, A. (1994). Playing the edge: Motivation and risk-taking in a high altitude wilderness-like environment. *Environment and Behavior, 26,* 3-24.

Ewert, A., and Hood, D. (1995). Urban-proximate and urban-distant wilderness: An exploratory comparison between two "types" of wilderness. *Journal of Park and Recreation Administration, 13,* 73-85.

Ewert, A. (1998). A comparison of urban-proximate and urban-distant wilderness users on selected variables. *Environmental Management, 22,* 927-35.

Ewing, G. (1980). Progress and problems in the development of recreational trip generation and trip distribution models. *Leisure Sciences, 3,* 1-24.

Faris, R., and Dunham, H. (1965). *Mental Disorders in Urban Areas.* Chicago: Phoenix Books.

Fazio, J., and Gilbert, D. (1974). Mandatory wilderness permits: Some indications of success. *Journal of Forestry, 72,* 753-56.

Fazio, J. (1979a). Communicating with the wilderness user. *Wildlife and Range Science Bulletin Number 28,* Moscow, ID: University of Idaho College of Forestry.

Fazio, J. (1979b). Agency literature as an aid to wilderness management. *Journal of Forestry, 77,* 97-98.

Fazio, J., and Ratcliffe, R. (1989). Direct-mail literature as a method to reduce problems of wild river management. *Journal of Park and Recreation Administration, 7,* 1-9.

Fedler, A., and Miles, A. (1989). Paying for backcountry recreation: Understanding the acceptability of use fees. *Journal of Park and Recreation Administration, 7,* 35-46.

Feldman, R. (1978). Effectiveness of audio-visual media for interpretation to recreating motorists. *Journal of Interpretation, 3,* 14-19.

Ferriss, A. (1962). *National Recreation Survey: Outdoor Recreation Resources Review Commission Study Report 19.* Washington, D.C.: U.S. Government Printing Office.

Ferriss, A. (1970). The social and personality correlates of outdoor recreation. *The Annals, 389,* 46-55.

Festinger, L. (1957). *A Theory of Cognitive Dissonance*. Stanford, CA: Stanford University Press.

Field, D., and O'Leary, J. (1973). Social groups as a basis for assessing participation in selected water activities. *Journal of Leisure Research, 5,* 16-25.

Field, D., and Creek, N., Jr. (1974). A basis for assessing differential participation in water-based recreation. *Water Resources Bulletin, 10,* 1218-27.

Field, D., and Johnson, D. (1983). The interactive process of applied research: A partnership between scientists and park and resource managers. *Journal of Park and Recreation Administration, 1,* 18-27.

Finn, K., and Loomis, D. (1998). Minority group participation in recreational fishing: The role of demographics and constraints. *Proceedings of the 1997 Northeastern Recreation Research Symposium*. USDA Forest Service General Technical Report NE-241, 64-69.

Fish, C., and Bury, R. (1981). Wilderness visitor management: Diversity and agency policies. *Journal of Forestry, 79,* 608-12.

Fishbein, M., and Ajzen, I. (1974). Attitudes toward objects as predictors of single and multiple behavioral criteria. *Psychological Review, 81,* 59-74.

Fishbein, M., and Ajzen, I. (1975). *Belief, Attitude, Interaction and Behavior: An Introduction to Theory and Research*. Reading, MA: Addison-Wesley Publishing Company.

Fisher, A., and Krutilla, J. (1972). Determination of optimal capacity of resource-based recreation facilities. *Natural Resources Journal, 12,* 417-44.

Flekke, G., McAvoy, L., and Anderson, D. (1996). The potential of an expert system to address congestion and crowding in the national park system. *Crowding and Congestion in the National Park System: Guidelines for Research and Management*. St. Paul, MN: University of Minnesota Agricultural Experiment Station Publication, 86-1996, 132-41.

Floyd, M., and Gramann, J. (1993). Effects of acculturation and structural assimilation in resource-based recreation: The case study of Mexican-Americans. *Journal of Leisure Research, 25,* 6-21.

Floyd, M., Gramann, J., and Saenz, R. (1993). Ethnic factors and the use of public outdoor recreation areas: The case of Mexican-Americans. *Leisure Sciences, 15,* 83-98.

Floyd, M., Shinew, K., McGuire, F., and Noe, F. (1994). Race, class, and leisure activity preferences: Marginality and ethnicity revisited. *Journal of Leisure Research, 26,* 158-73.

Floyd, M., and Gramann, J. (1995). Perceptions of discrimination in a recreation context. *Journal of Leisure Research, 27,* 192-99.

Floyd, M. (1997). Pleasure, arousal, and dominance: Exploring affective determinants of recreation satisfaction. *Leisure Sciences, 19,* 83-96.

Floyd, M., and Gramann, J. (1997). Experience-based setting management: Implications for market segmentation of hunters. *Leisure Sciences, 19,* 113-28.

Floyd, M. (1998). Getting beyond marginality and ethnicity: The challenge of race and ethnic studies in leisure research. *Journal of Leisure Research, 30,* 3-22.

Foster, R., and Jackson, E. (1979). Factors associated with camping satisfaction in Alberta Provincial Park campgrounds. *Journal of Leisure Research, 11,* 292-306.

Fractor, D. (1982). Evaluating alternative methods for rationing wilderness use. *Journal of Leisure Research, 14,* 341-49.

Frayer, W., and Butts, D. (1974). BUS: A processing system for records of backcountry use. *Journal of Leisure Research, 6,* 305-11.

Freedman, J., Levansky, S., and Ehrlich, P. (1971). The effect of crowding on human task performance. *Journal of Applied Social Psychology, 1,* 7-25.

Frissell, S., and Duncan, D. (1965). Campsite preference and deterioration. *Journal of Forestry, 63,* 256-60.

Frissell, S., and Stankey, G. (1972). Wilderness environmental quality: Search for social and ecological harmony. *Proceedings of the Society of American Foresters Annual Conference,* Hot Springs, AR: Society of American Foresters, 170-83.

Frissell, S., Lee, R., Stankey, G., and Zube, E. (1980). A framework for estimating the consequences of alternative carrying capacity levels in Yosemite Valley. *Landscape Planning, 7,* 151-70.

Frost, J., and McCool, S. (1988). Can visitor regulation enhance recreational experiences? *Environmental Management, 12,* 5-9.

Furuseth, O., and Altman, R. (1991). Who's on the Greenway: Socioeconomic, demographic, and locational characteristics of greenway users. *Environmental Management, 15,* 329-36.

Gans, H. (1962). Outdoor recreation and mental health. *Trends in American Living and Outdoor Recreation: Outdoor Recreation Resources Review Commission Study Report 22.* Washington, D. C.: U.S. Government Printing Office, 233-42.

Gerstl, J. (1961). Leisure, taste, and occupational milieu. *Social Problems, 9,* 56-68.

Gibbons, S., and Ruddell, E. (1995). The effect of goal orientation and place dependence on select goal interferences among winter backcountry users. *Leisure Sciences, 17,* 171-83.

Gibbs, K. (1977). Economics and administrative regulations of outdoor recreation use. *Outdoor Recreation: Advances in Application of Economics.* USDA Forest Service General Technical Report WO-2, 98-104.

Gibson, J. (1977). Theory of affordances. *Perceiving, Acting, and Knowing: Toward an Ecological Psychology.* Hallsdale, NJ: Lawrence Erlbaum Associates.

Gibson, J. (1979). *The Ecological Approach to Visual Perception.* Boston, MA:, Houghton Mifflin Company.

Gilbert, G., Peterson, G., and Lime, D. (1972). Towards a model of travel behavior in the Boundary Waters Canoe Area. *Environment and Behavior, 4,* 131-57.

Gilligan, C. (1982). *In a Different Voice.* Cambridge, MA: Harvard University Press.

Glancy, M. (1986). Participant observation in the recreation setting. *Journal of Leisure Research, 18,* 59-80.

Glass, R., Walton, G., and Echelberger, H. (1991). *Estimates of recreation use in the White River drainage, Vermont.* USDA Forest Service Research Paper NE-658.

Glass, R., and More, T. (1992). *Satisfaction, Valuation, and Views Toward Allocation of Vermont Goose Hunting Opportunities.* USDA Forest Service Research Paper NE-668.

Glass, R., and Walton, G. (1995). *Recreation Use of Upper Pemigewasset and Swift River Drainages, New Hampshire.* USDA Forest Service Research Note NE-701.

Glyptis, S. (1985). Women as a target group: The views of the staff of Action Sport–West Midlands. *Leisure Studies, 4,* 347-62.

Gobster, P., and Delgado, A. (1993). Ethnicity and recreation use in Chicago's Lincoln Park: In-park user survey findings. *Managing Urban and High-Density Recreation Settings*. USDA Forest Service General Technical Report NC-163, 75-81.

Godin, V., and Leonard, R. (1976). Guidelines for managing backcountry travel and usage. *Trends, 13*, 33-37.

Godin, V., and Leonard, R. (1977a). *Permit Compliance in Eastern Wilderness: Preliminary Results*. USDA Forest Service Research Note NE-238.

Godin, V., and Leonard, R. (1977b). Design capacity for backcountry recreation management planning. *Journal of Soil and Water Conservation, 32*, 161-64.

Godin, V., and Leonard, R. (1979). Management problems in designated wilderness areas. *Journal of Soil and Water Conservation, 34*, 141-43.

Godschalk, D., and Parker, F. (1975). Carrying capacity: A key to environmental planning? *Journal of Soil and Water Conservation, 30*, 160-65.

Graefe, A., Ditton, R., Roggenbuck, J., and Schreyer, R. (1981). Notes on the stability of the factor structure of leisure meanings. *Leisure Sciences, 4*, 51-65.

Graefe, A., Vaske, J., and Kuss, F. (1984). Resolved issues and remaining questions about social carrying capacity. *Leisure Sciences, 6*, 497-507.

Graefe, A., Vaske, J., and Kuss, F. (1984). Social carrying capacity: An integration and synthesis of twenty years of research. *Leisure Sciences, 6*, 395-431.

Graefe, A., and Fedler, A. (1986). Situational and subjective determinants of satisfaction in marine recreational fishing. *Leisure Sciences, 8*, 275-95.

Graefe, A., Kuss, F., and Loomis, L. (1986a). Visitor Impact Management in wildland settings. *Proceedings–National Wilderness Research Conference: Current Research*. USDA Forest Service General Technical Report INT-212, 432-39.

Graefe, A., Donnelly, M., and Vaske, J. (1986b). Crowding and specialization: A reexamination of the crowding model. *Proceedings–National Wilderness Research Conference: Current Research*. USDA Forest Service General Technical Report INT-212, 333-38.

Graefe, A., and Drogin, E. (1989). Factors affecting boating satisfaction at Raystown Lake. *Proceedings of the 1989 Northeastern Recreation Research Symposium*. USDA Forest Service General Technical Report NE-132, 31-38.

Graefe, A., Kuss, F., and Vaske, J. (1990). *Visitor Impact Management: The Planning Framework*. Washington, D.C.: National Parks and Conservation Association.

Graefe, A., and Moore, R. (1992). Monitoring the visitor experience at Buck Island Reef National Monument. *Proceedings of the 1991 Northeastern Recreation Research Symposium*. USDA Forest Service General Technical Report NE-160, 55-58.

Gramann, J., and Burdge, R. (1981). The effect of recreation goals on conflict perception: The case of water skiers and fishermen. *Journal of Leisure Research, 13*, 15-27.

Gramann, J. (1982). Toward a behavioral theory of crowding in outdoor recreation: An evaluation and synthesis of research. *Leisure Sciences, 5*, 109-126.

Gramann, J., and Vander Stoep, G. (1987). Prosocial behavior theory and natural resource protection: A conceptual synthesis. *Journal of Environmental Management, 24*, 247-57.

Gramann, J., Floyd, M., and Saenz, R. (1993). Outdoor recreation and Mexican American ethnicity: A benefits perspective. *Culture, Conflict, and Communication in the Wildland-Urban Interface*. Boulder, CO: Westview Press, 69-84.

Green, E., Hebron, S., and Woodward, D. (1987). *Leisure and Gender: A Study of Sheffield Women's Leisure Experience*. London: The Sports Council and Economic and Social Research Council.

Greenleaf, R., Echelberger, H., and Leonard, R. (1984). Backpacker satisfaction, expectations, and use levels in an eastern forest setting. *Journal of Park and Recreation Administration, 2*, 49-56.

Greist, D. (1975). Risk zone management: A recreation area management system and method of measuring carrying capacity. *Journal of Forestry, 73*, 711-14.

Griffitt, W., and Veitch, R. (1971). Hot and crowded: Influence of population density and temperature on interpersonal affective behavior. *Journal of Personality and Social Psychology, 17*, 92-98.

Groves, D., and Wolenski, R. (1977). Applied recreation research: The missing link between theoretical research and the practitioner. *Journal of Environmental Systems, 7*, 59-98.

Haas, G., Allen, D., and Manfredo, M. (1979). Some dispersed recreation experiences and the resource settings in which they occur. *Assessing Amenity Resource Values*. USDA Forest Service General Technical Report RM-68, 21-26.

Haas, G., Driver, B., and Brown, P. (1980a). Measuring wilderness recreation experiences. *Proceedings of the Wilderness Psychology Group*. Durham, New Hampshire: Wilderness Psychology Group, 20-40.

Haas, G., Driver, B., and Brown, P. (1980b). A study of ski touring experiences on the White River National Forest. *Proceedings of the North American Symposium on Dispersed Winter Recreation*. St. Paul, MN: University of Minnesota, Office of Special Programs, Education Series 2-3, 25-30.

Haas, G., Driver, B., Brown, P., and Lucas, R. (1987). Wilderness management zoning. *Journal of Forestry, 85*, 17-22.

Hadley, L. (1971). Perspectives on law enforcement in recreation areas. *Recreation Symposium Proceedings*. Upper Darby, PA: USDA Forest Service Northeastern Forest Experiment Station, 156-60.

Hall, T., and Shelby, B. (1996). Who cares about encounters? Differences between those with and without norms. *Leisure Sciences, 18*, 7-22.

Hall, T., Shelby, B., and Rolloff, D. (1996). Effect of varied question format on boaters' norms. *Leisure Sciences, 18*, 193-204.

Hammitt, W. (1980). Outdoor recreation: Is it a multi-phase experience? *Journal of Leisure Research, 12*, 107-15.

Hammitt, W. (1982). Cognitive dimensions of wilderness solitude. *Environment and Behavior, 14*, 478-93.

Hammitt, W., McDonald, C., and Cordell, H. (1982). Conflict perception and visitor support for management controls. *Forest and River Recreation: Research Update*. St. Paul, MN: University of Minnesota Agricultural Experiment Station Miscellaneous Publication 18, 45-48.

Hammitt, W. (1983). Toward an ecological approach to perceived crowding in outdoor recreation. *Leisure Sciences, 5*, 309-20.

Hammitt, W., and McDonald, C. (1983). Past on-site experience and its relationship to managing river recreation resources. *Forest Science, 29*, 262-66.

Hammitt, W., and Brown, G., Jr. (1984). Function of privacy in wilderness environments. *Leisure Sciences, 6*, 151-66.

Hammitt, W., and Hughes, J. (1984). Characteristics of winter backcountry use in Great Smoky Mountains National Park. *Environmental Management, 8,* 161-66.

Hammitt, W., McDonald, C., and Noe, F. (1984). Use level and encounters: Important variables of perceived crowding among non-specialized recreationists. *Journal of Leisure Research, 16,* 1-9.

Hammitt, W., McDonald, C., and Hughes, J. (1986). Experience level and participation motives of winter wilderness users. *Proceedings–National Wilderness Research Conference: Current Research.* USDA Forest Service General Technical Report INT-212, 269-77.

Hammitt, W. (1989). The spectrum of conflict in outdoor recreation. *Outdoor Recreation Benchmark 1988: Proceedings of the National Outdoor Recreation Forum.* USDA Forest Service General Technical Report SE-52, 439-50

Hammitt, W., Knauf, L, and Noe, F. (1989a). A comparison of user versus researcher determined level of past experience on recreation preference. *Journal of Leisure Research, 21,* 202-13.

Hammitt, W., McDonald, C., and Noe, F. (1989b). Wildlife management: Managing the hunt versus the hunting experience. *Environmental Management, 13,* 503-7.

Hammitt, W., and Madden, M. (1989). Cognitive dimensions of wilderness privacy: A field test and further explanation. *Leisure Sciences, 9,* 293-301.

Hammitt, W., and Patterson, M. (1991). Coping behavior to avoid visual encounters: Its relationship to wildland privacy. *Journal of Leisure Research, 23,* 225-37.

Hammitt, W., and Patterson, M. (1993). Use patterns and solitude preferences of shelter campers in Great Smoky Mountains National Park, U.S.A. *Journal of Environmental Management, 38,* 43-53.

Hammitt, W., and Rutlin, W. (1995). Use encounter standards and curves for achieved privacy in wilderness. *Leisure Sciences, 17,* 245-62.

Hammitt, W., and Cole, D. (1998). *Wildland Recreation: Ecology and Management.* New York: John Wiley.

Hancock, H. (1973). Recreation preference: Its relation to user behavior. *Journal of Forestry, 71,* 336-37.

Harmon, L. (1979). How to make park law enforcement work for you. *Parks and Recreation, 14,* 20-21.

Harmon, D. (1992). Using an interactive computer program to communicate with the wilderness visitor. *Proceedings of the Symposium on Social Aspects and Recreation Research.* USDA Forest Service General Technical Report PSW-132, 60.

Harrington, M., Dawson, D., and Bolla, P. (1992). Objective and subjective constraints on women's enjoyment of leisure. *Society and Leisure, 15,* 203-22.

Harris, C., Driver, B., and Bergersen, E. (1985). Do choices of sport fisheries reflect angler preferences for site attributes? *Proceedings–Symposium on Recreation Choice Behavior.* USDA Forest Service General Technical Report INT-184, 46-54.

Harris, C., and Driver, B. (1987). Recreation user fees: Pros and cons. *Journal of Forestry, 85,* 25-29.

Harry, J. (1972). Socio-economic patterns of outdoor recreation use near urban areas–A comment. *Journal of Leisure Research, 4,* 218-19.

Hartmann, L., and Cordell, H. (1989). An overview of the relationship between social and demographic factors and outdoor recreation participation. *Outdoor Recreation*

Benchmark 1988: Proceedings of the National Outdoor Recreation Forum. USDA Forest Service General Technical Report SE-52, 255-74.

Hartmann, L., Freilich, H., and Cordell, H. (1989). Trends and current status of participation in outdoor recreation. *Outdoor Recreation Benchmark 1988, Proceedings of the National Outdoor Recreation Forum.* USDA Forest Service General Technical Report SE-52, 147-65.

Hartmann, L., and Overdevest, C. (1990). Race, ethnicity, and outdoor recreation participation: A state-of-the-knowledge review and theoretical perspective. *Proceedings of the 1989 Southeastern Recreation Research Conference.* Athens, GA: University of Georgia, 53-63.

Harwell, R. (1987). A "no-rescue" wilderness experience: What are the implications? *Parks and Recreation.* 22, 34-37.

Hauser, P. (1962). Demographic and ecological changes as factors in outdoor recreation. *Trends in American Living and Outdoor Recreation: Outdoor Recreation Resources Review Commission Report #22.* Washington, DC: U.S. Government Printing Office, 27-59.

Hautaluoma, J., and Brown, P. (1978). Attributes of the deer hunting experience: A cluster analytic study. *Journal of Leisure Research, 10,* 271-87.

Hautaluoma, J., Brown, P., and Battle, N. (1982). Elk hunter consumer satisfaction patterns. *Forest and River Recreation: Research Update.* University of Minnesota Agricultural Experiment Station Miscellaneous Publication 18, 74-80.

Havighurst, R., and Feigenbaum, K. (1959). Leisure and life-style. *American Journal of Sociology, 64,* 396-404.

Hawes, D. (1978). Satisfaction derived from leisure time pursuits: An exploratory nationwide survey. *Journal of Leisure Research, 10,* 247-64.

Hazel, K., Langenau, E., Jr., and Levine, R. (1990). Dimensions of hunting satisfaction: Multiple-satisfactions of wild turkey hunting. *Leisure Sciences, 12,* 383-93.

Heberlein, T. (1973). Social psychological assumptions of user attitude surveys: The case of the wildernism scale. *Journal of Leisure Research, 5,* 18-33.

Heberlein, T. (1977). Density, crowding, and satisfaction: Sociological studies for determining carrying capacities. *Proceedings: River Recreation Management and Research Symposium.* USDA Forest Service General Technical Report NC-28, 67-76.

Heberlein, T., and Shelby, B. (1977). Carrying capacity, values, and the satisfaction model: A reply to Greist. *Journal of Leisure Research, 9,* 142-48.

Heberlein, T., and Dunwiddie, P. (1979). Systematic observation of use levels, campsite selection and visitor characteristics at a high mountain lake. *Journal of Leisure Research, 11,* 307-16.

Heberlein, T., Trent, J., and Baumgartner, R. (1982). The influence of hunter density on firearm deer hunters' satisfaction: A field experiment. *Transactions of the 47th North American Natural Resource and Wildlife Conference,* 665-76.

Heberlein, T., Alfano, G., and Ervin, L. (1986). Using a social carrying capacity model to estimate the effects of marina development at the Apostle Islands National Lakeshore. *Leisure Sciences, 8,* 257-74.

Heinrichs, J. (1982). Cops in the woods. *Journal of Forestry, 11,* 722-725, 748.

Helgath, S. (1975). *Trail Deterioration in the Selway-Bitterroot Wilderness.* USDA Forest Service Research Note INT-193.

Hendee, J., Catton, W., Jr., Marlow, L., and Brockman, C. (1968). *Wilderness Users in the Pacific Northwest–Their Characteristics, Values, and Management Preferences*. USDA Forest Service Research Paper PNW-61.

Hendee, J. (1969). Rural-urban differences reflected in outdoor recreation participation. *Journal of Leisure Research, 1,* 333-41.

Hendee, J., and Campbell, F. (1969). Social aspects of outdoor recreation—The developed campground. *Trends, 6,* 13-16.

Hendee, J., and Harris, R. (1970). Foresters' perceptions of wilderness user attitudes and preferences. *Journal of Forestry, 68,* 759-62.

Hendee, J. (1971). Sociology and applied leisure research. *Pacific Sociological Review, 14,* 360-68.

Hendee, J., Gale, R., and Catton, W., Jr. (1971). A typology of outdoor recreation activity preferences. *Journal of Environmental Education, 3,* 28-34.

Hendee, J., and Lucas, R. (1973). Mandatory wilderness permits: A necessary management tool. *Journal of Forestry, 71,* 206-9.

Hendee, J., and Stankey, G. (1973). Biocentricity in wilderness management. *Bioscience, 23,* 535-38.

Hendee, J. (1974). A multiple-satisfaction approach to game management. *Wildlife Society Bulletin, 2,* 104-13.

Hendee, J., and Burdge, R. (1974). The substitutability concept: Implications for recreation management and research. *Journal of Leisure Research, 6,* 157-62.

Hendee, J., and Lucas, R. (1974). Police state wilderness: A comment on a comment. *Journal of Forestry, 72,* 100-101.

Hendee, J., and Potter, D. (1975). Hunters and hunting: Management implications of research. *Proceedings of the Southern States Recreation Research Applications Workshop,* Asheville, North Carolina, 137-61.

Hendee, J., Hogans, M., and Koch, R. (1976). *Dispersed Recreation on Three Forest Road Systems in Washington and Oregon: First Year Data.* USDA Forest Service Research Note PNW-280.

Hendee, J., Clark, R., and Daily, T. (1977). *Fishing and Other Recreation Behavior at High Mountain Lakes in Washington State.* USDA Forest Service Research Note PNW-304.

Hendee, J., Stankey, G., and Lucas, R. (1990). *Wilderness Management.* Golden, CO: North American Press.

Henderson, K., and Rannells, J. (1988). Farm women and the meaning of work and leisure: An oral history perspective. *Leisure Sciences, 10,* 41-50.

Henderson, K., Bialeschki, M., Shaw, S., and Freysinger, V. (1989). *A Leisure of One's Own: A Feminist Perspective on Women's Leisure.* State College, PA: Venture Publishing.

Henderson, K. (1990). The meaning of leisure for women: An integrative review of the research. *Journal of Leisure Research, 22,* 228-43.

Henderson, K., and Allen, K. (1991). The ethic of care: Leisure possibilities and constraints for women. *Society and Leisure, 14,* 97-113.

Henderson, K. (1994a). Theory application and development in recreation, parks and leisure research. *Journal of Park and Recreation Administration, 12,* 51-64.

Henderson, K. (1994b). Perspectives on analyzing gender, women and leisure. *Journal of Leisure Research, 26,* 119-37.

Henderson, K. (1996). One size doesn't fit all: The meanings of women's leisure. *Journal of Leisure Research, 28,* 139-54.

Henderson, K. (1997). Just recreation: Ethics, gender, and equity. *Journal of Park and Recreation Administration, 15,* 16-31.

Hendricks, B., Ruddell, E., and Bullis, C. (1993). Direct and indirect park and recreation resource management decision making: A conceptual approach. *Journal of Park and Recreation Administration, 11,* 28-39.

Hendricks, J., and Burdge, R. (1972). The nature of leisure research: A reflection and comment. *Journal of Leisure Research, 4,* 215-17.

Hendricks, W. (1995). A resurgence in recreation conflict research: Introduction to the special issue. *Leisure Sciences, 17,* 157-58.

Heritage Conservation and Recreation Service. (1979). *The Third Nationwide Outdoor Recreation Plan.* Washington, D. C.: U. S. Government Printing Office.

Heywood, J. (1985). Large recreation group and party size limits. *Journal of Park and Recreation Administration, 3,* 36-44.

Heywood, J. (1986). Human use of parks. *A Literature Review: The President's Commission on Americans Outdoors.* Washington, D. C.: U. S. Government Printing Office, O-29-O-35.

Heywood, J. (1987). Experience preferences of participants in different types of river recreation groups. *Journal of Leisure Research, 19,* 1-12.

Heywood, J. (1991). Visitor inputs to Recreation Opportunity Spectrum allocation and monitoring. *Journal of Park and Recreation Administration, 9,* 18-30.

Heywood, J., Christensen, J., and Stankey, G. (1991). The relationship of biophysical and social setting factors in the Recreation Opportunity Spectrum. *Leisure Sciences, 13,* 239-46.

Heywood, J. (1993a). Behavioral conventions in higher density, day use wildland / urban recreation settings: A preliminary case study. *Journal of Leisure Research, 25,* 39-52.

Heywood, J. (1993b). Game theory: A basis for analyzing emerging norms and conventions in outdoor recreation. *Leisure Sciences, 15,* 37-48.

Heywood, J., and Engelke, R. (1995). Differences in behavioral convention: A comparison of United States-born and Mexican-born Hispanics, and Anglo-Americans. *Proceedings of the Second Symposium on Social Aspects and Recreation Research.* USDA Forest Service General Technical Report PSW-156, 35-40.

Heywood, J. (1996a). Social regularities in outdoor recreation. *Leisure Sciences, 18,* 23-37.

Heywood, J. (1996b). Conventions, emerging norms, and norms in outdoor recreation. *Leisure Sciences, 18,* 355-63.

Hof, M., Hammitt, J., Rees, M., Belnap, J., Poe, N., Lime, D., and Manning, R. (1994). Getting a handle on visitor carrying capacity–A pilot project at Arches National Park. *Park Science, 14,* 11-13.

Hof, M., and Lime, D. (1997). Visitor Experience and Resource Protection framework in the national park system: Rationale, current status, and future direction. *Proceedings–Limits of Acceptable Change and Related Planning Processes: Progress and Future Directions.* USDA Forest Service General Technical Report INT-371, 29-36.

Hogans, M. (1978). *Using Photography for Recreation Research.* USDA Forest Service Research Note PNW-327.

Holland, I., and Beazley, R. (1971). Personality, motivation, and education needed in professional forestry. *Journal of Forestry, 69*, 418-23.

Hollander, J. (1977). Motivational dimensions of the camping experience. *Journal of Leisure Research, 9*, 133-41.

Hollenhorst, S. (1990). What makes a recreation specialist? The case of rockclimbing. *Social Science and Natural Resource Recreation Management.* Boulder, CO: Westview Press, 81-90.

Hollenhorst, S., and Stull-Gardner, L. (1992) The indicator performance estimate (IPE) approach to defining acceptable conditions in wilderness. *Proceedings of the Symposium on Social Aspects and Recreation Research.* USDA Forest Service General Technical Report PSW-132, 48-49.

Hollenhorst, S., Whisman, S., and Ewert, A. (1992a). *Monitoring Visitor Use in Backcountry Wilderness.* USDA Forest Service General Technical Report PSW-134.

Hollenhorst, S., Olson, D., and Fortney, R. (1992b). Use of importance-performance analysis to evaluate state park cabins: The case of the West Virginia State Park system. *Journal of Park and Recreation Administration, 10*, 1-11.

Hollenhorst, S., and Gardner, L. (1994). The indicator performance estimate approach to determining acceptable wilderness conditions. *Environmental Management, 18*, 901-6.

Hollenhorst, S., Schuett, M., and Olson, D. (1995a). Conflicts and issues related to mountain biking in the national forests: A multi-methodological approach. *Proceedings of the Second Symposium on Social Aspects and Recreation Research.* USDA Forest Service General Technical Report PSW-156, 7-10.

Hollenhorst, S., Schuett, M., Olson, D., and Chavez, D. (1995b). An examination of the characteristics, preferences, and attitudes of mountain bike users of the national forests. *Journal of Park and Recreation Administration, 13*, 41-51.

Homans, G. (1950). *The Human Group.* New York: Harcourt, Brace.

Hope, J. (1971). Hassles in the park. *Natural History, LXXX*, 20-23, 82-91.

Hopkins, T., and More, R. (1995). The relationship of recreation specialization to the setting preferences of mountain bicyclists. *Proceedings of the 1994 Northeastern Recreation Research Symposium.* USDA Forest Service General Technical Report NE-198, 71-75.

Horna, J. (1987). The leisure component of the parental role. Paper presented at the meeting of the Fifth Canadian Congress on Leisure Research. Halifax, Nova Scotia.

Horsley, A. (1988). The unintended effects of a posted sign on littering attitudes and stated intentions. *Journal of Environmental Education, 19*, 10-14.

Hospodarsky, D., and Lee, M. (1995). Ethnic use of the Tonto: Geographic expansion of the recreation knowledge base. *Proceedings of the Second Symposium on Social Aspects and Recreation Research.* USDA Forest Service General Technical Report PSW-156, 45-47.

Howard, D. (1976). Multivariate relationships between leisure activities and personality. *Research Quarterly, 47*, 226-37.

Huffman, M., and Williams, D. (1986). Computer versus brochure information dissemination as a backcountry management tool. *Proceedings—National Wilderness Research Conference: Current Research.* USDA Forest Service General Technical Report INT-212, 501-8.

Huffman, M.., and Williams, D. (1987). The use of microcomputers for park trail information dissemination. *Journal of Park and Recreation Administration, 5*, 35-46.

Hulbert, J., and Higgins, J. (1977). BWCA visitor distribution system. *Journal of Forestry, 75*, 338-40.

Hull, R., Stewart, W., and Young, K. (1992). Experience patterns: Capturing the dynamic nature of a recreation experience. *Journal of Leisure Research, 24*, 240-52.

Hull, R., Michael, S., Walker, G., and Roggenbuck, J. (1996). Ebb and flow of brief leisure experiences. *Leisure Sciences, 18*, 299-314.

Hultsman, W. (1988). Applications of a touch-sensitive computer in park settings: Activity alternatives and visitor information. *Journal of Park and Recreation Administration, 6*, 1-11.

Hultsman, W., and Hultsman, J. (1989). Attitudes and behaviors regarding visitor-control measures in fragile environments: Implications for recreation management. *Journal of Park and Recreation Administration, 7*, 60-69.

Hutchison, R., and Fidel, K. (1984). Mexican-American recreation activities: A reply to McMillen. *Journal of Leisure Research, 16*, 344-49.

Hutchison, R. (1987). Ethnicity and urban recreation: Whites, blacks, and Hispanics in Chicago's public parks. *Journal of Leisure Research, 19*, 205-22.

Hutchison, R. (1988). A critique of race, ethnicity, and social class in recent leisure-recreation research. *Journal of Leisure Research, 20*, 10-30.

Hutchison, R. (1993). Hmong leisure and recreation activity. *Managing Urban and High-Use Recreation Settings.* USDA Forest Service General Technical Report NC-163, 87-92.

Hutchison, R. (1994). Women and the elderly in Chicago's public parks. *Leisure Sciences, 16*, 229-47.

Irwin, P., Gartner, W., and Phelps, C. (1990). Mexican-American/Anglo cultural differences as recreation style determinants. *Leisure Sciences, 12*, 335-48.

Iso-Ahola, S. (1980). *The Social Psychology of Leisure and Recreation.* Dubuque, IA: William C. Brown Co. Publishing.

Iso-Ahola, S., and Allen, J. (1982). The dynamics of leisure motivation: The effects of outcome on leisure needs. *Research Quarterly, 53*, 141-49.

Iso-Ahola, S. (1986a). Concerns and thoughts about leisure research. *Journal of Leisure Research, 18*, iv-x.

Iso-Ahola, S. (1986b). A theory of substitutability of leisure behavior. *Leisure Sciences, 8*, 367-89.

Ivy, M., Stewart, W., and Lue, C. (1992). Exploring the role of tolerance in recreational conflict. *Journal of Leisure Research, 24*, 348-60.

Jaakson, R. (1973). A preliminary bicultural study of value orientations and leisure activities. *Journal of Leisure Research, 5*, 10-22.

Jaakson, R. (1989). Recreation boating spatial patterns: Theory and management. *Leisure Sciences, 11*, 85-98. Jackson, J. (1965). Structural characteristics of norms. *Current Studies in Social Psychology.* New York, NY: Holt, Rinehart and Winston, Inc., 301-9.

Jackson, E. (1980). Socio-demographic variables, recreational resource use, and attitudes toward development in Camrose, Alberta. *Leisure Sciences, 3*, 189-211.

Jackson, E., and Wong, R. (1982). Perceived conflict between urban cross-country skiers and snowmobilers in Alberta. *Journal of Leisure Research, 14*, 47-62.

Jackson, E. (1987). Outdoor recreation participation and views in resource development and preservation. *Leisure Sciences, 9*, 235-50.

Jackson, E. (1988). Leisure constraints: A survey of past research. *Leisure Sciences, 10*, 203-15.

Jackson, E., and Henderson, K. (1995). Gender-based analysis of leisure constraints. *Leisure Sciences, 17*, 31-51.

Jacob, G., and Schreyer, R. (1980). Conflict in outdoor recreation: A theoretical perspective. *Journal of Leisure Research, 12*, 368-80.

Jacobi, C., Manning, R., Valliere, W., and Negra, C. (1996). Visitor use and conflict on the carriage roads of Acadia National Park. *Proceedings of the 1995 Northeastern Recreation Research Symposium*. USDA Forest Service General Technical Report NE-218, 109-12.

Jakes, P., Dwyer, J., and Carr, D. (1998). Demonstrating the value of a social science research program to a natural resource management agency. *Proceedings of the 1997 Northeastern Recreation Research Symposium*, USDA Forest Service General Technical Report NE-241, 228-33.

James, G. and Ripley, T. (1963). *Instructions for Using Traffic Counters to Estimate Recreation Visits and Use*. USDA Forest Service Research Paper SE-3.

James, G., and Rich, J. (1966). *Estimating Recreation Use on a Complex of Developed Sites*. USDA Forest Service Research Note SE-64.

James, G., and Tyre, G. (1967). *Use of Water-Meter Records to Estimate Recreation Visits and Use on Developed Sites*. USDA Forest Service Research Note SE-73.

James, G. (1968). *Pilot Test of Sampling Procedures for Estimating Recreation Use on Winter Sports Sites*. USDA Forest Service Research Paper SE-42.

James, G., and Henley, R. (1968). *Sampling Procedures for Estimating Mass and Dispersed Types of Recreation Use on Large Areas*. USDA Forest Service Research Paper SE-31.

James, G., and Cordell, H. (1970). *Importance of Shading to Visitors Selecting a Campsite at Indian Boundary Campground in Tennessee*. USDA Forest Service Research Note SE-130.

James, G. (1971). Inventorying recreation use. *Recreation Symposium Proceedings*. USDA Forest Service, 78-95.

James, G., and Schreuder, H. (1971). Estimating recreation use in the San Gorgonio Wilderness. *Journal of Forestry, 69*, 490-93.

James, G., Taylor, N., and Hopkins, M. (1971a). *Estimating Recreation Use of a Unique Trout Stream in the Coastal Plains of South Carolina*. USDA Forest Service Research Note SE-159.

James, G., Wingle, H., and Griggs, J. (1971b). *Estimating Recreation Use on Large Bodies of Water*. USDA Forest Service Research Paper SE-79.

James, G., and Quinkert, A. (1972). *Estimating recreational use at developed observation sites*. USDA Forest Service Research Paper SE-97.

James, G. and Schreuder, H. (1972). *Estimating Dispersed Recreation Use Along Trails and in General Undeveloped Areas with Electric-Eye Counters: Some Preliminary Findings*. USDA Forest Service Research Note SE-181.

Johnson, C., Horan, P., and Pepper, W. (1997a). Race, rural residence, and wildland visitation: Examining the influence of sociocultural meaning. *Rural Sociology, 62*, 89-110.

Johnson, C., Bowker, J., English, D., and Worthen, D. (1997b). *Theoretical Perspectives of Ethnicity and Outdoor Recreation: A Review and Synthesis of African-American and European American Participation.* USDA Forest Service General Technical Report SRS-11.

Johnson, C., Bowker, J., English, D., and Worthen, D. (1998). Wildland recreation in the rural south: An examination of marginality and ethnicity theory. *Journal of Leisure Research, 30,* 101-20.

Johnson, D., and Field, D. (1981). Applied and basic social research: A difference in social context. *Leisure Sciences, 4,* 269-79.

Johnson, D., and Vande Kamp, M. (1996). Extent and control of resource damage due to noncompliant visitor behavior: A case study from the U. S. National Parks. *Natural Areas Journal, 16,* 134-41.

Jones, P. and McAvoy, L. (1988). An evaluation of a wilderness user education program: A cognitive and behavioral analysis. *National Association of Interpretation 1988 Research Monograph,* 13-20.

Jubenville, A. (1971). A test of difference between wilderness recreation party leaders and party members. *Journal of Leisure Research, 3,* 116-19.

Jubenville, A., and Becker, R. (1983). Outdoor recreation management planning: Contemporary schools of thought. *Recreation Planning and Management.* State College, PA: Venture Publishing, 303-19.

Kaltenborn, B., and Emmelin, L. (1993). Tourism in the high north: Management challenges and recreation opportunity spectrum planning in Svalbard, Norway. *Environmental Management, 17,* 41-50.

Kaplan, M. (1960). *Leisure in America: A Social Inquiry.* New York: John Wiley and Sons, Inc.

Kaufman, H. (1960). *The Forest Ranger: A Study in Administrative Behavior.* Baltimore: Johns Hopkins University Press.

Kelly, J. (1974). Socialization toward leisure: A developmental approach. *Journal of Leisure Research, 6,* 181-93.

Kelly, J. (1977). Leisure socialization: Replication and extension. *Journal of Leisure Research, 9,* 121-32.

Kelly, J. (1980). Outdoor recreation participation: A comparative analysis. *Leisure Sciences, 3,* 129-54.

Kennedy, J. (1985). Conceiving forest management or providing for current and future social value. *Forest Ecology and Management, 13,* 121-32.

Kennedy, J. (1987a). Early career development of foresters, range conservationists, and wildlife/fisheries biologists in two western Forest Service regions. *Western Journal of Applied Forestry, 2,* 10-14.

Kennedy, J. (1987b). Career development of range conservationists in their first three years with the Forest Service. *Journal of Range Management, 40,* 249-53.

Kernan, A., and Drogin, E. (1995). The effect of a verbal interpretive message on day user impacts at Mount Rainier National Park. *Proceedings of the 1994 Northeastern Recreation Research Symposium.* USDA Forest Service General Technical Report NE-198, 127-29.

Kerr, G., and Manfredo, M. (1991). An attitudinal-based model of pricing for recreation services. *Journal of Leisure Research, 23,* 37-50.

Kim, N., and Graefe, A. (1997). Conceptual relationships between impact parameters of social carrying capacity and the Recreation Opportunity Spectrum. *Proceedings of the 1996 Northeastern Recreation Research Symposium*. USDA Forest Service General Technical Report NE-232, 109-14.

Kim, S., and Shelby, B. (1998). Norms for behavior and conditions in two national park campgrounds in Korea. *Environmental Management, 22*, 277-85.

King, D. (1965). *Characteristics of Family Campers Using the Huron-Manistee National Forests*. USDA Forest Service Research Paper LS-19.

King, D. (1966). *Activity Patterns of Campers* USDA Forest Service Research Note NC-18.

King, D. (1968). Socioeconomic variables related to campsite use. *Forest Science, 14*, 45-54.

Kliskey, A. (1998). Linking the wilderness perception mapping concept to the recreation opportunity spectrum. *Environmental Management, 22*, 79-88.

Klobus-Edwards, P. (1981). Race, residence, and leisure style: Some policy implications. *Leisure Sciences, 4*, 95-112.

Klukas, R., and Duncan, D. (1967). Vegetation preferences among Itasca Park visitors. *Journal of Forestry, 65*, 18-21.

Knetsch, J. (1969). Assessing the demand for outdoor recreation. *Journal of Leisure Research, 1*, 83-94.

Knetsch, J. (1977). Displaced facilities and benefit calculations. *Land Eonomics, 53*, 123-29.

Knopf, R., Driver, B., and Bassett, J. (1973). Motivations for fishing. *Human Dimensions in Wildlife Programs*. Washington, DC: The Wildlife Management Institute, 28-41.

Knopf, R., and Barnes, J. (1980). Determinants of satisfaction with a tourist resource: A case study of visitors to Gettysburg National Military Park. *Tourism Marketing and Management Issues*. Washington, DC: George Washington University, 217-33.

Knopf, R., and Lime, D. (1981). *The National River Recreation Study Questionnaires: An Aid to Recreation Management*. USDA Forest Service Research Paper NC-222.

Knopf, R. (1983). Recreational needs and behavior in natural settings. *Behavior and the Natural Environment*. New York: Plenum Publishing Company, 205-40.

Knopf, R., Peterson, G., and Leatherberry, E. (1983). Motives of recreational river floating: Relative consistency across settings. *Leisure Sciences, 5*, 231-55.

Knopf, R., and Lime, D. (1984). *A Recreation Manager's Guide to Understanding River Use and Users*. USDA Forest Service General Technical Report WO-38.

Knopp, T. (1972). Environmental determinants of recreation behavior. *Journal of Leisure Research, 4*, 129-38.

Knopp, T., and Tyger, J. (1973). A study of conflict in recreational land use: Snowmobiling versus ski-touring. *Journal of Leisure Research, 5*, 6-17.

Knopp, T., Ballman, G., and Merriam, L., Jr. (1979). Toward a more direct measure of river user preferences. *Journal of Leisure Research, 11*, 317-26.

Knudson, D., and Curry, E. (1981). Campers perceptions of site deterioration and crowding. *Journal of Forestry, 79*, 92-94.

Kohlberg, L. (1976). Moral stages and moral development. *Moral Development and Behavior: Theory, Research and Social Issues*. New York: Holt, Rinehart and Winston.

Kraus, R., and Lewis, C. (1986). Ethnic and racial minorities in urban recreation. *A Literature Review: President's Commission on Americans Outdoors*. Washington, DC: U.S. Government Printing Office, U19-U30.

Krumpe, E., and Brown, P. (1982). Using information to disperse wilderness hikers. *Journal of Forestry, 80*, 360-62.

Krumpe, E. and McCool, S. (1997). Role of public involvement in the Limits of Acceptable Change wilderness planning system. *Proceedings–Limits of Acceptable Change and Related Planning Processes: Progress and Future Directions*. USDA Forest Service General Technical Report INT-371, 16-20.

Krutilla, J. (1967). Conservation reconsidered. *American Economic Review, 57*, 777-86.

Kuentzel, W., and Heberlein, T. (1992a). Cognitive and behavioral adaptations to perceived crowding: A panel study of coping and displacement. *Journal of Leisure Research, 24*, 377-93.

Kuentzel, W., and Heberlein, T. (1992b). Does specialization affect behavioral choices and quality judgments among hunters? *Leisure Sciences, 14*, 211-26.

Kuentzel, W., and McDonald, C. (1992). Differential effects of past experience, commitment, and lifestyle dimensions on river use specialization. *Journal of Leisure Research, 24*, 269-87.

Kuentzel, W., and Heberlein, T. (1997). Social status, self-development, and the process of sailing specialization. *Journal of Leisure Research, 29*, 300-19.

Kuss, F., Graefe, A., and Vaske, J. (1990). *Visitor Impact Management: A Review of Research*. Washington, DC: National Parks and Conservation Association.

Lahart, D., and Barley, J. (1975). Reducing children's littering on a nature trail. *Journal of Environmental Education, 7*, 37-45.

LaPage, W. (1963). Some sociological aspects of forest recreation. *Journal of Forestry, 61*, 32-36.

LaPage, W. (1967). *Camper Characteristics Differ at Public and Commercial Campgrounds in New England*. USDA Forest Service Research Note NE-59.

LaPage, W. (1968). *The Role of Customer Satisfaction in Managing Commercial Campgrounds*. USDA Forest Service Research Paper NE-105.

LaPage, W. (1973). *Growth Potential of the Family Camping Market*. USDA Forest Service Research Paper NE-252.

LaPage, W., and Ragain, D. (1974). Family camping trends—An eight-year panel study. *Journal of Leisure Research, 6*, 101-12.

LaPage, W., Cormier, P., Hamilton, G., and Cormier, A. (1975). *Differential Campsite Pricing and Campground Attendance*. USDA Forest Service Research Paper NE-330.

LaPage, W. (Compiler). (1980). *Proceedings–1980 National Outdoor Recreation Trends Symposium, Volumes I and II*. USDA Forest Service General Technical Report NE-57.

LaPage, W., and Bevins, M. (1981). *Satisfaction Monitoring for Quality Control in Campground Management*. USDA Forest Service Research Paper NE-484.

LaPage, W. (1983a). Recreation resource management for visitor satisfaction. *Journal of Park and Recreation Administration, 1*, 37-44.

LaPage, W. (1983b). Recreation resource management for visitor satisfaction. *Recreation Planning and Management*. State College, PA: Venture, 279-85.

Larrabee, E., and Meyersohn, R. (Eds.). (1958). *Mass Leisure*. Glencoe, IL: The Free Press.

Lawler, E. (1973). *Motivations in Work Organizations*. Monterey, CA: Brooks/Cole Publishing Company.

Leatherberry, E. (1976). *Northern Wisconsin Snowmobilers: Their Characteristics and Management Preferences*. USDA Forest Service Research Paper NC-135.

Leatherberry, E. (1980). Comparing attitudes of Wisconsin residents and snowmobilers regarding use of snowmobiles on public land. *North American Symposium on Dispersed Winter Recreation*. St. Paul, MN: University of Minnesota, 78-81.

Leatherberry, E., and Lime, D. (1981). *Unstaffed Trail Registration Compliance in a Backcountry Recreation Area*. USDA Forest Service Research Paper NC-214.

Lee, H., Kersteller, D., Graefe, A., and Confer, J. Jr. (1997). Crowding at an art festival: A replication and extension of the outdoor recreation crowding model. *Proceedings of the 1996 Northeastern Recreation Research Symposium*. USDA Forest Service General Technical Report NE-232, 198-204.

Lee, R. (1972). The social definition of outdoor recreation places. *Social Behavior, Natural Resources, and the Environment*. New York: Harper and Row, 68-84.

Lee, R. (1975). *The Management of Human Components in the Yosemite National Park Ecosystem: Final Research Report*. Berkeley, CA: University of California.

Lee, R. (1977). Alone with others: The paradox of privacy in the wilderness. *Leisure Sciences, 1*, 3-19.

Lenskyj, H. (1988). Measured time: Women, sport, and leisure. *Leisure Studies, 7*, 233-40.

Leonard, R., Echelberger, H., and Schnitzer, M. (1978). *Use Characteristics of the Great Gulf Wilderness*. USDA Forest Service Research Paper NE-428.

Leonard, R., Echelberger, H., Plumley, H., and Van Meter, L. (1980). *Management Guidelines for Monitoring Use on Backcountry Trails*. USDA Forest Service Research Note NE-286.

Leopold, A. (1934). Conservation economics. *Journal of Forestry, 32*, 537-44.

Leopold, L., Clarke, F., Hanshaw, B., and Balsley, J. (1971). *A Procedure for Evaluating Environmental Impact*. Geological Survey Circular 645. Washington, DC: U.S. Geological Survey.

Leuschner, W., Cook, P., Roggenbuck, J., and Oderwald, R. (1987). A comparative analysis for wilderness user fee policy. *Journal of Leisure Research, 19*, 101-14.

Lewis, M., Lime, D., and Anderson, P. (1996a). Use of visitor encounter norms in natural area management. *Natural Areas Journal, 16*, 128-33.

Lewis, M., Lime, D., and Anderson, P. (1996b). Paddle canoeists encounter norms in Minnesota's Boundary Waters Canoe Area wilderness. *Leisure Sciences, 18*, 143-60.

Librarian of Congress. (1962). *Outdoor Recreation Literature: A Survey: Outdoor Recreation Resources Review Commission Study Report 27*. Washington, D. C.: U. S. Government Printing Office.

Lichtkoppler, R., and H. Clonts. (1990). Recreation Opportunity Spectrum reevaluated: Its application to the eastern U.S. *Social Science and Natural Resource Recreation Management*. Boulder, CO: Westview Press, 105-21.

Lime, D. (1971). *Factors Influencing Campground Use in the Superior National Forest of Minnesota*. USDA Forest Service Research Paper NC-60.

Lime, D., and Stankey, G. (1971). Carrying capacity: Maintaining outdoor recreation quality. *Recreation Symposium Proceedings*. USDA Forest Service, 174-84.

Lime, D. (1972a). Behavioral research in outdoor recreation management: An example of how visitors select campgrounds. *Environment and the Social Sciences: Perspectives and Applications*. Washington, D. C.: American Psychological Association, 198-206.

Lime, D. (1972b). *Large Groups in the Boundary Waters Canoe Area–Their Numbers, Characteristics, and Impact.* USDA Forest Service Research Note NC-142.

Lime, D. (1974). Locating and designing campgrounds to provide a full range of camping opportunities. *Outdoor Recreation Research: Applying the Results.* USDA Forest Service General Technical Report NC-9, 56-66.

Lime, D., and Lorence, G. (1974). *Improving Estimates of Wilderness Use from Mandatory Travel Permits.* USDA Forest Service Research Paper NC-101.

Lime, D., and Buchman, R. (1974). Putting wilderness permit information to work. *Journal of Forestry, 72,* 622-26.

Lime, D. (1976). Wilderness use and users: A summary of research. *Proceedings of the 54th Annual Winter Meeting, Allegheny Section, Society of American Foresters.* Dover, DE: Society of American Foresters.

Lime, D. (1977a). Principles of recreation carrying capacity. *Proceedings of the Southern States Recreation Research Applications Workshop.* Asheville, NC, 122-34.

Lime, D. (1977b). When the wilderness gets crowded . . . ? *Naturalist, 28,* 1-7.

Lime, D. (1977c). Alternative strategies for visitor management of western whitewater river recreation. *Managing Colorado River Whitewater: The Carrying Capacity Strategy.* Logan, UT: Utah State University, 146-55.

Lime, D., and Lucas, R. (1977). Good information improves the wilderness experience. *Naturalist, 28,* 18-20.

Lime, D. (1979). Carrying capacity. *Trends, 16,* 37-40.

Lime, D., Knopf, R., and Peterson, G. (1981). The national river recreation study: Growing new data base with exciting potential. *Some Recent Products of River Recreation Research,* USDA Forest Service General Technical Report NC-63, 1-8.

Lime, D. (1995). Principles of carrying capacity for parks and outdoor recreation areas. *Acta Environmentalica Universitatis Comemiane, 4,* 21-29.

Lindsay, J., and Ogle, R. (1970). Socioeconomic patterns of outdoor recreation use near urban areas. *Journal of Leisure Research, 4,* 19-24.

Little, B. (1976). Specialization and the varieties of environmental experience: empirical studies within the personality paradigm. *Experiencing the Environment.* New York: Plenum Press, 81-116.

Lloyd, R., and Fischer, V. (1972). *Dispersed versus concentrated recreation as forest policy.* Paper presented at the Seventh World Forestry Congress, Buenos Aries, Argentina.

London, M., Crandall, R., and Fitzgibbons, D. (1977). The psychological structure of leisure: Activities, needs, people. *Journal of Leisure Research, 9,* 252-63.

Lottier, S. (1938). Distribution of criminal offenses in metropolitan regions. *Journal of Criminal Law and Criminology, 29,* 39-45.

Love, L. (1964). *Summer Recreational Use of Selected National Forest Campgrounds in the Central Rocky Mountains.* USDA Forest Service Research Paper RM-5.

Lucas, R. (1963). Bias in estimating recreationists length of stay from sample surveys. *Journal of Forestry, 61,* 912-14.

Lucas, R. (1964a). *Recreational Use of the Quetico-Superior Area.* USDA Forest Service Research Paper LS-8.

Lucas, R. (1964b). *The Recreational Capacity of the Quetico-Superior Area.* USDA Forest Service Research Paper LS-15.

Lucas, R. (1964c). Wilderness perception and use: The example of the Boundary Waters Canoe Area. *Natural Resources Journal, 3,* 394-411.

Lucas, R. (1966). The contribution of environmental research to wilderness policy decisions. *Journal of Social Issues, 22,* 117-26.

Lucas, R. (1970). *User Evaluation of Campgrounds on Two Michigan National Forests.* USDA Forest Service Research Paper NC-44.

Lucas, R., and Oltman, J. (1971). Survey sampling wilderness visitors. *Journal of Leisure Research, 3,* 28-43.

Lucas, R., Schreuder, H., and James, G. (1971). *Wilderness Use Estimation: A Pilot Test of Sampling Procedures on the Mission Mountains Primitive Area.* USDA Forest Service Research Paper INT-109.

Lucas, R. (1973). Wilderness: A management framework. *Journal of Soil and Water Conservation, 28,* 150-54.

Lucas, R., and Stankey, G. (1974). Social carrying capacity for backcountry recreation. *Outdoor Recreation Research: Applying the Results.* USDA Forest Service General Technical Report NC-9, 14-23.

Lucas, R. (1975). *Low Compliance Rates at Unmanned Trail Registers.* USDA Forest Service General Technical Report INT-200.

Lucas, R. (1979). Perceptions of non-motorized recreational impacts: A review of research findings. *Recreational Impact on Wildlands.* USDA Forest Service, Pacific Northwest Region R-6-001-1979, 24-31.

Lucas, R. (1980). *Use Patterns and Visitor Characteristics, Attitudes, and Preferences in Nine Wilderness and Other Roadless Areas.* USDA Forest Service Research Paper INT-253.

Lucas, R. (1981). *Redistributing Wilderness Use Through Information Supplied to Visitors.* USDA Forest Service Research Paper INT-277.

Lucas, R., and Kovalicky, T. (1981). *Self-issued Wilderness Permits as a Use Measurement System.* USDA Forest Service Research Paper INT-270.

Lucas, R. (1982). Recreation regulations—When are they needed? *Journal of Forestry, 80,* 148-51.

Lucas, R. (1983). *Low and Variable Visitor Compliance Rates at Voluntary Trail Registers.* USDA Forest Service Research Note INT-326.

Lucas, R. (1983). The role of regulations in recreation management. *Western Wildlands, 9,* 6-10.

Lucas, R. (1985). Recreation trends and management of the Bob Marshall Wilderness Complex. *Proceedings of the 1985 National Outdoor Recreation Trends Symposium, Volume II.* Atlanta, GA: U.S. National Park Service, 309-16.

Lundberg, G., Komarovsky, M., and McInerny, M. (1934). *Leisure: A Suburban Study.* New York: Columbia University Press.

Lundgren, A. (Ed.). (1996). *Recreation Fees in the National Park Service—Issues, Policies and Guidelines for Future Action.* St. Paul, MN: University of Minnesota Cooperative Park Studies Unit.

Lynch, J., and Nelson, C. (1997). Updating the Recreation Opportunity Spectrum User Guide—Eastern Region Supplement. *Proceedings of the 1996 Northeastern Recreation Research Symposium.* USDA Forest Service General Technical Report NE-232, 157-59.

Lynd, R., and Lynd, H. (1929). *Middleton, a Study in American Culture.* New York: Harcourt Brace.

MacDonald, M., McGuire, C., and Havighurst, R. (1949). Leisure activities and the socioeconomic status of children. *American Journal of Sociology, 54*, 505-19.

Machlis. G., and Harvey, M. (1993). The adoption and diffusion of recreation research programs: A case study of the visitor services project. *Journal of Park and Recreation Administration, 11*, 49-65.

Magill, A. (1976) *Campsite Reservation Systems: The Campers' Viewpoint.* USDA Forest Service Research Paper PSW-121.

Magill, A. (1988). Natural resource professionals: The reluctant public servants. *The Environmental Professional, 10*, 295-303.

Manfredo, M., and Anderson, D. (1982). Recreation preferences of Oregon trout fishermen. *Forest and River Recreation Research Update.* St. Paul, MN: University of Minnesota Agricultural Experimental Station Miscellaneous Report 18, 64-68.

Manfredo, M., Driver, B., and Brown, P. (1983). A test of concepts inherent in experience-based setting management for outdoor recreation areas. *Journal of Leisure Research, 15*, 263-83.

Manfredo, M. (1984). The Comparability of onsite and offsite measures of recreation needs. *Journal of Leisure Research, 16*, 245-49.

Manfredo, M. and Anderson, D. (1987). The influence of activity importance and similarity on perception of recreation substitutes. *Leisure Sciences, 9*, 77-86.

Manfredo, M., and Shelby, B. (1988) The effect of using self-report measures in tests of attitude-behavior relationships. *Journal of Social Psychology, 128*, 731-43.

Manfredo, M. (1989). An investigation of the basis for external information search in recreation and tourism. *Leisure Sciences, 11*, 29-45.

Manfredo, M. and Bright, A. (1991). A model for assessing the effects of communication on recreationists. *Journal of Leisure Research, 23*, 1-20.

Manfredo, J. (Ed.). (1992). *Influencing Human Behavior: Theory and Applications in Recreation, Tourism, and Natural Resources Management.* Champaign, IL: Sagamore Publishing, Inc.

Manfredo, M., Yuan, S., and McGuire, F. (1992). The influence of attitude accessibility on attitude-behavior relationships: implications for recreation research. *Journal of Leisure Research, 24*, 157-70.

Manfredo, M., and Driver, B. (1996). Measuring leisure motivation: A meta-analysis of the recreation experience preference scales. *Journal of Leisure Research, 28*, 188-213.

Manning, R. (1979a). Behavioral characteristics of fishermen and other recreationists on four Vermont rivers. *Transactions of the American Fisheries Society, 108*, 536-41.

Manning, R. (1979b). Strategies for managing recreational use of national parks. *Parks, 4*, 13-15.

Manning, R., and Ciali, C. (1979). The computer hikes the Appalachian trail. *Appalachia, XL III*, 75-85.

Manning, R., and Moncrief, L. (1979). Land use analysis through matrix modeling: Theory and application. *Journal of Environmental Management, 9*, 33-40.

Manning, R., and Ciali, C. (1980). Recreation density and user satisfaction: A further exploration of the satisfaction model. *Journal of Leisure Research, 12*, 329-45.

Manning, R., and Cormier, P. (1980). Trends in the temporal distribution of park use. *Proceedings of the 1980 Outdoor Recreation Trends Symposium, Volume II.* USDA Forest Service General Technical Report NE-57, 81-87.

Manning, R. and Baker, S. (1981). Discrimination through user fees: Fact or fiction? *Parks and Recreation, 16,* 70-74.

Manning, R., and Ciali, C. (1981). Recreation and river type: Social-environmental relationships. *Environmental Management, 5,* 109-20.

Manning, R., and Potter, F. (1982). Wilderness encounters of the third kind. *Proceedings of the Third Annual Conference of the Wilderness Psychology Group.* Morgantown, WV: West Virginia University, 1-14.

Manning, R., Powers, L., and Mock, C. (1982). Temporal distribution of forest recreation: Problems and potential. *Forest and River Recreation: Research Update.* St. Paul, MN: University of Minnesota Agricultural Experiment Station Miscellaneous Publication 18, 26-32.

Manning, R., Callinan, E., Echelberger, H., Koenemann, E., and McEwen, D. (1984). Differential fees: Raising revenue, distributing demand. *Journal of Park and Recreation Administration, 2,* 20-38.

Manning, R., and Potter, F. (1984). Computer simulation as a tool in teaching park and wilderness management. *Journal of Environmental Education. 15,* 3-9.

Manning, R., and Powers, L. (1984). Peak and off-peak use: Redistributing the outdoor recreation/tourism load. *Journal of Travel Research, 23,* 25-31.

Manning, R. (1985a). Diversity in a democracy: Expanding the recreation opportunity spectrum. *Leisure Sciences, 7,* 377-99.

Manning, R. (1985b) Crowding norms in backcountry settings: A review and synthesis. *Journal of Leisure Research, 17,* 75-89.

Manning, R. (1986). Density and crowding in wilderness: Search and research for satisfaction. *Proceedings—National Wilderness Research Conference: Current Research.* USDA Forest Service General Technical Report INT-212, 440-48.

Manning, R., and Koeneman, E. (1986). Differential campsite pricing: An experiment. *Campgrounds: New perspectives on Management.* Carbondale, IL: Southern Illinois University, 39-48.

Manning, R. (1987). *The Law of Nature: Park Rangers in Yosemite Valley.* Brookline, MA: Umbrella Films.

Manning, R., and Fraysier, M. (1989) Expert and public opinion: conflicting or complementary views? *Journal of Park and Recreation Administration, 7,* 44-59.

Manning, R., and Zwick, R. (1990). The relationship between quality of outdoor recreation opportunities and support for recreation funding. *Proceedings of the 1989 Northeastern Recreation Research Symposium.* USDA Forest Service General Technical Report NE-145, 13-18.

Manning, R., Lime, D., Hof, M., and Freimund, W. (1995a). The visitor experience and resource protection process: The application of carrying capacity to Arches National Park. *The George Wright Forum, 12,* 41-55.

Manning, R., Lime, D., and McMonagle, R. (1995b). Indicators and standards of the quality of the visitor experience at a heavily-used national park. *Proceedings of the 1994 Northeastern Recreation Research Symposium.* USDA Forest Service General Technical Report NE-198, 24-32.

Manning, R., Lime, D., Hof, M., and Freimund, W. (1995c). The carrying capacity of national parks: Theory and application. *Proceedings of the Conference on Innovations and Challenges in the Management of Visitor Opportunities in Parks and Protected Areas.* Waterloo, Canada: University of Waterloo, 9-21.

Manning, R., and Lime, D. (1996). Crowding and carrying capacity in the national park system: Toward a social science research agenda. *Crowding and Congestion in the National Park System: Guidelines for Management and Research.* St. Paul, MN: University of Minnesota Agricultural Experiment Station Publication 86, 27-65.

Manning, R., and Valliere, W. (1996). Environmental values, environmental ethics, and wilderness management: An empirical study. *International Journal of Wilderness, 2,* 27-32.

Manning, R., Ballinger, N., Marion, J., and Roggenbuck, J. (1996a). Recreation management in natural areas: Problems and practices, status and trends. *Natural Areas Journal, 16,* 142-46.

Manning, R., Lime, D., and Hof, M. (1996b). Social carrying capacity of natural areas: theory and application in the U. S. National Parks. *Natural Areas Journal, 16,* 118-27.

Manning, R., Lime, D., Freimund, W., and Pitt, D. (1996c). Crowding norms at frontcountry sites: A visual approach to setting standards of quality. *Leisure Sciences, 18,* 39-59.

Manning, R., Johnson, D., and VandeKamp, M. (1996d). Norm congruence among tour boat passengers to Glacier Bay National Park. *Leisure Sciences, 18,* 125-41.

Manning, R., Graefe, A., and McCool, S. (1996e). Trends in carrying capacity planning and management. *Proceedings of the Fourth International Outdoor Recreation and Tourism Trends Symposium.* St. Paul, MN: University of Minnesota, 334-41.

Manning, R., LaPage, W., Griffall, K., and Simon, B. (1996f). Suggested principles for designing and implementing user fees and charges in the National Park System. *Recreation Fees in the National Park System.* St. Paul, MN: University of Minnesota Cooperative Park Studies Unit, 134-36.

Manning, R. (1997). Social carrying capacity of parks and outdoor recreation areas. *Parks and Recreation, 32,* 32-38.

Manning, R., Valliere, W., and Jacobi, C. (1997). Crowding norms for the carriage roads of Acadia National Park: Alternative measurement approaches. *Proceedings of the 1996 Northeastern Recreation Research Symposium.* USDA Forest Service General Technical Report NE-232, 139-45.

Manning, R. (1998). "To provide for the enjoyment": Recreation management in the National Parks. *The George Wright Forum, 15,* 6-20.

Manning, R., Jacobi, C., Valliere, W., and Wang, B. (1998). Standards of quality in parks and recreation. *Parks and Recreation, 33,* 88-94.

Manning, R., and Wang, B. (1998). Social science in the national park system: An assessment of visitor information. *Park Science, 18,* 1, 16-17.

Manning, R., Valliere, W. Wang, B., and Jacobi, C. (1999). Crowding norms: Alternative measurement approaches. *Leisure Sciences, 21,* 219-29.

Marcin, T., and Lime, D. (1977). Our changing population structure: What will it mean to future outdoor recreation use? *Outdoor Recreation: Advances in the Application of Economics.* USDA Forest Service General Technical Report WO-2, 42-53, 35-41.

Marion, J., and Lime, D. (1986). Recreational resource impacts: Visitor perceptions and management responses. *Wilderness and Natural Areas in the Eastern United States.* Nacodoches, TX: Stephen F. Austin University, 229-35.

Marion, J., Roggenbuck, J., and Manning, R. (1993). *Problems and Practices in Backcountry Recreation Management: A Survey of National Park Service Managers.* US National Park Service Natural Resources Report NPS/NRVT/NRR-93112, Denver, CO.

Marler, L. (1971). A study of anti-letter messages. *Journal of Environmental Education, 3,* 52-53.

Marquardt, R., McGaun, A., Ratlift, J., and Routson, J. (1972). The cognitive dissonance model as a predictor of customer satisfaction among camper owners. *Journal of Leisure Research, 4,* 275-83.

Marnell, L. (1977). Methods for counting river recreation users. *Proceedings: River Recreation Management and Research Symposium.* USDA Forest Service General Technical Report NC-28, 77-82.

Marsden, H. (1972). Crowding and animal behavior. *Environment and the Social Sciences: Perspectives and Applications.* Washington, DC: American Psychological Association, Inc., 5-16.

Marshall, N. (1972). Privacy and environment. *Human Ecology, 1,* 93-110.

Marshall, N. (1974). Dimensions of privacy preferences. *Multivariate Behavioral Research, 9,* 255-72.

Marshall, R. (1933). The forest for recreation. *A National Plan for American Forestry.* Washington, DC: Senate Document 12, 73rd Congress, 1st Session, Volume 1, 463-87.

Marshall, R. (1938). *The People's Forest.* New York: H. Smith and R. Haas.

Martin, B. (1986). Hiker's opinions about fees for backcountry recreation. *Proceedings– National Wilderness Research Conference: Current Research.* USDA Forest Service General Technical Report INT-212, 483-88.

Martin, S., McCool, S., and Lucas, R. (1989). Wilderness campsite impacts: Do managers and visitors see them the same? *Environmental Management, 13,* 623-29.

Martinson, K., and Shelby, B. (1992). Encounter and proximity norms for salmon anglers in California and New Zealand. *North American Journal of Fisheries Management, 12,* 559-67.

Maslow, A. (1943). A theory of human motivation. *Psychological Review, 50,* 370-96.

McAvoy, L., and Dustin, D. (1981). The right to risk in wilderness. *Journal of Forestry, 79,* 150-52.

McAvoy, L., and Dustin, D. (1983). Indirect versus direct regulation of recreation behavior. *Journal of Park and Recreation Administration, 1,* 12-17.

McAvoy, L., Dustin, D., Rankin, J., and Frakt, A. (1985). Wilderness and legal-liability: Guidelines for resource managers and program leaders. *Journal of Park and Recreation Administration, 3,* 41-49.

McAvoy, L., Gramann, J., Burdge, R., and Absher, J. (1986). Understanding the causes of conflict between commercial and recreational users of the Mississippi River. *Journal of Park and Recreation Administration, 4,* 49-60.

McAvoy, L. (1990). Rescue-free wilderness areas. *Adventure Education.* State College, PA: Venture Publishing, 329-34.

McCarville, R., Reiling, S., and White, C. (1986). The role of fairness in users' assessments of first-time fees for a public recreation service. *Leisure Sciences, 18,* 61-76.

McCarville, R., and Crompton, J. (1987). Propositions addressing perception of reference price for public recreation services. *Leisure Sciences, 9,* 281-91.

McCarville, R. (1996). The importance of price last paid in developing price expectations for a public leisure service. *Journal of Park and Recreation Administration, 14,* 52-64.

McCay, R. (1976). *Ohio Trail Users*. USDA Forest Service Research Note NE-228.

McCay, R., and Moeller, G. (1976). *Compatibility of Ohio Trail Users*. USDA Forest Service Research Note NE-225.

McClaskie, S., Napier, T., and Christensen, J. (1986). Factors influencing outdoor recreation participation: A state study. *Journal of Leisure Research, 18,* 190-205.

McConnell, K. (1977). Congestion and willingness to pay: A study of beach use. *Land Economics, 53,* 185-95.

McCool, S., Lime, D., and Anderson, D. (1977). Simulation modeling as a tool for managing river recreation. *Proceedings: River Recreation Management and Research Symposium*. USDA Forest Service General Technical Report NC-28, 304-11.

McCool, S., and Schreyer, R. (1977). Research utilization in wildland recreation management: A preliminary analysis. *Journal of Leisure Research, 9,* 98-109.

McCool, S. (1978). Recreation activity packages at water-based resources. *Leisure Sciences, 1,* 163-73.

McCool, S., and Utter, J. (1981). Preferences for allocating river recreation use. *Water Resources Bulletin, 17,* 431-37.

McCool, S., and Utter, J. (1982). Recreation use lotteries: Outcomes and preferences. *Journal of Forestry, 80,* 10-11, 29.

McCool, S., Stankey, G., and Clark, R. (1985). Choosing recreation settings: Processes, findings, and research directions. *Proceedings–Symposium on Recreation Choice Behavior*. USDA Forest Service General Technical Report INT-184, 1-8.

McCool, S., and Lime, D. (1989). Attitudes of visitors toward outdoor recreation management policy. *Outdoor Recreation Benchmark 1988: Proceedings of the National Outdoor Recreation Forum*. USDA Forest Service General Technical Report SE-52, 401-11.

McCool, S., and Reilly, M. (1993). Benefit segmentation analysis of state park visitor setting preferences and behavior. *Journal of Park and Recreation Administration, 11,* 1-14.

McCool, S., and Watson, A. (1995). *Linking Tourism, the Environment, and Sustainability*. USDA Forest Service General Technical Report INT-323.

McCool, S., and Christensen, N. (1996). Alleviating congestion in parks and recreation areas through direct management of visitor behavior. *Crowding and Congestion in the National Park System: Guidelines for Management and Research*. St. Paul, MN: University of Minnesota Agriculture Experiment Station Publication 86-1996, 67-83.

McCool, S., and Cole, D. (1997a). *Proceedings–Limits of Acceptable Change and Related Planning Processes: Progress and Future Direction*. USDA Forest Service General Technical Report INT-371.

McCool, S., and Cole, D. (1997b). Annotated bibliograhy of publications for LAC applications. *Proceedings–Limits of Acceptable Change and Related Planning Processes: Progress and Future Directions*. USDA Forest Service General Technical Report INT-371, 81-84.

McCormick, B. (1996). What can be learned from the single case? *Leisure Sciences, 18,* 365-69.

McCoy, K., Krumpe, E., Allen, S. (1995). Limits of acceptable change: Evaluating implementation by the U.S. Forest Service. *International Journal of Wilderness, 1,* 18-22.

McDonald, C., Noe, F., and Hammitt, W. (1987). Expectations and recreation fees: A dilemma for recreation resource administrators. *Journal of Park and Recreation Administration, 5*, 1-9.

McDonald, C. (1996). Normative perspectives on outdoor recreation behavior: Introductory comments. *Leisure Sciences, 18*, 1-6.

McDonald, J., and Hutchison, I. (1986). Minority and ethnic variation in outdoor recreation participation. *A Literature Review: The President's Commission on Americans Outdoors*. Washington, DC: US Government Printing Office, S-41-S-51.

McEwen, D., and Tocher, S. (1976). Zone management: Key to controlling recreational impact in developed campsites. *Journal of Forestry, 74*, 90-91.

McEwen, D. (1986). Recreation quality and the market for tent camping. *Journal of Park and Recreation Administration, 4*, 83-95.

McFarlane, B., Boxall, P., and Watson, D. (1998). Past experience and behavioral choice among wilderness users. *Journal of Leisure Research, 30*, 195-213.

McGuire, F., Dottavio, F., and O'Leary, J. (1987). The relationship of early life experiences to later life leisure involvement. *Leisure Sciences, 9*, 251-57.

McIntyre, N. (1989). The personal meaning of participation: Enduring involvement. *Journal of Leisure Research, 21*, 167-79.

McIntyre, N., and Pigram, J. (1992). Recreation specialization reexamined: The case of vehicle-based campers. *Leisure Sciences, 14*, 3-15.

McLaughlin, W., and Paradice, W. (1980). Using visitor preference information to guide dispersed winter recreation management for cross-country skiing and snowmobiling. *Proceedings of the North American Symposium on Dispersed Winter Recreation*. St. Paul, MN: University of Minnesota, Office of Special Programs, Education Series 2-3, 64-72.

McLean, D., and Johnson, R. (1997). Techniques for rationing public recreation services. *Journal of Park and Recreation Administration, 15*, 76-92.

McMillen, J. (1983). The social organization of leisure among Mexican-Americans. *Journal of Leisure Research, 15*, 166-73.

Meadows, D., Randers, J., and Behrens, W. (1972). *The Limits to Growth*. New York: Universe Books.

Meinecke, E. (1928). *A Report Upon the Effects of Excessive Tourist Travel on the California Redwood Parks*. Sacramento, CA: California State Printing Office.

Mengak, K., Dottavio, F., and O'Leary, J. (1986). The use of importance-performance analysis to evaluate a visitor center. *Journal of Interpretation, 11*, 1-13.

Mengak, K., and Perales, M. (1991). Estimating dispersed recreation use in multiple access settings using parked vehicles. *Proceedings of the 1990 Southeastern Recreation Research Conference*. USDA Forest Service General Technical Report SE-67, 53-59.

Merigliano, L. (1990). Indicators to monitor the wilderness recreation experience. *Managing America's Enduring Wilderness Resource*. St. Paul, MN: University of Minnesota, 156-62.

Merriam, L., Jr., and Ammons, R. (1968). Wilderness users and management in three Montana areas. *Journal of Forestry, 66*, 390-95.

Merriam, L., Jr, Wald, K., and Ramsey, C. (1972). Public and professional definitions of the state park: A Minnesota case. *Journal of Leisure Research, 4*, 259-74.

Merriam, L., Jr., and Smith, C. (1974). Visitor impact on newly developed campsites in the Boundary Waters Canoe Area. *Journal of Forestry, 72*, 627-30.

Merriam, L. (1986). Nearly a quarter of a century in the Bob Marshall Wilderness (1960-1984). *Proceedings–National Wilderness Research Conference: Current Research.* USDA Forest Service General Technical Report INT-212, 253-59.

Merrill, K., and Graefe, A. (1998). The relationship between activity specialization and preferences for setting and route attributes of selected rock climbers. *Proceedings of the 1997 Northeastern Recreation Research Symposium.* USDA Forest Service General Technical Report NE-241, 40-43.

Meyersohn, R. (1969). The sociology of leisure in the United States: Introduction and bibliography, 1945-1965. *Journal of Leisure Research, 1,* 53-68.

Milgram, S. (1970). The experience of living in cities. *Science, 167,* 1461-68.

Miller, R., Prato, A., and Young, R. (1977). Congestion, success, and the value of Colorado deer hunting experiences. *Transactions of the Forty-Second North American Wildlife and National Resources Conference.* Washington, DC: Wildlife Management Institute, 129-36.

Miller, M., and Van Maaneen, J. (1982). Getting into fishing: Observations on the social identities of New England fishermen. *Urban Life, 11,* 27-54.

Mills, A. (1985) Participation motivations for outdoor recreation: A test of Maslow's theory. *Journal of Leisure Research, 17,* 184-99.

Mitchell, L. (1969). Recreational geography: Evolution and research needs. *Professional Geographer, 21,* 117-19.

Mitchell, R. (1971). Some social implications of higher density housing. *American Sociological Review, 36,* 18-29.

Moeller, G., and Engelken, J. (1972). What fishermen look for in a fishing experience. *Journal of Wildlife Management, 36,* 1253-57.

Moeller, G., Larson, R., and Morrison, D. (1974). *Opinions of Campers and Boaters at the Allegheny Reservoir.* USDA Forest Service Research Paper NE-307.

Moncrief, L. (1970). Trends in outdoor recreation research. *Journal of Leisure Research, 2,* 127-30.

Moore, R. and Graefe, A. (1994). Attachment to recreation settings: the case of rail-trail users. *Leisure Sciences, 16,* 17-31.

Moore, S., Schockey, J., and Bruckler, S. (1990). Social encounters as a cue for determining wilderness quality. *Social Science and Natural Resource Recreation Management.* Boulder, CO: Westview Press, 69-79.

Moore, S., and McClaran, M. (1991). Symbolic dimensions of the packstock debate. *Leisure Sciences, 13,* 221-37.

More, T., and Payne, B. (1978). Affective responses to natural areas near cities. *Journal of Leisure Research, 10,* 7-12.

More, T., and Buhyoff, G. (1979). *Managing Recreation Areas for Quality Experiences: A Theoretical Framework.* USDA Forest Service Research Paper NE-432.

More, T. (1980a). *Trail Deterioration as an Indicator of Trail Use in an Urban Forest Recreation Area.* USDA Forest Service Research Note NE-292.

More, T. (1980b). *Emotional Responses to Recreation Environments.* USDA Forest Service Research Paper NE-461.

More, T., Echelberger, H., and Koenemann, E. (1990). *Factors Affecting Recreation Participation by Vermont Residents.* USDA Forest Service Research Paper NE-631.

More, T., Dustin, D., and Knopf, R. (1996). Behavioral consequences of campground user fees. *Journal of Park and Recreation Administration. 14,* 81-93.

Morehead, J. (1979). The ranger image. *Trends, 16*, 5-8.

Moss, W., Shackelford, L., and Stokes, G. (1969). Recreation and personality. *Journal of Forestry, 67*, 182-84.

Moss, W., and Lamphear, S. (1970). Substitutability of recreational activities in meeting stated needs and drives of the visitor. *Environmental Education, 1*, 129-31.

Mowen, A., Williams, D., and Graefe, A. (1997). Specialized participants and their environmental attitudes: Re-examining the role of "traditional" and psychological specialization dimensions. *Proceedings of the 1996 Northeastern Recreation Research Symposium.* USDA Forest Service General Technical Report NE-232, 134-38.

Mowen, A., Graefe, A., and Virden, R. (1998). A typology of place attachment and activity involvement. *Proceedings of the 1997 Northeastern Recreation Research Symposium.* USDA Forest Service General Technical Report NE-241, 89-92.

Mueller, E., and Gurin, G. (1962). *Participation in Outdoor Recreation: Factors Affecting Demand Among American Adults: Outdoor Recreation Resources Review Commission Study Report 20.* Washington, DC: US Government Printing Office.

Munley, V., and Smith, V. (1976). Learning-by-doing and experience: The case of whitewater recreation. *Land Economics, 52*, 545-53.

Murray, J. (1974). *Appalachian Trail Users in the Southern National Forests: Their Characteristics, Attitudes, and Management Preferences.* USDA Forest Service Research Paper SE-116.

Muth, R., and Clark, R. (1978). *Public Participation in Wilderness and Backcountry Litter Control: A Review of Research and Management Experience.* USDA Forest Service General Technical Report PNW-75.

Nash, R. (1982). *Wilderness and the American mind.* New Haven, CT: Yale University Press.

National Academy of Sciences. (1969) *A Program for Outdoor Recreation Research.* Washington, DC: National Academy of Sciences.

National Advisory Commission on Civil Disorders. (1970). Kerner Commission Report: Grievances. *Recreation and Leisure Service for the Disadvantaged.* Philadelphia, PA: Lea and Febiger, 41-48.

National Park Service. (1997). *VERP: The Visitor Experience and Resource Protection (VERP) Framework—A Handbook for Planners and Managers.* Denver, CO: Denver Service Center.

Neulinger, J and Miranda, B. (1969). Attitude dimensions of leisure. *Journal of Leisure Research, 1*, 255-61.

Neulinger, J., and Breit, M. (1971). Attitude dimensions of leisure: A replication study. *Journal of Leisure Research, 3*, 255-61.

Neumeyer, M., and Neumeyer, E. (1949). *Leisure and Recreation.* New York: A. S. Barnes and Company.

Nielson, C., and Buchanan, T. (1986). A comparison of the effectiveness of two interpretive programs regarding fire ecology and fire management. *Journal of Interpretation, 1*, 1-10.

Nielson, J., and Endo, R. (1977). Where have all the purists gone? An empirical examination of the displacement hypothesis in wilderness recreation. *Western Sociological Review, 8*, 61-75.

Nielson, J., and Shelby, B. (1977). River-running in the Grand Canyon: How much and what kind of use. *Proceedings: River Recreation Management and Research Symposium.* USDA Forest Service General Technical Report NC-28, 168-77.

Nielson, J., Shelby, B., and Haas, J. (1977). Sociological carrying capacity and the last settler syndrome. *Pacific Sociological Review, 20*, 568-81.

Nilsen, P., and Tayler, G. (1997). A comparative analysis of protected area planning and management frameworks. *Proceedings–Limits of Acceptable Change and Related Planning Processes: Progress and Future Directions*. USDA Forest Service General Technical Report INT-371, 49-57.

Noe, F., Wellman, J., and Buhyoff, J. (1981). Perception of conflict between off-road vehicle users in a leisure setting. *Journal of Environmental Systems, 11*, 243-53.

Noe, F., Hull, R., and Wellman, J. (1982). Normative response and norm activation among ORV users within a seashore environment. *Leisure Sciences, 5*, 127-42.

Noe, F. (1987). Measurement specification and leisure satisfaction. *Leisure Sciences, 9*, 163-72.

Noe, F. (1992). Further questions about the management and conceptualization of backcountry encounter norms. *Journal of Leisure Research, 24*, 86-92.

Odum, E. (1959). *Fundamentals of Biology*. Philadelphia: W. B. Saunders Company.

O'Leary, J., Field, D., and Schreuder, G. (1974). Social groups and water activity clusters: An exploration of interchangeability and substitutions. *Water and Community Development: Social and Economic Perspectives*. Ann Arbor, MI: Ann Arbor Science Publishers, Inc., 195-215.

O'Leary, J., and Pate, G. (1979). Water-based activity involvement for recreation consumers at state, federal, local, or private facilities. *Water Resources Bulletin, 15*, 182-88.

O'Leary, J., and Weeks, H. (1979). Using recreation consumer data in developing wildlife management strategies. *Wildlife Society Bulletin, 7*, 98-103.

O'Leary, J., Napier, T., Dottavio, D. (1982). Examining predictor variables used in outdoor recreation planning. *Guiding Land Use Management*. Baltimore: Johns Hopkins University Press.

O'Leary, J., Behrens-Tepper, J., McGuire, F., and Dottavio, F. (1987). Age of first hunting experience: Results from a nationwide recreation survey. *Leisure Sciences 9*, 225-33.

Oliver, S., Roggenbuck, J., and Watson, A. (1985). Education to reduce impacts in forest campgrounds. *Journal of Forestry, 83*, 234-36.

Olson, E., Bowman, M., and Roth, R. (1984). Interpretation and nonformal education in natural resources management. *Journal of Environmental Education, 15*, 6-10.

Ormrod, R., and Trahan, R. (1977). Can signs help visitors control their own behavior? *Trends, 10*, 25-27.

Outdoor Recreation Resources Review Commission. (1962). *Outdoor Recreation for America*. Washington DC: US Government Printing Office.

Owens, P. (1985). Conflict as a social interaction process in environment and behavior research: The example of leisure and recreation research. *Journal of Environmental Psychology, 5*, 243-59.

Parsons, D., Stohlgren, T., and Fodor, P. (1981). Establishing backcountry use quotas: The example from Mineral King, California. *Environmental Management, 5*, 335-40.

Parsons, D., Stohlgren, T., and Kraushaar, J. (1982). Wilderness permit accuracy: Differences between reported and actual use. *Environmental Management, 6*, 329-35.

Pastalan, L. (1970). Privacy as a behavioral concept. *Social Forces, 45*, 93-97.

Patterson, M. and Hammitt, W. (1990). Backcountry encounter norms, actual reported encounters, and their relationship to wilderness solitude. *Journal of Leisure Research, 22*, 259-75.

Pawelko, K., Drogin, E., and Graefe, A. (1997). The influence of recreationists' cultural or ethnic background upon their river recreation experiences. *Proceedings of the 1996 Northeastern Recreation Research Symposium.* USDA Forest Service General Technical Report NE-232, 49-54.

Perry, M. (1983). Controlling crime in the parks. *Parks and Recreation, 18*, 49-51, 67.

Peterson, D. (1987). Look ma, no hands! Here's what's wrong with no-rescue wilderness. *Parks and Recreation, 22*, 39-43, 54.

Peterson, G., and Neumann, E. (1969). Modeling and predicting human responses to the visual recreation environment. *Journal of Leisure Research, 1*, 219-38.

Peterson, G., and Lime, D. (1973). Two sources of bias in the measurement of human response to the wilderness environment. *Journal of Leisure Research, 5*, 66-73.

Peterson, G. (1974). A comparison of the sentiments and perceptions of canoeists and wilderness managers in the Boundary Waters Canoe Area. *Journal of Leisure Research, 6*, 194-206.

Peterson, G. (1977). Recreation preferences of urban teenagers: The influence of cultural and environmental attributes. *Children, Nature, and the Urban Environment: Proceedings of a Symposium Fair.* USDA Forest Service General Technical Report NE-30, 113-21.

Peterson, G., deBettencourt, J., and Wang, P. (1977). A Markov-based linear programming model of travel in the Boundary Waters Canoe Area. *Proceedings: River Recreation Management and Research Symposium.* USDA Forest Service General Technical Report NC-28, 342-50.

Peterson, G., and Lime, D. (1978). A research-management partnership grows in Minnesota's canoe country. *Naturalist, 15*, 5-11.

Peterson, G., and Lime, D. (1979). People and their behavior: A challenge for recreation management. *Journal of Forestry, 77*, 343-46.

Peterson, G., and deBettencourt, J. (1979). Flow metering of wilderness travel in the Quetico-Superior: New findings and research needs. *Modeling and Simulation, 10*, 1335-40.

Peterson, G., and Lime, D. (1980). Recreation policy analysis in wilderness management: A case study of the Quetico-Superior. *Proceedings of the Third Annual Applied Geography Conference.* Kent, OH: Kent State University, 4-13.

Peterson, G., Stynes, D., Rosenthal, D., and Dwyer, J. (1985). Substitution in recreation choice behavior. *Proceedings–Symposium on Recreation Choice Behavior.* USDA Forest Service General Technical Report INT-184, 19-30.

Peterson, G. (1992). Using fees to manage congestion at recreation areas. *Park Visitor Research for Better Management: Park Visitor Research Workshop.* Canberra, Australia: Phillip Institute of Technology, 57-67.

Peterson, M. (1981). *Trends in Recreational Use of National Forest Wilderness.* USDA Forest Service Research Paper INT-319.

Peterson, M. (1985). *Improving Voluntary Registration Through Location and Design of Trail Registration Stations.* USDA Forest Service Research Paper INT-336.

Pfister, R. (1977). Campsite choice behavior in the river setting: A pilot study on the Rogue River, Oregon. *Proceedings: River Recreation Management and Research Symposium.* USDA Forest Service General Technical Report NC-28, 351-58.

Pfister, R. (1993). Ethnic identity: A new avenue for understanding leisure and recreation preferences. *Culture, Conflict, and Communication in the Wildland-Urban Interface*. Boulder, CO: Westview Press, 53-68.

Philley, M., and McCool, S. (1981). Law enforcement in the national park system: Perceptions and practices. *Leisure Sciences, 4,* 355-71.

Pierce, R. (1980a). Dimensions of leisure. I: Satisfactions. *Journal of Leisure Research, 12,* 5-19.

Pierce, R. (1980b) Dimensions of leisure. II: Descriptions. *Journal of Leisure Research, 12,* 150-63.

Pierce, R. (1980c). Dimensions of leisure. III: Characteristics. *Journal of Leisure Research, 12,* 273-84.

Plager, A., and Womble, P. (1981). Compliance with backcountry permits in Mount McKinley National Park. *Journal of Forestry, 79,* 155-56.

Plumley, H., Peet, H., and Leonard, R. (1978.). *Records of Backcountry Use Can Assist Trail Managers*. USDA Forest Service Research Paper NE-414.

Potter, D., Hendee, J., and Clark, R. (1973). Hunting satisfaction: Game, guns or nature. *Human Dimensions in Wildlife Programs*. The Wildlife Management Institute, Washington, D. C., 62-71.

Potter, F., and Manning, R. (1984). Application of the wilderness travel simulation model to the Appalachian Trail in Vermont. *Environmental Management, 8,* 543-50.

Powers, R., Osborne, J., and Anderson, E. (1973). Positive reinforcement of litter removal in the natural environment. *Journal of Applied Behavioral Analysis, 6,* 579-80.

Prentice, R. (1993). Motivations of the heritage consumer in the leisure market: An application of the Manning-Hass demand hierarchy. *Leisure Sciences, 15,* 273-90.

Priest, S., and Bugg, R. (1991). Functions of privacy in Australian wilderness environments. *Leisure Sciences, 13,* 247-55.

Propst, D., and Lime, D. (1982). How satisfying is satisfaction research? *Forest and River Recreation: Research Update*. St. Paul, MN: University of Minnesota Agricultural Experiment Station Miscellaneous Publication 18, 124-33.

Ramthun, R. (1995). Factors in user group conflict between hikers and mountain bikers. *Leisure Sciences, 17,* 159-69.

Ramthun, R. (1996). Information sources and attitudes of mountain bikers. *Proceedings of the 1995 Northeastern Recreation Research Symposium*. USDA Forest Service General Technical Report NE-218, 14-16.

Rapaport, A. (1975). Toward a redefinition of density. *Environment and Behavior, 7,* 133-58.

Rawhouser, D., Harris, C., Grussing, L., Krumpe, E., and McLaughlin, W. (1989). Cooperative research for monitoring recreation use of the Lower Salmon River. *Journal of Park and Recreation Administration, 7,* 41-57.

Rechisky, A., and Williamson, B. (1992). Impact of user fees on day use attendance at New Hampshire State Parks. *Proceedings of the 1991 Northeastern Recreation Research Symposium*. USDA Forest Service General Technical Report NE-160, 106-8.

Reid, L. (1987). The policy connection: Linking research and management. *Proceedings of the 1986 Southeastern Recreation Research Conference*. Athens, GA: University of Georgia, 87-98.

Reiling, S., Criner, G., and Oltmanns, S. (1988). The influence of information on users' attitudes toward campground user fees. *Journal of Leisure Research, 20,* 208-17.

Reiling, S., Cheng, H., and Trott, C. (1992). Measuring the discriminatory impact associated with higher recreational fees. *Leisure Sciences, 14*, 121-37.

Reiling, S., and Cheng, H. (1994). Potential revenues from a new day-use fee. *Proceedings of the 1994 Northeastern Recreation Research Symposium.* USDA Forest Service General Technical Report NE-198, 57-60.

Reiling, S., McCarville, R., and White, C. (1994). *Demand and Marketing Study at Army Corps of Engineers Day-Use Areas.* Vicksburg, MS: U.S. Army Corps of Engineers Waterways Experiment Station.

Reiling, S., Cheng, H., Robinson, C., McCarville, R., and White, C. (1996). Potential equity effects of a new day-use fee. *Proceedings of the 1995 Northeastern Recreation Research Symposium.* USDA Forest Service General Technical Report NE-218, 27-31.

Reiling, S., and Kotchen, M. (1996). Lessons learned from past research on recreation fees. *Recreation Fees in the National Park Service: Issues, Policies and Guidelines for Future Action.* St. Paul, MN: University of Minnesota Cooperative Park Studies Unit, 49-69.

Reissman, L. (1954). Class, leisure, and social participation. *American Sociological Review, 19,* 76-84.

Relph, E. (1976). *Place and Placelessness.* London: Pion.

Riddick, C., DeSchriver, M., and Weissinger, E. (1984). A methodological review of research in *Journal of Leisure Research* from 1978 to 1982. *Journal of Leisure Research, 16*, 311-21.

Ritchie, J. (1975). On the derivation of leisure activity types—A perceptual mapping approach. *Journal of Leisure Research, 7*, 128-40.

Ritter, D. (1997). Limits of acceptable change planning in the Selway-Bitterroot Wilderness: 1985-1997. *Proceedings–Limits of Acceptable Change and Related Planning Processes: Progress and Future Directions.* USDA Forest Service General Technical Report INT-371, 25-28.

Robertson, R. (1982). Visitor knowledge affects visitor behavior. *Forest and River Recreation: Research Update.* St. Paul, MN: University of Minnesota Agricultural Experiment Station Miscellaneous Publication 18, 49-51.

Robertson, R., and Regula, J. (1994). Recreational displacement and overall satisfaction: A study of central Iowa's licensed boaters. *Journal of Leisure Research, 26,* 174-81.

Roggenbuck, J., and Schreyer, R. (1977). Relations between river trip motives and perception of crowding, management preference, and experience satisfaction. *Proceedings: River Recreation Management and Research Symposium.* USDA Forest Service General Technical Report NC-28, 359-64.

Roggenbuck, J., and Berrier, D. (1981). Communications to disperse wilderness campers. *Journal of Forestry, 75*, 295-97.

Roggenbuck, J., and Berrier, D. (1982). A comparison of the effectiveness of two communication strategies in dispersing wilderness campers. *Journal of Leisure Research, 14*, 77-89.

Roggenbuck, J., and Ham, S. (1986). Use of information and education in recreation management. *A Literature Review: The President's Commission on Americans Outdoors.* Washington, D. C.: U.S. Government Printing Office, M-59-M-71.

Roggenbuck, J. and Passineau, J. (1986). Use of the field experiment to assess the effectiveness of interpretation. *Proceedings of the Southeastern Recreation Research*

Conference. Athens, GA: University of Georgia Institute of Community and Area Development, 65-86.

Roggenbuck, J., and Lucas, R. (1987). Wilderness use and users: A state-of-knowledge review. *Proceedings—National Wilderness Research Conference: Issues, State-of-Knowledge, Future Directions*. USDA Forest Service General Technical Report INT-220, 204-45.

Roggenbuck, J., Williams, D., Bange, S., and Dean, D. (1991). River float trip encounter norms: Questioning the use of the social norms concept. *Journal of Leisure Research, 23*, 133-53.

Roggenbuck, J. (1992). Use of persuasion to reduce resource impacts and visitor conflicts. *Influencing Human Behavior: Theory and Applications in Recreation, Tourism, and Natural Resources*. Champaign, IL: Sagamore Publishing, 149-208.

Roggenbuck, J., Williams, D., and Bobinski, C. (1992). Public-private partnership to increase commercial tour guides' effectiveness as nature interpreters. *Journal of Park and Recreation Administration, 10*, 41-50.

Roggenbuck, J., Williams, D., and Watson, A. (1993). Defining acceptable conditions in wilderness. *Environmental Management, 17*, 187-97.

Roggenbuck, J., Marion, J., and Manning, R. (1994). Day users of the backcountry: The neglected national park visitor. *Trends, 31*, 19-24.

Rollins, R., and Chambers, D. (1990). Camper satisfaction with Canadian Park Service campgrounds. *Social Science and Natural Resource Recreation Management*. Boulder, CO: Westview Press, 91-103.

Romesburg, H. (1974). Scheduling models for wilderness recreation. *Journal of Environmental Management, 4*, 159-77.

Romsa, G. (1973). A method of deriving outdoor recreational activity patterns. *Journal of Leisure Research, 5*, 34-46.

Rosenthal, D., Waldman, D., and Driver, B. (1982). Construct validity of instruments measuring recreationists preferences. *Leisure Sciences, 5*, 89-108.

Rosenthal, D., and Driver, B. (1983). Managers' perceptions of experiences sought by ski tourers. *Journal of Forestry, 81*, 88-90, 105.

Rosenthal, D., Loomis, J., and Peterson, G. (1984). Pricing for efficiency and revenue in public recreation areas. *Journal of Leisure Research, 16*, 195-208.

Rosenthal, D., Loomis, J., and Peterson, G. (1984). *The Travel Cost Model: Concepts and Applications*. USDA Forest Service General Technical Report RM-109.

Ross, T., and Moeller, G. (1974). *Communicating Rules in Recreation Areas*. USDA Forest Service Research Paper NE-297.

Rossi, P., and Berk, R. (1985). Varieties of normative consensus. *American Sociological Review, 50*, 333-47.

Rossman, B., and Ulehla, Z. (1977). Psychological reward values associated with wilderness use: A functional-reinforcement approach. *Environment and Behavior, 9*, 41-46.

Rowell, A. (1986). A wilderness travel simulation model with graphic presentation of trail data. *Proceedings–National Wilderness Research Conference: Current Research*. USDA Forest Service General Technical Report INT-212, 478-82.

Ruddell, E. and Gramann, J. (1994). Goal orientation, norms, and noise induced conflict among recreation area users. *Leisure Sciences, 16*, 93-104.

Rugg, R. (1973). Map records of forest recreational itineraries. *Journal of Leisure Research, 5,* 60-66.

Rutlin, W., and Hammitt, W. (1994). Functions of privacy in the Ellicott Rock Wilderness. *Proceedings of the 1993 Southeastern Recreation Research Conference.* USDA Forest Service General Technical Report SE-90, 19-27.

Saunders, P. (1982). Monitoring and reporting recreation use: A case study. *Proceedings of the Southeastern Recreation Research Conference.* Athens, GA: Institute of Ecology, University of Georgia, 143-63.

Schechter, M., and Lucas, R. (1978). *Simulation of Recreational Use for Park and Wilderness Management.* Baltimore: Johns Hopkins University Press.

Schmitz-Scherzer, R., Rudinger, G., Angeleiner, A., and Bierhoff-Altermann, D. (1974). Notes on a factor analysis comparative study of the structure of leisure activities in four different samples. *Journal of Leisure Research, 6,* 77-83.

Schmidt, D., and Keating, J. (1979). Human crowding and personal control: An integration of the research. *Psychological Bulletin, 86,* 680-700.

Schneider, I., Anderson, D., and Jakes, P. (1993). *Innovations in Recreation Management: Importance, Diffusion, and Implementation.* USDA Forest Service General Technical Report NC-155.

Schneider, I., and Hammitt, W. (1995). Visitor response to outdoor recreation conflict: A conceptual approach. *Leisure Sciences, 17,* 223-34.

Schoenfeld, C. (1976). Who's minding the wilderness store? *Journal of Soil and Water Conservation, 31,* 242-47.

Schomaker, J., and Knopf, R. (1982a). Effect of question context on a recreation satisfaction measure. *Leisure Sciences, 5,* 35-43.

Schomaker, J., and Knopf, R. (1982b). Generalizability of a measure of visitor satisfaction with outdoor recreation. *Applied Psychological Measurement, 6,* 173-83.

Schomaker, J., and Leatherberry, E. (1983). A test for inequity in river recreation reservation systems. *Journal of Soil and Water Conservation, 38,* 52-56.

Schomaker, J. (1984). Writing quantifiable river recreation management objectives. *Proceedings of the 1984 National River Recreation Symposium,* 249-53.

Schreuder, H., Tyre, G., and James, G. (1975). Instant- and interval-count sampling: Two new techniques for estimating recreation use. *Forest Science, 21,* 40-44.

Schreyer, R., Roggenbuck, J., McCool, S., Royer, L., and Miller, J. (1976). *The Dinosaur National Monument Whitewater River Recreation Study.* Logan, UT: Utah State University.

Schreyer, R., and Roggenbuck, J. (1978). The influence of experience expectations on crowding perceptions and social-psychological carrying capacities. *Leisure Sciences, 1,* 373-94.

Schreyer, R., and Roggenbuck, J. (1981). Visitor images of national parks: The influence of social definitions of places on perceptions and behavior. *Some Recent Products of Recreation Research.* USDA Forest Service General Technical Report NC-63, 39-44.

Schreyer, R. (1982). Experience level affects expectations for recreation participation. *Forest and River Recreation: Research Update.* St. Paul, MN: University of Minnesota Agricultural Experiment Station Miscellaneous Publication 18, 154-59.

Schreyer, R., and Knopf, R. (1984). The dynamics of change in outdoor recreation environments—Some equity issues. *Journal of Park and Recreation Administration, 2,* 9-19.

Schreyer, R., and Lime, D. (1984). A novice isn't necessarily a novice: The influence of experience use history on subjective perceptions of recreation participation. *Leisure Sciences, 6,* 131-49.

Schreyer, R., Lime, D., and Williams, D. (1984). Characterizing the influence of past experience on recreation behavior. *Journal of Leisure Research, 16,* 34-50.

Schreyer, R., and Beaulieu, J. (1986). Attribute preferences for wildland recreation settings. *Journal of Leisure Research, 18,* 231-47.

Schreyer, R., and Driver, B.. (1989). The benefits of outdoor recreation participation. *Outdoor Recreation Benchmark 1988: Proceedings of the National Outdoor Recreation Forum.* USDA Forest Service General Technical Report SE-52, 472-82.

Schreyer, R. (1990). Conflict in outdoor recreation: The scope of the challenge to resource planning and management. *Social Science and Natural Resource Recreation Management.* Boulder, CO: Westview Press, 13-31.

Schultz, J., McAvoy, L., and Dustin, D. (1988). What are we in business for? *Parks and Recreation, 23,* 52-53.

Schuett, M. (1993). Information sources and risk recreation: The case of whitewater kayakers. *Journal of Park and Recreation Administration, 11,* 67-72.

Schuett, M. (1995). Predictors of social group participation in whitewater kayaking. *Journal of Park and Recreation Administration, 13,* 42-54.

Schwartz, E. (1973). Police services in the parks. *Parks and Recreation, 8,* 72-74.

Schweitzer, D., and Randall, R. (1974). The key to getting research applied: Manager-researcher cooperation. *Journal of Forestry, 72,* 418-19.

Scott, D. (1993). Use and non-use of public parks in northeast Ohio: Differences between African-Americans and whites. *Proceedings of the 1993 Northeastern Recreation Research Symposium.* USDA Forest Service General Technical Report NE-185, 224-27.

Scott, D., and Munson, W. (1994). Perceived constraints to park usage among individuals with low incomes. *Journal of Park and Recreation Administration, 12,* 79-96.

Scott, D. (1995). Gender differences in the use of public parks in northeast Ohio. *Proceedings of the 1994 Northeastern Recreation Research Symposium.* USDA Forest Service General Technical Report NE-198, 155-58.

Scotter, G. (1981). Response rates at unmanned trail registers, Waterton Lakes National Park, Alberta, Canada. *Journal of Leisure Research, 13,* 105-111.

Searle, M., and Jackson, E. (1985). Socioeconomic variations in perceived barriers to recreation participation among would-be participants. *Leisure Sciences, 7,* 227-49.

Selin, S., and Howard, D. (1988). Ego involvement and leisure behavior: A conceptual specification. *Journal of Leisure Research, 20,* 237-44.

Sessons, H. (1961). *A Review of Selected Results of Recreation Studies.* Washington, D. C.: Outdoor Recreation Resources Review Commission.

Sessons, H. (1963). An analysis of selected variables affecting outdoor recreation patterns. *Social Forces, 42,* 112-15.

Shafer, C., and Hammitt, W. (1994). Management conditions, and indicators of importance in wilderness recreation experiences. *Proceedings of the 1993 Southeastern Recreation Research Conference.* USDA Forest Service General Technical Report SE-90, 57-67.

Shafer, C. and Hammitt, W. (1995a). Purism revisited: Specifying recreational conditions of concern according to resource intent. *Leisure Sciences, 17,* 15-30.

Shafer, C., and Hammitt, W. (1995b). Congruency among experience dimensions, cognitive indicators, and coping behaviors in wilderness. *Leisure Sciences, 17,* 263-79.

Shafer, E., Jr. (1965). Socio-economic characteristics of Adirondack campers. *Journal of Forestry, 63,* 690-94.

Shafer, E., Jr., and Burke, H. (1965). Preferences for outdoor recreation facilities in four state parks. *Journal of Forestry, 63,* 512-18.

Shafer, E., Jr., and Thompson, R. (1968). Models that describe use of Adirondack campgrounds. *Forest Science, 14,* 383-91.

Shafer, E., Jr. (1969). *The Average Camper Who Doesn't Exist.* USDA Forest Service Research Paper NE-142.

Shafer, E., Jr., and Mietz, J. (1969). Aesthetic and emotional experiences rate high with northeastern wilderness hikers. *Environment and Behavior, 1,* 187-97.

Shafer, E., Jr., and Lucas, R. (1979). Research needs and priorities for dispersed recreation management. *Journal of Leisure Research, 10,* 311-21.

Shanks, B. (1976). Guns in the parks. *The Progressive, 40,* 21-23.

Shaull, S., and Gramann, J. (1998). The effect of cultural assimilation on the importance of family-related and nature-related recreation among Hispanic Americans. *Journal of Leisure Research, 30,* 47-63.

Shaw, S. (1985). Gender and leisure: Inequality in the distribution of leisure time. *Journal of Leisure Research, 17,* 266-82.

Shaw, S. (1992). Dereifying family leisure? An examination of women's and men's everyday experiences and perceptions of family time. *Leisure Sciences, 14,* 271-86.

Shaw, S. (1994a). Constraints to women's leisure. *Journal of Leisure Research, 25,* 8-22.

Shaw, S. (1994b). Gender, leisure, and constraint: Toward a framework for the analysis of women's leisure. *Journal of Leisure Research, 26,* 8-22.

Shelby, B. (1980a). Crowding models for backcountry recreation. *Land Economics, 56,* 43-55.

Shelby, B. (1980b). Contrasting recreational experiences: Motors and oars in the Grand Canyon. *Journal of Soil and Water Conservation, 35,* 129-31.

Shelby, B., Lowney, D., and McKee, P. (1980). *Problems with satisfaction as a criterion for management and change.* Paper presented at the annual meeting of the Rural Sociological Society, Ithaca, New York.

Shelby, B. (1981a). Encounter norms in backcountry settings: Studies of three rivers. *Journal of Leisure Research, 13,* 129-38.

Shelby, B. (1981b). Research, politics, and resource management decisions: A case study of river research in Grand Canyon. *Leisure Sciences, 4,* 281-96.

Shelby, B., and Colvin, R. (1982). Encounter measures in carrying capacity research: Actual, reported and diary contacts. *Journal of Leisure Research, 14,* 350-60.

Shelby, B., Danley, B., Gibbs, M., and Peterson, M. (1982). Preferences of backpackers and river runners for allocation techniques. *Journal of Forestry, 80,* 416-19.

Shelby, B., Heberlein, T., Vaske, J., and Alfano, G. (1983). Expectations, preferences, and feeling crowded in recreation activities. *Leisure Sciences, 6,* 1-14.

Shelby, B., and Heberlein, T. (1984). A conceptual framework for carrying capacity determination. *Leisure Sciences, 6,* 433-51.

Shelby, B. (1985). Resource and activity substitutes for recreational salmon fishing in New Zealand. *Proceedings — Symposium on Recreation Choice Behavior*. USDA Forest Service General Technical Report INT-184, 79-85.

Shelby, B., and Harris, R. (1985). Comparing methods for determining visitor evaluations of ecological impacts: Site visits, photographs, and written descriptions. *Journal of Leisure Research, 17*, 57-67.

Shelby, B., and Heberlein, T. (1986). *Carrying Capacity in Recreation Settings*. Corvallis, OR: Oregon State University Press.

Shelby, B., Bregenzer, N., and Johnson, R. (1988a). Displacement and product shift: Empirical evidence from Oregon rivers. *Journal of Leisure Research, 20*, 274-88.

Shelby, B., Vaske, J., and Harris, R. (1988b). User standards for ecological impacts at wilderness campsites. *Journal of Leisure Research, 20*, 245-56.

Shelby, B., Vaske, J., and Heberlein, T. (1989a). Comparative analysis of crowding in multiple locations: Results from fifteen years of research. *Leisure Sciences, 11*, 269-91.

Shelby, B., Whittaker, D., and Danley, M. (1989b). Allocation currencies and perceived ability to obtain permits. *Leisure Sciences, 11*, 137-44.

Shelby, B., Whittaker, D., and Danley, M. (1989c). Idealism versus pragmatism in user evaluations of allocation systems. *Leisure Sciences, 11*, 61-70.

Shelby, B., and Vaske, J. (1991a). Using normative data to develop evaluative standards for resource management: A comment on three recent papers. *Journal of Leisure Research, 23*, 173-87.

Shelby, B., and Vaske, J. (1991b). Resource and activity substitutes for recreational salmon fishing in New Zealand. *Leisure Sciences, 13*, 21-32.

Shelby, B., Brown, T., and Taylor, J. (1992a). *Streamflow and Recreation*. USDA Forest Service General Technical Report RM-209.

Shelby, B., Brown, T., and Baumgartner, R. (1992b). Effects of streamflows on river trips on the Colorado River in Grand Canyon, Arizona. *Rivers, 3*, 191-201.

Shelby, B., and Shindler, B. (1992). Interest group standards for ecological impacts at wilderness campsites. *Leisure Sciences, 14*, 17-27.

Shelby, B., and Whittaker, D. (1995). Flows and recreation quality on the Dolores River: Integrating overall and specific evaluations. *Rivers, 5*, 121-32.

Shelby, B., Vaske, J., and Donnelly, M. (1996). Norms, standards and natural resources. *Leisure Sciences, 18*, 103-23.

Shepard, J. (1974). A status recognition model of work-leisure relationships. *Journal of Leisure Research, 6*, 58-63.

Shin, W., and Jaakson, R. (1997). Wilderness quality and visitors' wilderness attitudes: Management implications. *Environmental Management, 21*, 225-32.

Shindler, B. (1992). Countering the law of diminishing standards. *Defining Wilderness Quality: The role of Standards in Wilderness Management — A Workshop Proceedings*. USDA Forest Service General Technical Report PNW-305, 53-60.

Shindler, B., and Shelby, B. (1992). User assessment of ecological and social campsite attributes. *Defining Wilderness Quality: The Role of Standards in Wilderness Management — A Workshop Proceedings*. USDA Forest Service General Technical Report PNW-305, 107-14.

Shindler, B., and Shelby, B. (1993). Regulating wilderness use: An investigation of user group support. *Journal of Forestry, 91*, 41-44.

Shindler, B., and Shelby, B. (1995). Product shift in recreation settings: Findings and implications from panel research. *Leisure Sciences, 17*, 91-104.

Shinew, K., Floyd, M., McGuire, F., and Noe, F. (1995). Sex, race, and subjective social class and their association with leisure preferences. *Leisure Sciences, 17*, 75-89.

Sieg, G., Roggenbuck, J., and Bobinski, C. (1988). The effectiveness of commercial river guides as interpreters. *Proceedings of the 1987 Southeastern Recreation Research Conference*. Athens, GA: University of Georgia, 12-20.

Smith, S., and Haythorn, W. (1972). The effects of compatibility, crowding, group size, and leadership seniority on stress, anxiety, hostility, and annoyance in isolated groups. *Journal of Personality and Social Psychology, 22*, 67-69.

Smith, S. (1975). Toward meta-recreation research. *Journal of Leisure Research, 7*, 235-39.

Smith, S. (1980). Intervening opportunities and travel to urban recreation centers. *Journal of Leisure Research , 12*, 296-308.

Smith, V., and Krutilla, J. (1974). A simulation model for the management of low density recreational areas. *Journal of Environment Economics and Management, 1*, 187-201.

Smith, V., and Headly, R. (1975). The use of computer simulation models in wilderness management. *Management Science Applications to Leisure Time*. Amsterdam: North Holland.

Smith, V., and Krutilla, J. (1976). *Structure and Properties of a Wilderness Travel Simulator*. Baltimore, MD: Johns Hopkins University Press for Resources for the Future, Inc.

Sofranko, A., and Nolan, M. (1972). Early life experiences and adult sports participation. *Journal of Leisure Research, 4*, 6-18.

Solomon, M., and Hansen, E. (1972). *Canoeists' Suggestions for Stream Management in the Manistee National Forest in Michigan*. USDA Forest Service Research Paper NC-77.

Stamps, S., and Stamps, M. (1985). Race, class, and leisure activities of urban residents. *Journal of Leisure Research, 17*, 40-56.

Stankey, G. (1970). An appeal for uniform income categories in outdoor recreation studies. *Journal of Leisure Research, 2*, 88.

Stankey, G. (1971). Myths in wilderness decision-making. *Journal of Soil and Water Conservation, 26*, 183-88.

Stankey, G. (1972). A strategy for the definition and management of wilderness quality. *Natural Environments: Studies in Theoretical and Applied Analysis*. Baltimore: The Johns Hopkins University Press, 88-114.

Stankey, G. (1973). *Visitor Perception of Wilderness Recreation Carrying Capacity*. USDA Forest Service Research Paper INT-142.

Stankey, G., and Lime, D. (1973). *Recreational Carrying Capacity: An Annotated Bibliography*. USDA Forest Service General Technical Report INT-3.

Stankey, G., Lucas, R., and Ream. R. (1973). Relationships between hunting success and satisfaction. *Proceedings of the Thirty-Eighth North American Wildlife and Natural Resources Conference*. Washington, DC: The Wildlife Management Institute, 77-84.

Stankey, G. (1974). Criteria for the determination of recreational carrying capacity in the Colorado River Basin. *Environmental Management in the Colorado River Basin*. Logan, UT: Utah State University Press.

Stankey, G., Lucas, R., and Lime, D. (1976). Crowding in parks and wilderness. *Design and Environment, 7*, 38-41.

Stankey, G., and Baden, J. (1977). *Rationing Wilderness Use: Methods, Problems, and Guidelines*. USDA Forest Service Research Paper INT-192.

Stankey, G. (1979). Use rationing in two southern California wildernesses. *Journal of Forestry, 77,* 347-49.

Stankey, G. (1980a). *A Comparison of Carrying Capacity Perceptions Among Visitors to Two Wildernesses*. USDA Forest Service Research Paper INT-242.

Stankey, G. (1980b). Wilderness carrying capacity: Management and research progress in the United States. *Landscape Research, 5,* 6-11.

Stankey, G. (1980c). Integrating wildland recreation research into decisionmaking: Pitfalls and promises. *Symposium Proceedings—Applied Research for Parks and Recreation in the 1980s*. Victoria, British Columbia: University of Victoria, 43-56.

Stankey, G., and McCool, S. (1984). Carrying capacity in recreational settings: Evaluation, appraisal, and application. *Leisure Sciences, 6,* 453-73.

Stankey, G., McCool, S., and Stokes, G. (1984). Limits of Acceptable Change: A new framework for managing the Bob Marshall Wilderness Complex. *Western Wildlands, 10,* 33-37.

Stankey, G., Cole, D., Lucas, R., Peterson, M., Frissell, S., and Washburne, R. (1985). *The Limits of Acceptable Change (LAC) System for Wilderness Planning*. USDA Forest Service General Technical Report INT-176.

Stankey, G., and Manning, R. (1986). Carrying capacity of recreation settings. *A Literature Review: The President's Commission on Americans Outdoors*. Washington, D.C.: U.S. Government Printing Office, M-47-M-57.

Stankey, G., and Schreyer, R. (1987). Attitudes toward wilderness and factors affecting visitor behavior: A state-of-knowledge review. *Proceedings—National Wilderness Research Conference: Issues, State-of-Knowledge, Future Directions*. USDA Forest Service General Technical Report INT-220, 246-93.

Stankey, G. (1989). Solitude for the multitudes: Managing recreational use in wilderness. *Public Places and Spaces*. New York: Plenum Press, 277-99.

Stankey, G. (1997). Institutional barriers and opportunities in application of the limits of acceptable change. *Proceedings–Limits of Acceptable Change and Related Planning Processes: Progress and Future Direction*. USDA Forest Service General Technical Report INT-371, 10-15.

Steele, R., Burr, S., and Iaicone, D. (1990). Pennsylvania trout fishing: A consideration of specialization and social interaction. *Proceedings of the 1990 Northeastern Recreation Research Symposium*. USDA Forest Service General Technical Report NE-145, 139-45.

Stein, T., and Lee, M. (1995). Managing recreation resources for positive outcomes: An application of benefits-based management. *Journal of Park and Recreation Administration, 13,* 52-70.

Stevenson, S. (1989). A test of peak load pricing on senior citizen recreationists: A case study of Steamboat Lake State Park. *Journal of Park and Recreation Administration, 7,* 58-68.

Stewart, W. (1989). Fixed itinerary systems in backcountry management. *Journal of Environmental Management, 29,* 163-71.

Stewart, W., and Carpenter, E. (1989). Solitude at Grand Canyon: An application of expectancy theory. *Journal of Leisure Research, 21,* 4-17.

Stewart, W. (1991). Compliance with fixed itinerary systems in water-based parks. *Environmental Management, 15,* 235-40.

Stewart, W. (1992). Influence of the onsite experience on recreation experience preference judgments. *Journal of Leisure Research, 24,* 185-98.

Stewart, W., and Hull, R. (1992). Satisfaction of what? Post hoc versus real-time construct validity. *Leisure Sciences, 14,* 195-209.

Stodolska, M., and Jackson, E. (1998). Discrimination in leisure and work experienced by a white ethnic minority group. *Journal of Leisure Research, 30,* 23-46.

Stokols, D. (1972a). On the distinction between density and crowding: Some implications for future research. *Psychological Review, 79,* 275-77.

Stokols, D. (1972b). A social psychological model of human crowding phenomena. *Journal of the American Institute of Planners, 38,* 72-83.

Stokowski, P. (1990). Extending the social groups model: Social network analysis in recreation research. *Leisure Sciences, 12,* 251-63.

Stokowski, P., and Lee, R. (1991). The influence of social network ties on recreation and leisure: An exploratory study. *Journal of Leisure Research, 23,* 95-113.

Stone, G., and Traves, M. (1958). Camping in the wilderness. *Mass Leisure.* New York: The Free Press of Glencoe, 290-305.

Stynes, D., Bevins, M., and Brown, T. (1980). Trends or methodological differences? *Proceedings of the 1980 Outdoor Recreation Trends Symposium, Volume I.* USDA Forest Service General Technical Report NE-57, 223-31.

Stynes, D. (1994). Recreation and tourism monitoring systems: Conceptual and methodological issues. *Proceedings of the 1991 Southeastern Recreation Research Conference.* USDA Forest Service General Technical Report SE-89, 1-10.

Sumner, E. (1936). *Special Report on a Wildlife Study in the High Sierra in Sequoia and Yosemite National Parks and Adjacent Territory.* Washington, DC: U.S. National Park Service Records, National Archives.

Swearingen, T., and Johnson, D. (1995). Visitors' responses to uniformed park employees. *Journal of Park and Recreation Administration, 13,* 73-85.

Tarbet, D., Moeller, G., and McLoughlin, K. (1977). Attitudes of Salmon River users toward management of wild and scenic rivers. *River Recreation Management and Research Symposium.* USDA Forest Service General Technical Report NC-28, 365-71.

Tarrant, M., Manfredo, M., and Driver, B. (1994). Recollections of outdoor recreation experiences: A psychophysiological perspective. *Journal of Leisure Research, 26,* 357-71.

Tarrant, M. (1996). Attending to past outdoor recreation experiences: Symptom reporting and changes in affect. *Journal of Leisure Research, 28,* 1-17.

Tarrant, M., and English, D. (1996). A crowding-based model of social carrying capacity: Applications for whitewater boating use. *Journal of Leisure Research, 28,* 155-68.

Tarrant, M., Cordell, H., and Kibler, T. (1997). Measuring perceived crowding for high-density river recreation: The effects of situational conditions and personal factors. *Leisure Sciences, 19,* 97-112.

Tatham, R., and Dornoff, R. (1971). Market segmentation for outdoor recreation. *Journal of Leisure Research, 3,* 5-16.

Taylor, D. (1993). Urban park use: Race, ancestry, and gender. *Managing Urban and High-Use Recreation Settings.* USDA Forest Service General Technical Report NC-163, 82-86.

Taylor, D., and Winter, P. (1995). Environmental values, ethics, and depreciative behavior in wildland settings. *Proceedings of the Second Symposium on Social Aspects and Recreation Research.* USDA Forest Service General Technical Report PSW-156, 59-66.

Thomas, L. (1956). Leisure pursuits by socio-economic strata. *Journal of Educational Sociology, 29,* 367-77.

Thompson, J., Lime, D., Gartner, B., and Sames, W. (Compliers). (1995). *Proceedings of the Fourth International Outdoor Recreation and Tourism Trends Symposium and the 1995 National Recreation Resources Planning Conference.* St. Paul, MN: University of Minnesota Extension Service.

Tierney, P. (1995). Development and testing of a cultural identity construct for recreation and tourism studies. *Proceedings of the Second Symposium on Social Aspects and Recreation Research.* USDA Forest Service General Technical Report PSW-156, 41-43.

Tinsley, H., Barrett, T., and Kass, R. (1977). Leisure activities and need satisfaction. *Journal of Leisure Research, 9,* 110-20.

Tinsley, H., and Kass, R. (1978). Sex effects in the study of leisure activities and need satisfaction: A replication and extension. *Journal of Leisure Research, 10,* 191-202.

Tinsley, H., and Kass, R. (1979). The latent structure of the need satisfying properties of leisure activities. *Journal of Leisure Research, 11,* 278-91.

Tinsley, H. (1984). Limitations, explorations, aspirations: A confession of fallibility and a promise to strive for perfection. *Journal of Leisure Research, 16,* 93-98.

Tinsley, H., and Johnson, T. (1984). A preliminary taxonomy of leisure activities. *Journal of Leisure Research, 16,* 234-44.

Titre, J., and Mills, A. (1982). Effect of encounters on perceived crowding and satisfaction. *Forest and River Recreation: Research Update.* St. Paul, MN: University of Minnesota Agricultural Experiment Station Miscellaneous Publication 18, 146-53.

Todd, S., and Graefe, A. (1989). Level of experience and perception of conflict among canoeists on the Delaware River. *Proceedings of the 1989 Northeastern Recreation Research Symposium.* USDA Forest Service General Technical Report NE-132, 147-56.

Tombaugh, L., and Love, L. (1964). *Estimating Number of Visitors to National Forest Campgrounds.* USDA Forest Service Research Note RM-17.

Toth, J., Jr. (1997). Racial and gender meanings of why people participate in recreational fishing. *Leisure Sciences, 19,* 129-46.

Towler, W. (1977). Hiker perception of wilderness: A study of the social carrying capacity of Grand Canyon. *Arizona Review, 26,* 1-10.

Tuan, Y. (1974). *Topophilia: A Study of Environmental Perception, Attitudes, and Values.* Englewood Cliffs, NJ: Prentice-Hall, Inc.

Tuan, Y. (1977). *Space and Place: The Perspective of Experience.* Minneapolis, MN: University of Minnesota Press.

Twight, B., and Catton, W., Jr. (1975). The politics of images: Forest managers versus recreation publics. *Natural Resources Journal, 15,* 297-306.

Twight, B., Smith, K., and Wissinger, G. (1981). Privacy and camping: Closeness to the self vs. closeness to others. *Leisure Sciences, 4,* 427-41.

Twight, B., and Lyden, F. (1988). Multiple-use vs. organizational commitment. *Forest Science, 34,* 474-86.

Twight, B., and Lyden, F. (1989). Measuring Forest Service bias. *Journal of Forestry, 87,* 35-41.

Tyre, G., and Siderlis, C. (1979). Instant-count sampling: A technique for estimating recreation use in municipal settings. *Leisure Sciences, 2,* 173-79.

Underhill, H., Xaba, A., and Borkan, R. (1986). The wilderness use simulation model applied to Colorado River Boating in Grand Canyon National Park, USA. *Environmental Management, 10,* 367-74.

Utter, J., Gleason, W., and McCool, S. (1981). User perceptions of river recreation allocation techniques. *Some Recent Products of River Recreation Research.* USDA Forest Service General Technical Report NC-63, 27-32.

Uysal, M., McDonald, C., and Reid, L. (1990). Sources of information used by international visitors to U.S. parks and natural areas. *Journal of Park and Recreation Administration, 8,* 51-59.

Valins, S., and Baum, A. (1973). Residential group size, social interaction and crowding. *Environment and Behavior, 5,* 421-40.

Valliere, W., and Manning, R. (1995). Environmental ethics and wilderness management: An empirical study. *Proceedings of the 1994 Northeastern Recreation Research Symposium.* USDA Forest Service General Technical Report NE-198, 195-98.

Vander Stoep, G., and Gramann, J. (1987). The effect of verbal appeals and incentives on depreciative behavior among youthful park visitors. *Journal of Leisure Research, 19,* 69-83.

Vander Stoep, G., and Roggenbuck, J. (1996). Is your park being "loved to death?": Using communication and other indirect techniques to battle the park "love bug." *Crowding and Congestion in the National Park System: Guidelines for Research and Management.* St. Paul, MN: University of Minnesota Agricultural Experiment Station Publication 86-1996, 85-132.

Van Doren, C., and Lentnek, B. (1969). Activity specialization among Ohio's recreation boaters. *Journal of Leisure Research, 1,* 296-315.

Van Doren, C., and Heit, M. (1973). Where it's at: A content analysis and appraisal of the *Journal of Leisure Research. Journal of Leisure Research, 5,* 67-73.

Van Horne, M., Szwak, L., and Randall, S. (1985). Outdoor recreation activity trends—Insights from the 1982-83 nationwide recreation survey. *Proceedings of the 1985 National Outdoor Recreation Trends Symposium, Volume II.* Atlanta, GA: U.S. National Park Service, 109-30.

Van Horne, M., Szwak, L., and Randall, S. (1986). *1982-83 Nationwide Recreation Survey.* U.S. Department of the Interior, National Park Service.

Van Meter, D. (1988). Educating natural resource managers for the 21st century. *Journal of Forestry, 86,* 64.

Van Wagtendonk, J. (1980). Visitor use patterns in Yosemite National Park. *Journal of Travel Research, 19,* 12-17.

Van Wagtendonk, J., and Benedict, J. (1980). Wilderness permit compliance and validity. *Journal of Forestry, 78,* 399-401.

Van Wagtendonk, J. (1981). The effect of use limits on backcountry visitation trends in Yosemite National Park. *Leisure Sciences, 4,* 311-23.

Van Wagtendonk, J. and Colio, P. (1986). Trailhead quotas: Rationing use to keep wilderness wild. *Journal of Forestry, 84,* 22-24.

Vaske, J., Donnelly, M., and Heberlein, T. (1980). Perceptions of crowding and resource quality by early and more recent visitors. *Leisure Sciences, 3,* 367-81.

Vaske, J., Donnelly, M., Heberlein, T., and Shelby, B. (1982a). Differences in reported satisfaction ratings by consumptive and nonconsumptive recreationists. *Journal of Leisure Research, 14,* 195-206.

Vaske, J., Graefe, A., and Demptster, A. (1982b). Social and environmental influences on perceived crowding. *Proceedings of the Wilderness Psychology Group Conference.* Morgantown, WV: West Virginia University, 211-27.

Vaske, J., Donnelly, M., and Tweed, D. (1983). Recreationist-defined versus researcher-defined similarity judgments in substitutability research. *Journal of Leisure Research, 15,* 251-62.

Vaske, J., Fedler, A., and Graefe, A. (1986a). Multiple determinants of satisfaction from a specific waterfowl hunting trip. *Leisure Sciences, 8,* 149-66.

Vaske, J., Graefe, A., Shelby, B., and Heberlein, T. (1986b). Backcountry encounter norms: Theory, method, and empirical evidence. *Journal of Leisure Research, 18,* 137-53.

Vaske, J., Donnelly, M., and Deblinger, R. (1990a). Norm activation and the acceptance of behavioral restrictions among over sand vehicle users. *Proceedings of the 1990 Northeastern Recreation Research Symposium.* USDA Forest Service General Technical Report NE-145, 153-59.

Vaske, J., Donnelly, M., and Shelby, B. (1990b). Comparing two approaches for identifying recreation activity substitutes. *Leisure Sciences, 12,* 289-302.

Vaske, J., Donnelly, M., and Williamson, B. (1991). Monitoring for quality control in state park management. *Journal of Park and Recreation Administration, 9,* 59-72.

Vaske, J., Donnelly, M., and Shelby, B. (1992). Establishing management standards: Selected examples of the normative approach. *Defining Wilderness Quality: The Role of Standards in Wilderness Management—A Workshop Proceedings.* USDA Forest Service General Technical Report PNW-305, 23-37.

Vaske, J., Donnelly, M., and Shelby, B. (1993). Establishing management standards: Selected examples of the normative approach. *Environmental Management, 17,* 629-43.

Vaske, J., Donnelly, M., Wittmann, K., and Laidlaw, S. (1995a). Interpersonal versus social-values conflict. *Leisure Sciences, 17,* 205-22.

Vaske, J., Wittmann, K., Laidlaw. S., and Donnelly, M. (1995b). Recreation conflicts on Mt. Evans. *Proceedings of the 1994 Northeastern Recreation Research Symposium.* USDA Forest Service General Technical Report NE-198, 96-99.

Vaske, J., Donnelly, M., Doctor, R., and Petruzzi, J. (1995c). Frontcountry encounter norms among three cultures. *Proceedings of the 1994 Northeastern Recreation Research Symposium.* USDA Forest Service General Technical Report NE-198, 162-65.

Vaske, J., Donnelly, M., and Petruzzi, J. (1996). Country of origin, encounter norms and crowding in a frontcountry setting. *Leisure Sciences, 18,* 161-76.

Vaux, H., Jr. (1975). The distribution of income among wilderness users. *Journal of Leisure Research, 7,* 29-37.

Veblen, T. (1912). *Theory of the Leisure Class.* New York: MacMillen.

Virden, R., and Schreyer, R. (1988). Recreation specialization as an indicator of environmental preference. *Environment and Behavior, 20,* 721-39.

Virden, R., and Knopf, R. (1989). Activities, experiences, and environmental settings: A case study of Recreation Opportunity Spectrum relationships. *Leisure Sciences, 11,* 159-76.

Virden, R. (1990). A comparison study of wilderness users and nonusers: Implications for managers and policymakers. *Journal of Park and Recreation Administration, 8,* 13-24.

Virden, R., and Brooks, R. (1991). Wilderness managers in the southwest: The relationship between wilderness philosophy, experience, and practice. *Journal of Park and Recreation Administration, 9,* 71-84.

Vogelsong, H., Graefe, A., Confer, J., Solan, D., and Kramp, J. (1998). Relationships between motivations, activities and settings: The recreation opportunity spectrum within the Delaware State Park System. *Proceedings of the 1997 Northeastern Recreation Research Symposium.* USDA Forest Service General Technical Report NE-241,124-27.

Vork, M. (1998). Visitor response to management regulation—A study among recreationists in southern Norway. *Environmental Management, 22,* 737-46.

Wade, J. (1979). Law enforcement in the wilderness. *Trends, 16,* 12-15.

Wagar, J. V. (1946). Services and facilities for forest recreationists. *Journal of Forestry, 44,* 883-87.

Wagar, J. V. (1951). Some major principles in recreation land use planning. *Journal of Forestry, 49,* 431-35.

Wagar, J. A. (1963a). *Campgrounds for Many Tastes.* USDA Forest Service Research Paper INT-6.

Wagar, J. A. (1963b). *Relationships between Visitor Characteristics and Recreational Activities on Two National Forests.* USDA Forest Serce Research Paper NE-7.

Wagar, J. A. (1964). The carrying capacity of wild lands for recreation. *Forest Science Monograph 7,* Washington, DC: Society of American Foresters.

Wagar, J. A. (1966). Quality in outdoor recreation. *Trends, 3,* 9-12.

Wagar, J. A. (1968). The place of carrying capacity in the management of recreation lands. *Third Annual Rocky Mountain-High Plains Park and Recreation Conference Proceedings.* Fort Collins, CO: Colorado State University.

Wagar, J. A. (1969). *Estimation of Visitor Use from Self-Registration at Developed Recreation Sites.* USDA Forest Service Research Paper INT-70.

Wagar, J. A., and Thalheimer, J. (1969). *Trial Results of Net Count Procedures for Estimating Visitor Use at Developed Recreation Sites.* USDA Forest Service Research Note INT-105.

Wagar, J. A. (1974). Recreational carrying capacity reconsidered. *Journal of Forestry, 72,* 274-78.

Wagner, F., and Donahue, T. (1986). The impact of inflation and recession on urban leisure in New Orleans. *Journal of Leisure Research, 8,* 300-6.

Wagstaff, M., and Wilson, B. (1988). The evaluation of litter behavior modification in a river environment. *Proceedings of the 1987 Southeastern Recreation Research Conference.* Athens, GA: University of Georgia, 21-28.

Walker, G., and Kiecolt, K. (1995). Social class and wilderness use. *Leisure Sciences, 17,* 295-308.

Wallace, G. and Smith, M. (1997). A comparison of motivations, preferred management actions, and setting preferences among Costa Rican, North American, and European visitors to five protected areas in Costa Rica. *Journal of Park and Recreation Administration, 15,* 59-82.

Walsh, R. (1986). *Recreation Economic Decisions.* State College, PA: Venture Publishing.

Wang, B., and Manning, R. (1999). Computer simulation modeling for recreation management: A study on carriage road use in Acadia National Park, Maine, USA. *Environmental Management, 23,* 193-203.

Warren, G. (1997). Recreation management in the Bob Marshall, Great Bear, and Scapegoat Wildernesses: 1987-1997. *Proceedings–Limits of Acceptable Change and Related Planning Processes: Progress and Future Directions.* USDA Forest Service General Technical Report INT-371, 21-24.

Washburne, R. (1978). Black under-participation in wildland recreation: Alternative explanations. *Leisure Sciences, 1,* 175-89.

Washburne, R., and Wall, P. (1980). *Black-White Ethnic Differences in Outdoor Recreation.* USDA Forest Service Research Paper INT-249.

Washburne, R. (1981). Carrying capacity assessment and recreational use in the national wilderness preservation system. *Journal of Soil and Water Conservation, 36,* 162-66.

Washburne, R. (1982). Wilderness recreational carrying capacity: Are numbers necessary? *Journal of Forestry, 80,* 726-28.

Washburne, R., and Cole, D. (1983). *Problems and Practices in Wilderness Management: A Survey of Managers.* USDA Forest Service Research Paper INT-304.

Watson, A., Williams, D., and Daigle, J. (1991a). Sources of conflict between hikers and mountain bikers in the Rattlesnake NRA. *Journal of Park and Recreation Administration, 9,* 59-71.

Watson, A., Roggenbuck, J., and Williams, D. (1991b). The influence of past experience on wilderness choice. *Journal of Leisure Research, 23,* 21-36.

Watson, A., and Niccolucci, M. (1992a). Place of residence and hiker-horse conflict in the Sierras. *Proceedings of the Symposium on Social Aspects and Recreation Research.* USDA Forest Service General Technical Report PSW-132, 71-72.

Watson, A. and Niccolucci, M. (1992b). Defining past-experience dimensions for wilderness recreation. *Leisure Sciences, 14,* 89-103.

Watson, A., Williams, D., Roggenbuck, J., and Daigle, J. (1992). *Visitor Characteristics and Preferences for Three National Forest Wildernesses in the South.* USDA Forest Service Research Paper INT-455.

Watson, A. (1993). *Characteristics of Visitors Without Permits Compared to Those With Permits at the Desolation Wilderness, California.* USDA Forest Service Research Note INT-414.

Watson, A., Niccolucci, M., and Williams, D. (1993). *Hikers and Recreational Packstock Users: Predicting and Managing Recreation Conflicts in Three Wildernesses.* USDA Forest Service Research Paper INT-468.

Watson, A., Niccolucci, M., and Williams, D. 1994. The nature of conflict between hikers and recreational stock users in the John Muir Wilderness. *Journal of Leisure Research, 26,* 372-85.

Watson, A. (1995a). An analysis of recent progress in recreation conflict research and perceptions of future challenges and opportunities. *Leisure Sciences, 17,* 235-38.

Watson, A. (1995b). Opportunities for solitude in the Boundary Waters Canoe Area Wilderness. *Northern Journal of Applied Forestry, 12,* 12-18.

Watson, A., and Niccolucci, M. (1995). Conflicting goals of wilderness management: Natural conditions vs. natural experiences. *Proceedings of the Second Symposium on Social Aspects and Recreation Research.* USDA Forest Service General Technical Report PSW-156, 11-15.

Watson, A., Hendee, J., and Zaglauer, H. (1996a). Human values and codes of behavior: Changes in Oregon's Eagle Cap Wilderness visitors and their attitudes. *Natural Areas Journal, 16,* 89-93.

Watson, A., Zaglauer, H., and Stewart, S. (1996b). Activity orientation as a discriminant variable in recreation conflict research. *Proceedings of the 1995 Northeastern Recreation Research Symposium.* USDA Forest Service General Technical Report NE-218, 103-8.

Wearing, B., and Wearing, S. (1988). "All in a day's leisure": Gender and the concept of leisure. *Leisure Studies, 7,* 111-23.

Webb, E., Campbell, D., Schwartz, R., and Sechrest, L. (1966). *Unobtrusive Measures: Nonreactive Research in the Social Sciences.* Chicago: Rand McNally and Company.

Wellman, J., Roggenbuck, J., and Smith, A. (1982a). Recreation specialization and norms of depreciative behavior among canoeists. *Journal of Leisure Research, 14,* 323-40.

Wellman, J., Dawson, M., and Roggenbuck, J. (1982b). Park managers predictions of the motivations of visitors to two national park areas. *Journal of Leisure Research, 14,* 1-15.

Wenger, W., Jr. (1964). *A Test of Unmanned Registration Stations on Wilderness Trails: Factors Influencing Effectiveness.* USDA Forest Service Research Paper PNW-16.

Wenger, W., Jr., and Gregersen, H. (1964). *The Effect of Non-Response on Representativeness of Wilderness-Trail Register Information.* USDA Forest Service Research Paper PNW-17.

Wenger, W., Jr., and Videbeck, R. (1969). Eye pupillary measurement of aesthetic response to forest scenes. *Journal of Leisure Research, 1,* 149-62.

West, P. (1977). A status group dynamics approach to predicting participation rates in regional recreation demand studies. *Land Economics, 53,* 196-211.

West, P. (1981a). *On-Site Social Surveys and the Determination of Social Carrying Capacity in Wildland Recreation Management.* USDA Forest Service Research Note NC-264.

West, P. (1981b). Perceived crowding and attitudes toward limiting use in backcountry recreation areas. *Leisure Sciences, 4,* 419-26.

West, P. (1982a). A nationwide test of the status group dynamics approach to outdoor recreation demand. *Leisure Sciences, 5,* 1-18.

West, P. (1982b). Effects of user behavior on the perception of crowding in backcountry forest recreation. *Forest Science, 28,* 95-105.

West, P. (1983). A test of the projection accuracy of the status group dynamics approach to recreation demand. *Leisure Sciences, 6,* 15-45.

West, P. (1984). Status differences in interpersonal influence in the adoption of outdoor recreation activities. *Journal of Leisure Research, 16,* 350-54.

West, P. (1985). Predicting the direction of participation rate trends with the status group dynamics approach to recreation demand. *Proceedings of the 1985 Outdoor Recreation Trends Symposium, Volume II.* Atlanta, GA: U.S. National Park Service, 362-70.

West, P. (1989). Urban regional parks and black minorities: Subculture, marginality, and interracial relations in park use in the Detroit metropolitan area. *Leisure Sciences, 11*, 11-28.

West, P., Fly, J., Larkin, F., and Marans, R. (1992). Minority anglers and toxic fish consumption: Evidence from a statewide survey of Michigan. *Race and the Incidence of Environmental Hazards: A Time for Discourse*. Boulder, CO: Westview Press, 100-113.

West, P. (1993). The tyranny of metaphor: Interracial relations, minority recreation, and the wildland-urban interface. *Culture, Conflict, and Communication in the Wildland-Urban Interface*. Boulder, CO: Westview Press, 109-15.

Westin, A. (1967). *Privacy and Freedom*. New York: Atheneaum Books.

Westover, T., Flickenger, T., and Chubb, M. (1980) Crime and law enforcement. *Parks and Recreation, 15*, 28-33.

Westover, T. (1986). Park use and perception: Gender differences. *Journal of Park and Recreation Administration, 4*, 1-8.

Westover, T., and Collins, J. (1987). Perceived crowding in recreation settings: An urban case study. *Leisure Sciences, 9*, 87-99.

Westover, T. (1989). Perceived crowding in recreational settings: An environment-behavior model. *Environment and Behavior, 21*, 258-76.

Whisman, S., and Hollenhorst, S. (1998). A path model of whitewater boating satisfaction on the Cheat River of West Virginia. *Environmental Management, 22*, 109-17.

White, R. (1955). Social class differences in the uses of leisure. *American Journal of Sociology, 61*, 145-50.

White, T. (1975). The relative importance of education and income as predictors in outdoor recreation participation. *Journal of Leisure Research, 7*, 191-99.

Whittaker, D., and Shelby, B. (1988). Types of norms for recreation impact: Extending the social norms concept. *Journal of Leisure Research, 20*, 261-73.

Whittaker, D. (1992). Selecting indicators: Which impacts matter more? *Defining Wilderness Quality: The role of Standards in Wilderness Management — A Workshop Proceedings*. USDA Forest Service General Technical Report PNW-305, 13-22.

Whittaker, D., and Shelby, B. (1992). Developing good standards: Criteria, characteristics, and sources. *Defining Wilderness Quality: The Role of Standards in Wilderness Management — A Workshop Proceedings*. USDA Forest Service General Technical Report PNW-305, 6-12.

Wicker, A. (1969). Attitudes versus actions: The relationship of verbal and overt behavioral responses to attitude objects. *Journal of Social Issues, 25*, 41-78.

Wicker, A., and Kirmeyer, S. (1976). What the rangers think. *Parks and Recreation, 11*, 28-30, 42.

Wicks, B., and Crompton, J. (1986). Citizen and administrator perspectives of equity in the delivery of park services. *Leisure Sciences, 8*, 341-65.

Wicks, B. (1987). The allocation of recreation and park resources: The courts' intervention. *Journal of Park and Recreation Administration, 5*, 1-9.

Wicks, B., and Crompton, J. (1987). An analysis of the relationships between equity choice preferences, service type and decision making groups in a U.S. city. *Journal of Leisure Research, 19*, 189-204.

Wicks, B., and Crompton, J. (1989). Allocation services for parks and recreation: A model for implementing equity concepts in Austin, Texas. *Journal of Urban Affairs, 11*, 169-88.

Wicks, B., and Crompton, J. (1990). Predicting the equity preferences of park and recreation department employees and residents of Austin, Texas. *Journal of Leisure Research, 22*, 18-35.

Wikle, T. (1991). Comparing rationing policies used on rivers. *Journal of Park and Recreation Administration, 9*, 73-80.

Wildland Research Center, University of California. (1962). *Wilderness and Recreation—A Report on Resources, Values, and Problems: Outdoor Recreation Resources Review Commission Study Report 3*. Washington, D. C.: U.S. Government Printing Office.

Williams, D. (1985). A developmental model of recreation choice behavior. *Proceedings—Symposium on Recreation Choice Behavior*. USDA Forest Service General Technical Report INT-184, 31-37.

Williams, D., and Knopf, R. (1985). In search of the primitive-urban continuum—The dimensional structure of outdoor recreation settings. *Environment and Behavior, 17*, 351-70.

Williams, D., and Huffman, M. (1986). Recreation specialization as a factor in backcountry trail choice. *Proceedings—National Wilderness Research Conference: Current Research*. USDA Forest Service General Technical Report INT-212, 339-44.

Williams, D. (1988a). Measuring perceived similarity among outdoor recreation activities: A comparison of visual and verbal stimulus presentations. *Leisure Sciences, 10*, 153-66.

Williams, D. (1988b). Recreational specialization: A complex issue for visitor management. *Western Wildlands, 14*, 21-26.

Williams, D., Ellis, G., Nickerson, N., and Shafer, C. (1988). Contributions of time, format, and subject to variation in recreation experience preference measurement. *Journal of Leisure Research, 20*, 57-68.

Williams, D. (1989). Great expectations and the limits of satisfaction: A review of recreation and customer satisfaction research. *Outdoor Recreation Benchmark 1988: Proceedings of the National Outdoor Recreation Forum*. USDA Forest Service General Technical Report SE-52, 422-38.

Williams, D., Schreyer, R., and Knopf, R. (1990). The effect of experience use history on the multidimensional structure of motivations to participate in leisure activities. *Journal of Leisure Research, 22*, 36-54.

Williams, D., Roggenbuck, J., and Bange, S. (1991). The effect of norm-encounter compatibility on crowding perceptions, experience, and behavior in river recreation settings. *Journal of Leisure Research, 23*, 154-72.

Williams, D., Roggenbuck, J., Patterson, M., and Watson, A. (1992a). The variability of user-based social impact standards for wilderness management. *Forest Science, 38*, 738-56.

Williams, D., Patterson, M., Roggenbuck, J., and Watson, A. (1992b). Beyond the commodity metaphor: Examining emotional and symbolic attachment to place. *Leisure Sciences, 14*, 29-46.

Williams, D. (1993). Conflict in the great outdoors. *Parks and Recreation, 28*, 28-34.

Williamson, B., Vaske, J., and Donnelly, M. (1990). Monitoring for quality control in New Hampshire state parks. *Proceedings of the 1990 Northeastern Recreation Research Symposium*. USDA Forest Service General Technical Report NE-145, 111-18.

Willis, C., Canavan, J., and Bond, R. (1975). Optimal short-run pricing policies for a public campground. *Journal of Leisure Research, 7*, 108-13.

Witt, P., and Bishop, D. (1970). Situational antecedents to leisure behavior. *Journal of Leisure Research, 2*, 64-77.

Witt, P. (1971). Factor structure of leisure behavior for high school age youth in three communities. *Journal of Leisure Research, 3*, 213-20.

Witt, P., and Goodale, T. (1981). The relationship between barriers to leisure enjoyment and family stages. *Leisure Sciences, 4*, 29-49.

Witt, P. (1984). Research in transition: Prospects and challenges. *Parks and Recreation, 19*, 60-63.

Witter, D., Haverland, P., Belusz, L., and Hicks, C. (1982). Missouri trout park anglers: Their motives and opinions of management. *Forest and River Recreation: Research Update*. St. Paul, MN: University of Minnesota Agricultural Experiment Station Miscellaneous Publication 18, 69-73.

Wolf, N. (1991). *The Beauty Myth: How Images of Beauty Are used Against Women*. New York: William Morrow.

Wohlwill, J., and Heft, H. (1977). A comparative study of user attitudes toward development and facilities in two contrasting natural recreation areas. *Journal of Leisure Research, 9*, 264-80.

Womble, P., and Studebaker, S. (1981). Crowding in a national park campground. *Environment and Behavior, 13*, 557-73.

Woodard, M. (1988). Class, regionality, and leisure among urban black Americans: The post-civil rights era. *Journal of Leisure Research, 20*, 87-105.

Yoesting, D., and Burkhead, D. (1973). Significance of childhood recreation experience on adult leisure behavior: An exploratory analysis. *Journal of Leisure Research, 5*, 25-36.

Yoesting, D., and Christensen, J. (1978). Re-examining the significance of childhood recreation patterns on adult leisure behavior. *Leisure Sciences, 1*, 219-29.

Young, J., Williams, D., and Roggenbuck, J. (1991). The role of involvement in identifying users' preferences for social standards in the Cohutta Wilderness. *Proceedings of the 1990 Southeastern Recreation Research Conference*. USDA Forest Service General Technical Report SE-67, 173-83.

Young, R. (1983). Toward an understanding of wilderness participation. *Leisure Sciences, 5*, 339-57.

Young, R., and Kent, A. 1985. Using the theory of reasoned action to improve the understanding of recreation behavior. *Journal of Leisure Research, 17*, 90-106.

Yu, P. (1996). The relationship among self-esteem, acculturation, and recreation participation of recently arrived Chinese immigrant adolescents. *Journal of Leisure Research, 28*, 251-73.

Yuan, M., and McEwen, D. (1989). Test for campers' experience preference differences among three ROS setting classes. *Leisure Sciences, 11*, 177-85.

Zuzanek, J. (1978). Social differences in leisure behavior: Measurement and interpretation. *Leisure Sciences, 1*, 271-93.

Index